IMPLEMENTING THE IT BALANCED SCORECARD

Aligning IT with Corporate Strategy

Other CRC/Auerbach Publications in Software Development, Software Engineering, and Project Management

IMPLEMENTING THE IT BALANCED SCORECARD

Aligning IT with Corporate Strategy

Jessica Keyes

Auerbach Publications
Taylor & Francis Group

Boca Raton   London   New York   Singapore

Published in 2005 by
Auerbach Publications
Taylor & Francis Group
6000 Broken Sound Parkway NW
Boca Raton, FL 33487-2742

© 2005 by Taylor & Francis Group
Auerbach is an imprint of Taylor & Francis Group

No claim to original U.S. Government works
Printed in the United States of America on acid-free paper
10 9 8 7 6 5 4 3

International Standard Book Number-10: 0-8493-2621-4 (Hardcover)
International Standard Book Number-13: 978-0-8493-2621-9 (Hardcover)
Library of Congress Card Number 2004059480

Library of Congress Cataloging-in-Publication Data

Keyes, Jessica, 1950-
 Implementing the IT balanced scorecard: aligning IT with corporate strategy / Jessica Keyes.
  p. cm.
 Includes bibliographical references and index.
 ISBN 0-8493-2621-4 (alk. paper)
 1. Information technology--Management. 2. Management information systems. 3. Business-Data processing--Management. 4. Strategic planning. I. Title.

HD30.2.K465 2004
658'.05--dc22   2004059480

Taylor & Francis Group
is the Academic Division of T&F Informa plc.

Visit the Taylor & Francis Web site at
http://www.taylorandfrancis.com

and the Auerbach Publications Web site at
http://www.auerbach-publications.com

Dedication

This book is dedicated to my family and friends.

Table of Contents

About the Author

Jessica Keyes is president of New Art Technologies, Inc., a high-technology and management consultancy and development firm started in New York in 1989. She is also a founding partner of New York City-based Manhattan Technology Group.

Keyes has given seminars for such prestigious universities as Carnegie Mellon, Boston University, University of Illinois, James Madison University, and San Francisco State University. She is a frequent keynote speaker on the topics of competitive strategy and productivity and quality. She is former advisor for DataPro, McGraw-Hill's computer research arm, as well as a member of the Sprint Business Council. Keyes is also a founding Board of Directors member of the New York Software Industry Association. She has recently completed a two-year term on the Mayor of New York City's Small Business Advisory Council. She is currently a professor of computer science at Fairleigh Dickinson University's graduate center as well as the University of Phoenix, where she is an Area Chair, and Virginia Tech. She has been the editor for WGL's *Handbook of eBusiness* and Auerbach Publications' *Systems Development Management* and *Information Management*.

Prior to founding New Art, Keyes was Managing Director of R&D for the New York Stock Exchange and has been an officer with Swiss Bank Co. and Banker's Trust, both in New York City. She holds a Masters of Business Administration degree from New York University, where she did her research in the area of artificial intelligence.

A noted columnist and correspondent with over 200 articles published, Keyes is the author of 19 books, including Auerbach's *Software Engineering Handbook* and *Software Configuration Management*.

Preface

A company's technology strategy is often subordinate to its business strategy. Here, a management committee, or some other planning body, meticulously plans the company's long-range plan. The technology chiefs are called from their basement perches only to plan for one or another automated system as it meets a comparatively short-term goal from one or more of the business units. In some companies, this planning process is akin to weaving cloth. In weaving, thread after thread is woven so tightly that, when complete, the cloth's individual threads are nearly impossible to distinguish from one another. The strength and resiliency of the completed cloth are the result of this careful weaving.

A company, too, is made up of many threads, each with its own strategy. Only when all of these unmatched threads, or strategies, are woven evenly together can a successful general business strategy be formulated. This, then, is the premise behind a **balanced** strategic vision. But first, those crafting the corporate (and IT) strategy have to understand exactly what strategy is.

Components of Strategy

There are three factors that define strategy and strategic processes: (1) the scope of strategic decision making, (2) the factors or forces to be considered in formulating a strategy, and (3) the approach to strategic planning.

The scope of decision making defines the decision's impact on the organization. For it to be strategic, it must deal with the organization's relationship with the external environment and must have some impact on the success of the organization as a whole.

In his excellent book on competitive strategy, Michael Porter (1980) identifies several competing forces that should be considered in business strategy formulation:

- Bargaining power of customers
- Bargaining power of suppliers
- Current competitors
- Threat of new entrants into the market
- Threat of substitute products or services

Barriers to entering or exiting markets affect these forces. Porter advises that a company should flexibly employ its assets to ease its entry into, mobility within, and exit from a market area. Alternatively, the company can attempt to put up barriers to other companies entering the marketplace. Advantages of this strategy include "cornering the market," but this may be more than offset by the expense involved in doing so.

The process of strategy formulation consists of many activities, according to Uyterhoeven et al. (1977):

- Create a strategic profile that includes how the company defines itself as well as the steps it has taken to be competitive.
- Develop a strategic forecast of the environment. This should encompass political, economic, market, product, competitive, and technological issues.
- Perform an audit of the strengths and weaknesses of the organization.
- Compare the audit results with the environmental scan; from this comparison, create a set of strategic alternatives.
- Test the consistency of the alternatives to make sure they fit the capabilities of the organization as well as the external opportunities defined by the organization. These alternatives must also be consistent with the profile that the organization has created for itself. This step permits the alignment of what it is possible for the company to do in its particular environment versus what the company has the capability to do.
- Review the alternatives and make a choice.

Strategic Use of Information Technology

Most corporations are besieged by demands from their internal divisions and departments for funding to automate one or another system based on the strategy or strategies upon which those departments have

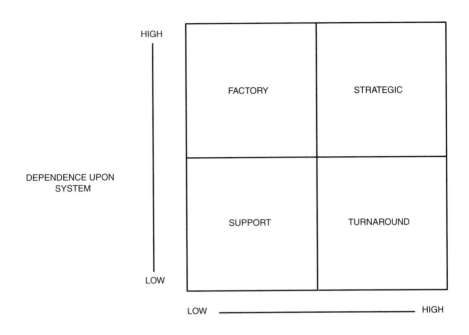

FIGURE 1   Framework for assessment of strategic importance of an IT system.

embarked. Even in the best of economic times, it is foolhardy for an organization to invest in all comers. The savvy organization should attempt to separate the wheat from the chafe and fund only those projects that offer a positive contribution to the organization's bottom line — economics, productivity, or customer satisfaction.

Because of this necessity, it is important to be able to determine the strategic level of an existing, or potential, system. One useful tool is the framework developed by Harvard professors F. Warren McFarlan and James Cash (1989), which assesses the strategic significance of a system to an organization.

A matrix function can be used to assist in determining a company's classification and to determine the appropriate way to manage the technology resource based on whether it serves a support or strategic role in the organization. As shown in Figure 1, the McFarlan-Cash grid is two-dimensional, showing four different types of management environments:

1. Strategic firms have a very tight relationship of firm to technology. These firms have an "excruciating" dependence on technology. Systems that these companies develop are critical to their competitive success.

2. Turnaround firms, while considering technology to be very important, do not quite have the dependence on technology as do strategic firms. These firms are making the transition to the strategic level. Their current systems are not considered strategic but the development of new ones are making them crucial to the competitiveness of the organization.
3. In factory-type firms, while technology is heavily depended upon for smooth running of their operations, it is not seen as a major differentiator.
4. In support-type firms, technology is considered important and useful but not on the short list of things this company needs to do.

The many forms of technology in relation to business strategy require different sets of techniques. In using technology to support the mission and strategy of the organization, a well-known technique, and one that should be employee by all organizations, is strategy set transformation (Parsons, 1983):

- Identify the *strategy set* of the organization. This consists of a firm's mission statement, its organizational objectives, the organizational strategy, and strategic organizational attributes.
- Identify stakeholder groups within the organization.
- Identify the operating objectives of the stakeholder groups and the constraints related to the development of systems.
- Develop information strategies using these results.

This set of questions is quite elegant in its simplicity. Its employment assures the organization that the proper fit between technology and business is, indeed, being achieved.

Organizational Performance Measurement

All systems and the business processes they automate should be measured. Time and motion studies performed in the 1920s and 1930s used quantitative performance data that had been collected internally within the organization to identify exactly what each worker should do to achieve maximum production efficiency.

In the 1960s, the quality movement began when Deming and Juran's total quality management (TQM) philosophies were widely adopted in Japan, and ultimately in the United States in the 1980s. Right on the heel of these innovations came the Malcolm Baldridge National Quality Award (http://www.quality.nist.gov), a summary of which appears in Appendix G.

There is no lack of measurement approaches. Thor's (1994) Family of Measures approach focuses on the identification of five categories of metrics:

1. Profitability
2. Productivity
3. External quality
4. Internal quality
5. Other metrics, including innovation, safety, and organizational culture

It is Thor's contention that a family of metrics is needed at every step in the process, not just at the strategic level. Indeed, some metrics are used at the lowest levels and others are rolled up into organizationwide metrics.

The Family of Measures approach utilizes a brainstorming technique. A representative gathering of personnel is used to identify, analyze, and ultimately select metrics. Each family of measures developed is referred to as a metric set. Each metric set should be evaluated using appropriate data and a trial or break-in period established to identify problems.

Like Baldridge, the Family of Measures approach provides a framework in terms of categories of metrics. Balanced scorecard and other approaches also use the framework approach.

The Balanced Scorecard and IT

The goals of an information technology (IT) balanced scorecard are simplistic in scope but complex to execute:

1. Align IT plans with business goals and needs.
2. Establish appropriate measures for evaluating the effectiveness of IT.
3. Align employees' efforts toward achieving IT objectives.
4. Stimulate and improve IT performance.
5. Achieve balanced results across stakeholder groups.

The keyword here is "balanced." It reflects the balance between the five goals listed above, the four balanced scorecard perspectives (customer, business processes, learning, and innovation and financial), long- and short-term objectives, as well as between qualitative and quantitative performance measures.

The remainder of this book provides detailed explanations on how to implement the IT balanced scorecard. This book reviews more than a few sample scorecards, metrics, and techniques, while providing insight, experience, and research into the process as a whole. However, as Kaplan and Norton themselves readily admit, the balanced scorecard is only a template, a template that must be customized for the specific elements of an organization or industry.

For it to work effectively within an IT department, the balanced scorecard approach must be adopted by the organization as a whole. That is, IT departments crafting balanced scorecards in isolation are doomed to failure. It is only when the organization develops an organizationwide set of linked, or cascading, scorecards that there can be any hope of success.

What Is This Book About?

This book is about the balanced scorecard. While it does thoroughly explain the concept of the scorecard framework from both the corporate and IT perspectives, it does something even more important: it lays the groundwork for implementation of the scorecard approach. It does this by providing examples, case histories, and current research and thinking for some very important concepts — performance measurement and management, continuous process improvement, benchmarking, metrics selection, even people management — and then discusses how to integrate all of this into the four perspectives of the balanced scorecard. Essentially, this book provides a comprehensive one-stop-shopping "how-to" approach that will lead you to success. One would not want anything less.

References

McFarlan, F.W. and J.I. Cash. (1989). *Competing through Information Technology*. Boston: Harvard Business School Video Series.

Porter, M. (1980). *Competitive Strategy*. New York: Macmillan.

Thor, Carl G. (1994). *Doing and Rewarding: Inside a High-Performance Organization*. Portland, OR: Productivity Press.

Uyterhoeven, H., R. Ackerman, and J. Rosenblum.(1977). *Strategy and Organization*. Homewood, IL: Richard D. Irwin, Inc.

Chapter 1

Why Balanced Scorecard?

95 Percent of a typical workforce does not understand its organization's strategy.

90 Percent of organizations fail to execute their strategies successfully.

86 Percent of executive teams spend less than one hour per month discussing strategy.

70 Percent of organizations do not link middle management incentives to strategy.

60 Percent of organizations do not link strategy to budgeting.

—Balanced Scorecard Collaborative (2004)

McKinsey and Company (2002) studied the impact of information technology (IT) in its controversial *Productivity Report 1995–2000*. This report challenged the long-held view that IT has been the engine responsible for widespread productivity gains. The McKinsey report relates productivity gains to IT investments in only six economic sectors: retail, wholesale, securities, telecom, semiconductors, and computer manufacturing.

While most in the IT field disagree with its findings the McKinsey report, given the renown and influence of its authors, has caused a bit of a stir in corporate boardrooms far and wide. Carr (2003) reports that the percentage of capital expenditures devoted to IT in the United States grew from 5 percent in 1965 to 15 percent in the early 1980s, reached 30 percent by the middle of the 1990s, and exploded to almost 50 percent by the end of the millennium. As a result, senior managers have redoubled their efforts to judge the true benefits of IT.

What Is Balanced Scorecard?

The technique that many companies have selected, and not coincidentally the topic of this book, is the *balanced scorecard*, as shown in Figure 1.1. Heralded by the *Harvard Business Review* as one of the most significant management ideas of the past 75 years, the balanced scorecard has been implemented in companies to both measure as well as manage the IT effort.

Robert S. Kaplan and David P. Norton developed the balanced scorecard approach in the early 1990s to compensate for their perceived shortcomings of using only financial metrics to judge corporate performance. They recognized that in this "New Economy" it was also necessary to value intangible assets. Because of this, they urged companies to measure such esoteric factors as quality and customer satisfaction. By the middle 1990s, the balanced scorecard became the hallmark of a well-run company. Kaplan and Norton often compare their approach for managing a company to that of pilots viewing assorted instrument panels in an airplane's cockpit — both have a need to monitor multiple aspects of their working environment.

In the scorecard scenario, a company organizes its business goals into discrete, all-encompassing perspectives: financial, customer, internal process, and learning/growth. The company then determines cause–effect relationships; for example, satisfied customers buy more goods, which increases revenue. Next, the company lists measures for each goal, pinpoints targets, and identifies projects and other initiatives to help reach those targets.

Departments create scorecards tied to the company's targets, and employees and projects have scorecards tied to their department's targets. This cascading nature provides a line of sight between each individual, what they are working on, the unit they support, and how that impacts the strategy of the whole enterprise.

Bain & Co's (2003) *Management Tools* report, which surveyed more than 6000 global businesses, found that 62 percent were using a balanced

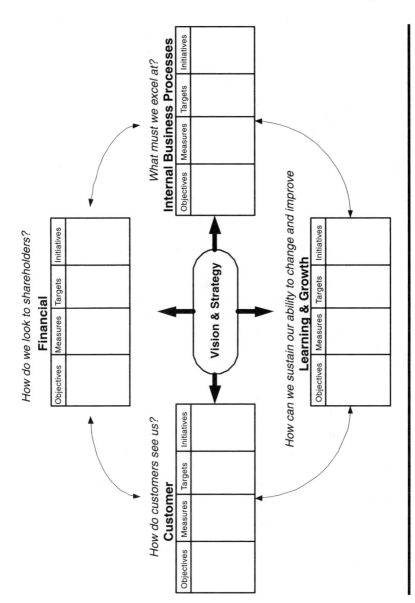

FIGURE 1.1 The balanced scorecard and its four perspectives.

scorecard approach. General Electric, Home Depot, Wal-Mart, and Mobil are among the many well-publicized companies using this approach.

Kaplan and Norton (2001) both emphasize that the approach is more than just a way to identify and monitor metrics. It is also a way to manage change and increase a company's effectiveness, productivity, and competitive advantage. Essentially, as Kaplan and Norton put it, a company that uses the scorecard to identify and then realize strategic goals is a *strategy-focused organization*. Cigna is a good example of this. According to Norton, when Cigna started its balanced scorecard process, the company had negative shareholder value. The parent company was trying to sell Cigna but had no takers. Five years and a few balanced scorecards later, Cigna was sold for $3 billion.

For IT managers, the balanced scorecard is an invaluable tool that will finally permit IT to link to the business side of the organization using a "cause-and-effect" approach. Some have likened the balanced scorecard to a new language, which enables IT and business line managers to think together about what IT can do to support business performance. A beneficial side effect of the use of the balanced scorecard is that, when all measures are reported, one can calculate the strength of relations between the various value drivers (Van Der Zee and De Jong, 1999). For example, if the relation between high development costs and high profit levels is weak for a long time, it can be inferred that the developed software docs not sufficiently contribute to results as expressed by the other (e.g., financial) performance measures.

So, how does a company adopt a successful scorecard approach? According to Kaplan and Norton (2001):

> Each organization we studied did it a different way, but you could see that, first, they all had strong leadership from the top. Second, they translated their strategy into a balanced scorecard. Third, they cascaded the high-level strategy down to the operating business units and the support departments. Fourth, they were able to make strategy everybody's everyday job, and to reinforce that by setting up personal goals and objectives and then linking variable compensation to the achievement of those target objectives. Finally, they integrated the balanced scorecard into the organization's processes, built it into the planning and budgeting process, and developed new reporting frameworks as well as a new structure for the management meeting.

The key, then, is to develop a scorecard that naturally builds in cause-and-effect relationships, includes sufficient performance drives, and, finally, provides a linkage to appropriate financial measures.

At the very lowest level, a discrete software system can be evaluated using the balanced scorecard. The key, here, is the connectivity between the system and the objectives of the organization as a whole.

Attributes of Successful Performance Measurement Systems

Various governmental groups, including the National Partnership for Reinventing Government (*Guide to a Balanced Scorecard Performance Management Methodology*, 1999), found that there were certain attributes that set apart successful performance measurement and management systems, including:

- *A conceptual framework is needed for the performance measurement and management system.* Every organization, regardless of type, needs a clear and cohesive performance measurement framework that is understood by all levels of the organization and that supports objectives and the collection of results.
- *Effective internal and external communications are the keys to successful performance measurement.* Effective communication with employees, process owners, customers, and stakeholders is vital to the successful development and deployment of performance measurement and management systems.
- *Accountability for results must be clearly assigned and well-understood.* High-performance organizations clearly identify what it takes to determine success and make sure that all managers and employees understand what they are responsible for in achieving organizational goals.
- *Performance measurement systems must provide intelligence for decision makers, not just compile data.* Performance measures should be limited to those that relate to strategic organizational goals and objectives, and that provide timely, relevant, and concise information for use by decision makers — at all levels — to assess progress toward achieving predetermined goals. These measures should produce information on the efficiency with which resources are transformed into goods and services, on how well results compare to a program's intended purpose, and on the effectiveness of organizational activities and operations in terms of their specific contribution to program objectives.
- *Compensation, rewards, and recognition should be linked to performance measurements.* Performance evaluations and rewards should be tied to specific measures of success by linking financial

and nonfinancial incentives directly to performance. Such a linkage sends a clear and unambiguous message to the organization as to what is important.

■ *Performance measurement systems should be positive, not punitive.* The most successful performance measurement systems are not "gotcha" systems, but learning systems that help the organization identify what works — and what does not — so as to continue with and improve on what is working and repair or replace what is not working.

■ *Results and progress toward program commitments should be openly shared with employees, customers, and stakeholders.* Performance measurement system information should be openly and widely shared with an organization's employees, customers, stakeholders, vendors, and suppliers.

If used *properly,* the balanced scorecard approach provides a framework to accomplish these ends. Notice the emphasis on the word "properly." The balanced scorecard is not a panacea for all organizational problems. Just implementing it willy-nilly is neither going to solve performance problems, nor will it enhance alignment between the business units and IT. For the balanced scorecard to work, it must be carefully planned and executed.

Case Studies

They say that a picture is worth a thousand words. The same can be said about examples. This book is filled with them. The last half of this first chapter presents several case studies of companies and federal agencies that went through the balanced scorecard process. It is worthwhile noting that commercial entities are famously reticent about sharing their performance measurement systems. These are often closely guarded due to their proprietary nature and the competitive posture of the organization. This is why one will find that quite a few of the examples in this book are based on governmental efforts.

Federal Express

Mention Federal Express (FedEx) to anybody and the first image conjured up is overnight delivery. Most laypeople are quite astounded by FedEx's ability to pick up a package today and deliver it by 10:30 a.m. tomorrow — even if the package needs to travel thousands of miles. They are even more impressed when they find that all FedEx planes converge on a single airport in Tennessee in the middle of the night to redistribute their loads and fly to all points north, south, east, and west. Few realize how large a role technology plays in this somewhat super-logistical feat.

It all started when Fred Smith, founder and still head of the multi-billion dollar company, conceived the idea for express delivery as a project in business school. No matter how or why he came up with the idea, Smith was certainly a visionary by understanding, as far back as the 1970s, the importance of technology and quality measurements to the success of his scheme.

Smith's reliance on technology to build the foundation of his business is more uncommon than first meets the eye. Smith was not, and is not, a technologist. However, he does understand the relationship between information technology and business strategy, and actively embarks on policies and projects that reflect this commitment. Understanding and commitment are quite different.

Smith represents this most perfect combination. He's a businessman with a keen interest in what technology can do for FedEx. In fact, his interest is so pronounced that it is said he personally reads voluminous computer trades to keep abreast of any new development that can be leveraged by his company.

FedEx tech centers, which process millions of transactions on a daily basis, are scattered across the globe. The main unit is located at FedEx's headquarters in Memphis, with others in Los Angeles and London. The most interesting unit is located in Colorado Springs. When FedEx began its quest for the perfect system, it had trouble hiring the technical people that it needed. Many balked at making a move to Memphis, mostly famous as the birthplace of Elvis.

In the 1970s, FedEx did a study to determine where the most ideal place to relocate to would be in order to attract the best talent. This turned out to be Colorado Springs. To this day, FedEx senior management believes that this concession to staff morale was instrumental in its ultimate success.

Even in the early 1970s, Smith clearly understood the growing closeness of the world, now called "globalization" but referred to by Smith then as "worldwide logistics." At the same time, FedEx's strategic planning sessions were questioning where the business was going and what the competitors were doing. They asked themselves what would FedEx have to do to stay competitive over the next decade or two. Some interesting things about FedEx set it apart from most of its contemporaries in the 1970s (and even today). First, it understood the coming push toward globalization — although this trend is one that it did not begin to pursue until at least ten years later. Second, FedEx's planning horizon stretched out over two decades, which was more Japanese oriented than its American counter-parts, who usually worked in a window of two to five years. Third, technology was considered the key part of its strategy. Finally, and most importantly, it understood the concept of the balanced scorecard long before the term was invented by Kaplan and Norton. FedEx has certainly been a strategy-focused organization since the day Smith conceived it three decades ago.

FedEx and the Balanced Scorecard

According to Threat (1999), there are three key measurement indicators applied at FedEx. The goal of the *customer-value creation indicator* is to define a customer value that is not currently being met and then use technology to meet that need. Ultimately, the information produced by the system should be stored for analysis.

A hallmark of the "FedEx way" is that FedEx really listens to its customers and creates services and technology to fulfill core needs. When FedEx initiated its overnight services in the 1970s, customers told FedEx that "their peace of mind" required access to more extensive delivery information. The original tracking service was a tedious manual process requiring numerous telephone calls to a centralized customer service center. In turn, customer service had to call one or more of the 1400 operations centers to track a single package. This process was expensive and slow. Today's rapid online tracking capability was conceived to meet this need.

FedEx's tracking system also fulfills another important company requirement. The system automatically calculates whether the commitment to the customer was met by comparing ship date and service type to delivery date and time. This information forms the basis of FedEx's money-back guarantee, and appears on customer invoices. More importantly, this statistic is aggregated for the internal index on service quality that Threat describes as the focal point for corporate improvement activities.

Another key FedEx indicator is *performance support*. The goal here is to create appropriate tools that enable front-line employees to improve their personal performance using the information in FedEx's vast databases. Individual performance is then aggregated to location, geographic unit, and ultimately make their way into the corporatewide statistics. These statistics are available on every desktop in the company.

Examples of performance support indicators, from the perspective of a courier, include:

- Does the count of packages delivered equal the Enhanced Tracker's count of deliverables?
- Does the count of revenue forms equal the Enhanced Tracker's count of shipments picked up?

As the courier is closing out his day's activities, he uses his hand-held device, the Enhanced Tracker, to guide him through this series of performance measurements. During the day, the Tracker records activity information and time per activity as the courier does his job. Information from the hand-held Tracker gets ported to the corporate database with the aggregated historical information ultimately used for manpower tracking, or comparison of actual achievements to performance standards.

Perhaps the most important indicator is *business goal alignment*. This is used to align the incentives of employees and management with corporate and customer objectives.

These indicators, then, form the basis for FedEx's balanced scorecard. The FedEx corporate philosophy — called "People, Service, Profit" — guides all decisions. As founder and president Fred Smith says, "Putting our people first allows them to take care of customers, and if we do that in the right way, our customers will take care of us — completing a cycle that must be balanced as we move forward rapidly" (Threat, 1999).

Federal Acquisition System

In 1993, the Procurement Executives' Association (PEA) of the U.S. Government created the Performance Measurement Action Team (PMAT). Its task was to assess the state of the acquisition system, identify a structured methodology to measure and improve acquisition performance, and develop strategies for measuring the health of agency acquisition systems.

The PMAT found that organizations were using top-down management reviews to determine compliance with established process-oriented criteria and to certify the adequacy of the acquisition system. This method was found to lack focus on the outcomes of the processes used and was largely ineffective in obtaining dramatic and sustained improvements in the quality of the operations.

The PMAT did extensive research and made site visits to leaders in performance measurement and management in an attempt to identify an assessment methodology appropriate for federal organizations. The model chosen was the Balanced Scorecard (BSC) model. As modified by the PMAT, the measurement model identified critical success factors for acquisition systems and developed performance measures within the four perspectives discussed below. Agencies that implemented the PMAT model utilized generic survey instruments and statistics obtained from the Federal Procurement Data System and other available data systems to determine the overall health of the system and how effectively it met its performance goals.

The lessons learned, and the best practices and strategies resulting from the PMAT experience, were used to create an expanded and enhanced BSC model. The PEA believes this revised methodology to be the best for deploying an organization's strategic direction, communicating its expectations, and measuring its progress toward agreed-to objectives.

In the government arena, the "financial" perspective differs from that of the traditional private sector. Private-sector financial objectives generally represent clear, long-range targets for profit-seeking organizations, operating in a purely commercial environment. Financial considerations for public organizations have an enabling or a constraining role but will rarely be the primary objective for business systems. Success for public organizations should be measured by how effectively and efficiently they meet the needs of their constituencies. Therefore, in the government, the financial perspective emphasizes cost efficiency, that is, the ability to deliver maximum value to the customer.

The "customer" perspective captures the ability of the organization to provide quality goods and services, the effectiveness of their delivery, and overall customer service and satisfaction. In the governmental model, the principal driver of performance is different than in the strictly commercial environment; namely, customers and stakeholders take preeminence over financial results. In general, public organizations have a different, perhaps greater, stewardship/fiduciary responsibility and focus than do private-sector entities.

The "internal business processes" perspective focuses on the internal business results that lead to financial success and satisfied customers. To meet organizational objectives and customer expectations, organizations must identify the key business processes at which they must excel. Key processes are monitored to ensure that outcomes will be satisfactory. Internal business processes are the mechanisms through which performance expectations are achieved.

The "learning and growth" perspective looks at the ability of employees, the quality of information systems, and the effects of organizational alignment in supporting the accomplishment of organizational goals. Processes will only succeed if adequately skilled and motivated employees, supplied with accurate and timely information, are driving them. This perspective takes on increased importance in organizations, like those of the PEA members, that are undergoing radical change. To meet changing requirements and customer expectations, employees may be asked to take on dramatically new responsibilities, and may require skills, capabilities, technologies, and organizational designs that were not available previously.

The PEA endorses the balanced scorecard approach for a variety of reasons, including:

- Implementing the BSC agency-wide will provide:
  - A common methodology and coordinated framework for all agency performance measurement efforts
  - A common "language" for agency managers

- A common basis for understanding measurement results
- An integrated picture of the agency overall
■ Helping agencies to develop BSCs for additional functions (e.g., program, human resources, finance, IT) will strengthen the link among the acquisition system, those additional functions, and agency missions and goals. This will highlight how performance improvement initiatives in one area positively or negatively affect performance in another area. Also, this will promote cross-functional coordination of improvement efforts and help break down "stovepipes" in the agency.
■ Acquisition executives may serve as advocates to promote the benefits of the BSC agency-wide by advertising successful improvement efforts, and by discussing the BSC methodology in meetings with the Secretary, Administrator, or senior-level managers in other functional areas.
■ The BSC will provide sound data on which to base business decisions, from allocation of available resources to future direction. This will enable the agency to manage its activities and its resources more effectively. For example, the BSC could form a common basis to support a business case for more resources.

The balanced scorecard core measures were determined by consensus of the participating agencies, given two key constraints: (1) the need to minimize development of new systems for collecting and reporting data and (2) the need to have measures that could be used by each of the participating agencies.

In developing its balanced scorecard measurements, the PEA team identified several performance objectives common to world-class purchasing systems, both public and private. These performance objectives, and the supporting performance measures associated with them, are considered the "core" for assessing system health and strategic performance. They are listed in Table 1.1 within each of the four perspectives.

Customer Perspective

For this perspective, "customer" means the government end user of the contract. This includes direct internal customers and, for multi-agency acquisitions, direct or external customers.

Percent of customers satisfied with timeliness. This is the customer's degree of satisfaction with the timeliness of the delivery of products or services and other factors affecting the acquisition schedule. The timeliness category may include an assessment of the following:

TABLE 1.1   Core Purchasing System Measurements within the Balanced Scorecard Framework

Customer Perspective

Customer Satisfaction
- Percent of customers satisfied with timeliness
- Percent of customers satisfied with quality

Effective Service Partnership
- Percent of customers satisfied with the responsiveness, cooperation, and communication skills of the acquisition office

Learning and Growth Perspective

Information Availability for Strategic Decision-Making
- The extent of reliable management information

Quality Workforce
- Percent of employees meeting mandatory qualification standards

Employee Satisfaction: Quality Work Environment
- Percent of employees satisfied with the work environment

Employee Satisfaction: Executive Leadership
- Percent of employees satisfied with the professionalism, culture, values, and empowerment

Internal Business Processes Perspective

Acquisition Excellence: Effective Quality Control System
- Ratio of protests sustained by General Accounting Office and Court of Federal Claims

Acquisition Excellence: Effective Use of Alternative Procurement Practices
- Number of actions using electronic commerce

Fulfilling Public Policy Objectives
- Percent achievement of socio-economic goals
- Percent competitive procurement of total procurements

Financial Perspective

Minimizing Administrative Costs
- Cost to spend ratio

Maximizing Contract Cost Avoidance
- Cost avoidance through use of purchase cards
- Percent of prompt payment interest paid of total dollars disbursed

---

- Are products and services delivered when needed?
- Are milestones consistently met?
- Is planning performed early in the acquisition process?
- Is communication consistent and effective?
- Does the acquisition office do a good job in preventing problems that might lead to delays?

Data for this measure will come from a customer survey.

Percent of customers satisfied with quality. This is the customer's satisfaction with the quality of goods and services delivered. "Quality" also includes an assessment of whether or not contractors selected for awards offer the best combination of quality and price. Data for this measure will come from a customer survey.

Percent of customers satisfied with the responsiveness, cooperation, and communication skills of the acquisition office. The perceptions, choices, and behavior of all participants in the acquisition process affect the outcome of any acquisition. This element is based upon the degree of responsiveness of the acquisition team, the success of mechanisms that support teaming, and the degree of satisfaction with communications and problem solving. Data for this measure will come from a customer survey.

Finance Perspective

Cost to spend ratio. This element represents the cost for each office to spend one dollar of its customers' funds. This figure is calculated by dividing the operating cost of each office by the total obligations of that office. The cost of operating each office includes salaries, benefits, training, travel, information technology, and contractor support. It is recognized that these elements of cost may not capture the entire cost of the acquisition system, but the decision was made not to attempt to quantify the costs of developing statements of work, conducting inspections, making payments, etc.

In addition, due to the variation in acquisition system organizational structures across the federal agencies, the result of this cost to spend measure may not be directly comparable, one agency to another. Cost to spend measurements should be looked at as only one of the indicators of the current status of the acquisition system's efficiency. The most important focus should be on improvements themselves. Benchmarking across, and outside of, federal agencies can provide avenues of inquiry for identifying best practices for possible adoption, and should also be one of the techniques used to facilitate performance improvement.

Cost avoidance through use of purchase cards. This element represents the number of purchase card transactions multiplied by the estimated costs avoided by using purchase cards versus issuing a purchase order.

Percent of prompt payment interest paid of total dollars disbursed. This element represents the amount of interest penalties paid as a percentage of total disbursements by the agency. This element is calculated by taking the total interest penalties paid by each office and dividing by the amount of total disbursements paid. Data for this measure can be extracted from the Treasury's annual Prompt Pay report or from local financial systems.

Internal Business Processes Perspective

Ratio of protests sustained by the General Accounting Office (GAO) or the Court of Federal Claims (COFC). This element measures the ratio of protests upheld by the GAO or COFC. For this measure, a protest is defined as a written objection by a vendor(s) concerning an acquisition action. This measure is calculated by dividing the number of protests upheld by the total number of new contract awards. GAO data for this measure can be extracted from the GAO's annual Competition in Contracting Act report to Congress, and COFC data can be extracted from local protest control files.

Percent of actions using electronic commerce. This element represents the total number of acquisition actions through use of electronic commerce.

Percent achievement of socioeconomic goals. This element tracks each agency's achievement of the socioeconomic goals established for the agency. This element will comprise several separate measures. For each defined category, the agency's achievements for that category, as reported to the Small Business Administration, is divided by the goal established for that category. The individual measures for the categories are not averaged together. Data for this measure can be extracted from the files of the local Office of Small and Disadvantaged Business Utilization.

Percent competitive procurement of total procurements. This element assumes that cost savings, greater quality, or better sourcing are generally achieved through the use of competition versus noncompetition. This element tracks the agency's percentage of competitive procurements as a percentage of total procurements greater than $25,000. Two data elements will be tracked for this measure. The first is the total number of competitive actions divided by the total number of actions. The second element is the total number of competitive actions plus the number of follow-on actions, divided by the total number of actions minus the number of actions not available for competition.

Learning and Growth Perspective

Extent of reliable management information. This measure captures the extent to which the managers of the procuring activities believe they have timely, accurate, and complete information to make management decisions. The measurement information will come from an appropriate survey instrument.

Percent of employees meeting mandatory qualification standards. This measure identifies the percentage of acquisition employees who meet the mandatory education, training, and experience requirements as identified in the Contract Specialist Qualification Standards. It will be calculated by dividing the number of acquisition employees who meet the education, training, and experience requirements by the total number of acquisition employees in the organization. Data will be derived from the local Acquisition Career Development data system.

Percent of employees satisfied with the work environment. To retain high-quality acquisition professionals and enhance worker performance, the work environment must be pleasant and include the necessary resources for accomplishment of work. This measure represents the employees' degree of satisfaction with items such as tools provided (e.g., information technology, reference material, etc.), working conditions, and reward mechanisms. Data for this measure comes from an employee survey.

Percent of employees satisfied with the professionalism, culture, values, and empowerment. Management plays a vital role in the operation of each acquisition team by directing, motivating, and leading its personnel. Acquisition leadership should foster a professional environment that promotes the efficient and effective acquisition of goods and services from responsible contractors. This measure includes an assessment of the employees' perceptions of organizational professionalism, culture, values, and empowerment. Data for this measure comes from an employee survey.

Contractor Purchasing System

The Department of Energy (DOE) crafted a balanced scorecard for a contractor purchasing system. The mission, vision, and strategy of the system are as follows:

- ▪ Mission: To provide acquisition and assistance services to support accomplishment of the Department's programmatic goals and objectives.
- ▪ Vision: To deliver on a timely basis the best value product or service to our customers while maintaining the public's trust and fulfilling public policy objectives.
- ▪ Strategy: To change the present system's culture, management systems, and line processes consistent with the principles of Quality Management, in order to establish and maintain: a customer focus, a sense of urgency, continuous and breakthrough process improvement, and an emphasis on results.

The system's mission, vision, and strategy are surrounded by the four balanced scorecard perspectives: customer, internal processes, learning and growth, and financial. Each of these perspectives has one or more objectives:

- *Customer* — customer satisfaction. This perspective captures the ability of the organization to provide quality goods and services, effective delivery, and overall customer satisfaction. For purposes of this model, both the recipient of goods and services (the internal customer) and the sponsor or overseer (DOE) are regarded as customers of the business processes. In a governmental model, or for the major DOE contractors, the principal driver of performance is different than in the strictly commercial environment; namely, customers and stakeholders take preeminence over financial results. Recognizing that budgets are limiting factors, public organizations and the major DOE contractors have a greater stewardship responsibility and focus than do private-sector entities.

- *Internal business processes* — effective internal controls, effective supplier management, use of effective competition, effective utilization of alternate procurement approaches, acquisition process, good corporate citizenship through purchasing. This perspective provides data regarding the internal business results against measures that lead to financial success and satisfied customers. To meet the organizational objectives and customers' expectations, organizations must identify the key business processes in which they must excel. Key processes are monitored to ensure that outcomes are satisfactory. Internal business processes are the mechanisms through which performance expectations are achieved.

- *Learning and growth* — employee satisfaction, employee alignment. This perspective captures the ability of employees, information systems, and organizational alignment to manage the business and adapt to change. Processes will only succeed if adequately skilled and motivated employees, supplied with accurate and timely information, are driving them. This perspective takes on increased importance in organizations, such as the DOE and its contractors, that are undergoing radical change. To meet changing requirements and customer expectations, employees may be asked to take on dramatically new responsibilities, and may require skills, capabilities, technologies, and organizational designs that were not available previously.

- *Financial* — optimum cost efficiency of purchasing operations. In government, and with the DOE's major contractors, the "financial" perspective differs from that of the traditional private sector. Private-sector financial objectives generally represent clear, long-range targets for profit-seeking organizations, operating in a purely commercial environment. Financial considerations for public organizations, to include the DOE's major contractors, have an enabling or a constraining role but will rarely be the primary objective for business systems. Success for such organizations should be measured by how effectively and efficiently these organizations meet the needs of their constituencies. In government, and for the DOE's major contractors, this perspective captures cost efficiency, delivering maximum value to the customer for each dollar spent.

Each objective should be supported by at least one measure that will indicate an organization's performance against that objective. Measures should be precisely defined, including the population to be measured, the method of measurement, the data source, and the time period for the measurement. Measures should be written as mathematical formulas wherever possible.

Ideally, measures should be:

- *Objective* — not judgment calls
- *Controllable* — the results substantially in the hands of the organization with the effects of potential outside influences minimized
- *Simple* — easily understood and measuring only one thing
- *Timely* — frequently available indicators of recent or current performance
- *Accurate* — reliable, precise, sensitive indicators of results
- *Graded* — trackable data available before system failure, not binary yes/no measures
- *Cost effective* — providing data worth the cost of gathering it
- *Useful* — providing data necessary for the organization to manage the business
- *Motivating* — achieving the targets should drive good business decisions, not overexpenditure, overcompliance, or other suboptimization

Table 1.2 shows the measures and targets for the four balanced scorecard perspectives.

On to Chapter 2

This first chapter discussed the concept of the balanced scorecard and provided a few working examples. It is hoped that, by now, readers will fully understand that the balanced scorecard must not be done in isolation from the rest of the company. It simply will not work that way. Indeed, the success of the balanced scorecard framework relies on the entire organization taking part in the creation of a series of cascading scorecards that are linked by cause and effect (e.g., if the new system permits

TABLE 1.2   Measures and Targets for Four Balanced Scorecard Perspectives

Objective	Measure	Target
Customer Service		
Customer satisfaction Data source: annual customer climate survey or real-time transactional survey Data generation: accomplished using appropriate survey instrument Data verification: purchasing directors are responsible for accuracy of survey data generation, and for retention of records in accordance with records management requirements Records will be made available for compliance or DOE reviews.	Core: Customer satisfaction rating Percent of customer satisfaction with the timeliness, quality, and level of communication provided by the procurement office The customer satisfaction rating must address the following elements: ■ Timeliness: extent of customer satisfaction with timeliness of procurement processing, planning activities, and ongoing communications ■ Quality: extent of customer satisfaction with the quality of procurement services ■ Communications: extent to which procurement communicates accurate information that impacts the work of the customer's organization The customer satisfaction rating is to be determined using one of the following two alternatives (note: use of one or the other is required): 1. Annual Customer Climate Survey 2. Real-Time Transactional Survey	92%

TABLE 1.2 (continued)   Measures and Targets for Four Balanced Scorecard Perspectives

Objective	Measure	Target
Internal Business Processes		
Effective internal controls Data source: purchasing files, compliance reviews, review boards, and local purchasing information systems (LPIS) Data generation: based on results of compliance reviews, transactional review of purchasing files, review boards, LPIS, etc. Data verification: purchasing/directors are responsible for the retention of records in accordance with records management requirements; records will be made available for compliance or DOE reviews Effective supplier management Data source: LPIS Data generation: data is generated from the LPIS Data verification: purchasing directors are responsible for the accurate reporting of results and for retention of records in accordance with records management requirements; records will be made available for compliance or DOE reviews	Core: Assessment of the degree to which the purchasing system is in compliance with stakeholder requirements including applicable laws, regulations, terms and conditions of contracts, ethics, good business practices, etc. The assessment result is to be expressed in percentage form (Note: In assessing performance under this measure, contractors are to rely primarily on the results of the most recent formal compliance review, information gained from the periodic review of purchasing files, formal review boards, and other appropriate sources. The cognizant DOE Contracting Officer is required to review and approve the contractor's self-assessment method-ology and score under this measure as part of the CO's review of the contractor's BSC self-assessment activities.) Core: Percent delivery on-time (includes JIT, excludes purchase cards)	(Appropriate targets will be negotiated between the Cognizant DOE Contracting Officer and the contractor purchasing organization.) 83 Percent (Appropriate targets will be negotiated) (Appropriate targets will be negotiated) (For all three measures, appropriate targets will be negotiated) 8–10 days for ≤$100,000 30–35 days for >$100,000 10–13 days for all actions Specific negotiations with local DOE office

TABLE 1.2 (continued)   Measures and Targets for Four Balanced Scorecard Perspectives

Objective	Measure	Target

Internal Business Processes (continued)

Objective	Measure	Target
Use of effective competition Data source: LPIS Data generation: data is generated from the LPIS Data verification: purchasing directors are responsible for the accurate reporting of results and for retention of records in accordance with records management requirements; records will be made available for compliance or DOE reviews	Optional: Customer satisfaction with supplier performance Core: Percent of total dollars obligated on actions over $100,000 that were awarded using effective competition (Note: This measure applies to any dollars obligated during the fiscal year on a subcontract or purchase order that was awarded using effective competition and whose current dollar value exceeds $100,000.	
Effective utilization of alternate procurement approaches Data source: LPIS Data generation: data is generated from the LPIS Data verification: purchasing directors are responsible for the accurate reporting of results and for retention of records in accordance with records management requirements; records will be made available for compliance or DOE reviews	Effective competition means, given the size and complexity of the requirement, a sufficient number of potential sources are solicited with the expectation of receiving competitive proposals to support the reasonableness of price or cost. The placement of delivery orders, task orders, or releases against indefinite delivery, indefinite quantity, requirements-	
Acquisition process Data source: LPIS Data generation: data is generated from the LPIS	type or other similar contracts are considered competitive if the underlying contract was awarded using effective competition.)	

TABLE 1.2 (continued)   Measures and Targets for Four Balanced Scorecard Perspectives

Objective	Measure	Target

Internal Business Processes (continued)

Objective	Measure	Target
Data verification: purchasing directors are responsible for the accurate reporting of results and for retention of records in accordance with records management requirements; records will be made available for compliance or DOE reviews	Core: Rapid Purchasing Techniques: 1. Percent of transactions placed by users (number of transactions placed by users divided by the sum of total transactions— including JIT, Purchase Card, etc.)	
Good corporate citizenship through purchasing	2. Percent of transactions placed through Rapid Purchasing Tech- niques (number of transactions placed through Rapid Purchasing techniques divided by the sum of total transactions— including purchase cards, long-term purchasing agreements, e-commerce (see below), JIT, ICPT, oral purchasing orders, strategic agreements and supplier programs)	
Data source: local goals as negotiated with cognizant DOE office		
Data generation: data is generated from the LPIS		
Data verification: purchasing directors are responsible for the accurate reporting of results and for retention of records in accordance with records management requirements; records will be made available for compliance or DOE reviews	3. Percent of transactions placed through electronic commerce (number of transactions placed through e-commerce divided	

TABLE 1.2 (continued)   Measures and Targets for Four Balanced Scorecard Perspectives

Objective	Measure	Target

Internal Business Processes (continued)

by the sum of total transactions. E-commerce means that all communication with the vendor(s) throughout the pre-award and award process is done by electronic means (i.e., paperless). E-commerce tools include the internet, use of CD-ROMs, e-catalogs, e-mail, etc. Use of fax machines is not included unless it is a paperless fax.)

Core:

Average cycle time (exception: purchase card) for each of the following dollar ranges:

Average cycle time for ≤$100,000

Average cycle time for >$100,000

Average cycle time for all actions

Core:

Percent of economic and social diversity and local participation program goals achieved, including SB, SDB, Women-owned SB Goals, HubZone, and Disabled Veterans.

TABLE 1.2 (continued)   Measures and Targets for Four Balanced Scorecard Perspectives

Objective	Measure	Target
Learning and Growth		
Employee satisfaction	Core:	(Appropriate targets
Data source: employee	Employee satisfaction	will be negotiated)
climate survey, focus	rating: percent of	98 Percent aligned
groups, and other	employees satisfied with	
methods as appropriate	the work environment,	
Data generation:	and the organization's	
accomplished by using	professionalism, culture	
appropriate survey	and values. This rating	
instrument and other	may include data from	
information sources.	employee survey, focus	
Data verification:	groups, or other	
purchasing directors	methods	
are responsible for	Core:	
accuracy of survey data	Employee alignment:	
generation, and other	percent of employees	
information sources,	whose performance	
and for retention of	evaluation plans are	
records in accordance	aligned with	
with records manage-	organizational goals and	
ment requirements.	objectives	
Records will be made		
available for compliance		
and/or DOE reviews		
Employee alignment		
Data source: employee		
performance appraisals		
and LPIS as appropriate		
Data generation: data is		
generated from the LPIS		
Data verification:		
purchasing directors		
are responsible for the		
accurate reporting of		
results and for		
retention of records in		
accordance with		
records management		
requirements. Records		
will be made available		
for compliance and/or		
DOE reviews		

TABLE 1.2 (continued)   Measures and Targets for Four Balanced Scorecard Perspectives

Objective	Measure	Target
Financial		
Optimum cost efficiency of purchasing operations Data source: LPIS Data generation: data is generated from the LPIS Data verification: purchasing directors are responsible for the accurate reporting of results and for retention of records in accordance with records management requirements; records will be made available for compliance or DOE reviews	Core: Cost to spend ratio purchasing operation's operating costs (labor plus overhead) divided by purchasing obligations Optional: negotiated cost savings: this consists of negotiated cost savings and costs avoided, plus savings from system improvements all divided by the cost of the purchasing function	(Appropriate targets will be negotiated) (Appropriate targets will be negotiated)

20 percent additional customers to purchase our products online, our profits should rise by 30 percent).

Chapter 2 delves into the concepts of performance measurement, the basis of a scorecard approach, and discusses the use of the balanced scorecard at the organizational level.

References

Bain & Co. (2003). *Management Tools 2003 Highlights.* http://www.bain.com/management_tools/2003_Tools_Highlights.pdf.

Balanced Scorecard Collaborative. (2004). www.bscol.com.

Carr, N. (May 2003). IT Doesn't Matter. *Harvard Business Review.*

Kaplan, R.S. and D.P. Norton. (2001, February). On Balance. (Interview). *CFO, Magazine for Senior Financial Executives.*

McKinsey and Co. (2002). *U.S. Productivity Report. 1995–2000.* www.mckinsey.com.

National Partnership for Reinventing Government, U.S. Department of Commerce. (1999). *Guide to a Balanced Scorecard Performance Management Methodology.* United States Department of Commerce, Washington, D.C.

Solving the Paradox. (September 23, 2000). *The Economist.*

Threat, H. (1999, May-June). Measurement Is Free. *Strategy & Leadership*, 27(3), 16(4).

Van Der Zee, J. and B. De Jong. (1999, Fall). Alignment is Not Enough: Integrating Business Information Technology Management with the Balanced Business Scorecard. *Journal of Management Information Systems*, 16(2), 137–156.

Chapter 2

Understanding Performance Management: Balanced Scorecard at the Corporate Level

---

You can't manage what you don't measure!

Utilizing a balanced scorecard approach requires the company, and each of its departments (including IT), to become *organizationally ready* to implement this new framework. This means that the process of performance improvement, measurement, and management must first be intimately understood. As one reads through this chapter, one needs to think in two dimensions: (1) how this applies to the organization as a whole, and (2) how one can implement these ideas within the IT department. A word of warning: performance improvement must be an organizationwide endeavor. While there will be some positive effects when implementing these programs solely within the IT department, the effect will be diminished by a lack of cohesiveness within the organization.

There are a wide range of definitions for performance objective, performance goal, performance measure, performance measurement, and performance management (*Guide to a Balanced Scorecard Performance Management Methodology*, 1999). To frame the dialog and move forward with a common baseline, certain key concepts must be clearly defined and understood, such as:

- *Performance objective:* a critical success factor in achieving the organization's mission, vision, and strategy, which if not achieved would likely result in a significant decrease in customer satisfaction, system performance, employee satisfaction or retention, or effective financial management.
- *Performance goal:* a target level of activity expressed as a tangible measure, against which actual achievement can be compared.
- *Performance measure:* a quantitative or qualitative characterization of performance.
- *Performance measurement:* a process of assessing progress toward achieving predetermined goals, including information on the efficiency with which resources are transformed into goods and services (outputs), the quality of those outputs (how well they are delivered to clients and the extent to which clients are satisfied) and outcomes (the results of a program activity compared to its intended purpose), and the effectiveness of government operations in terms of their specific contributions to program objectives.
- *Performance management:* the use of performance measurement information to effect positive change in organizational culture, systems, and processes by helping to set agreed-upon performance goals, allocating and prioritizing resources, informing managers to either confirm or change current policy or program directions to meet those goals, and sharing results of performance in pursuing those goals.
- *Output measure:* a calculation or recording of activity or effort that can be expressed in a quantitative or qualitative manner.
- *Outcome measure:* an assessment of the results of a program compared to its intended purpose.

A leading-edge organization seeks to create an efficient and effective performance management system to:

- Translate vision into clear measurable outcomes that define success, and that are shared throughout the organization and with customers and stakeholders.
- Provide a tool for assessing, managing, and improving the overall health and success of business systems.

- Continue to shift from prescriptive, audit- and compliance-based oversight to an ongoing, forward-looking strategic partnership involving agency headquarters and field components.
- Include measures of quality, cost, speed, customer service, and employee alignment, motivation, and skills to provide an in-depth, predictive performance management system.
- Replace existing assessment models with a consistent approach to performance management.

Understanding Performance Management

Several steps must be undertaken to establish performance measures that make sense and are workable throughout the organization.

Step 1: Define Organizational Vision, Mission, and Strategy

The balanced scorecard (BSC) methodology requires the creation of a vision, mission statement, and strategy for the organization. This ensures that the performance measures developed in each perspective support accomplishment of the organization's strategic objectives. It also helps employees visualize and understand the links between the performance measures and successful accomplishment of strategic goals.

The key is to first identify where one wants the organization to be in the near future and then set a vision that seems somewhat out of reach. In this way, as Kaplan and Norton contend, managers have the instrumentation they need to navigate to future competitive success.

Step 2: Develop Performance Objectives, Measures, and Goals

Next, it is essential to identify what the organization must do well (i.e., the performance objectives) to attain the identified vision. For each objective that must be performed well, it is necessary to identify measures and set goals covering a reasonable period of time (e.g., three to five years). Although this sounds simple, many variables actually impact how long this exercise will take. The first, and most significant, variable is how many people are employed in the organization and the extent to which they will be involved in setting the vision, mission, measures, and goals.

The BSC translates an organization's vision into a set of performance objectives distributed among four perspectives: financial, customer, internal business processes, and learning and growth. Some objectives are maintained to measure an organization's progress toward achieving its vision. Other objectives are maintained to measure the long-term drivers of success. Through the use of the BSC, an organization monitors both its current performance (financial, customer satisfaction, and business process results) and its efforts to improve processes, motivate and educate employees, and enhance information systems — its ability to learn and improve.

When creating performance measures, it is important to ensure that they link directly to the strategic vision of the organization. The measures must focus on the outcomes necessary to achieve the organizational vision and the objectives of the strategic plan. When drafting measures and setting goals, ask whether or not achievement of the identified goals will help achieve the organizational vision.

Each objective within a perspective should be supported by at least one measure that will indicate an organization's performance against that objective. Define measures precisely, including the population to be measured, the method of measurement, the data source, and the time period for the measurement. If a quantitative measure is feasible and realistic, then its use should be encouraged.

When developing measures, it is important to include a mix of quantitative and qualitative measures. Quantitative measures provide more objectivity than qualitative measures. They may help to justify critical management decisions on resource allocation (e.g., budget and staffing) or systems improvement. The company should first identify any available quantitative data and consider how it can support the objectives and measures incorporated in the BSC. Qualitative measures involve matters of perception, and therefore of subjectivity. Nevertheless, they are an integral part of the BSC methodology. Judgments based on the experience of customers, employees, managers, and contractors offer important insights into acquisition performance and results.

Step 3: Adjustments May Be Necessary

Finally, it takes time to establish measures, but it is also important to recognize that they might not be perfect the first time. Performance management is an evolutionary process that requires adjustments as experience is gained in the use of performance measures.

Mission, Vision, and Strategy

If it is not possible to demonstrate a genuine need to improve the organization, failure is a virtual certainty.

- *Make realistic initial attempts at implementation.* If initial attempts are too aggressive, the resulting lack of organizational "buy-in" will limit the chance of success. Likewise, if implementation is too slow, one may not achieve the necessary organizational momentum to bring the BSC to fruition.
- *Integrate the scorecard into the organization.* Incorporating performance measurement and improvement into the existing management structure, rather than treating it as a separate program, will greatly increase the balanced scorecard's long-term viability.
- *Change the corporate culture.* To achieve long-term success, it is imperative that the organizational culture evolve to the point where it cultivates performance improvement as a continuous effort. Viewing performance improvement as a one-time event is a recipe for failure.
- *Institutionalize the process.* Creating, leveraging, sharing, enhancing, managing, and documenting balanced scorecard knowledge will provide critical "corporate continuity" in this area. A knowledge repository will help minimize the loss of institutional performance management knowledge that may result from retirements, transfers, promotions, etc.

Techniques for Performance Assessment, Management, and Improvement

The Department of Defense (*DoD Performance Assessment Guide*, 1996) studied a wide variety of assessment and improvement techniques. This section summarizes the findings.

Awareness of Strategic Challenge

Can American companies compete in the world economy? Most advocates of quality and productivity improvement cite the deterioration of the U.S. competitive position with respect to the quality of its products and services. Because the competition is always improving, an organization must be aware of the need to focus on the continuous improvement of its services and products. Continuous improvement, according to Deming and others, is a process of continually improving the design of products, the delivery of service, and all aspects of the way work is carried out. Continuous improvement requires planning, doing the work, evaluating the results, and modifying the way work is accomplished based on those evaluations. Continuous improvement requires a high degree of "people" involvement at all levels and a constant stream of innovative ideas. Some possible actions to promote an awareness of a strategic challenge among organizational members include:

- Publicize the organization's mission and its importance. Use newsletters, bulletin boards, and posters.
- Discuss with a supervisor how one's job is tied to mission accomplishment.
- Find out what the people one serves think about one's services and products.
- Talk about the impact of quality improvement with others in the organization.

Vision for the Future

How will the organization as we know it survive — let alone succeed — in the face of increased global competition and rapid changes in technology? Organizations must be aware of their competition and changing economic conditions in order to thrive in the future. All companies utilize business or strategic plans that begin with determining direction. The direction to be pursued depends on answers to such questions as: What is the purpose of this organization? What does this organization have to do in the future to remain competitive?

Innovation

How many things are being done in your organization or department just because "this is the way that it has always been done?" Many times, there are good reasons for the tried-and-true approach. However, there are likely to be more than a few instances where a fresh approach can be a better approach. The best source of ideas about these new approaches is the people involved. Here are some ideas about tapping into this source.

- Make sure people are not afraid to try something new. Do not punish creativity but rather encourage calculated risk taking.
- Publicize success stories and give credit to the initiators.
- Institute a suggestion system — attach a bonus for the best suggestion.
- Allow more freedom for people to guide their own work.
- Introduce formal mechanisms for the implementation of new ideas.

Quality Philosophy

Simply telling staff to "think quality" will have little effect. To be effective, everyone in the organization must be aware of and committed to a quality policy or philosophy. Some actions include:

- Adopt a quality philosophy or policy.
- Write it down and publicize it.
- Provide training so that people can implement it.
- Get people involved in "making it happen."

Establishing a quality policy demands that senior executives and managers come to grips with defining quality and defining means for measuring quality. A policy should make clear to staff what is expected from them. To be most effective, the policy should:

- Be written
- Contain specific goals and objectives
- Be published and widely disseminated
- Hold people accountable for successes and failures
- Be taken seriously by organizational members

Value Systems

Every organization promotes a set of values that guide people in their work. This can be done consciously, as in cases where specific values are promoted in policy statements, or unconsciously, by values conveyed through the actions and examples of senior executives. People in an organization may be receiving a message that is inconsistent with quality and productivity improvement. Some possible actions include:

- Make values you wish to promote explicit — incorporate them into a quality policy.
- Demonstrate the values in every way possible — make sure words and actions of senior executives are consistent with the values.

Ethics

Honesty and integrity can provide a cornerstone to the quality and productivity improvement process. Quality, flexibility, and innovation require wholesale involvement by organizational members and a willingness to work together, all of which rely on trust. Some ways to promote this attitude include:

- Make only those commitments one can live up to.
- Put ethics policy in writing — try to keep gray areas to a minimum.
- Demand total integrity — both inside and outside the organization.

Senior Executive Involvement

A successful quality or productivity improvement process needs the active participation of senior executives. Such involvement sends a clear, positive message throughout the organization. Some possible actions include:

- Hold regular meetings to review progress.
- Ask organizational members for their ideas about how to improve.
- Follow up on suggestions from organizational members.
- Attempt to find out why the organization may not be meeting a particular goal or objective.

Visible Senior Executive Commitment

Senior executive commitment is a prerequisite for quality and productivity improvement. Unless a leader's commitment is visible and real, those involved in the performance efforts do not see the quality process as important. A leader's day-to-day behavior is an important clue to others as to what value performance improvement has to that person. Some possible actions include:

- Practice what is preached. Set examples of quality and productivity improvement at top levels.
- Regularly review the organization's progress toward meeting its goals and objectives.
- Find out why goals have not been reached.
- Pick a few important areas and demonstrate your commitment through visible personal involvement (e.g., personal phone calls to customers).

Supervisor Role in Quality Improvement

People need to know that their supervisors have the capability, desire, and resources to help them solve problems and to provide advice on quality and productivity improvement.

Make sure middle managers and supervisors:

- Follow up on problems brought to attention.
- Learn about quality and productivity tools and techniques.
- Serve as coaches for quality improvement projects.

Supervisor Concern for Improvement

The managers (at all levels) in an organization, by their words, actions, support, and choices, make it clear to organizational members what is important. For everyone in the organization to become committed to quality or productivity improvement, it must be clear that the managers are so committed. Some ways to send this message include:

- Listen to organizational members.
- Emphasize quality and productivity improvement at all levels of the organization.
- Hold regular meetings attended by representatives from all levels of the organization to discuss progress and barriers to improvement.
- Recognize and publicize success stories.
- Establish an Executive Council for Total Quality Management implementation.

System or Structure for Quality Improvement

Sometimes, the barriers to quality improvement exist in the structure or system. It may be beneficial to examine the system as it supports or inhibits quality improvement. While much of the structure or system cannot be changed, it is likely that there are some areas where change is possible. Some actions include:

- Construct flowcharts depicting inputs, outputs, customers, and interfaces with other organizations. These can be constructed for various levels of the organization. Attempt to identify likely quality improvement areas.
- Implement quality teams.
- Ask the people involved for ideas about changing the structure or system.
- Track improvement progress after a change has been made.

Awareness of Quality Issues

Staff members should be aware of the importance of a quality or productivity improvement process. To promote awareness, some actions include:

- If a quality or productivity improvement process is already in place, publicize it. Use newsletters, bulletin boards, etc.
- Write down the organization's quality or productivity improvement policy and then make sure everyone sees it.

Attitudes and Morale

People are the most basic quality and productivity factor in any organization. The attitudes and morale of the workforce are important determinants of quality and productivity improvement. Motivation underlies every person's performance. Motivation is affected by quality of leadership, job fulfillment, personal recognition, and the overall support present in the working environment. Here are some things to consider to improve morale:

- Resolve complaints.
- Assign jobs in an equitable manner.
- Recognize top performance.
- Make sure appropriate training is available for advancement.

Cooperation

It is important that a spirit of cooperation and teamwork exists in all areas of the organization. When individuals are rewarded only for their own accomplishments, team efforts can suffer. Some actions include:

- Reward team accomplishments — utilize recognition, increased responsibilities, some time off.
- Set aside a few hours every few months for team members to sit down together to discuss how they are working together or any problems they may be having.
- Encourage teams to develop group identities (a logo, team name). Locate members in the same area if possible.
- Establish cross-functional quality teams.

Workforce Involvement

People want to have their ideas and opinions given careful consideration. When initiating a quality improvement process, everyone should be involved because people's support and commitment are necessary for success. Some ideas to get people involved include

- Use a team approach to clarify mission, define performance measures, set goals, etc.
- If a total team approach is not appropriate, allow workgroup members to "vote" and to suggest alternative performance measures, goals, etc.

Perceptions of Work Environment

People must perceive that there are enough of the appropriate personnel to get the job done and that their work goals or standards are fair. Some actions include:

- Reexamine workloads and reassign people if necessary.
- Allow organizational members to participate in setting work goals and standards. If participation is not possible, perhaps voting among a set of alternatives could be utilized.

Social Interactions

Social interactions may not appear to be related to quality improvement at first glance. However, in most organizations, people need to work together for a common goal to accomplish their work successfully. It is certainly easier and more enjoyable to work together in a friendly atmosphere and, most likely, more productive as well. To promote a friendly work environment, one may want to:

- Encourage after-work recreational activities.
- Encourage fair treatment of all organizational members.
- Make sure work is assigned equitably.
- Ensure that work goals and standards are reasonable.
- Discourage favoritism.

Tasks and Characteristics

Sometimes, barriers to quality improvement can be found in the tasks themselves. People need the appropriate supplies, equipment, information, and time to accomplish their work. Work delays can often be attributed to one or more of these barriers. Some actions include:

- Find out why there is never enough time to complete a certain job(s); the reasons might include:
  - Equipment may be outdated.
  - Equipment may be unknowingly abused and so needs frequent repair.
  - Timely information may be a problem.
- Take steps to correct these situations, to include:
  - Assign a performance action team to work the problems.
  - An outside organization may be required to perform a job analysis.

Rewards and Recognition

People are influenced by the consequences of their actions. When establishing goals and improvement plans, consider the informal and formal rewards that are in place. In addition to money, people work for things such as achievement, influence, advancement, job satisfaction, autonomy, and recognition. Here are some ideas:

- Make sure promotions are tied to performance.
- Encourage supervisors to give credit to their top performers.
- Recognize top performance:
  - Picture in newsletter
  - Special job title
  - Note of thanks
  - Parking space
  - Special badge or insignia
  - Special privileges
  - Prizes, trophies, or certificates
- Compensate top performers in some way:
  - An afternoon off
  - Incentive awards
  - Gain sharing
  - Provide increased responsibility or work restructuring

Customer Orientation

Keeping in mind that there are internal as well as possible external customers, the encouragement of customer orientation can lead to some real gains in quality and productivity.

- Promote an awareness of internal and external customers who deserve and demand one's best efforts.
- Ask customers about ways to improve:
  - Call them.
  - Establish cross-functional action teams and invite customers to participate.
  - Survey customers.
  - Ask your front-line service providers about what customers want.
- Tie good performance to rewards such as recognition.
- Make sure all organizational members are treated as they are expected to treat their "customers."

Communications

It is very important that staff members get the information they need to do their jobs. Some actions include:

- Open channels of communication between work units organizations:
  - Have representatives hold monthly meetings to exchange information.
  - Establish "regular" correspondence that contains the needed information.

Automate if possible. The information may already be available through another source, for example, via computer printouts used for other purposes. Have copies of the relevant portions sent to additional locations.

Work Unit Input Measures

To establish goals (and evaluate performance against them), input measures must be developed and regularly monitored. Input measures describe the resources, time, and staff utilized for a program. Financial resources can be identified as current dollars, or discounted, based on economic or accounting practices. Nonfinancial measures can be described in proxy measures. These measures are not described in terms of ratios. They are often used as one element of other measures such as efficiency and effectiveness measures, which are described in other sections of this book.
Examples include:

1. Total funding
2. Actual number of labor hours

Work Unit Output Measures

To establish goals (and evaluate performance against them), output measures must be developed and regularly monitored. Output measures describe goods or services produced. Outputs can be characterized by a discrete definition of the service or by a proxy measure that represents the product. Highly dissimilar products can be rolled up into a metric. As with input measures, these measures are not described in terms of ratios. They are often used as one element of other measures, such as efficiency and effectiveness measures, which are described later.

Examples:

1. Number of line items shipped
2. Number of pay accounts maintained
3. Dollar of sales for commissary
4. Net operating result
5. Total number of transactions for the period

Work Unit Efficiency Measures

To establish goals (and evaluate performance against them), efficiency measures must be developed and regularly monitored. Efficiency is the measure of the relationship of outputs to inputs and is usually expressed as a ratio. These measures can be expressed in terms of actual expenditure of resources as compared to expected expenditure of resources. They can also be expressed as the expenditure of resources for a given output.

Examples include:

1. Unit cost per output

$$\frac{\text{Total cost of operations}}{\text{Number of completed transactions (or units produced)}}$$

2. Labor productivity

$$\frac{\text{Number of completed transactions (or units produced)}}{\text{Actual number of labor hours}}$$

3. Cycle time

$$\frac{\text{Number of days to complete job order}}{\text{Number of job orders completed}}$$

Work Unit Effectiveness Measures

To establish goals (and evaluate performance against them), effectiveness measures must be developed and regularly monitored. Effectiveness measures are measures of output conformance to specified characteristics. Examples include:

1. Quantity

$$\frac{\text{Number of engines repaired}}{\text{Number of engines requiring repair}}$$

2. Timeliness

$$\frac{\text{Number of transactions completed by target time}}{\text{Total number of transactions for period}}$$

3. Quality

$$\frac{\text{Number of defect-free products received by customers}}{\text{Number of products received by customers}}$$

4. Customer satisfaction:
   a. Customer satisfaction survey results
   b. Complaint rates

Work Unit Direct Outcomes

To establish goals (and evaluate performance against them), direct outcome measures must be developed and regularly monitored. Direct outcomes measures assess the effect of output against a given objective standard. Examples include:

1. Materiel readiness rate
2. Health status of eligible population provided with medical care

Work Unit Impact Measures

To establish goals (and evaluate performance against them), impact measures must be developed and regularly monitored. Impact measures describe how the outcome of a program affects strategic organization or mission objectives. An example:

1. Impact of materiel readiness on execution of Operation Desert Storm

Diagnosis

To implement a customer-driven strategy in an organization, one must first learn what one is (and is not) doing now that will drive or impede the quality improvement process. An internal evaluation, or diagnosis, of key areas and processes in the organization can help determine what one is doing right and where improvement is needed. Doing things right means:

- Defining customer requirements
- Turning customer requirements into specifications
- Identifying key indicators that can be tracked to learn which requirements are being met and which are not

Warranties and Guarantees

Warranties and guarantees demonstrate the organization's commitments to customers. Whether explicit or implicit, they are promises made to customers about products or services. These commitments should promote trust and confidence among customers in the organization's products, services, and relationships. Make sure that the organization's commitments:

- Address the principal concerns of customers
- Are easily understandable
- Are specific and concise
- Are periodically revisited to ensure that quality improvements are reflected
- Compare favorably with those of competing companies

Supplier Activities

Quality results demand that supplies, materials, commodities, and services required by the organization meet quality specifications. One of the best ways to ensure this is to develop long-term relationships with suppliers. The purchase of supplies should not be made on the basis of price tag alone. The development of a long-term relationship requires that the supplier also be concerned with quality and work with the organization as part of a team to reduce costs and improve quality. Some ways to involve suppliers as part of a team include:

- Have suppliers review a product or service throughout the development cycle.
- Make sure suppliers know how you define quality requirements.
- Work with suppliers to agree on quality goals.

Definition (Senior Executives)

To successfully improve organizational performance, senior executives must clearly define:

- The organization's strategic plan
- The organization's annual performance plan
- Performance measures

Performance Measurement

Strategic planning is a disciplined effort to produce fundamental decisions and actions that shape and guide what an organization is, what it does, and why it does it. It requires broad-scale information gathering, an exploration of alternatives, and an emphasis on the future implications of present decisions. Each strategic plan should include a mission statement, general performance goals and objectives, a description of how the goals will be achieved, and an indication of how program evaluations were used in establishing or revising the goals.

The mission of an organization describes its reason for existence. Mission statements are broad and expected to remain in effect for an extended period of time. The statement should be clear and concise, summarizing what the organization does by law and presenting the main purposes for all its major functions and operations. This is often accompanied by an overarching statement of philosophy or strategic purpose intended to convey a vision for the future and an awareness of challenges from a top-level perspective.

Performance goals are sometimes referred to as objectives by other organizations. Note that the terms can be used interchangeably. Performance goals or objectives elaborate on the mission statement and constitute a specific set of policy, programmatic, or management objectives for the programs and operations covered in the strategic plan. They must be expressed in a manner that allows a future assessment of whether a goal has been achieved.

A description of how the goals will be achieved must also be included in a strategic plan. The description should include a schedule for significant actions, a description of resources required to achieve the goals, and the identification of key external factors that might affect achievement of the goals.

Program evaluation is an analytic process used to measure program outcomes. The results of program evaluations are used to help establish and revise goals.

Annual performance plans are derived from the strategic plan and set specific performance goals for a particular period of time. A performance plan should include performance goals and the performance indicators that will be used to assess whether performance goals have been attained. These performance goals are to be expressed in objective, quantifiable, and measurable form.

Performance measures are used to measure goal attainment. They provide a basis for comparing actual program results with established performance goals. A range of measures should be developed for each program.

There are three major categories of performance measures: (1) factor of production measures, (2) outcome measures, and (2) work process measures. It is usually desirable for all three categories to be represented among an organization's set of measures to achieve balanced measurement across a mission.

Factor of Production Measures

These measures typically describe the resource to output relationship. They often focus on different aspects of the resources to output relationship. There are four distinct types of factor of production measures: input, output, efficiency, and effectiveness.

Input Measures

These measures describe the resources, time, and staff utilized for a program. Financial resources can be identified as current dollars, or discounted, based on economic or accounting practices. Nonfinancial measures can be described in proxy measures. These measures are not described in terms of ratios. They are often used as one element of other measures, such as efficiency and effectiveness measures, which are described later. Examples include:

1. Total funding
2. Actual number of labor hours

Output Measures

These measures describe goods or services produced. Outputs can be characterized by a discrete definition of the service or by a proxy measure that represents the product. Highly dissimilar products can be rolled up into a metric. As with input measures, these measures are not described in terms of ratios. They are often used as one element of other measures, such as efficiency and effectiveness measures, which are described later. Examples include:

1. Number of line items shipped
2. Number of pay accounts maintained
3. Dollars of sales for commissary
4. Net operating result
5. Total number of transactions for the period

Efficiency Measures

Efficiency is the measure of the relationship of outputs to inputs and is usually expressed as a ratio. These measures can be expressed in terms of *actual* expenditure of resources as compared to *expected* expenditure of resources. They can also be expressed as the expenditure of resources for a given output. Examples include:

1. Unit cost per output

$$\frac{\text{Total cost of operations}}{\text{Number of completed transactions (or units produced)}}$$

2. Labor productivity

$$\frac{\text{Number of completed transactions (or units produced)}}{\text{Actual number of labor hours}}$$

3. Cycle time

$$\frac{\text{Number of days to complete job order}}{\text{Number of job orders completed}}$$

Effectiveness Measures

These are measures of output conformance to specified characteristics. Examples include:

1. Quantity

$$\frac{\text{Number of engines repaired}}{\text{Number of engines requiring repair}}$$

2. Timeliness

$$\frac{\text{Number of transactions completed by target time}}{\text{Total number of transactions for period}}$$

3. Quality

$$\frac{\text{Number of defect-free products received by customers}}{\text{Number of products received by customers}}$$

4. Customer satisfaction:
   a. Customer satisfaction survey results
   b. Complaint rates

Outcome Measures

Outcome measures describe the results achieved by the product being produced with given characteristics. There are two types of outcome measures: direct and impact.

Direct Outcome Measures

These measures assess the effect of output against given objective standards. Examples include:

1. Material readiness rate
2. Health status of eligible population provided with medical care

Impact Measures

Impact measures describe how the outcome of a program affects strategic organization or mission objectives. An example:

1. Impact of material readiness on product launch

Work Process Measures

Work process measures are indicators of the way work gets done in producing the output at a given level of resources, efficiency, and effectiveness. These measures are a direct by-product of the technique, but do not measure the attributes of the final product per se. These measures are typically processes, or tools, to evaluate and help improve work processes. Some of the common measures include the following.

Cost Effectiveness

This is an evaluation process to assess changes in the relationship of resources to (1) an outcome, (2) an efficiency rate, or (3) an effectiveness rate. Examples include:

1. *Outcome:* Is it cost effective to spend 10 percent more resources to improve base security by 5 percent?
2. *Efficiency:* Will an investment in equipment whose depreciation increases unit cost by 5 percent reduce operating costs by more than that amount?
3. *Effectiveness:* Will a change in the process result in the same efficiency rate but at a much improved effectiveness rate as measured by quality, timeliness, etc.?

Efficiency Reviews or Management Analysis

These basic industrial engineering approaches:

■ Identify the essential output.
■ Flowchart the existing work processes used to achieve that output.
■ Identify resources associated with those processes.
■ Identify and eliminate unnecessary tasks.
■ Perform methods analyses to complete necessary tasks in the most efficient or effective manner.
■ Estimate cost benefits of investment necessary to support alternative methods of performing tasks.

Flowcharting

This is a work process evaluation tool that graphically maps the activities that make up a process. It illustrates how different elements and tasks fit together. They can be used to describe a business process and the physical flow over space and time. They thus provide insight about efficiency and effectiveness opportunities.

Cost-Based Activity Modeling System (IDEF Modeling)

These are widely used techniques to capture the processes and structure of information in an organization. The analysis charts work processes, identifies and eliminates non-value-added tasks, identifies costs of remaining tasks, and focuses on process changes to accomplish needed tasks at reduced costs.

Theory of Constraints

This is a work engineering process that specifically focuses on maximizing throughput, inventory reduction, and turnaround time as key work process indicators.

Macro Management Analysis Reviews

These reviews typically use economic analysis techniques rather than industrial engineering approaches to assess alternative organizations or work processes. An example of this type of review includes a consolidation study of alternative work methods that consolidates organizations or work processes to achieve economies of scale.

Benchmarking

Benchmarking systematically compares performance measures such as efficiency, effectiveness, or outcomes of an organization against similar measures from other internal or external organizations. This analysis helps uncover best practices that can be adopted for improvement.

Statistical Process Control

This is a measurement method used for assessing the performance of processes. Statistical evaluation techniques identify whether a process is in control (e.g., produces results in a predictable manner) and assess the impact of method changes on process results.

Status of Conditions Indicators

These are measures such as accident rates, absenteeism, and turnover rates. They are indirect measures of the quality of work life that impact efficiency and effectiveness.

Organizational Assessment Tools

These are measurement tools designed to identify organization culture and management style, workforce and management knowledge, application of quality and process improvement tools, and organizational outcomes. This form of measurement is increasingly used in leading private-sector corporations to assess potential for innovation, employee empowerment, and internal and external customer relations and satisfaction.

Innovation

These measures are typically qualitative indicators of the rate of introduction of managerial or technological innovations into the work process. Innovation can be used as a barometer of organizational health and openness to new methods and processes.

Quality

These indicators for work processes are various methods of identifying the costs of waste due to work processes or methods that produce less than standard output. These include such indicators as defect rates, rework, and "cost of quality" such as the total resources of time, personnel, and materials engaged in inspection, rework, scrap, etc.

Definition (work units)

To successfully implement a quality improvement process, the various work units within the organization must:

- Know how senior executives define quality improvement
- Have defined long term-goals
- Have defined short-term objectives
- Have defined performance measures to monitor progress

Definition (workforce)

To successfully implement a quality improvement process, organizational members must be able to:

- Specify what goals and objectives they are working toward
- Know how these goals and objectives relate to their work unit's mission
- Know how performance measures relate to the monitoring of goal and objective accomplishment

A good way to ensure this is to invite organizational members or representatives to participate in setting goals and defining performance measures. In the event that this is not possible, make sure that organizational members know what goals they are working toward and how performance measurement relates to them.

Internal Customer Activities

The ability to meet requirements and external customer expectations requires a quality process in place to create the product or service. A quality process is one that converts raw materials or information into completed products or services with each step in the process adding value toward completing the final product or service. Because these steps are "value-adding activities" and usually produce intermediate outputs, their effect on the final output's quality can be substantial.

The recipients of intermediate outputs (materials or information) are internal customers. Their needs and requirements are equally important as those of external customers.

- Analyze your quality process. Construct flowcharts depicting inputs, outputs, internal customers, interfaces with other organizations, and external customers.
- Find out what the requirements and needs of your internal customers are:
  - Ask them.
  - Establish a cross-functional action team.

External Customer Activities

How do your products or services measure up? The best way to find out is by asking the customers. Waiting for complaints is not the most helpful method because complaints usually do not point out what one is doing right. Better methods include:

- Periodically asking customers to complete a short survey
- Phoning some customers to ask them about your service

- Catching people while they are being served to ask them what they think
- Asking your front-line personnel about ways to improve
- Trying out the service as a customer
- Asking the people who are *not* using your service why they are not

Strategic Quality Planning

A very thorough planning process is crucial whether an organization is developing its overall strategic plan or developing plans for specific quality and productivity improvements. Quality and productivity improvement planning should be integrated with strategic planning. Planning can help identify the primary targets for improvement. It can also provide a basis for estimating the resources needed to do the job.

Identifying quality and productivity improvement priorities can be an important part of the planning process. Consider the development and use of criteria to select those areas most in need of improvement. Some criteria that have proven useful for others include:

- Investment plans (potential that investment will lead to increased quality and productivity)
- Net benefit (greatest resource savings for given investment)
- Information or data gathering system (easy to track, automated)
- Quality and productivity improvement potential
- Size of input variables (high burners of labor or capital)

After some likely candidate areas for quality or productivity improvement have been identified, a variety of possible strategies for improvement can be considered. Any strategy considered should be evaluated against and subsequently integrated into the overall business plan. The strategies presented below represent a "checklist" for consideration. They are not always appropriate for every situation.

- Change in strategy
- Improved procedures or work methods
- Better employee utilization
- Training
- Technological improvements

Organizational Streamlining

Obviously, the structure of an organization is not easily open to dramatic or sweeping changes. However, working within the basic structure, there may be opportunities for streamlining that can enhance the organization's ability to support its mission.

- ■ Is timely information getting to the people and work units that need it?
  - − Rerouting or opening channels may solve this problem.
- ■ Are there "chronic complaints" often expressed between work units?
  - − Set up a cross-functional team to define problems and suggest solutions.

Investment and Technology

The lack of appropriate technology (or abuse of existing technology) may be hampering the organization's quality improvement process. Budget constraints play a major role in the acquisition of "needed improvements." In addition to a healthy budget, here are some other things to consider:

- ■ Make sure people are trained in a timely fashion to use the equipment they do have.
- ■ Regularly review and update a realistic schedule for replacing outdated equipment or investing in appropriate technology.
- ■ Plan ahead when purchasing new equipment. Who will be using it? How will they receive needed training?

Methods and Process Improvement

Work processes or methods can often be streamlined or restructured resulting in significant quality and productivity improvement. The ways in which work is accomplished should be reviewed on a regular basis. Some techniques and tools to use are root cause analysis, statistical process control, and the design of experiments.

Good Ideas

The people who are doing the job are often the people with the best information and ideas about how to improve the process. A formal suggestion program is one vehicle used to obtain "good ideas." But sometimes people do not bother to use suggestion programs. Someone might feel that "others must have certainly suggested this earlier, so why bother?" Some other methods include:

- Walk through work units and ask people for ideas about how to improve.
- Have supervisors periodically schedule short meetings to gather suggestions.
- Use quality teams or performance action teams.

Creativity

The success of a quality and productivity improvement process depends on everyone in the organization. Some creativity-inducing techniques include:

- *Brainstorming:* a technique used by a group of people for thought generation. The aim is to elicit as many ideas as possible within a given timeframe.
- *Nominal group technique:* a technique used by a group of people to define and solve problems.
- *Modified Delphi technique:* a technique used to select the "best" or "most important" idea or solution from among a set of suggested ideas or solutions.
- *Quality teams:* these teams are also referred to as Performance Action Teams, or Quality Improvement Teams. These teams might be composed of volunteers who meet regularly to review progress toward goal attainment, plan for changes, decide upon corrective actions, etc. Members are usually from the same work unit.
- *Cross-functional teams:* these teams are similar to quality teams but the members are from several work units that interface with one another. These teams are particularly useful when work units depend on one another for materials, information, etc.
- *Quality circles:* a group of workers and their supervisors who voluntarily meet to identify and solve job-related problems. The group uses structured processes to accomplish its task.
- *Scanlon committees:* committees comprised of managers, supervisors, and employees who work together to implement a philosophy of management or labor cooperation that is believed to enhance productivity. There are a number of principles and techniques involved, with employee participation being a major component.

Quality Training

Successful customer-driven organizations make sure that everyone in the organization receives the appropriate training. Everyone needs to know not only what to do, but also how to do it. Training often takes place on four levels:

1. Senior executives trained in the customer-driven management strategies and skills needed to power and model a service-driven corporate culture
2. Managers or supervisors trained in customer championship, empowerment, team building, coach-counseling, and skills needed to integrate the quality process throughout the organization
3. Front-line customer contact people trained in strategies, skills, and attitudes required to put customer needs first
4. Everyone else in organization trained in service quality awareness and needs of "internal customers"

The above-described training emphasizes the strategies, skills, and attitudes needed to support customers. Additional training for selected organizational members is usually necessary to acquire the skills needed to define performance measures, evaluate improvements, design experiments, etc. Formal training programs can be costly. Here are some possibilities to supplement the ongoing training programs:

- Encourage attendance at outside seminars.
- Provide resources in-house and publicize them.
- Encourage people to take advantage of ongoing training programs. Make sure they know the advantages of participating.

Feedback

The data concerning a quality improvement process that is collected must be seen by the people involved so that they are aware of how they are doing. Feedback should be provided as soon as possible after data collection:

- Report data in summary form — perhaps bulletin boards.
- Include any comparative data (such as trends over time, or goals).
- Spread the word — share comments about any improvements noted by "customers."

Reward Systems

While salary increases and promotions can be powerful rewards, there are other reasons that people find work to be rewarding. Other possibilities include:

- Awards (formal and informal): it is always possible to set up an in-house award for "best effort" or "most improved."
- Recognition: publicize success stories.
- Pats on the back: everyone likes to be told he or she is doing a great job.
- Increased responsibility.

Assessments

Formal surveys are not always necessary. However, surveys can often be conducted by in-house personnel and can provide a quick means to gather important information. Surveys are also another way to get organizational members involved in quality and productivity improvement. People appreciate the chance to provide input into a process that affects them. But be careful! Be prepared to act upon the results and let people know about what is being done. Surveys can be used to assess people's opinions about the:

- Need for quality and productivity improvements
- Goals and objectives that have been proposed
- Data that is being collected or being proposed for collection
- Outcomes of ongoing quality and productivity improvement efforts

Definition (Teams)

Some tools involving group participation that can be utilized to define missions, goals, and objectives are described below:

- *Nominal group technique:* a tool for idea generation, problem solving, mission and key result area definition, performance measure definition, goals and objectives definition. Participants should include a variety of levels (i.e., workers, supervisors, managers). A group leader addresses the subject and presents the problem or issue to be dealt with by the group. Participants spend a few minutes writing down their ideas. The leader conducts a round-robin listing of the ideas by asking each participant in turn for one idea. All ideas are written on a flipchart as stated and no judgments or evaluations are made at this time. Each item is then discussed in turn. Some ideas are combined, some are discarded, and some new ideas are added. The leader then asks participants to vote for the top three, five, or seven priority items. The results are tallied, and the top five priority items (based on the voting results) are discussed. For example, as applied to key result area definition, the top five priority items would be the five key result areas chosen by the group as most important for mission accomplishment.

■ *Roadblock identification analysis:* a tool that focuses on identifying roadblocks to performance improvement or problems that are causing the group to be less productive than it could be. This tool utilizes the nominal group technique to identify and prioritize performance roadblocks. Action teams are formed to analyze barriers and develop proposals to remove roadblocks. The proposals are implemented, tracked, and evaluated.

■ *Productivity by objectives:* a systematic process for involving everyone in a comprehensive plan to achieve selected goals and objectives. This process involves a hierarchical system with councils, teams, and coordinators.

■ *Management by objectives:* an approach that stresses mutual goal setting by managers and subordinates, clarity and specificity in the statement of goals, and frequent feedback concerning progress toward goals. Goals should be couched in terms of specific measurable outcomes (such as units produced, product quality). Goals should be realistic and attainable.

Measurement

Measurement, a method for tracking progress, is fundamental to management even without a formal quality improvement process. There are many types of data that can be collected and monitored concerning quality and productivity improvement progress. Generally, people often refer to six types of data, or performance indicators. These include the measurement of inputs, outputs, efficiency, effectiveness, direct outcomes, and impacts.

The data regarding quality and productivity improvement that can be collected are the "performance indicators" that are described in the section entitled "Definition (Senior Executives)." This data includes the measurement of inputs, outputs, efficiency, effectiveness, direct outcomes, and impacts. This data is just "numbers" unless it is compared to something meaningful. Some meaningful comparisons include:

■ Data compared to benchmarks (similar organizations and world class organizations)
■ Data compared at time intervals (are we doing better? worse? the same?)
■ Data compared to goals and objectives

The data that is collected concerning a quality improvement process needs to be evaluated periodically. For example, suppose data has been collected and tracked over time. Results indicate that improvement has occurred steadily. How much improvement is good enough? When should priorities shift? Some strategies to use for evaluative purposes include:

■ Assign a task force or establish performance action teams to periodically review the data.
■ Use the data to identify problems and barriers.
■ Revise the data being collected to reflect changes in emphasis, etc.

Measurement and Process Analysis

Some tools that can be utilized to analyze performance data or analyze work processes are described below.

Root Cause Analysis

A root cause is the bottom line of a problem. Often, problems present themselves only as symptoms. Symptoms do not explain problems — they point to them. A root cause is the reason for the problem or symptom. Root cause analysis, then, is a method used to identify potential root causes of problems, narrow those down to the most significant causes, and analyze them using the following tools:

1. *Fishbone diagram:* a diagram (see Figure 2.1) that depicts the characteristics of a problem or process and the factors or root causes that contribute to them. To construct a fishbone diagram:

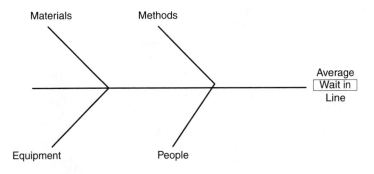

FIGURE 2.1   Fishbone diagram.

    a. Define problem clearly and objectively.

    b. Write problem statement in box at right of diagram.

    c. Define major categories of possible causes (use generic branches). Factors to consider include data and information systems, dollars, environment, hardware, materials, measurements, methods, people, training, and equipment.

    d. Construct the diagram by inserting the major categories at ends of lines.

    e. Brainstorm possible and specific causes and list them under appropriate category.

    f. Vote to identify the likely root causes.

    g. Gather data to construct a Pareto chart to verify most likely cause.

2. *Pareto chart:* a chart (see Figure 2.2) used to classify problems or causes by priority. It helps highlight the vital few as opposed to the trivial many. It also helps to identify which cause or problem is the most significant. To construct a Pareto chart:

    a. Select a problem you want to analyze.

    b. Determine the categories of the problem and collect the data you want to display.

    c. Note the categories on the horizontal axis in descending order of value.

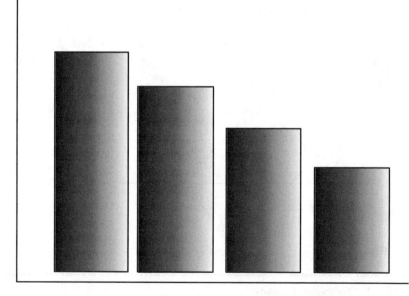

FIGURE 2.2 Pareto chart.

    d. Determine measurement scale (cost, frequency, etc.) and note it on left vertical axis.

    e. Draw a cumulative line from left to right that shows the cumulative percent of the categories.

3. *Statistical process control:* a disciplined way of identifying and solving problems in an effort to improve performance. It involves use of fishbone diagrams to identify the causes and effects of problems. Data is then collected and organized in various ways (e.g., graphs, fishbone diagrams, Pareto charts, and histograms) to further examine problems. The data can be tracked over time (control charts) to determine variation in the process. The process is then changed in some way and new data is collected and analyzed to determine whether the process has been improved.

4. *Control charts*, or run charts (see Figure 2.3), are constructed as follows:

    a. Put what you are going to measure on the vertical axis.

    b. Choose a time interval for taking measurements and put this on the horizontal axis.

    c. Collect data and plot results.

    d. Calculate control limits by finding mean and standard deviation of data and calculating three standard deviations above and three below the mean.

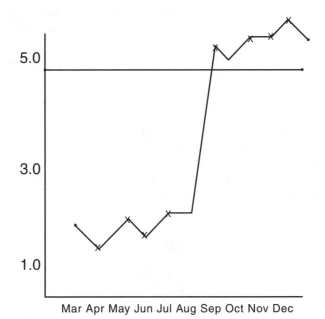

FIGURE 2.3   Run chart.

    e. Draw the control limits and mean on graph.

    f. Results that fall outside the control limits indicate where improvement is needed and should be investigated.

5. *Design of experiments:* an approach using several tools that seeks to reduce variation (similar to purpose of control charts). Some of the tools include multi-vari charts, a components search, and scatter plots. These tools are relatively simple to use and do not require prior statistical knowledge.

Organizational Development

Some tools used in organizational development include those discussed below:

1. *Force field analysis:* a technique involving the identification of forces "for" and "against" a certain course of action. The nominal group technique could be used in conjunction with force field analysis. The group might prioritize the forces for and against by assessing their magnitude and probability of occurrence. The group might then develop an action plan to minimize the forces against and maximize the forces for.

2. *Team building:* a process of developing and maintaining a group of people who are working toward a common goal. Team building usually focuses on one or more of the following objectives: (1) clarifying role expectations and obligations of team members; (2) improving superior–subordinate or peer relationships; (3) improving problem solving, decision making, resource utilization, or planning activities; (4) reducing conflict; and (5) improving the organizational climate.

3. *Transactional analysis:* a process that helps people change to become more effective on the job and can also help organizations change. The process involves several exercises that help identify organizational scripts and games that people may be playing. The results help point the way toward change.

Awareness and Communication

For any process to be effective, people throughout the organization must know about it and understand it. Special publicity efforts may be necessary when a process is first established. There should be a regular mechanism for keeping people informed about progress. Some possibilities include:

- Use newsletters or bulletin boards to publicize the successful results and information about the people who made those results possible.
- Keep informed about what programs and processes are effective in other organizations.
- Establish a quality and productivity library.
- Arrange workshops.

Work Flow and Work Delays

An analysis of work methods and processes may be appropriate to pinpoint common causes for delays. One potential cause may be that members of one work unit are waiting for materials or information from another work unit before they can proceed. Another potential cause could be that equipment is frequently "down" for repair. One may wish to consider the following:

- Assign people (or ask for volunteers) to quality teams. The teams may or may not be cross-functional.
- The teams might use root cause analysis to identify potential causes for delays.
- The teams might then identify potential solutions, implement the solutions, and track data to determine whether or not the situation is improving.

Staffing

In the face of budget constraints, there is probably not much that can be done about understaffing. However, in the spirit of "making the most with what you've got," analyzing work methods and processes may offer some insights for reorganization of work, which would then have an impact upon workload.

High turnover can occur for a wide variety of reasons: lack of opportunity for advancement, too little work to do, too much work to do, repetitive work, working conditions, etc. Some possible actions include:

- Ask members about why people do not remain with the organization. You may be surprised at the answers.
- Use surveys, or ask people informally.
- Depending on the reasons, there may be some things that can be done to improve the situation.

Work Priorities

Sometimes, shifting work priorities is inevitable due to the nature of the jobs. Often, restructuring the group can alleviate some of the problems.

- Give people responsibility to make decisions and be flexible.
- Check on information flow — especially between work units and between organizations.
- Use task teams or project teams when appropriate.
- Assign a quality team to investigate the problem.

Quality

It is important that customers be satisfied with the quality of work they receive. Many of the tools and techniques that have been described in this section can be applied to improve this outcome. Some ideas include:

- Find out what the customers think. Ask them about ways to improve.
  - Call them.
  - Survey customers.
  - Establish cross-functional action teams and invite customers to participate.
  - Ask the employees who have contact with the customers.
- Once you know what the customers think, look for ways to make sure you can "deliver."
  - Analyze work methods using process analysis.
  - Define goals, objectives, and performance indicators for improving quality.
  - Reward people for achieving goals and objectives.
  - Periodically evaluate the results.

Timeliness

It is important that customers be pleased with the timeliness of work being produced. One may need to investigate ways to speed up work processes or deadlines without adversely affecting the quality of work.

Some delays may be caused by waiting for information, supplies, etc. from other work units or organizations with whom you interface. Should this be the case, invite members from those work units or organizations to participate in cross-functional teams. There may be ways to increase the speed with which you obtain your "inputs," thereby increasing your speed in delivering "outputs."

- Analyze work methods using process analysis.
- Define goals, objectives, and performance indicators for improving delivery time.
- Reward people for achieving goals and objectives.
- Periodically evaluate the results.

Balanced Scorecard at the Corporate Level

From an organizational perspective, the concepts of performance management are very much the base that supports the balanced scorecard (BSC) framework. Indeed, the BSC approach becomes very understandable when one realizes that, instead of being a radical new approach to performance management and measurement, it merely brings together and organizes tried and true performance-enhancing "best practices" that companies have been practicing for decades.

On to Chapter 3

This chapter discussed performance measurement and management as the basis for the balanced scorecard. IT managers will need to realize that it is up to them to understand and digest the concepts discussed in this chapter. Not only do these concepts form the foundation for figuring out (1) how to link to other business units within the organization, and (2) how to develop performance drivers, metrics, and targets, but these concepts are also fundamental to implementing a quality and productivity-oriented technology department.

Chapter 3 delves into the key elements of the balance scorecard even more granularly than discussed thus far. Chapter 3 discusses the dual concepts of benchmarking and selecting metrics.

References

DoD Performance Assessment Guide. (1996). Comptroller of the Department of Defense Directorate for Performance Measures and Results.

Guide to a Balanced Scorecard Performance Management Methodology. (1999). United States Department of Commerce.

Chapter 3

Key Elements of a Balanced Scorecard Project

> Not everything that can be counted counts, and not everything that counts can be counted.

> **—Albert Einstein**

Van Der Zee and De Jong (1999) suggest that the following questions be asked before embarking on an integrated balanced scorecard (BSC) effort:

1. Whom Do We Want to Be?

It is important to understand the direction in which the company is moving. What products and services will the company ultimately sell? What markets and distribution channels will it enter? To answer these questions will require the company to look at customer or market positioning, competitive positioning, and core competencies.

Most companies embark on their strategy formulation process by organizing a series of meetings. At times, an external consultant is used to facilitate the process. In all cases, both IT and business line management should be represented.

2. How Will We Get There, and What Goals Do We Have to Achieve?

Once the strategy has been formulated, it is now time to figure out how to get from where one is to where one wants to be. Here, a balanced scorecard (BSC) approach can be used as a framework for discussion. The balanced scorecard cause-and-effect relationships guarantee that cross-functional discussions always promote a common business strategy.

3. What Do We Have to Measure?

Each goal should be a mixture of quantifiable measures and performance drivers. A small European bank, for example, added target measures to selected high-level performance indicators. It decided that operational costs would have to go down by 25 percent and more than 10 percent of sales had to come through new distribution channels within three years. Department managers had to translate the general scorecard into specific scorecards for their departments. Their own appraisals were directly linked to their measured performance.

Getting Ready

The U.S. Government's Procurement Managers Association (*Guide to a Balanced Scorecard Performance Management Methodology, 1999*) recommends the following steps to ensure success when implementing the balanced scorecard:

Step 1: Make a Commitment at All Levels — Especially at the Top Level

Research clearly shows that strong leadership is paramount in creating a positive organizational climate for nurturing performance improvements. Senior management leadership is vital throughout the performance measurement and improvement process. Senior management refers to the organizational level that can realistically foster cross-functional, mission-oriented performance improvements. Senior management should have frequent formal and informal meetings with employees and managers to show support for improvement efforts and implementation initiatives. Also, senior management should frequently review progress and the results of improvement efforts.

Step 2: Develop Organizational Goals

Goals must be specified and publicized to provide focus and direction to the organization. Vision statements and strategic or tactical plans (including systematic ways to evaluate performance) are important for methodically planning acquisition performance improvements. To be meaningful, they must include measurable objectives, along with realistic timetables for their achievement.

Step 3: Offer Training in Improvement Techniques

Training should be provided to appropriate personnel to help them properly make process improvements. The scope of training should include the operation of integrated project improvement teams, the role employees play in exercising sound business judgment, and the specific techniques for making process improvements (e.g., flowcharts, benchmarking, cause-and-effect diagrams, etc.). Comprehensive training is needed to expand employees' technical capabilities and to achieve "buy-in" for undertaking meaningful improvement efforts. Use of facilitators can provide "just-in-time" training to members of process action teams.

Step 4: Establish a Reward and Recognition System to Foster Performance Improvements

Rewards and recognition systems should be tied to performance improvement, as measured by the balanced scorecard. Thus, employee incentives will tend to reinforce the organizational objectives being measured by the scorecard. While handing out rewards to individual employees has its place, group reward and recognition systems are also needed to encourage integrated, cross-functional teams of employees, customers, and managers to undertake acquisition performance improvement.

Step 5: Break Down Organizational Barriers

To overcome unfounded fears about the perceived adverse effects of performance measurement and improvement, the official uses of the balanced scorecard must be spelled out to employees and managers. Managers should explain that the performance measurement data should be used to promote self-assessment, self-improvement, progress in acquisition reform, linkage to the overall mission and goals, and collaborative departmental benchmarking — not to take reprisals against individuals or departments. Also a good idea is the presentation of "success stories" that demonstrate the nonthreatening nature of the BSC methodology. Stakeholders must be shown that a cooperative effort toward performance improvement is the most appropriate course of action — that supporting the BSC is in their best interest.

Step 6: Coordinate Corporate and Departmental Responsibilities

Implementation should be a collaborative effort between the corporate office and the individual departments within the company. These entities should jointly decide on their respective roles and responsibilities relative to the balanced scorecard. In most cases, the corporate office is in the best position to provide leadership, oversight, and a well-defined methodology.

Developing Benchmarks

The central component of the balanced scorecard (BSC) is benchmarking. The dictionary definition of benchmark is "a point of reference from which measurements may be made." It is something that serves as a standard by which others can be measured.

The purpose of benchmarking is to assist in the performance improvement process. Specifically, benchmarking can:

- Identify opportunities
- Set realistic but aggressive goals
- Challenge internal paradigms on what is possible
- Understand methods for improved processes
- Uncover strengths within an organization
- Learn from the leaders' experiences
- Better prioritize and allocate resources

Table 3.1 describes the ramifications of not using benchmarking (Kendall, 1999).

Obviously, benchmarking is critical to an organization. However, benchmarking must be done with great care. There are actually times when one should not benchmark:

- One is targeting a process that is not critical to the organization.
- One does not know what customers require from one's process.
- Key stakeholders are not involved in the benchmarking process.
- Inadequate resources, including budgetary, have been committed.

TABLE 3.1   Benchmarking versus Not Benchmarking

	Without Benchmarking	*With Benchmarking*
Defining Customer Requirements	Based on history/gut feel Acting on perception	Based on market reality Acting on objective evaluation
Establishing Effective Goals	Lack external focus Reactive Lagging industry	Credible, customer-focused Proactive Industry leadership
Developing True Measures of Productivity	Pursuing pet projects Strengths and weaknesses not understood	Solving real problems Performance outputs known, based on best in class
Becoming Competitive	Internally focused Evolutionary change Low commitment	Understand the competition Revolutionary ideas with proven performance High commitment
Industry Practices	Not invented here Few solutions	Proactive search for change Many options Breakthroughs

- One is benchmarking a process rather than a process.
- There is strong resistance to change.
- One is expecting results instantaneously.

Most organizations use a four-phase model to implement benchmarking:

1. Plan
2. Collect
3. Analyze
4. Adapt

Phase 1: Plan

When planning a benchmarking effort, considerable thought should be given to who is on the benchmarking team. In some cases, team members will require training in the different tools and techniques of the benchmarking process.

The creation of a benchmarking plan is similar to the creation of a project plan for a traditional systems development effort, with a few twists:

1. The scope of the benchmarking study must be established. All projects must have boundaries. In this case, one will need to determine which departmental units or processes will be studied.
2. A purpose statement should be developed. This should state the mission and goals of the plan.
3. If benchmarking partners (i.e., other companies in your peer grouping who agree to be part of your effort) are to be used, specific criteria for their involvement should be noted. In addition, a list of any benchmarking partners should be provided. Characteristics of benchmarking partners important to note include policies and procedures, organizational structure, financials, locations, quality, productivity, competitive environment, and products and services.
4. Define a data collection plan and determine how the data will be used, managed, and ultimately distributed.
5. Finally, the plan should discuss how implementation of any improvements resulting from the benchmarking effort will be accomplished.

Phase 2: Collect

The collection phase of a benchmarking effort is very similar to the requirements elicitation phase of software engineering. The goal is to collect data and turn it into knowledge.

During the collection phase, the focus is on developing data collection instruments. The most widely used is the questionnaire with follow-up telephone interviews and site visits. Other methods include interviewing, observation, participation, documentation, and research. Appendix E provides a quick primer on "elicitation" techniques from a software engineering perspective.

Phase 3: Analyze

Once the data has been collected, it should be analyzed. Hopefully, one has managed to secure the cooperation of one or more benchmarking partners so that the analysis will be comparative rather than introspective.

The goal of data analysis is to identify any gaps in performance. Having found these, one will need to:

1. Identify the operational best practices and enablers. In other words, what are your partners doing right that you are not? Then find out exactly "how" they are doing it.

2. Formulate a strategy to close these gaps by identifying opportunities for improvement.
3. Develop an implementation plan for these improvements.

The analysis phase uses the outputs of the data collection phase — that is, the questionnaires, interviews, observations, etc. It is during this phase that process mapping and the development of requisite process performance measurements is performed.

Kendall (1999) suggests that process performance measurements be:

■ Tied to customer expectations
■ Aligned with strategic objectives
■ Clearly reflective of the process and not influenced by other factors
■ Monitored over time

Stewart and Mohamed (2001) suggest a metric template that enables the organization to clearly define a measurement and then track its performance. Table 3.2 details a measurement description card format for a typical process metric while Table 3.3 shows the reported results.

Phase 4: Adapt

Once the plan has been formulated and receives approval from management, it will be implemented in this phase. Traditional project management techniques should be used to control, monitor, and report on the project. It is also during this phase that the continuous improvement plan is developed. In this plan, new benchmarking opportunities should be identified and pursued.

The American Productivity and Quality Center (2001) recommends the Benchmarking Maturity Matrix for a periodic review of the benchmarking initiative. They stress that to understand an initiative's current state and find opportunities for improvement, the organization must examine its approach, focus, culture, and results. The Benchmarking Maturity Matrix demonstrates the maturity of eleven key elements derived from five core focus areas: management culture (e.g., expects long-term improvement), benchmarking focal point (e.g., team), processes (e.g., coaching), tools (e.g., intranet), and results.

The eleven key elements within the matrix are:

1. Knowledge management/sharing
2. Benchmarking
3. Focal point

TABLE 3.2   Measurement Description Card for Measure OP1-M1

Field	*Description*
Decision-making tier:	Project
Performance perspective (criteria):	Operational (OP)
Performance indicator (subcriteria):	Facilitate document transfer and handling (OP1)
Indicator objectives:	IT assists in the efficient transfer and handling of project documents Project staff are proficient in the use of IT-based procedures
Performance measure:	OP1-M1
Measure weight:	50 Percent of performance indicator
Measure description:	Percent of users proficient with IT-based procedures employed on the project
Performance metric:	Percent (%)
Measure outcome:	Ensure that 90 percent of users are proficient with IT-based project procedures
Performance baseline:	50 Percent of users are proficient with IT-based project procedures
Performance targets:	Degree of Performance Improvement / Degree of Proficiency None — 50 Minor — 60 Moderate — 70 High — 80 Excellent — 90
Data source:	Staff will undertake computer proficiency exams
Responsible component:	Project IT manager
Data collector:	Project IT professional
Collection frequency:	Tests will be taken monthly
Report frequency:	Measure is reported on completion of project
Remarks:	None

TABLE 3.3   Monthly Measurement Results for Measure OP1-M1

Month	1	2	3	4	5	6	7
Result (%)	52	55	57	60	61	65	68

4. Benchmarking process
5. Improvement enablers
6. Capture storage
7. Sharing dissemination
8. Incentives
9. Analysis
10. Documentation
11. Financial impact

The five maturity levels are, from lowest to highest:

1. Internal financial focus, with short-term focus that reacts to problems
2. Sees need for external focus to learn
3. Sets goals for knowledge sharing
4. Learning is a corporate value
5. Knowledge sharing is a corporate value

Based on these two grids, a series of questions are asked and a score calculated:

■ Key 1: Which of the following descriptions best defines your organization's orientation toward learning?
■ Key 2: Which of the following descriptions best defines your organization's orientation toward improving?
■ Key 3: How are benchmarking activities and inquiries handled within your organization?
■ Key 4: Which of the following best describes the benchmarking process in your organization?
■ Key 5: Which of the following best describes the improvement enablers in place in your organization?
■ Key 6: Which of the following best describes your organization's approach for capturing and storing best practices information?
■ Key 7: Which of the following best describes your organization's approach for sharing and disseminating best practices information?
■ Key 8: Which of the following best describes your organization's approach for encouraging the sharing of best practices information?
■ Key 9: Which of the following best describes the level of analysis done by your organization to identify actionable best practices?
■ Key 10: How are business impacts that result from benchmarking projects documented within your organization?
■ Key 11: How would you describe the financial impact resulting from benchmarking projects?

The maturity matrix is a good tool for internal assessment as well as for comparisons to other companies.

Choosing Metrics

A wide variety of metrics are discussed in this book. You will have to determine which metrics are right for your organization. However, before even selecting the metrics you will be using, you will need to gear your company up for the process. Berk (2001) has identified the six steps of a benchmarking initiative:

1. *Select the process and build support.* It is more than likely that there will be many processes to benchmark. Berk advises that you break down a large project into discrete manageable sub-projects. These sub-projects should be prioritized, with those critical to the goals of the organization taking priority.

2. *Determine current performance.* Quite a few companies decide to benchmark because they have heard the wonderful success stories of Motorola or General Electric. During this author's days with the New York Stock Exchange, the chairman was forever touting the latest current management fad and insisting that we all follow suit. The problem is that all organizations are different and, in the case of benchmarking, extremely issue specific. Before embarking on a benchmarking effort, the planners need to really investigate and understand the business environment and the impact of specific business processes on overall performance.

3. *Determine where performance should be.* Perhaps just as importantly, the organization should benchmark itself against one of its successful competitors. This is how you can determine where "you should be" in terms of your own organization's performance. Both competitive analysis and phantom analysis, discussed later on in this chapter, are useful tools for this purpose.

4. *Determine the performance gap.* You now know where you are (item 2 on this list) as well as where you would like to be (item 3 on this list). The difference between the two is referred to as the *performance gap.* The gap must be identified, organized, and categorized. That is, the causal factor should be attributed to people, process, technology, or cultural influences and then prioritized.

5. *Design an action plan.* Technologies are most comfortable with this step, as an action plan is really the same thing as a project plan. It should list the chronological steps for solving a particular problem as identified in item 4 above. Information in this plan should also include problem-solving tasks, who is assigned to each task, and the timeframe.

6. *Continuously improve.* In the process improvement business, there are two catch phrases: "process improvement" and "continuous

improvement." The former is reactive to a current set of problems and the latter is proactive, meaning that the organization should continuously be searching for ways to improve.

One of the reasons why there is more than a handful of balanced scorecard implementation failures is that the metrics were poorly defined (Schneiderman, 1999).

Therefore, one of the most critical of tasks confronting the balanced scorecard implementation team is the selection of metrics. A variety of sample scorecards (see Appendix I) as well as metrics are listed throughout this book. However, one cannot just select some from column A and some from column B. Different messages work differently for different companies, and even within different divisions of the same company.

Developed by Thomas Saaty (1994), the Analytic Hierarchy Process (AHP) is a framework of logic and problem solving that organizes data into a hierarchy of forces that influence decision results. It is a simple, adaptable methodology in use by government as well as many commercial organizations. One of the chief selling points of this methodology is that it is participative, promotes consensus, and does not require any specialized skill sets to utilize.

AHP is based on a series of paired comparisons in which users provide judgments about the relative dominance of the two items. Dominance can be expressed in terms of preference, quality, importance, or any other criterion.

Four sets of metrics should be determined, one for each of the four BSC perspectives. Metric selection usually begins by gathering participants together for a brainstorming session. The number of participants selected should be large enough to ensure that a sufficient number of metrics are initially identified.

Participants, moderated by a facilitator, brainstorm a set of possible metrics and the most important metrics are selected. Using a written survey, each participant is asked to compare all possible pairs of metrics in each of the four areas as to their relative importance using a scale as shown in Table 3.4.

From the survey responses, the facilitator computes the decision model for each participant that reflects the relative importance of each metric. Each participant is then supplied with the decision models of all other participants and is asked to rethink his or her original metric choices. The group meets again to determine the final set of metrics for the scorecard. The beauty of this process is that it makes readily apparent any inconsistencies in making paired comparisons and prevents metrics from being discarded prematurely.

TABLE 3.4   AHP Pairwise Comparisons Based on Saaty (1994)

Comparative Importance	Definition	Explanation
1	Equally important	Two decision elements (e.g., indicators) equally influence the parent decision element
3	Moderately more important	One decision element is moderately more influential than the other
5	Strongly more important	One decision element has stronger influence than the other
7	Very strongly more important	One decision element has significantly more influence over the other
9	Extremely more important	The difference between influences of the two decision elements is extremely significant
2, 4, 6, 8	Intermediate judgment values	Judgment values between equally, moderately, strongly, very strongly, and extremely
Reciprocals		If v is the judgment value when i is compared to j, then 1/v is the judgment value when j is compared to i

Clinton, Webber, and Hassell (2002) provide an example of using ADP to determine how to weight the relative importance of the categories and metrics. A group of participants meets to compare the relative importance of the four balanced scorecard categories in the first level of the ADP hierarchy. They may want to consider the current product life-cycle stage when doing their comparisons. For example, while in the product introduction stage, formalizing business processes may be of considerable relative importance. When dealing with a mature or declining product, on the other hand, the desire to minimize variable cost per unit may dictate that the financial category be of greater importance than the other three scorecard categories. They provide the following illustrative sample survey question that might deal with this issue:

> Survey question: In measuring success in pursuing a differentiation strategy, for each pair, indicate which of the two balanced scorecard categories is more important. If you believe that the categories being compares are equally important in the scorecard process, you should mark a "1." Otherwise, mark the box with the number that corresponds to the intensity on the side that you consider more important described in the above scale.

Consider the following examples:

Customer	9	8	7	6	5	4	3	2	1	2	3	4	5	6	7	8	9	Financial
					X													

In this example, the customer category is judged to be strongly more important than the financial category.

Customer	9	8	7	6	5	4	3	2	1	2	3	4	5	6	7	8	9	Internal Business Processes
									X									

In this example, the customer category is judged to be equally important to the internal business processes category.

The values can then be entered into AHP software, such as Expert Choice (http://www.expertchoice.com/software/), which will compute local and global weights with each set of weights always equal to "1." Local weights are the relative importance of each metric within a category, and global weights constitute the relative importance of each metric to the overall goal. The software will show the relative importance of all metrics and scorecard categories. For example, in the prior example, the results might have been:

Category	Relative Weight
Innovation and Learning	.32
Internal Business Processes	.25
Customer	.21
Financial	.22
Total	1.00

The results show that the participants believe that the most important category is innovation and learning. If, within the innovation and learning category, it is determined that the market share metric is the most important, with a local weight of .40, then one can calculate the global outcome by multiplying the local decision weights from Level 1 (categories) by the local decision weights for Level 2 (metrics).

Clinton, Webber, and Hassell (2002) provide a good example of the final calculation, as shown in Table 3.5. These results indicate that the least important metric is revenue from the customer category and the most important metric is market share, from the innovation and learning category.

TABLE 3.5   AHP Global Outcome Worksheet

Balanced Scorecard

Strategic Objective: Success in pursuing a differentiation strategy

Categories and Metrics	Level 1 ✗ Level 2	Global Outcome
Innovation and Learning		
Market share	(.40 × .32)	.128
Number of new products	(.35 × .32)	.112
Revenue from new products	(.25 × .32)	.080
Total: Innovation and learning		.320
Internal Business Processes		
Number of product units produced	(.33 × .25)	.08333
Minimizing variable cost per unit	(.33 × .25)	.08333
Number of on-time deliveries	(.33 × .25)	.08333
Total internal business processes		.250
Customer		
Revenue	(.20 × .21)	.042
Market share	(.38 × .21)	.080
QFD (Quality Function Deployment) score	(.42 × .21)	.088
Total customer		.210
Financial		
Cash value-added	(.28 × .22)	.062
Residual income	(.32 × .22)	.070
Cash flow ROI	(.40 × .22)	.088
Total financial		.220
Sum of the Global Weights		1.00

Looking Outside the Organization for Key Indicators

Competitive analysis serves a useful purpose. It helps organizations devise their strategic plans and gives them insight into how to craft their performance indicators.

The philosophy behind the Combustion Engineering's technique (Conference Board, 1988) is that information coupled with the experience of a seasoned industry manager is more than adequate to take the place of expensive experts in the field of competitive analysis.

The goal behind the Combustion Engineering's technique is to analyze one competitor at a time to identify strategies and predict future moves. The key difference between this technique and others is the level of involvement of senior managers of the firm. In most companies, research is delegated to staff who prepare a report on all competitors at once. The Combustion Engineering's method is to gather the information on one competitor, and then use senior managers to logically deduce the strategy of the competitor in question.

Combustion Engineering uses a five-step approach to performing competitive analyses, as described below.

Step 1: Preliminary Meeting

Once the competitor is chosen, a preliminary meeting is scheduled. It should be attended by all senior managers who might have information or insight to contribute concerning this competitor. This includes the chief executive officer as well as the general manager and managers from sales, marketing, finance, and manufacturing. A broader array of staff attending is important to this technique because it serves to provide access to many diverse sources of information. This permits the merger of external information sources — as well as internal sources — collected by the organization, such as documents, observations, and personal experiences.

At this meeting, it is agreed that all attendees spend a specified amount of time collecting more recent information about a competitor. At this time, a second meeting is scheduled in which to review this more recent information.

Step 2: Information Meeting

At this meeting, each attendee will receive an allotment of time to present his or her intimation to the group.

The group will then perform a relative strengths-versus-weaknesses analysis. This will be done for all areas of interest uncovered by the information obtained by the group. The analysis will seek to draw conclusions about two criteria. First, is a competitor stronger or weaker than your company? Second, does the area have the potential to affect customer behavior?

Combustion Engineering rules dictate that unless the area meets both of these criteria, it should not be pursued further — either in analysis or discussion. Because managers do not always agree on what areas to include or exclude, it is frequently necessary to appoint a moderator who is not part of the group.

Step 3: Cost Analysis

At this point, with areas of concern isolated, it is necessary to do a comparative cost analysis. The first step here is to prepare a breakdown of costs for the product. This includes labor, manufacturing, cost of goods, distribution, sales, administrative, as well as other relevant items of interest as necessary.

At this point, compare the competitor's cost for each of these factors according to the following scale:

- Significantly higher
- Slightly higher
- Slightly lower
- Significantly lower

Now translate these subjective ratings to something a bit more tangible, such as slightly higher is equivalent to 15 percent. By weighting each of these factors by its relative contribution to the total product cost, it is now possible to calculate the competitor's total costs.

Step 4: Competitor Motivation

This is perhaps the most intangible step. The group must now attempt to analyze the competitor's motivation by determining how the competitor measures success as well as what its objectives and strategies are.

During the research phase, the senior manager or his or her staff gathered considerable information on this topic. Using online databases and Web sites, it is possible to collect information about self-promotions, annual reports, press releases, and the like. In addition, information from former employees, the sales force, investment analysts, suppliers, and mutual clients is extremely useful and serves to broaden the picture.

Based on the senior managers' understanding of the business, it is feasible to be able to deduce the competitor's motivation. Motivation can often be deduced by observing the way the competitor measures itself. Annual reports are good sources for this information. For example, a competitor that wants to reap the benefits of investment in a particular industry will most likely measure success in terms of return on investment.

Step 5: Total Picture

By reviewing information on the competitor's strengths and weaknesses, relative cost structure, goals, and strategies, the total picture of the firm can be created.

Using this information, the group should be able to use individual insights into the process of running a business in a similar industry to determine the competitor's next likely move(s).

For example, analysis shows that a competitor is stronger in direct sales, has a cost advantage in labor, and is focused on growing from a regional to national firm. The group would draw the conclusion that the competitor will attempt to assemble a direct sales effort nationwide, while positioning itself on the basis of low price.

Combustion Engineering also devised an approach for dealing with the situation in which an outsider enters the marketplace. Here, the strategy above obviously would not work.

Using the same group of people gathered to analyze competitor strategy, this exercise requests the group to look at the market as an objective third party would. The task is to design a fictitious company that would be able to successfully penetrate the market.

Compare this fictitious company with the competitor firms in the industry to see if any of the traditional competitors can easily adopt this approach.

When Combustion Engineering's phantom analysis uncovers a strategy that traditional competitors might easily adopt, they adopt this strategy as a preemptive move. When this same analysis reveals that an outsider could penetrate the industry by following this strategy, Combustion Engineering attempts to create additional barriers to entry. This includes forming an alliance with an outside company to pursue the phantom strategy itself.

Hruby's Missing Piece Analysis (1989) also attempts to anticipate competitor moves, but it does this by identifying key weaknesses in the competitor. By concentrating on the competitor's weakness, the great wealth of information on that competitor can be turned into usable, action-oriented intelligence.

The methodology for performing Hruby's Missing Piece Analysis is to analyze the strengths and weaknesses of the competitor in six areas. In each of these areas, the competitor is compared to the company doing the analysis:

1. *Product.* Compare the strength of the competitor's product from a consumer point of view.
2. *Manufacturing.* Compare capabilities, cost, and capacity.
3. *Sales and marketing.* How well does the competitor sell a product? Compare positioning, advertising, sales force, etc.
4. *Finance.* Compare financial resources to performance. How strong are these relative to requirements for launching a strong competitive thrust?

5. *Management.* How effective, aggressive, and qualified are the competitor's managers?
6. *Corporate culture.* Examine values and history to determine whether the competitor is likely to enter or attempt to dominate a market.

The goal of this exercise is to identify weaknesses in each of these areas, as well as to see whether any one of these weaknesses stands out as a major vulnerability. According to Hruby, most companies have a key weakness — or missing piece — that can be exploited.

To perform this technique requires that the competitor be rated in each of the six areas listed. Ratings are done on a scale of 1 to 5, with 1 being very weak, 2 is weak/uncompetitive, 3 is adequate/average, 4 is very strong/competitive, and 5 is excellent/superior.

Hruby recommends summarizing the scores in a competitive strengths matrix as shown in Table 3.6. This matrix lists the names of the competitors down the right-hand side and the competitive areas of interest across the top. Scores are entered into the appropriate cells. The worst score for each competitor should be highlighted. This is their weakest point and should be monitored accordingly.

In our example, Company A and Company B are both weak in the finance area. This means that they do not have enough strength to launch a major advertising campaign to bolster a new product. What this means is that if the company doing this analysis is ready, willing, and able to spend a lot of money, a new product launch would most probably be successful.

TABLE 3.6   Competitive Strengths Matrix

	Competitive Areas					
Competitor	1	2	3	4	5	6
Company A	5	3	4	2	4	3
Company B	4	4	3	2	3	4
Company C	1	3	3	5	2	3
Company D	4	5	4	4	5	4

Area 1: Product   Key: 1 = Weak to 5 = Excellent
Area 2: Manufacturing
Area 3: Sales & Marketing
Area 4: Finance
Area 5: Management
Area 6: Corporate Culture

Company C scored a 1 in the product category. This means that its product is not as good as the company doing the analysis. In this case, an advertising campaign emphasizing product differences would serve to grab some market share from Company C.

Company D, on the other hand, scored strongly in all matrix areas. Given a strong product and an aggressive management team, this company is likely to make an aggressive move, perhaps a new product launch or major advertising on an existing product. It might even reduce costs. Company D certainly bears watching.

Company C, on the other hand, has a weak product but a good financial position. It just might launch a new product. However, its weak management structure might defer any product launch.

In summary, upon analysis of the competitive strengths matrix, one would deduce that a combination of strong financial position and competent management provides a mix that indicates a strong likelihood of aggressive action on the part of the competitor. Using this analysis of information obtained from various sources, it is quite possible to keep tabs on what the competition is up to, as well as provide a wealth of performance indicators and measures that could be useful for performance management.

Process Mapping

In 1994, Sandia National Laboratories, with funding from the New Mexico Highway Department and the Federal Highway Administration via the New Mexico-based Alliance for Transportation Research, took on the challenge of finding a way to expedite the movement of freight across the U.S.–Mexico border (Sandia, 1997).

Three years later, the ATIPE computer system (Advanced Technologies for International Intermodal Ports of Entry) was born. Sandia developed ATIPE specifically to expedite the movement of commercial traffic back and forth across the border more safely, securely, and efficiently. ATIPE is built on three technologies: (1) an automated tracking system, (2) a process map that shows all the steps in shipping goods across the border, and (3) a collaborative information system.

A process map shows the entire shipment process. The map actually reads like a flowchart. It depicts all the steps involved in both the physical handling of the material (such as the truck moving across the border, paying tolls, being weighed) and the informational part of the process (such as filling out the forms, the permits, the reports, and making sure U.S. and Mexican customs have the all the paperwork they need to approve a border crossing). The ATIPE process map was based on hundreds of interviews with affected parties on both sides of the border.

The How and Why of Process Mapping

Process mapping is an approach for systematically analyzing a particular process. It provides a focal point for the performance improvement and measurement processes required when implementing the balanced scorecard.

Process mapping involves mapping each individual step, or unit operation, undertaken in that process in chronological sequence. Once individual steps are identified, they can be analyzed in more detail.

Because it is best done in small teams, process mapping is an important focal point for employee involvement. The act of defining each unit operation of a given process gives a much deeper understanding of the process to team members — sometimes leading to ideas for immediate operational improvements.

The following six steps will help when applying process mapping to a company's operational processes.

Step 1: Understand the basic process mapping tool.
Step 2: Create a flowchart of the product's life cycle.
Step 3: Use the flowchart to define boundaries.
Step 4: Identify the processes within the boundaries that have been set.
Step 5: Apply the basic process mapping tool to each process.
Step 6: Compile the results.

Step 1: Understand the Basic Process Mapping Tool

There are two basic components to process mapping:

1. Developing a process map
2. Analyzing each unit operation

Developing a Process Map: Breaking Down a Process into Unit Operations

The first basic step in process mapping is to break down a process into its component steps, or unit operations. The process map depicts these steps and the relationship between them.

Analyzing Each Unit Operation

The second basic step in process mapping is to analyze each unit operation in the form of a diagram that answers the following questions:

- What is the *product input* to each unit operation? (The product input to a given unit operation is generally the product output of the preceding unit operation. For the first unit operation of a process, there may not be any "product input.")
- What are the *non-product inputs* to the unit operation? (These include raw materials and components, as well as energy, water, and other resource inputs.)
- What is the *product output* of the unit operation?
- What are the *non-product outputs* of the unit operation? (These include solid waste, water discharge, air emissions, noise, etc.)
- What are the *environmental aspects* of the unit operation? (These may have been designated as inputs or outputs.)

Step 2: Create a Process Map of the Product's Life Cycle

The first application of the basic process mapping approach is to create a simple flowchart or process map showing the main stages of the life cycle of your product — from raw material extraction to end-of-life disposal (or reuse or recycling). Follow the process mapping guidelines given in Step 1, using the entire life cycle of the product.

Step 3: Use the Flowchart to Define the Boundaries

On the simple process map constructed in Step 2, draw a dotted line around the processes that you want to include in your analysis, as shown in Figure 3.1.

Step 4: Identify the Processes within the Boundaries that Have Been Set

The next step is to identify the processes included in the scope you selected. Looking at the life-cycle process map, most of the basic processes will be obvious. However, there may be some processes or operations that are not central to making the product, but have an impact nonetheless.

Step 5: Apply the Basic Process Mapping Tool to Each Process

Now you need to apply the process mapping tool to each of these processes to generate a process map showing the unit operations for each process. Then use a unit operation diagram to identify the relevant aspects of each unit operation. Be sure to include employees familiar with the operation in question on the team that identifies the aspects.

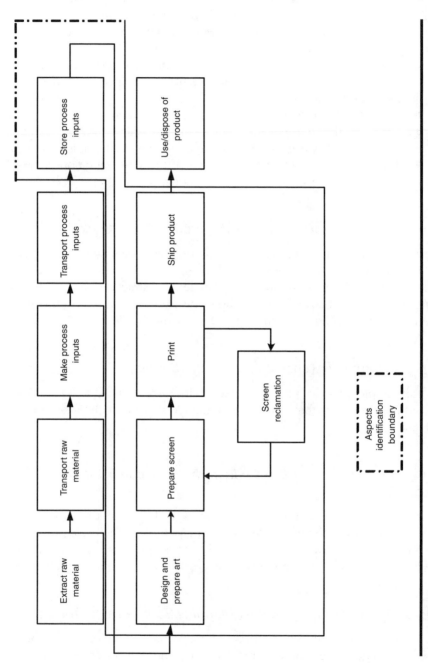

FIGURE 3.1 Life-cycle process map for a screen printing operation with boundaries defined.

The FAA's Cost Activity Measurement System (http://www.faa.gov/ait/bpi/handbook/appndxc.htm) provides a great example of the initial stages of process mapping. In the following excerpt, the process map definitions are defined:

5.3 Manage Work Force: Plan, develop, implement, and evaluate initiatives that support the effective utilization of human resources. These processes include recruitment, selection, training and development, retention, performance management, compensation/benefits, labor/employee/organizational relations, etc. This process provides the agency with a diverse, highly qualified, and productive work force to accomplish its operational mission.

> **5.3.1 Fill Positions and Set Pay:** Define the jobs needed to meet mission requirements and locate, select, determine pay, and hire people to perform the work.
> Outputs from the process:
> 1. New employees on duty,
> 2. Updated CPMIS/CUPS records,
> 3. Filed and distributed SF-50, and
> 4. Unsuccessful applicants.

> > **5.3.1.1 Initiate Request:** Process used by FAA organizations to initiate the filling of positions. Determine the need to fill a position; verify resource availability to fill the position; establish specific position requirements; and initiate SF-52 action.
> > Outputs from the process:
> > 1. Decision not to fill a position,
> > 2. Classified existing position description,
> > 3. Unclassified position description, and
> > 4. SF-52 with supporting documentation.

> > **5.3.1.2 Determine Job Requirements:** Classify, verify and establish positions to fill.
> > Outputs from the process:
> > 1. Classified established position description,
> > 2. SF-52 with supporting documentation,
> > 3. Updated POS (position) file, and
> > 4. Returned position description — incorrect, not classified.

> > **5.3.1.3 Locate Candidates:** Publicize and announce job vacancies, and recruit candidates from internal and external sources for various types of appointments.

Outputs from the process:
1. Unsuccessful applicants,
2. Tentative selectee,
3. Classified established position description (PD),
4. Pool of applications, and
5. Crediting plan.

5.3.1.4 Evaluate Candidates: Screen, assess, and certify candidates for positions under Merit Promotion Program (MPP) and other competitive and noncompetitive procedures. Evaluation of candidates involves testing applicants, assessing basic qualifications, rating and ranking applicants, etc.

Outputs from the process:
1. Unsuccessful applicants,
2. Selection list,
3. Tentative selectee,
4. Unsuccessful test results,
5. Assessment instruments,
6. Assessment reports,
7. Recycled applicants, and
8. Trained interviewers.

5.3.1.5 Process Selection: Determine employee's pay, initiate pre-employment processing (i.e., drug testing and physical), make the formal job offer, and complete employee processing by entering personnel data into the Consolidated Personnel Management Information System (CPMIS) and distributing the SF-50.

Outputs from the process:
1. Unsuccessful applicants,
2. SF-52 with salary determination,
3. Filed and distributed SF-50,
4. Completed entry on duty forms (EOD),
5. New employee on duty, and
6. Updated CPMIS/CUPS record.

Step 6: Compile the Results

Having completed the previous five steps, you have identified unit operations for all of your organization's processes and identified the relevant aspects for each unit operation. What next? To incorporate this data, enter it into a spreadsheet, following the example below. Then use this data to evaluate which of the aspects you selected for analysis are significant.

The Balanced Scorecard Plan

This chapter introduced the elements for successful balanced scorecard (BSC) implementation.

IT managers know the value of a good project plan so it should make sense to them that planning is of paramount importance. Key milestones in this phase include formulating the objectives of your plan and team building. This also includes getting commitment from management and training staff to understand the process and what is required of them. The plan must then be formulated and disseminated to all sponsors and team members.

During the development phase, the framework of the scorecard must be dissected and understood. The mission and objectives of each perspective must be developed, along with indicators and performance metrics (e.g., benchmarks). Each perspective should be linked with the other three perspectives, where possible, and the scorecard as a whole should be linked to the organizational scorecard.

This chapter concludes with a discussion of a number of common mistakes companies make when trying to measure performance (Ittner and Larcker, 2003), including:

- *Not linking measures to strategy.* Successful companies select performance measures on the basis of causal models, which lay out the plausible cause-and-effect relationships that exist between the chosen drivers of strategic success and outcomes.
- *Not validating the links.* Businesses need to scrupulously uncover the fundamental drivers of performance and then prove that actual improvements in non-financial performance measures affect future financial results.
- *Not setting the right performance targets.* Some companies focus on initiatives that promise short-term financial results, although other initiatives might have higher, long-term gains. Ittner and Larcker insist that there is a point of diminishing returns. For example, in one case, customers who were 100 percent satisfied spent no more money than those that were 80 percent satisfied.
- *Measuring incorrectly.* Some 70 percent of the companies that Ittner and Larker studied employed metrics that lacked statistical validity and reliability. They provide the example of companies trying to assess extremely complex performance dimensions using surveys containing only a few questions. They compound the problem by offering respondents only a small number of point scales (e.g., 1 = low, and 5 = high). These surveys are far too simplistic to discern superior performance or predict financial results.

On to Chapter 4

This chapter discussed a wide variety of topics relevant to implementing the balanced scorecard. To do so successfully requires the manager to understand the nature of benchmarking and how to go inside and outside of the organization (i.e., competitive analysis and phantom analysis) to develop a viable set of benchmarks. Chapter 4 will use everything discussed in the first few chapters to understand how to align IT to organizational strategy.

References

American Productivity and Quality Center. (2001, May). *A New Approach to Assessing Benchmarking Progress.* http://www.apqc.org/portal/apqc/ksn/ New%20Approach%20to%20Benchmarking.pdf?paf_gear_id=contentgear-home&paf_dm=full&pageselect=contentitem&docid=106955.

Berk, J. (2001, March 11). The Six Benchmarking Steps You Need. *Workforce Management Magazine.* http://www.workforce.com/archive/feature/22/28/ 08/index.php.

Clinton, B., S.A. Webber, and J.M. Hassell. (2002, Spring). Implementing the Balanced Scorecard Using the Analytic Hierarchy Process. *Management Accounting Quarterly*, Vol. 3, No. 3.

Conference Board. (1988, October-November). Calculating Competitor Action: Combustion Engineering's Strategy. *Management Briefing: Marketing.*

Guide to a Balanced Scorecard Performance Management Methodology. (1999). United States Department of Commerce.

Hruby, F.M. (1989, January 2). Missing Piece Analysis Targets the Competitor's Weakness. *Marketing News.*

Ittner, C.D. and D.F. Larcker. (2003, November). Coming Up Short on Nonfinancial Performance Measurement. *Harvard Business Review.*

Kendall, K. (1999, November). Benchmarking from A to Z. http://www.orau.gov/ pbm/presentation/kendall.pdf.

Saaty, T.L. (1994). *Fundamentals of Decision Making and Priority Theory with the Analytic Hierarchy Process.* Pittsburgh: RWS Publications.

Sandia National Labs. (1997, June 24). Sandia-Developed System Could Lead to More Efficient Movement of Cargo across US–Mexican Border. http://www.sandia.gov/media/usmexico.htm.

Schneiderman, A.M. (1999, January). Why Balanced Scorecards Fail. *Journal of Strategic Performance Management.*

Stewart, R.A. and S. Mohamed. (2001, April). Utilizing the Balanced Scorecard for IT/IS Performance Evaluation in Construction. *Construction Innovation*, pp. 147–163.

Van Der Zee, J. and B. De Jong. (1999, Fall). Alignment is Not Enough: Integrating Business Information Technology Management with the Balanced Business Scorecard. *Journal of Management Information Systems*, 16(2), 137–156.

Chapter 4

Aligning IT to Organizational Strategy

Seven deadly sins of the IT scorecard:
1. An IT-centric view of IT performance
2. Measures that don't matter
3. Lack of standard metrics definitions
4. Over-reliance on tools
5. Lack of drill-down capability hindering interpretation
6. Too many metrics
7. No individual impact

**—Working Council for Chief
Information Officers (2003)**

In the late 1980s, the deficiency in measuring IT using purely financial measures was addressed by Parker, Benson, and Trainor (1988) in their book on information economics.

Information economics assigns numerical scores to value and risk categories by a joint committee of end users and IT staff. For example, a value category of "0" would signify "no positive contribution" while a "5" would indicate a "large positive contribution." In the same vein, in the risk category, a "0" would mean no risk and a "5" would indicate a "large risk." Each of the categories is assigned a weight. By summing the weighted scores of the value categories and subtracting the weighted scores of the risk categories, one can calculate the total score of each project. *Value linking* incorporates the benefits and cost in other functional areas, while *value restructuring* refers to the efficiency and effectiveness of employees (e.g., does the new system free up employee time so that they can do their own jobs more effectively?). The balanced scorecard (BSC) extends the information economics theory into a set of constructs understandable and immediately usable throughout the organization.

This chapter discusses how the balanced scorecard can be used within the IT department to assess its own performance as well as to integrate itself to the organization as a whole. One quickly discovers that there are a variety of approaches to implementing an IT scorecard.

The IT Balanced Scorecard

Over the past decade, many CIOs have realized that it is not sufficient to manage merely the IT end of the business. The integration of IT strategy to business strategy must be managed as well. The tool chosen for this task is the balanced scorecard.

The Working Council for Chief Information Officers (2003) did an extensive review of IT scorecards and found that the most advanced scorecards shared the following six structural attributes:

1. *Simplicity of presentation.* The very best scorecards are limited to a single page of from 10 to 20 metrics written in nontechnical language.
2. *Explicit links to IT strategy.* The scorecard should be tightly coupled to the IT strategic planning process and assist in tracking progress against IT's key goals and objectives.
3. *Broad executive commitment.* Both senior IT as well as senior business managers should be involved in the scorecard process — both creation and ongoing.
4. *Enterprise-standard metrics definitions.* Consensus should be quickly achieved on metrics definitions. The review meetings should focus on decisions rather than debate over metrics.
5. *Drill-down capability and available context.* The high-level IT scorecard should allow for detailed review of trends or variance by providing more granularity on component elements.
6. *Individual manager compensation* should be linked to scorecard performance.

Progressive scorecard practitioners track metrics in five key categories:

1. *Financial performance.* IT spending in the content of service levels, project progress, etc. Sample metrics include cost of data communications per seat and relative spending per portfolio category.
2. *Project performance.* Sample metrics include percentage of new development investment resulting in new revenue streams and percentage of IT R&D investment leading to IT service improvements.
3. *Operational performance.* Instead of concentrating measurement efforts on day-to-day measures, best-in-class practitioners seek to provide an aggregate, customer-focused view of IT operations. Sample metrics include peak time availability and critical process uptime.
4. *Talent management.* This category of metrics seeks to manage IT human capital. Measures include staff satisfaction and retention as well as attractiveness of the IT department to external job seekers. Metrics include retention of high-potential staff and external citations of IT achievement.
5. *User satisfaction.* Sample metrics include focused executive feedback and user perspective.

The Working Council also found that best-of-breed practitioners included two additional metric categories:

1. *Information security.* These metrics monitor remediation efforts for known vulnerabilities and track proactive policy and certification efforts. (Also see Appendix K for a discussion of E-business auditing.) Sample metrics include percentage of staff receiving security training and percentage of external partners in compliance with security standards.
2. *Enterprise initiatives.* Best-of-breed practitioners also use the scorecard to highlight IT's contributions to initiatives of corporate strategic importance. Sample metrics include percentage of acquired company systems integrated in the Merger and Acquisition category and the number of business process steps enabled by technology in the Process Reengineering category.

Bowne & Co. (www.bowne.com), a New York City-based documents management company, initiated an IT balanced scorecard in 1997. Their process consisted of seven steps:

1. Kick-off training for IT staff.
2. *Ongoing strategy mapping.* The annual IT strategy, like most companies, is derived from the corporate strategy.

3. *Metrics selection.* A team, including the chief technology officer, created a list of metrics. The list was refined using analysis of each potential metric's strengths and weaknesses. The CIO approved the final list.
4. *Metrics definition.* A set of standard definitions is created for each metric. It defines the measurement technique as well as the data collection process. It outlines initiatives that must be completed to allow tracking of the metrics.
5. *Assigning metric ownership.* Owners are assigned to each metric. This person is responsible for scorecard completion. Their bonuses are related to their scorecard-related duties.
6. *Data collection and quality assurance.* Data frequency varies by metric, based on cost of collection, the corporate financial reporting cycle, and the volatility of the business climate.
7. CIO, CTO, and corporate officers review scorecard every six months; metrics are revisited annually.

Bowne & Co. is a good example of a departmentwide IT scorecard but this process can also be used to develop a scorecard for a particular system. The Central Intelligence Agency (Hagood and Friedman, 2002) did just this for a human resource information system (HRIS). The program director developed six criteria for success that would drive the balanced scorecard development effort:

1. Deliver each new program segment on time and within budget
2. Deliver each functionality as promised
3. Maintain high system performance standards
4. Reduce reliance on legacy systems
5. Increase customer satisfaction
6. Employee satisfaction

The resulting scorecard can be seen in Table 4.1.

Altering the Balanced Scorecard for IT

Martinsons, Davison, and Tse (1999) suggest that the four balanced scorecard perspectives might require some modification to be effective as an IT scorecard. Their reasoning is that the IT department is typically an internal rather than external service supplier, and projects are commonly carried out for the benefit of both the end users and the organization as a whole — rather than individual customers within a large market.

TABLE 4.1   The CIA's HRIS Balanced Scorecard

Goals	Objectives	Measures	Sources
Customer Perspective			
Provide HR information systems that meet agency needs	Incorporate stakeholder feedback into strategic planning Provide timely and accurate responses to customer service requests	Component HR officer survey HRIS help desk performance Level of participation in CIA IT forums percent with collaboration	HR front office Help desk personnel
Deliver all projects for customers in conformance with an acceptable plan	All projects have plans negotiated with customers and are baselined	Percent of baselined projects with a plan	Chief of operations
Manage HRIS work in conformity with published strategic and tactical plans	Maintain HR roadmap as basis for resource allocation Communicate HRIS strategic direction to stakeholders	Roadmap reviewed every two weeks and updated Number of projects performed for direct customers Level of participation in CIA IT forums with collaborations	Personnel Chief of operations
Internal Process Perspective			
HRIS data is available for users to conduct their business	Improve accuracy of data entry Maintain data accurately within the HRIS Make HRIS available to users for input 97 percent of the time Ensure retrievable data is no older than 24 hours	Data entry error rates HRIS hourly availability data Payroll processing time Age of data	Compensation group System engineer

TABLE 4.1 (continued)   The CIA's HRIS Balanced Scorecard

Goals	Objectives	Measures	Sources
Achieve the optimal balance between technical and strategic activities	Maintain balance between repair and new work Reduce demand for customer service needing intervention	Rework cost/unit of service Percent of time devoted to ad hoc work	Budget officer
Achieve the minimum architecture effective for HRIS	Implement an HRIS integration strategy Maintain alignment with CIA IS direction/initiatives	Number of non-Lawson apps in HRIS Total number of interfaces	System architect

Resource Perspective (Financial)

Goals	Objectives	Measures	Sources
Maximize the cost efficiency of operating and evolving the HRIS	Execute the budget consistent with strategic plan Understand and manage the cost drivers of HRIS	Percent of employees who have up-to-date information Cost/unit of service HRIS overhead as percent of total Total number of direct labor hours	Budget officer
Each project delivers its product as advertised	Scope, budget, and schedule are baselined at Project Initial Review for 100 percent of projects Project performance meets or exceeds baseline expectations	Schedule data Budget data Scope performance data	Chief of operations

Learning and Growth Perspective

Goals	Objectives	Measures	Sources
Maintain a skilled and productive workforce to operate and evolve the HRIS	Implement an effective strategic workforce plan Recruit skilled workers who have initiative, innovation, and flexibility	Number of employees with COTR certification Project management training levels Percent of technical training goals met	Personnel

TABLE 4.1 (continued)   The CIA's HRIS Balanced Scorecard

Goals	Objectives	Measures	Sources
	Retain employees by giving opportunities and incentives		
	Enhance employees' knowledge and skills		
Maintain a high degree of HRIS employee satisfaction	Enhance employees' knowledge and skills Provide opportunities for individual career growth	Project management training levels Percent of technical training goals met Job Description Index (JDI) scores Percent of voluntary separations	Personnel
Ensure that HRIS learns from the past for better future performance	Record, analyze, and use lessons learned Develop best practices for HRIS	Percent of leaders' time devoted to mentoring Percent of projects with lessons learned in database	Personnel

Martinsons et al. (1999) suggested four perspectives:

1. User orientation (end-user view):
   - Mission: deliver value-adding products and services to end users
   - Objectives: establish and maintain a good image and reputation with end users; exploit IT opportunities, establish good relationships with the user community, satisfy end-user requirements, and be perceived as the preferred supplier of IT products and services
2. Business value (management's view):
   - Mission: contribute to the value of the business
   - Objectives: establish and maintain a good image and reputation with management, ensure that IT projects provide business value, control IT costs, and sell appropriate IT products and services to third party
3. Internal processes (operations-based view):
   - Mission: deliver IT products and services in an efficient and effective manner
   - Objectives: anticipate and influence requests from end users and management, be efficient in planning and developing IT

applications, be efficient in operating and maintaining IT applications, be efficient in acquiring and testing new hardware and software, and provide cost-effective training that satisfies end users

4. Future readiness (innovation and learning view):
   ■ Mission: deliver continuous improvement and prepare for future challenges
   ■ Objectives: anticipate and prepare for IT problems that could arise, continuously upgrade IT skills through training and development, regularly upgrade IT applications portfolio, regularly upgrade hardware and software, conduct cost-effective research into emerging technologies and their suitability for the business

Martinsons et al. then drill down to provide IT-specific measures for each of these four perspectives. Most of the metrics have been derived from mainstream literature and include those presented in Table 4.2.

Martinsons et al. also explain that the three key balanced scorecard principles of:

1. Cause-and-effect relationships
2. Sufficient performance drivers
3. Linkage to financial measures

are built into their IT scorecard. They explain that cause-and-effect relationships can involve one or more of the four perspectives. For example, better staff skills (future readiness perspective) will reduce the frequency of bugs in an application (internal operations perspective).

Great-West Life Case Study

Van Grembergen, Saull, and De Haes (2003) performed an intensive study of the methodology used by Canada-based Great-West Life to develop their IT balanced scorecard. Great-West Life is the result of a merger between three financial services companies, each with its own IT services department. Stakeholders were quite concerned that they would lose control of their IT groups after the merger, so the merged IT department decided to utilize the balanced scorecard approach to formalize the controls and measures required to ensure IT success.

The merged IT department consisted of seven units: career centers, management services, account management, application delivery, technology services, corporate technology, and the E-business solutions center.

TABLE 4.2   IT Scorecard Metrics

Perspective	Metric
User orientation	Customer satisfaction
Business value:	
Cost control	Percent over/under IT budget
	Allocation to different budget items
	IT budget as a percent of revenue
	IT expenses per employee
Sales to third parties	Revenue from IT-related products or services
Business value of an IT project	Traditional measures (e.g., ROI, payback)
	Business evaluation based on information economics: value linking, value acceleration, value restructuring, technological innovation
	Strategic match with business contribution to product/service quality, customer responsiveness, management information, process flexibility
Risks	Unsuccessful strategy risk, IT strategy risk, definitional uncertainty (e.g., low degree of project specification), technological risk (e.g., bleeding edge hardware or software), development risk (e.g., inability to put things together), operational risk (e.g., resistance to change), IT service delivery risk (e.g., human/computer interface difficulties)
Business value of the IT department/ functional area	Percent resources devoted to strategic projects
	Percent time spent by IT manager in meetings with corporate executives
	Perceived relationship between IT management and top management
Internal processes:	
Planning	Percent resources devoted to planning and review of IT activities
Development	Percent resources devoted to applications development
	Time required to develop a standard-sized new application
	Percent of applications programming with reused code
	Time spent to repair bugs and fine-tune new applications

TABLE 4.2 (continued)   IT Scorecard Metrics

Perspective	Metric
Operations	Number of end-user queries handled
	Average time required to address an end-user problem
Future readiness:	
IT specialist capabilities	IT training and development budget as a percent of overall IT budget
	Expertise with specific technologies
	Expertise with emerging technologies
	Age distribution of IT staff
Satisfaction of IT staff	Turnover/retention of IT employees
	Productivity of IT employees
Applications portfolio	Age distribution
	Platform distribution
	Technical performance of applications portfolio
	User satisfaction with applications portfolio
Research into emerging technologies	IT research budget as percentage of IT budget
	Perceived satisfaction of top management with reporting on how specific emerging technologies may or may not be applicable to the company

At the time of the study, the IT department employed 812 full-time and part-time employees.

The organizational structure of the IT department is quite interesting. Application delivery was created as a stand-alone unit to focus on continuous improvement of delivery performance. Account management was created to ensure effective communications with the company's end users. This department takes great pains to educate end users on IT corporate agendas and translate business needs into IT processes. As its name implies, the career center focuses on the professional development of IT staff. The corporate technology group utilizes a centralized approach to the development of a common enterprise architecture and technology policies. Finally, the management services group focuses on running IT as a business and provides for effective financial reporting and adherence to the IT scorecard.

As one can see, the organizational structure of the IT department roughly parallels that of the four perspectives of the balanced scorecard:

1. Financial perspective — management services
2. Customer perspective — account management
3. Internal perspective — application delivery, technology services, corporate technology, E-business solutions
4. Learning and growth perspective — career centers

Senior management of the three companies questioned the benefits of large investments in IT and wanted IT to be better aligned with corporate strategy. Some of the concerns of the different stakeholder groups included:

- Senior management:
  - Does IT support the achievement of business objectives?
  - What value does the expenditure on IT deliver?
  - Are IT costs being managed effectively?
  - Are IT risks being identified and managed?
  - Are targeted inter-company IT synergies being achieved?
- Business unit executives:
  - Are IT services delivered at a competitive cost?
  - Does IT deliver on its service level commitments
  - Do IT investments positively affect business productivity or the customer experience?
  - Does IT contribute to the achievement of our business strategies?
- Corporate compliance internal audit:
  - Are the organization's assets and operations protected?
  - Are the key business and technology risks being managed?
  - Are proper processes, practices, and controls in place?
- IT organization:
  - Are we developing the professional competencies needed for successful service delivery?
  - Are we creating a positive workplace environment?
  - Do we effectively measure and reward individual and team performances?
  - Do we capture organizational knowledge to continuously improve performance?
  - Can we attract and retain the talent we need to support the business?

TABLE 4.3 Moving IT from Service Provider to Strategic Partner

Service Provider	Strategic Partner
IT is for efficiency	IT is for business growth
Budgets are driven by external benchmarks	Budgets are driven by business strategy
IT is separable from the business	IT is inseparable from the business
IT is seen as an expense to control	IT is seen as an investment to manage
IT managers are technical experts	IT managers are business problem solvers

One of the most important initiatives the new CIO undertook was to migrate the new information services group to a strategic partner, as opposed to an IT services provider. As articulated by Venkatraman (1999) and summarized in Table 4.3, there are some important differences.

Great-West Life's IT scorecard, as described by Van Grembergen, Saull, and De Haes (2003), encompasses the following four quadrants:

1. *Customer orientation:* to be the supplier of choice for all information services, either directly or indirectly through supplier relationships.
2. *Corporate contribution:* to enable and contribute to the achievement of business objectives through effective delivery of value-added information services.
3. *Operational excellence:* to deliver timely and effective services at targeted service levels and costs.
4. *Future orientation:* to develop the internal capabilities to continuously improve performance through innovation, learning, and personal organization growth.

Van der Zee (1999) and Van Grembergen (2000) proposed that the relationship between IT and business can be more explicitly expressed through a cascade of balanced scorecards, as shown in Figure 4.1.

Cascading was used effectively at Great-West Life, similar to the example in Figure 4.1, with the addition of "governance services" scorecards. Notice the use of the term "scorecards" — plural. Each set of scorecards is actually composed of one or more unit scorecards. For example, the IT Operations scorecard also includes a scorecard for IT Service Desk. Great-West Life's four-quadrant IT scorecard consists of the following objectives, measures, and benchmarks, as shown in Tables 4.4, 4.5, 4.6, and 4.7.

The measures of each of these unit scorecards are aggregated into the IT balanced scorecard. This, in turn, is fed into and evaluated against the business balanced scorecard.

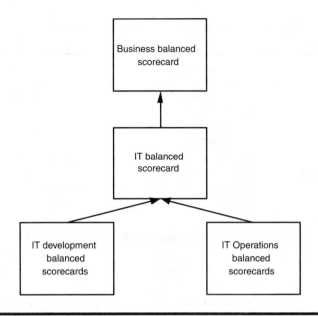

FIGURE 4.1   **Cascade of balanced scorecards.**

Representative IT Balanced Scorecard Value Metrics

There are a wide variety of metrics that an organization can utilize. Arveson (1998), writing for the Balanced Scorecard Institute, recommends the metrics outlined in Table 4.8. Readers should also review Appendix C, which contains a list of standard IT metrics, and Appendix B, which provides the metrics capability evaluation guide employed by the U.S. Air Force.

Drilling Down to the Specific System

Hopefully by now one understands the importance of developing cascading sets of interlinked balanced scorecards. From a departmental perspective, one will need to review, understand, and adhere to the organizational balanced scorecard from a macro perspective. However, one will need to review the departmental- and system-level scorecards from a micro level.

The beginning of this chapter discussed an example of a balanced scorecard used by the CIA to assess the performance of a human resource information system. Another example of a micro-level scorecard is one that can be built for the implementation of a customer relationship management (CRM) system. Brewton (2003) provides an illustration of a balanced CRM scorecard in Table 4.9.

TABLE 4.4 Corporate Contribution Scorecard Evaluates IT from the Perspective of Senior Management

Objective	Measures	Benchmarks
Business/ IT alignment	1. Operational plan/budget approval	1. Not applicable
Value delivery	2. Measured in business unit performance	2. Not applicable
Cost management	3. Attainment of expense and recovery targets	3. Industry expenditure comparisons
	4. Attainment of unit cost targets	4. Compass operational "top performance" levels
Risk management	5. Results of internal audits	5. Defined sound business practices
	6. Execution of security initiative	6. Not applicable
	7. Delivery of disaster recovery assessment	7. Not applicable
Inter-company synergy achievement	8. Single system solutions	8. Merger and acquisition guidelines
	9. Target state architecture approval	9. Not applicable
	10. Attainment of targeted integrated cost reductions	10. Not applicable
	11. IT organization integration	11. Not applicable

Like Brewton (2003), Rosemann and Wiese (1999) demonstrate that the balanced scorecard can be used at the system level. Enterprise resource planning (ERP) is one of the most sophisticated and complex of all software systems. It is a customizable software package that includes integrated business solutions for core business processes such as production planning and control and warehouse management. The major ERP vendors (SAP, Baan, Oracle, and PeopleSoft) have seen their profitability soar in recent years.

Rosemann and Wiese (1999) use a modified balanced scorecard approach to:

■ Evaluate the implementation of ERP software
■ Evaluate the continuous operation of the ERP installation

Along with the four balanced scorecard perspectives of financial, customer, internal processes, and innovation and learning, they have

TABLE 4.5   Customer Orientation Scorecard Evaluated the Performance of IT from the Perspective of Internal Business Users

Objective	Measures	Benchmarks
Customer satisfaction	1. Business unit survey ratings a. Cost transparency and levels b. Service quality and responsiveness c. Value of IT advice and support d. Contribution to business objectives	1. Not applicable
Competitive costs	2. Attainment of unit cost targets	2. Compass operational "Top-Level" performing levels
	3. Blended labor rates	3. Market comparisons
Development services performance	4. Major project success scores a. Recorded goal attainment b. Sponsor satisfaction ratings c. Project governance rating	4. Not applicable
Operational services performance	5. Attainment of targeted service levels	5. Competitor comparisons

added a fifth for the purposes of ERP installation — the project perspective. The individual project requirements, such as identification of critical path, milestones, etc., are covered by this fifth perspective, which represents all the project management tasks. Figure 4.2 represents the Rosemann-Wiese approach.

Rosemann and Wiese contend that most ERP implementers concentrate on the financial and business processes aspects of ERP implementation. Using the ERP balanced scorecard would enable them to also focus on customer and innovation and learning perspectives. The latter is particularly important because it enables the development of alternative values for the many conceivable development paths that support a flexible system implementation.

Implementation measures might include:

- *Financial:* total cost of ownership, which would enable identification of modules where over-customization took place
- *Project:* processing time along the critical path, remaining time to the next milestone, time delays that would affect financial perspective

TABLE 4.6 Operational Excellence Scorecard Views IT from the Perspective of IT Managers and Audit and Regulatory Bodies

Objective	Measures	Benchmarks

Development process performance	1. Function point measures of:
	  a. Productivity
	  b. Quality
	  c. Delivery rate
		1. To be determined

Operational process performance	2. Benchmark based measures of:
	  a. Productivity
	  b. Responsiveness
	  c. Change management effectiveness
	  d. Incident occurrence levels
		2. Selected compass benchmark studies

Process maturity	3. Assessed level of maturity and compliance in priority processes within:
	  a. Planning and organization
	  b. Acquisition and implementation
	  c. Delivery and support
	  d. Monitoring
		3. To be defined

Enterprise architecture management	4. Major project architecture approval	4. OSFI sound business practices
	5. Product acquisition compliance with technology standards	5. Not applicable
	6. "State of the infrastructure" assessment	6. Not applicable

- *Internal processes:* processing time before and after ERP implementation, coverage of individual requirements for a process
- *Customer:* linkage of customers to particular business processes automated, resource allocation per customer
- *Innovation and learning:* number of alternative process paths to support a flexible system implementation, number of parameters representing unused customizing potential, number of documents describing customizing decisions

As in all well-designed balanced scorecards, this one demonstrates a very high degree of linkage in terms of cause-and-effect relationships. For example, "customer satisfaction" within the Customer perspective might affect "total cost of ownership" in the Financial perspective, "total project time" in the Project perspective, "Fit with ERP solution" in the Internal

TABLE 4.7 Future Orientation Perspective Shows IT Performance from the Perspective of the IT Department Itself: Process Owners, Practitioners, and Support Professionals

Objective	Measures	Benchmarks

Human resource management	1. Results against targets:
	  a. Staff complement by skill type
	  b. Staff turnover
	  c. Staff "billable" ratio
	  d. Professional development days per staff member
		a. Not applicable
		
		b. Market comparison
		c. Industry standard
		d. Industry standard

Employee satisfaction	2. Employee satisfaction survey scores in:
	  a. Compensation
	  b. Work climate
	  c. Feedback
	  d. Personal growth
	  e. Vision and purpose
		2. North American technology dependent companies

Knowledge management	3. Delivery of internal process improvements to library 4. Implementation of "lessons learned" sharing process	3. Not applicable 4. Not applicable

Process perspective, and "User suggestions" in the Innovation and Learning perspective.

Rosemann and Wiese do not require the Project perspective in the balanced scorecard for evaluating the continuous operation of the ERP installation. Here, the implementation follows a straightforward balanced scorecard approach. Measures include:

- Financial:
  - Compliance with budget for hardware, software, consulting
- Customer:
  - Coverage of business processes: percent of covered process types, percent of covered business transactions, percent of covered transactions valued good or fair
  - Reduction of bottlenecks: percent of transactions not finished on schedule, percent of cancelled telephone order processes due to noncompetitive system response time
- Internal process:
  - Reduction of operational problems: number of problems with customer order processing system, percent of problems with

TABLE 4.8   Recommended Metrics

System/Service/Function	Possible Metric(s)
R&D	Innovation capture
	Number of quality improvements
	Customer satisfaction
Process improvement	Cycle time, activity costs
	Number of supplier relationships
	Total cost of ownership
Resource planning, account	Decision speed
management	Lowering level of decision authority
Groupware	Cycle time reduction
	Paperwork reduction
Decision support	Decision reliability
	Timeliness
	Strategic awareness
	Lowering level of decision authority
Management information systems	Accuracy of data
	Timeliness
E-commerce	Market share
	Price premium for products or services
Information-based products and	Operating margins
services	New business revenues
	Cash flow
	Knowledge retention

      customer order processing system, number of problems with
warehouse processes, number of problems with standard
reports, number of problems with reports on demand
- Availability of the ERP system: average system availability, average downtime, maximum downtime
- Avoidance of operational bottlenecks: average response time in order processing, average response time in order processing at peak time, average number of OLTP transactions, maximum number of OLTP transactions
- Actuality of the system: average time to upgrade the system, release levels behind the actual level
- Improvement in system development: punctuality index of system delivery, quality index
- Avoidance of developer bottlenecks: average workload per developer, rate of sick leave per developer, percent of modules covered by more than two developers

TABLE 4.9   CRM Scorecard

Perspective	Success Factor	Metric
Financial	Maximize customer lifetime value Maximize share of wallet	Customer lifetime value ($) Share of wallet (%)
Customer	Increase retention Increase penetration Increase win-backs Increase new business Increase satisfaction	Retention percent (%) Penetration ratio (number) Win-back percent (%) Customer acquisitions (number) Customers highly satisfied (%)
Process	Maximize sales productivity Maximize marketing effectiveness Maximize service quality	Conversion rate per sales channel (%) Revenue per conversion rate per sales channel ($) Cost of sales per sales channel ($) Number of leads per marketing channel (number) Service level per channel (%) Cost per service encounter ($)
Staff	Increase employee satisfaction Maintain high employee retention Increase core CRM competencies	CRM employees highly satisfied, by CRM function (%) CRM employee retention (%) Strategic CRM core competency coverage, by CRM function (%)

- ▪ Innovation and learning:
  - – Qualification: number of training hours per user, number of training hours per developer, qualification index of developer (i.e., how qualified is this developer to do what he or she is doing)
  - – Independence of consultants: number of consultant days per module in use for more than two years, number of consultant days per module in use for less than two years
  - – Reliability of software vendor: number of releases per year, number of functional additions, number of new customers

Keeping Track of What Is Going On

Operational awareness is the continuous attention to those activities that enable an organization to determine how well it is meeting predetermined

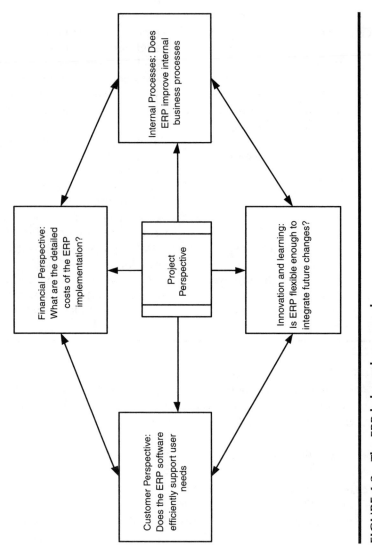

FIGURE 4.2   The ERP balanced scorecard.

performance objectives. It is a necessary component of scorecard-type endeavors.

Factors influencing the level of operational awareness include the nature of the work, the type of organization, and past performance. Accordingly, oversight organizations should maintain a relationship with the overseen organization and its management staff that affords ongoing awareness of that organization's strengths and weaknesses, if any. This monitoring or surveillance is a fundamental part of operational awareness.

Surveillance

Surveillance includes both formal and informal activities. Formal surveillance activities, based on specific criteria, are typically established in writing and provided to the organization. Surveillance, general in nature and usually conducted and reported orally, is an effective approach when circumstances require flexibility to accommodate changing emphasis, shifting priorities, or establishing rapport. There should be scheduled activities that provide for sufficient levels of operational awareness, a sampling of which follows:

1. Hold periodic meetings between management staff with agenda items designed to fully communicate subjects such as current initiatives, status of problem areas and actions taken to date, scheduled and planned training, and policy and procedure revision status of organizational or contract change implementation, as appropriate.
2. Review status reports and trend analyses of performance measures. Perform limited on-site review (if applicable) of selected areas of significant risk as appropriate.
3. Maintain awareness and involvement at a level such that a "for cause" issue is not a surprise.

When a "for cause" condition exists, certain surveillance activities may be assigned to other disciplines or functional areas. In these instances, supporting documentation resulting from the findings should be provided to the organization. Reports generated as a result of internal audits should be considered valuable diagnostic tools.

Selected significant risk areas typically refer to those actions or activities that require compliance with laws, regulations, and contract terms and conditions. There should be various control systems employed as necessary to ensure compliance and to test the currency and adequacy of the business system.

Validation and Verification

Validation is the process of determining the degree of accuracy and completeness of the measurement techniques and the resulting data. Assessment practices and results should be periodically validated. The success of the self-assessment will depend largely on the mutually agreed-upon and understood performance objectives, measures, and expectations; the scope, depth, and effectiveness of the self-assessment; and the integrity of the self-assessment.

Verification is the process of substantiating a set of data results by means such as checking stated facts, citations, measurements, or attendant circumstances.

Verification of data resulting, for example, from the self-assessment and other operational awareness activities will, in part, formulate the basis of the approval of the business system. The data should be analyzed to determine its accuracy and that comparisons or benchmarks are valid.

Verification of narrative or statistical data should be tailored by data type. For example, reports and documentation could substantiate the self-assessment results of measures designed to demonstrate efficiency. Likewise, interviews with selected internal and external customers and the organization's employees may also verify reported survey results. Trend analysis of the self-assessment results should reflect the factual information provided by the interviews with staff.

The following suggestions can assist in the validation and verification of the self-assessment process and results:

- Mutually understand what and how the organization will measure performance.
- Become familiar with the data sources and methods that will be used in the calculations.
- Confirm that the collection methodology is accurate, complete, and timely.
- Confirm that the data is properly controlled.
- Become familiar with the trend analysis techniques to be used and gain assurances that the organization's personnel are qualified in this area.

On to Chapter 5

This chapter discussed the unique concept of the IT scorecard and discovered that some researchers and many organizations have *fine-tuned* the idea of the balanced scorecard to suit their own particular purposes. This chapter also discussed a variety of IT-specific scorecard examples, along with their associated metrics. Hopefully, one is now becoming a lot more comfortable with the topic — as well as the process — and is getting ready to embark on a balanced scorecard project of one's own.

Chapters 5 through 8 embark on very specific discussions of each scorecard perspective. Chapter 5 specifically delves into the financial perspective of the balanced scorecard.

References

Arveson, P. (1998). The Value of Corporate IT Initiatives. http://www.balanced-scorecard.org/bscit/value_add.html.

Brewton, J. (2003, December 15). How Can We Use a Scorecard to Maximize Our CRM Performance. *CRM Magazine.* http://www.destinationcrm.com/articles/default.asp?ArticleID=3689&KeyWords=balanced.

Hagood, W. and L. Friedman. (2002, Winter). Using the Balanced Scorecard to Measure the Performance of Your HR Information System. *Public Personnel Management,* Vol. 31, No. 4.

Martinsons, M., R. Davison, and D. Tse. (1999, February). The Balanced Scorecard: A Foundation for the Strategic Management of Information Systems. *Decision Support Systems,* 25(1), 71–88.

Parker, M., R. Benson, and H. Trainor. (1988). *Information Economics: Linking Business Performance to Information Technology.* Englewood Cliffs, NJ: Prentice Hall.

Rosemann, M. and J. Wiese. (1999). Measuring the Performance of ERP Software — A Balanced Scorecard Approach. *Proceedings of the 10th Australasian Conference on Information Systems.* http://www2.vuw.ac.nz/acis99/Papers/PaperRosemannWiese-089.pdf.

Van der Zee, J. (1999, March). Alignment Is Not Enough: Integrating Business and IT Management with the Balanced Scorecard. *Proceedings of the 1st Conference on the IT Balanced Scorecard,* pp. 1–21.

Van Grembergen, W., R. Saull, and S. De Haes. (2003). Linking the IT Balanced Scorecard to the Business Objectives at a Major Canadian Financial Group. *Journal of Information Technology Cases and Application,* Vol. 5, No. 1.

Van Grembergen, W. (2000). The balanced scorecard and IT governance. *Information Systems Control Journal,* 2, 40–43.

Venkatraman, N. (1999). Valuing the IS contribution to the business. *Computer Sciences Corporation Report.*

Working Council for Chief Information Officers. (2003). *IT Balanced Scorecards.* http://www.cio.executiveboard.com/Images/CIO/PDF/CIO73748.pdf.

Chapter 5

Aligning IT to Meet Financial Objectives

How do we want our stakeholders to view us?
Sample indicators: profit, income, working capital, inventory

A study by Utunen (2003) determined the following priorities for financially based technology measurement: commercialization of technology, customer focus, technology stock, technology protection, technology acquisition, competence of personnel, and management focus. For each indicator, one or more metrics were established, as shown in Table 5.1.

This chapter summarizes a variety of financially based indicators and metrics that can be used within the financial perspective of the IT balanced scorecard.

Cost-Benefit Analysis

Cost-benefit analysis is quite easy to understand. The process compares the costs of the system to the benefits of having that system. Everyone does this on a daily basis. For example, if one goes out to buy a new $1000 personal computer, one weighs the cost of expending that $1000 against the benefits of owning the personal computer. For example, these benefits might include:

TABLE 5.1   Financially Based Financial Measurement

Indicator	Metric
Commercialization of Technology	
Product cost savings	Total product costs
	Costs of acquired technology
	Total R&D expenditure
Sales of new or improved product	Total sales
Customer Focus	
Customer complaints	Number of technical problems solved
Customer intelligence expenditure	Amount of R&D invested in researching R&D ideas among customers
Number of projects aligned with customers	Number of technology projects performed in cooperation with customers
Technology Stock	
Stock amount	Number of technologies owned or possessed by the company
Stock competitiveness	Qualitative evaluation of technology compared to competitors
Technology Protection	
Patenting activity	Number of new patents generated by R&D
Patentable innovations	Number of patentable innovations that are not yet patented
Importance of patents	Number of patents protecting the core of a specific technology or business area
Technology Acquisition	
Allocation of R&D	Total R&D expenditure
R&D efficiency and effectiveness	Amount of R&D expenditure spent on successfully commercialized technologies
New projects	Total number of new R&D projects started
Merger and acquisition	Amount of new technology acquired through mergers and acquisitions

TABLE 5.1 (continued)   Financially Based Financial Measurement

Indicator	Metric
Personnel Competence	
Personnel competence level	Qualitative evaluation of the level of personnel competencies
Management Focus	
Top management focus	Total number of working hours
Top management reaction time	Top management reaction time to strategic or environmental changes
R&D link to strategy	Percent of R&D directly in line with business strategy

- They no longer have to rent a computer — cost savings of $75 per month.
- It may be possible to earn extra money by typing term papers for students — potential earnings of $300 per month.

This can be summarized as follows:

One-Time Costs	Benefits per Year
$1000	1. Rental computer savings: $75 × 12 = $900
	2. Typing income: $300 × 12 = $3600
$1000/one time	$4500/year
Potential savings/earnings	$3500/first year; $4500 in subsequent years

One-time capital costs such as computers are usually amortized over a certain period of time. For example, a computer costing $1000 can be amortized over five years, which means that instead of comparing a one-time cost of $1000 to the benefits of purchasing the PC, one can compare a monthly cost instead.

Not all cost-benefit analyses are so clear-cut, however. In the example above, the benefits were both financially based. Not all benefits are so easily quantifiable. Benefits that cannot be quantified are called intangible benefits. Examples are:

- Reduced turnaround time
- Improved customer satisfaction
- Compliance with mandates
- Enhanced inter-agency communication

Aside from having to deal with both tangible and intangible benefits, most cost-benefit analyses must also deal with several alternatives. For example, assume that a bank is using a loan processing system that is old and often has problems. There might be several alternative solutions, including:

- ▪ Rewrite the system from scratch
- ▪ Modify the existing system
- ▪ Outsource the system

In each case, a spreadsheet should be created that details one-time as well as continuing costs. These should then be compared to the benefits of each alternative, both tangible as well as intangible.

An associated formula is the benefit-to-cost ratio (BCR). The computation of the financial benefit-to-cost ratio is done within the construct of the following formula: benefits/cost.

Break-Even Analysis

All projects have associated costs. All projects will also have associated benefits. At the outset of a project, costs will far exceed benefits. However, at some point the benefits will start outweighing the costs. This is called the *break-even point*. The analysis that is done to figure out when this break-even point will occur is called *break-even analysis*. In the calculation below, one can see that the break-even point comes during the first year.

One-Time Costs	Benefits per Year
$1000	1. Rental computer savings: $75 × 12 = $900
	2. Typing income: $300 × 12 = $3600
$1000/one time	$4500/year
Potential savings/earnings	$3500/first year; $4500 in subsequent years

Calculating the break-even point in a project with multiple alternatives enables the project manager to select the optimal solution. The project manager will generally select the alternative with the shortest break-even point.

Estimating ROI for an IT Project

Most organizations want to select projects that have a positive return on investment. The return on investment, or ROI as it is most commonly known, is the additional amount earned after costs are earned back. In the "buy versus not buy" PC decision discussed above, one can see that the ROI is quite positive during the first, and especially during subsequent years of ownership.

The IT and finance departments need to be joint owners of the ROI process. The International Data Group (IOMA, 2002), a technology research firm, provides two examples of where this failed and where it succeeded. Lanier International is a copy machine manufacturer. Unfortunately, all discussions between finance and IT about projects were more like confrontations. The finance department battled every facet of IT's methodology for arriving at their numbers. On the other hand, Owens-Corning, a building materials company, assigns a finance department person to each IT project. The finance person tracks the progress of benefits during and after the project. In this way, the IT department jointly owns the ROI numbers with the business.

The basic formula for ROI is:

$$ROI = \frac{(Benefit - Cost)}{Cost}$$

ROI calculations require the availability of large amounts of accurate data, which is sometimes unavailable to the project manager. Many variables must be considered and decisions made regarding which factors to calculate and which to ignore.

Before starting an ROI calculation, identify the following factors:

- *Know what you are measuring.* Successful ROI calculators isolate their true data from other factors, including the work environment and the level of management support.
- *Do not saturate.* Instead of analyzing every factor involved, pick a few. Start with the most obvious factors that can be identified immediately.
- *Convert to money.* Converting data into hard monetary values is essential in any successful ROI study. Translating intangible benefits into dollars is challenging and might require some assistance from the accounting or finance department. The goal is to demonstrate the impact on the bottom line.
- *Compare apples to apples.* Measure the same factors before and after the project.

According to Berry (2001), there are a variety of ROI techniques:

- *Treetop.* Treetop metrics investigate the impact on profitability for the entire company. Profitability can take the form of cost reductions because of IT's potential to reduce workforce size for any given process.

- *Pure cost.* There are several varieties of pure cost ROI techniques. Total cost of ownership (TCO) details the hidden support and maintenance costs over time that provide a more concise picture of the total cost. The Gartner Group's NOW (or normalized cost of work produced) index measures the cost of one's conducting a work task versus the cost to others doing similar work.
- *Holistic IT.* This is the same as the IT scorecard, where the IT department tries to align itself with the traditional balanced scorecard performance perspective of financial, customer, internal operations, and employee learning and innovation.
- *Financial.* Aside from ROI, *economic value added* tries to optimize a company's shareholder wealth.

There are also a variety of ways to actually calculate ROI. Davidson (1998) suggests measuring the following:

- *Productivity:* output per unit of input
- *Processes:* systems, workflow
- *Human resources:* costs and benefits for a specific initiative
- *Employee factors:* retention, morale, commitment, and skills

Phillips (1997) contends that the ROI calculation is not complete until the results are converted to dollars. This includes looking at combinations of hard and soft data. Hard data includes such traditional measures as output, time, quality, and costs. In general, hard data is readily available and relatively easy to calculate. Soft data, which is difficult to calculate, includes morale, turnover rate, absenteeism, loyalty, conflicts avoided, new skills learned, new ideas, successful completion of projects, etc., as shown in Table 5.2.

After the hard and soft data have been determined, they must be converted to monetary values:

Step 1: Focus on a single unit.

Step 2: Determine a value for each unit.

Step 3: Calculate the change in performance. Determine the performance change after factoring out other potential influences on the training results.

Step 4: Obtain an annual amount. The industry standard for an annual performance change is equal to the total change in performance data during one year.

Step 5: Determine the annual value. The annual value of improvement equals the annual performance change, multiplied by the unit value.

TABLE 5.2   Hard Data versus Soft Data

Hard Data

Output	Units produced
	Items assembled or sold
	Forms processed
	Tasks completed
Quality	Scrap
	Waste
	Rework
	Product defects or rejects
Time	Equipment downtime
	Employee overtime
	Time to complete projects
	Training time
Cost	Overhead
	Variable costs
	Accident costs
	Sales expenses

Soft Data

Work habits	Employee absenteeism
	Tardiness
	Visits to nurse
	Safety-rule violations
Work climate	Employee grievances
	Employee turnover
	Discrimination charges
	Job satisfaction
Attitudes	Employee loyalty
	Employee self-confidence
	Employee's perception of job responsibility
	Perceived changes in performance
New skills	Decisions made
	Problems solved
	Conflicts avoided
	Frequency of use of new skills
Development and advancement	Number of promotions or pay increases
	Number of training programs attended
	Requests for transfer
	Performance-appraisal ratings

TABLE 5.2 (continued) Hard Data versus Soft Data

Initiative	Implementation of new ideas
	Successful completion of projects
	Number of employee suggestions

Compare the product of this equation to the cost of the program using this formula: ROI = Net annual value of improvement − Program cost.

Hawkins et al. (1998) did a case study of a system implementation within the U.S. Department of Veterans Affairs. Spreadsheets were used to calculate the ROI at various stages of the project: planning, development, and implementation.

Initial Benefits Worksheet

Calculation:

$$\text{Hours/person average} \times \text{cost/hour} \times \text{number of people}$$

$$= \text{Total dollars saved}$$

■ Reduced time to learn system or job (worker hours)
■ Reduced supervision (supervision hours)
■ Reduced help from co-workers (worker hours)
■ Reduced calls to help line
■ Reduced downtime (waiting for help, consulting manuals, etc.)
■ Fewer or no calls from help line to supervisor about overuse of help service

Continuing Benefits Worksheet

Calculation:

$$\text{Hours/person average} \times \text{cost/hour} \times \text{number of people}$$

$$= \text{Total dollars saved}$$

■ Reduced time to perform operation (worker time)
■ Reduced overtime
■ Reduced supervision (supervisor hours)

- Reduced help from co-workers (worker hours)
- Reduced calls to help line
- Reduced downtime (waiting for help, consulting manuals, etc.)
- Fewer or no calls from help line to supervisor about overuse of help service
- Fewer mistakes (e.g., rejected transactions)
- Fewer employees needed
- Total savings in one year
- Expected life of system in years

Quality Benefits Worksheet

Calculation:

$$\text{Unit cost} \times \text{number of units} = \text{Total dollars saved}$$

- Fewer mistakes (e.g., rejected transactions)
- Fewer rejects — ancillary costs
- Total savings in one year
- Expected life of system, in years

Other Benefits Worksheet

Calculation:

$$= \text{Dollars saved per year}$$

- Reduced employee turnover
- Reduced grievances
- Reduced absenteeism and tardiness (morale improvements)

ROI Spreadsheet Calculation

Calculation:

$$\text{ROI} = (\text{Benefits} - \text{Costs/Costs})$$

- Initial time saved, total over life of system
- Continuing worker hours saved, total over life of system
- Quality improvements with fixed costs, total over life of system
- Other possible benefits, total over life of system
- Total benefits
- Total system costs (development, maintenance, and operation)

Phillips' (1997) ROI calculations are based on valuations of improved work product, which is referred to as a cost-effectiveness strategy.

ROI evaluates an investment's potential by comparing the magnitude and timing of expected gains to the investment costs. For example, a new initiative costs $500,000 and will deliver an additional $700,000 in increased profits. Simple ROI = Gains – Investment costs/Investment costs. ($700,000 – $500,000 = $200,000; $200,000/$500,000 = 40 percent.) This calculation works well in situations where benefits and costs are easily known, and is usually expressed as an annual percentage return.

However, technology investments frequently involve financial consequences that extend over several years. In this case, the metric has meaning only when the time period is clearly stated. Net present value (NPV) recognizes the time value of money by discounting costs and benefits over a period of time, and focuses either on the impact on cash flow rather than net profit, or savings.

A meaningful NPV requires sound estimates of the costs and benefits and use of the appropriate discount rate. An investment is acceptable if the NPV is positive. For example, an investment costing $1 million has an NPV of savings of $1.5 million. Therefore, ROI = NPV of savings – Initial investment cost/Initial investment cost. ($1,500,000 – $1,000,000 = $500,000. $500,000/$1,000,000 = 50 percent.) This can also be expressed as ROI = $1.5 million (NPV of savings)/$1 million (Initial investment) × 100 = 150 percent.

The internal rate of return (IRR) is the discount rate that sets the NPV of the program or project to zero. While the internal rate of return does not generally provide an acceptable decision criterion, it does provide useful information, particularly when budgets are constrained or there is uncertainty about the appropriate discount rate.

The U.S. CIO Council developed (see Appendix H) the Value Measuring Methodology (VMM) to define, capture, and measure value associated with electronic services unaccounted for in traditional ROI calculations, to fully account for costs, and to identify and consider risk.

Earned-Value Management

Most companies track the cost of a project using only two dimensions: planned costs versus actual costs. Using this particular metric, if managers spend all the money that has been allocated to a particular project, they are right on target. If they spend less money, they have a cost underrun — a greater expenditure results in a cost overrun. Fleming (2003) contends that this method ignores a key third dimension: the value of work performed.

Earned-value management (or EVM) enables the measurement of the true cost of performance of long-term capital projects. Although EVM has been in use for over a decade, government contractors are the major practitioners of this method.

The key tracking EVM metric is the cost performance index (CPI), which has proven remarkably stable over the course of most projects, according to Fleming. The CPI shows the relationship between the value of work accomplished ("earned value") and the actual costs. Fleming provides the following example to show how it works:

> If the project is budgeted to have a final value of $1 billion, but the CPI is running at 0.8 when the project is, say, one-fifth complete, the actual cost at completion can be expected to be around $1.25 billion ($1 billion/0.8). You are earning only 80 cents of value for every dollar you are spending. Management can take advantage of this early warning by reducing costs while there is still time.

Several software tools, including Microsoft Project, have the capability of working with EVM. PMPlan (http://www.pmplan.com) was written specifically to handle EVM, as shown in Figure 5.1.

Governance One also offers an interesting Flash-driven demo of its EVM offering at http://www.governanceone.com/flash/governance_demo.swf.

Rapid Economic Justification

Microsoft developed the Rapid Economic Justification framework (http://www.microsoft.com/windows/windowsmedia/Enterprise/AboutWM/BusinessValue/default.aspx) as an assessment and justification process that helps organizations align IT solutions with business requirements and then quantify the direct financial benefits of the proposed solutions. This approach combines the total cost of ownership (TCO) with project substantiation.

Freedman (2003) describes the five-step REJ process as follows:

1. *Understand the business.* IT managers should first evaluate the company's overall strategic direction and goals, along with any tactical problems and opportunities. This is done to ensure that the initiatives being considered actually do fit with the organization's overall objectives.
2. *Understand the solutions.* Both technical and business leaders need to work together to design possible alternative solutions to the

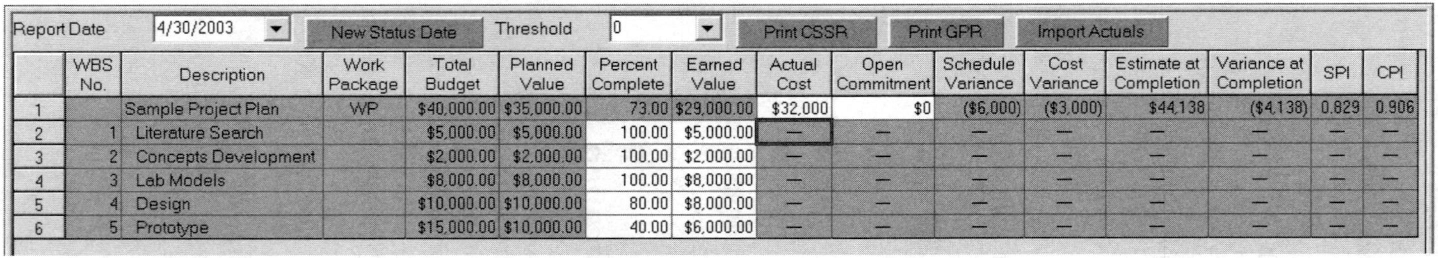

Report Date 4/30/2003 | New Status Date | Threshold 0 | Print CSSR | Print GPR | Import Actuals

	WBS No.	Description	Work Package	Total Budget	Planned Value	Percent Complete	Earned Value	Actual Cost	Open Commitment	Schedule Variance	Cost Variance	Estimate at Completion	Variance at Completion	SPI	CPI
1		Sample Project Plan	WP	$40,000.00	$35,000.00	73.00	$29,000.00	$32,000	$0	($6,000)	($3,000)	$44,138	($4,138)	0.829	0.906
2	1	Literature Search		$5,000.00	$5,000.00	100.00	$5,000.00	—	—	—	—	—	—	—	—
3	2	Concepts Development		$2,000.00	$2,000.00	100.00	$2,000.00	—	—	—	—	—	—	—	—
4	3	Lab Models		$8,000.00	$8,000.00	100.00	$8,000.00	—	—	—	—	—	—	—	—
5	4	Design		$10,000.00	$10,000.00	80.00	$8,000.00	—	—	—	—	—	—	—	—
6	5	Prototype		$15,000.00	$10,000.00	40.00	$6,000.00	—	—	—	—	—	—	—	—

FIGURE 5.1 EVM calculation.

identified problems. This often includes a "build versus buy" analysis to determine whether it is possible to solve the problem by using third-party software.

3. *Understand the cost-benefit equation.* This step calculates the summation of costs found under traditional TCO models. It incorporates hard financial benefits as well as intangible benefits (e.g., enhanced responsiveness).

4. *Understand the risks.* Standard risk analysis and development of risk mitigation strategies are performed.

5. *Understand the financial metrics.* Finally, the team projects the impact of the proposed IT investment in financial terms (i.e., payback, NPV, etc.) used by the specific company.

Portfolio Management

Kutnick and Cearley (2002) of the META Group found that if companies manage IT from an investment perspective — with a continuing focus on value, risk, cost, and benefits — it would help businesses reduce IT costs by up to 30 percent with a 2x to 3x increase in value. This is often referred to as portfolio management.

Freedman (2003) provides a stepwise plan for implementation:

1. *Take inventory.* A complete inventory of all IT initiatives should be developed. Information should include the project's sponsors and champion, a stakeholder list, strategic alignment with corporate objectives, estimated costs, and project benefits.

2. *Analyze.* Once the inventory is completed and validated, all projects on the list should be analyzed. A steering committee should be formed that has enough insight into the organization's strategic goals and priorities to place IT projects in the overall strategic landscape.

3. *Prioritize.* The output of the analysis step is a prioritized project list. The order of prioritization is based on criteria that the steering committee selects. This is different for different organizations. Some companies might consider strategic alignment to be the most important, while other companies might decide that the cost-benefit ratio is a better criterion for prioritization.

4. *Manage.* Portfolio management is not a one-time event. It is a constant process that must be managed. Projects must be continually evaluated based on changing priorities and market conditions.

Calculating the Net Worth of Organizational Information

Many organizations suffer from a proliferation of data that is either redundant or underutilized. The same organizations often suffer from not recognizing the true value of their data.

Calculating the value of information (or VOI) (Keyes, 1993) is a useful exercise that assists an organization in determining the true worth of its investment in information.

The following exercise is not meant to be performed by the technology group in a vacuum. Calculating the worth of the company's data is very much a group exercise that cuts across the organization. This is also not an exercise that can be rushed through and, in fact, can even harm the organization if hastily prepared.

Preparing the Field

Before any meetings are held to debate the relative worth of data, a *data dictionary* should be prepared that describes all automated systems as well as systems to be automated but still on the drawing board. This task is not as onerous as it sounds if the technology department employs an automated data dictionary. In those shops where an automated dictionary is not employed, a bit of work must be done to uncover this intimation and organize it logically. One of the key tasks of this assignment is to track all data elements that are being used by more than one system. The reason for this will become clearer as we proceed with this exercise.

At a minimum, prepare a chart that looks similar to the one in Table 5.3. Although it is common, from a data definition perspective, to break down each data element into its component parts, it should not be done in this case. For example, a customer address might be composed of four

TABLE 5.3   Creating the Data Dictionary for the VOI Process

Custfile	Customer File
Cust_name	Customer name
Cust_addr	Customer address
Cust_phone	Customer phone
Cust_credit	Customer credit score
Cust_line	Customer credit line
Cust_last	Customer last order number
Cust_date	Customer date of entry

individual data elements: street address, city, state, and zip code. For the purposes of the VOI exercise, we are interested in customer addresses as a single entity only. A corresponding document should be made available that carries complete explanations of the rather cryptic system names contained within the chart.

A Monetary Value of Information

The ultimate goal of this exercise is to assign a monetary value to each unitary piece of information. In this way, an organization — accustomed to calculating relative worth based on bottom-line statistics — can instantly recognize the value of information in terms that it understands.

With this in mind, the team should be assembled that is composed of representatives from the technology and user groups. Bear in mind that because this task is somewhat judgmental, a senior manager who is in the position to act as a corporate tiebreaker should be in attendance at the assignment of relative worth to any individual data element.

The team is now ready to evaluate each data element and apply a weighting algorithm that will ultimately tie the data element back to the organization in a monetary sense. The steps that should be taken for this assessment include:

1. Assign each system a weighting relative to its importance to the organization. Permissible weights for the entirety of this exercise are "1" for a low relative value, "2" for a middle relative value, and "3" for a high relative value.
2. For each data element within the system, assign a weighting that indicates that data element's importance relative to that system. Again, use the weightings "1," "2," or "3."
3. Multiply these two numbers together to get the total weighting of the data element relative to all data in the organization.
4. Each data element should have an annotation next to it indicating the number of systems in which this data element is cross-referenced. For example, it is possible that customer name is used in the sales system, the inventory system, and the marketing system. This will give us a total of three systems. The product calculated in Step 3 is now multiplied by the number determined in this instruction.
5. Convert this number to a percentage.
6. Using the last audited net income amount for the organization, calculate the VOI by multiplying the percentage calculated in instruction six by the net income amount. A completed chart is shown in Table 5.4.

TABLE 5.4 VOI Calculation Based on Net Income of $5 Million

Custfile	Customer File	Corp. Weighting	System Weighting	Cross-References	VOI (million)
Cust_name	Customer name	2	3 = 6	5 = 30	$1.5
Cust_addr	Customer address	2	2 = 4	2 = 8	$0.4
Cust_phone	Customer phone	2	3 = 6	1 = 6	$0.3
Cust_credit	Credit score	3	3 = 9	3 = 27	$1.35
Cust_line	Credit line	3	3 = 9	1 = 9	$0.45
Cust_last	Last order	2	2 = 4	3 = 12	$0.6
Cust_date	Date of entry	1	1 = 1	2 = 2	$0.1
			= Total weighting		In millions

IAM: Intangible Assets Monitor

Karl-Erik Sveiby (1997) developed a scorecard-like measure to monitor the value of intangible assets. The value of IAM is that it depends on the addition of intangible and tangible assets, as listed in Table 5.5.

IAM is based on very simplistic accounting but enables a powerful demonstration of the value of intangible assets.

The Prediction Market

Managers have long sought to "predict" particular targets — for example, sales exceeding $200 million for the month, new customers between 20 and 50 per quarter, etc. Developed by research universities, the prediction market is based on the notion that a marketplace can be a better predictor of the future than individuals (Kiviat, 2004).

Companies such as Microsoft and Hewlett-Packard have brought the Wall Street trading concept inside and have workers play-trading futures markets on such "commodities" as sales, product success, and supplier behavior. The key premise behind the market prediction market is that the typical workforce contains vast amounts of underutilized and untapped knowledge that only a market can unlock.

Before this can work, an internal software-based trading system must be implemented, presumably on the corporate intranet. Next, employees

TABLE 5.5   IAM Table of Metrics

Intangible Assets Monitor		
External Structure Indicators	Internal Structure Indicators	Competence Indicators
Indicators of growth/renewal	Indicators of growth/renewal	Indicators of growth/renewal
Profitability per customer	Investment in IT	Number of years in the profession
Organic growth	Structure-enhancing customers	Level of education
Image enhancing customers		Training and education costs
		Marking
		Competence turnover
		Competence-enhancing customers
Indicators of efficiency	Indicators of efficiency	Indicators of efficiency
Satisfied customers index	Proportion of support staff	Proportion of professionals
Sales per customer	Values/attitudes index	Leverage effect
Win/loss index		Value added per employee
		Value added per professional
		Profit per employee
		Profit per professional
Indicators of stability	Indicators of stability	Indicators of stability
Proportion of big customers	Age of the organization	Professionals turnover
Age structure	Support staff turnover	Relative pay
Devoted customers ratio	Rookie ratio	Seniority
Frequency of repeat orders	Seniority	

(all or a select few) are given accounts and "virtual" money in individual trading accounts. Each employee then gets to trade (e.g., buy or sell) selected commodities. For example, if the employee thought that the company would sell between $200 and $210 million worth of product, he or she would buy a futures contract that would signal to the rest of the market that this was a probable scenario. He or she could buy and sell as many times as desired. When trading stops, the scenario behind the highest priced stock is the one that the market deems most likely — and becomes the strategy selected. At Hewlett-Packard, the use of predictive markets has proven quite effective. In one case, the official forecast of the marketing manager was off by 13 percent while the stock market was off by just 6 percent. It was found that the predictive market beat official forecasts a whopping 75 percent of the time.

You may want to try this out for yourself. MIT's Technology Review has an Innovation Futures Web site (http://innovationfutures.com/bk/index.html) where registered users are given $10,000 worth of virtual cash with which to trade.

On to Chapter 6

In this chapter we put on our finance caps and learned a great deal about how to assign metrics to software systems and other computer-related assets. Our discussions included cost-benefit analysis, return on investment, net prevent value, rapid economic justification, portfolio management, and value of information. Proper use of these techniques will have you speaking the same language as management in no time.

Chapter 6 delves into the art and science of working with customers — both internal and external — as we move on to the customer perspective of the balanced scorecard.

References

Berry, J. (2001, July 30). IT ROI Metrics Fall into Four Groups. *Internetweek*, 869, p. 45.

Davidson, L. (1998, September 1). Measure What You Bring to the Bottom Line. *Workforce Magazine*, 77, 34–40

Fleming, Q. (2003, September). What's Your Project's Real Price Tag? *Harvard Business Review*, 81(9), p20, 2p, 1c.

Freedman, R. (2003, September). Helping Clients Value IT Investments. *Consulting to Management*, Vol. 14. No. 3.

Hawkins, C.H., Jr., K.L. Gustafson, and T. Nielson. (1998, July/August). Return on Investment (ROI) for Electronic Performance Support Systems: A Web-Based System. *Educational Technology*, 38(4), 15–22.

IOMA. (2002, October). How to Develop a Repeatable and Accurate ROI Process for IT. *IOMA's Report On Financial Analysis and Reporting*, Issue 02-10.

Keyes, J. (1993). *Infotrends: The Competitive Use of Information*. New York: McGraw-Hill.

Kiviat, B. (2004, July 12). The End of Management. *Time Magazine*, Vol. 164. No. 2. Bonus Section.

Kutnick, D. and D. Cearley. (2002, Jan./Feb.). *The Business of IT Portfolio Management*. META Group white paper.

Phillips, J.J. (1997). *Handbook of Training Evaluation and Measurement Methods* (3rd ed.). Houston: Gulf Publishing Company.

Sveiby, K. (1997, December). *The Value of Intangible Assets.* http://www.sveiby.com/articles/IntangAss/CompanyMonitor.html.

Utunen, P. (2003). Identify, Measure, Visualize Your Technology Assets. *Research Technology Management,* May/June, 31–39.

Chapter 6

Aligning IT to Meet Customer Objectives

How do we want our customers to view us?

Sample indicators: rank, market share, repeat orders, complaints

Treacy and Wiersma (1997) discuss three primary sources of differentiation vis-à-vis the balanced scorecard customer perspective:

1. *Product innovation.* Create new products and services that keep you ahead of competitors.
2. *Customer intimacy.* Develop intimate knowledge of customer needs and ways of satisfying these needs.
3. *Operational excellence.* Deliver acceptable quality and product characteristics at the lowest possible cost.

These three sources of differentiation should be kept in mind when dealing with IT end users as well as external customers of the organization.

Customer Intimacy and Operational Excellence

A customer satisfaction survey done by the Marketing Science Institute (1996) found that customers want their products and services delivered with the following four characteristics:

1. *Reliability*. Customers want dependability, accuracy, and consistency.
2. *Responsiveness*. Customers want prompt delivery and continuous communication.
3. *Assurance*. Customers want to be assured that the project team will deliver its project on time, with quality, within budget, and within scope.
4. *Empathy*. Customers want the project team to listen to and understand them. The customer really wants to be treated like a team member.

The goal is to select or develop and then deploy initiatives and accompanying metrics that fulfill these four requirements.

An 8 percent drop in quarterly profits accompanied by a 10 percent rise in service costs does not tell a customer service team what its service technicians should do differently on their service calls. However, knowing that several new technician hires dropped the average skill level such that the average time spent per service call rose 15 percent — and that, as a result, the number of late calls rose 10 percent — would explain why service costs had gone up and customer satisfaction and profits had gone down (Meyer, 1997). The key, then, is to select metrics wisely.

The U.S. Government uses an interesting variety of customer-centric measures as part of its E-services initiative, including:

- Customer satisfaction index
- Click count
- Attrition rate
- Complaints
- Customer frustration (abandoned transactions divided by total completed transactions)
- Visibility into the government process
- Efficient use of taxpayer dollars
- Effective sharing of information
- Trust
- Consistent quality of services
- Compliance with Section 508 (handicapped access)
- Compliance with security and privacy policies
- Partner satisfaction
- Political image
- Community awareness
- Negative and positive publicity

Stewart and Mohamed (2001) write about replacing the "customer" perspective with the more familiar, IT-specific "user" perspective. This more aptly broadens the customer perspective to include the internal as well as external customers that are using the IT application or its output. From an end-user's perspective, the value of a software system is based largely on the extent to which it helps the user do the job more efficiently and productively. Stewart and Mohamed (2001) emphasize indicators such as tool utilization rate, availability of training and technical support, and satisfaction with the tool. Table 6.1 summarizes their proposed indicators and metrics for an IT system for a system in the construction industry.

TABLE 6.1   Customer-Driven Indicators and Metrics for a Computer System

Performance Indicator	Key Aspects	Performance Measure
Facilitate document transfer and handling	Staff members are proficient in the use of IT-based handling procedures	Percent user proficient in IT-based procedures Percent documents transferred using IT tools
Enhance coordination between staff	Improved coordination More efficient utilization of contractors and subcontractors	Number of conflicts resulting from lack of coordination, reduced by a percent Time spent on rework arising from lack of coordination, reduced by a percent
Reduce response time to answer queries	IT application or tool facilitates quicker response to project queries	Response time to answer design queries, reduced by a percent
Empower staff to make decisions	Better and faster decision making	Time taken to provide information needed to arrive at decision, reduced by a percent
Enable immediate reporting and receive feedback	Information is made available to the project team as soon as it is ready	Time taken to report changes to management Time spent on reporting to total time at work, reduced by a percent
Identify errors or inconsistencies	Reduced number of QA nonconformances through IT	The ratio of the number of QA nonconformances for the IT-based system to the number of QA nonconformances for the traditional system

The Customer Satisfaction Survey

The easiest and most typical way to find out what customers think about an organization, its products, services, or systems, is to ask them. The instrument that performs this task is the *customer satisfaction survey*.

Those doing business on the Internet will find it rather easy to deploy a customer survey. It can be brief, such as the one in Figure 6.1, or a bit more lengthy, such as the one on the Port Authority of New York and New Jersey Web site (http://www.panynj.gov/aviation/jacsframe.htm), which asks customers for their thoughts on airport customer service.

There are quite a few survey hosting services available on a pay-per-use basis. KeySurvey (keysurvey.com) and Zoomerang (zoomerang.com) are just two.

If a Web- or e-mail-based survey is not practical, then one can opt for either doing a survey via traditional mail or phone. Because traditional mail surveys suffer from a comparatively low return rate — 1 to 3 percent — it is recommended that one utilize the telephone approach.

The steps to a successful customer survey include:

1. *Assemble the survey team.* The makeup of the survey team depends on the type of survey and the target customer base. If one will be calling external customers, then the best people for the job will be found in the marketing, sales, or customer services departments. If this is an IT-derived survey, and the customer base is composed of internal customers, then project leaders would be the best candidates for the job.
2. *Develop the survey.* Appendix E on requirements elicitation contains some relevant information on developing questionnaires and surveys, as well as on interviewing.
3. *Collect customer contact data.* Name, company, address, and phone number are the minimum pieces of information needed for this process. One might also want to capture sales to this client, years as a client, and other relevant data.
4. *Select a random sample of customers for the survey.* One cannot, and should not, survey *all* customers unless the customer base is very small. Random sampling is the most popular approach to reducing the number of surveys one will be sending out. Alternatively, one can use a systematic sampling approach. Using this method, one selects every Nth customer to include in the survey population.
5. *Mail a postcard alerting customers about the survey.* The postcard or letter should take the following form:

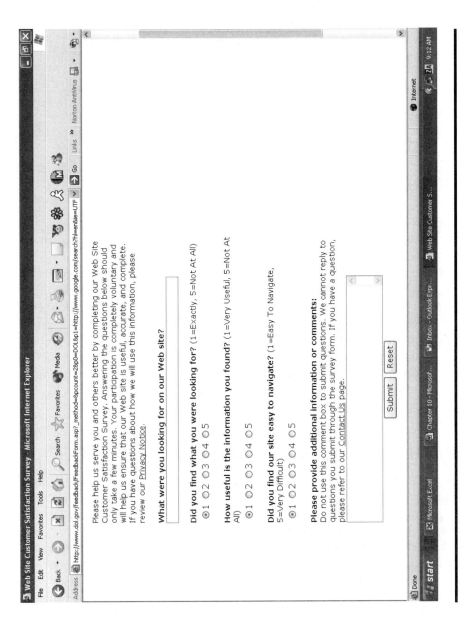

FIGURE 6.1 Brief customer satisfaction survey.

Dear Mr. Smith,

According to our records you purchased our *training services*. We are interested in knowing how helpful our services were and will be calling next week to ask for your comments. Your responses will help us find out what we are doing well and where we need to improve.

Our questions will take only a few minutes, so please give us a hand. Thank you in advance for your help.

Cordially,

Someone in authority
Their Title

6. Conduct interviewer training for staff.
7. Call customers and complete a Customer Satisfaction Survey instrument for each person.
8. Send the completed surveys and call sheets to the designated survey analysis team. This might be someone in the marketing department or, in the case of an internal IT survey, the manager designated for this task.
9. *Summarize survey results and prepare a report.* If using a Web-based or other automated surveying tools, one will be provided with analytical capabilities (see Figure 6.2). If doing this manually, then it is advisable to use Excel or another spreadsheet package for analysis.

Using Force Field Analysis to Listen to Customers

Nelson (2004) discusses a common problem when dealing with customers — haggling about the product's feature list. She recommends using force field analysis to more quickly and effectively brainstorm and prioritize ideas with a group of customers.

The power of this technique, usable in small as well as in large groups, lies in uncovering the driving as well as restraining forces for products or services. Driving forces can be features, services, a Web site, etc. — anything that helps customers drive toward success. Restraining forces can be quality issues, complex implementation, convoluted processes, support, unclear procedures — anything that prevents customers from being successful.

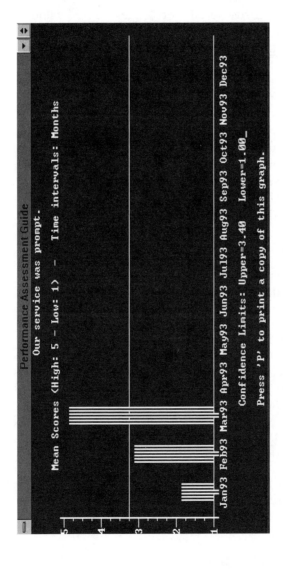

FIGURE 6.2   The DoD's performance assessment guide (discussed in Chapter 10) produces reports such as this.

The procedure is simple to follow:

1. State the problem, goal, or situation where you want feedback.
2. Divide the customer feedback group into smaller groups of eight to ten members. Sit them around a table and elect a scribe. A facilitator should also be appointed for each table.
3. Each discussion should take no longer than 30 minutes.
4. The table facilitator goes around the table asking each person to contribute one force. The table scribe records each new force.
5. Go around the table one or two more times until everyone is in agreement that their top three forces have been listed.
6. Review the list with the group.
7. Each person gets three votes for their top three forces.
8. The scribe will tally the votes for each force.
9. A meeting moderator should go around the room soliciting the top three driving forces from each table.
10. A meeting scribe should document the forces in a spreadsheet projected at the front of the room.
11. Each person in the room gets three votes for their top three forces.
12. The meeting scribe should enter the number of votes for each driving force.
13. When finished, sort the list by votes to rank them.

The process is then repeated for the restraining forces. A sample list follows:

- Driving forces:
  - Integration across modules   50 votes
  - Excellent tech support   45 votes
  - Standards-based technology   38 votes
- Restraining forces:
  - Product quality not always consistent   70 votes
  - Difficult to migrate from release to release   60 votes
  - User security is inadequate   30 votes

Force field analysis enables one to really listen to customers, which should lead to increased customer satisfaction and perhaps an improvement in the quality and competitiveness of products and services.

The Customer Economy

MacRae (2002) discards the idea of the *new economy* in favor of what he refers to as the *customer economy*. In this model, the customer is firmly in control. The key indicator in this economy is ETDBW, or "easy to do business with." In this economy, the customary metrics of profit and loss and return on assets are much less important than customer loyalty. The new customer-friendly manager focuses on the following metrics:

- Retention
- Satisfaction
- Growth
- Increases in customer spending
- Rate of defection and predicted rate of defection

MacRae recommends going to the source to maintain customer loyalty. One way to do this is to create a Customer Advisory Council. This is most effective when the leaders of the organization participate as well.

The Customer Advisory Council can be used to help answer the following questions, as recommended by Simoudis (1999):

- What are the customer's needs?
- How has the customer's behavior toward the enterprise changed since the customer was acquired?
- How does the customer use these products, and what products could the customer own?
- Which channels does the customer use most, and for what types of transactions?
- What channels should each customer be using?
- What kind of Web-based experience does the customer have?
- How much does it cost to service each customer's transaction?

The Patricia Seybold Group has developed two customer-focused metrics for the IT scorecard (Aldrich, 2001). The quality of experience (QoE) provided by IT services impacts employee productivity, channel revenue, as well as customer satisfaction. The metric assesses the user's experience with IT in terms of responsiveness and availability. Responsiveness is a measure of how long the user is waiting for information to be displayed. This is usually referred to as response time or download time. QoE expands on this definition to address everyone's experiences with IT — customers, employees, partners, etc.

One year after introducing QoE in 2000, Seybold introduced the Quality of Customer Experience (QCE). This is a set of metrics that allows the organization to assess, monitor, and manage the customer experience. The customer experience, according to this definition, is far more expansive than just accessing the company Web site. It also might include:

- Phone interactions
- E-mails

- Visits to your offices
- Direct-mail marketing
- Advertising
- Employee behavior
- How the product actually performs
- How the service is performed
- How the company is perceived by the community; alternatively, how the department is perceived by the rest of the company

Seybold considers the heart of QCE to be *customer outcomes* and resulting *moments of truth*. A customer measures the success of his experience in terms of reaching his desired outcome. Moments of truth are those points in the customer's experience where the quality of a company's execution substantially affects the customer's loyalty to the company and its products or services. That is, moments of truth signify key points in the customer's experience where he is judging the quality of the experience. Therefore, the heart of the QCE assessment is measuring the customer's success in executing the steps necessary within the company's system(s) to achieve the customer's desired outcomes.

For QCE to work properly, these moments of truth (or key success metrics) must be determined. They can be different for different people, so the best way to tackle this exercise is to develop a case study or scenario and run through it, pinpointing the moments of truth for each stakeholder involved in the scenario. Seybold calls this process Customer Scenario^SM Mapping. Consider the scenario of a company that needs a replacement motor — fast. The maintenance engineer needs to get production back up by 6 a.m. the next morning. His "moments of truth" are that (1) the motor is right for the job, (2) he has all the parts and tools he needs, and (3) he finishes before the shift supervisor shows up to bug him. The maintenance engineer must order his motor through his company's purchasing agent. The purchasing agent has his own "moments of truth": (1) find and order a motor in 15 minutes, delivery confirmed; (2) the best choice for motor is in first page of search results; (3) enough information is offered to enable a decision; (4) order department quickly confirms delivery without making the purchasing agent wait or repeat himself; and (5) the invoicing is correct.

Some of the metrics derived from this mapping include those presented in Table 6.2.

Innovation

Citibank understands innovation and how to measure it. The company has long had an Innovation Index (Tucker, 2002). This index measured

TABLE 6.2   Representative QCE Metrics

	Navigation	Performance	Operations	Environment
Customers find and purchase in 15 minutes	Average number of searches per order line item Average number of support calls per order Average elapsed time to select product and place the order	Average elapsed time to search Average elapsed time to select and purchase Number of steps required to select and purchase Average time to answer incoming phone call	Number of seconds average response time experienced by customers Number of seconds average response time experienced by employees who are interacting with customers Percent availability of customer-facing applications Number of customers on hold waiting for customer service	Internet performance index

revenues derived from new products but Citibank deemed this index insufficient to meet its needs. It created an Innovation Initiative, staffed by a special task force. This group was challenged to come up with more meaningful metrics that could be used to track progress and be easily integrated into Citibank's balanced scorecard. The task force eventually developed a set of metrics, which included new revenue from innovation, successful transfer of products from one country or region to another, the number and type of ideas in the pipeline, and time from idea to profit.

There are two types of innovation:

1. *Sustaining:* advances that give our most profitable customers something better, in ways that they define as "better"
2. *Disruptive:* advances that impair or "disrupt" the traditional fashion in which a company has gone to market and made money, because the innovation offers something its best customers *do not* want

Most software companies continually enhance their line of software products to provide their customers with the features that they (the customers) have stated they truly desired. This is *sustaining* innovation. These companies might also strive to come up with products that are radically different from what their customers want in order to expand their base of customers, compete with the competition, or even jump into a completely new line of business. This is *disruptive* innovation.

Most people equate innovation with a new invention, but it can also refer to a process improvement, continuous improvement, or even new ways to use existing things. Innovation can, and should, occur within every functional area of the enterprise. Good managers are constantly reviewing the internal and external landscapes for clues and suggestions about what might come next.

- *Research results from R&D.* One of the challenges is being alert to market opportunities that might be very different from the inventor's original vision.
- *Competitors' innovations.* Microsoft leveraged Apple's breakthrough graphical user interface and ultimately became far more dominant and commercially successful than Apple.
- Breakthroughs outside industry.
- *Customer requests.* A "customer-focused" organization's products and services will reflect a coherent understanding of customer needs.
- Employee suggestions.
- Newsgroups and trade journals.
- Trade shows and networking.

Some experts argue that a company's product architecture mirrors and is based on its organizational structure This is because companies attack that first project or customer opportunity in a certain way; and if it works, the company looks to repeat the process and this repetition evolves into a company's "culture." So when someone says that a company is "bureaucratic," what they are really saying is that it is incapable of organizing differently to address different customer challenges, because they have been so successful at the original model.

There are a variety of workplace structures that promote innovation, including:

- *Cross-functional teams.* Selecting a representative from the various functional areas and assigning them to solve a particular problem can be an effective way to quickly meld a variety of relevant perspectives and also efficiently pass the implementation stress test, avoiding, for example, the possibility that a particular functional group will later try to block a new initiative. Some variations include:

- *"Lightweight project manager" system.* Each functional area chooses a person to represent it on the project team. The project manager (PM) serves primarily as a coordinator. This function is "lightweight" in that the PM does not have the power to reassign people or reallocate resources.
- *"Tiger team."* Individuals from various areas are assigned and completely dedicated to the project team, often physically moving into shared office space together. This does not necessarily require permanent reassignment, but is obviously better suited for longer-term projects with a high level of urgency within the organization.

■ *Cross-company teams or industry coalitions.* Some companies have developed innovative partnership models to share the costs and risks of these high-profile investments, such as:
- Customer advisory boards
- Executive retreats
- Joint ventures
- Industry associations

According to Lyon (2002), there are several managerial techniques that can be utilized to spur innovation, as shown in Table 6.3.

Managing for Innovation

At a very high level, every R&D process will consist of:

■ *Generation of ideas.* From the broadest visioning exercises to specific functionality requirements, the first step is to list the potential options.
■ *Evaluation of ideas.* Having documented everything from the most practical to the far-fetched, the team can then coolly and rationally analyze and prioritize the components, using agreed-upon metrics.
■ *Product/service design.* These "ideas" are then converted into "requirements," often with very specific technical parameters.

There are two core elements of this longer-term, competency-enhancing work. The first is the generation of ideas. Most companies utilize a standard process to ensure that everyone has time and motivation to contribute. The second element is to promote an environment conducive to innovation. This includes:

TABLE 6.3   Promoting Innovation

Technique	Definition and Examples
Commitment to problem solving	Ability to ask the "right questions" Build in time for research and analysis
Commitment to openness	Analytical and cultural flexibility
Acceptance of "out-of-box" thinking	Seek out and encourage different viewpoints, even radical ones
Willingness to reinvent products and processes that are already in place	Create a "blank slate" opportunity map, even for processes that appear to be battle-tested and comfortable
Willingness to listen to everyone (employees, customers, vendors)	"Open door" Respect for data and perspective without regard to seniority or insider status
Keeping informed of industry trends	Constantly scanning business publications and trade journals, and clipping articles of interest "FYI" participation with fellow managers
Promotion of diversity, cross-pollination	Forward-thinking team formation, which also attempts to foster diversity Sensitive to needs of gender, race, and even work style
Change of management policies	Instill energy and "fresh start" by revising established rules
Provision of incentives for all employees, not just researchers and engineers	Compensation schemes to align individual performance with realization of company goals
Use of project management	Clear goals and milestones Tracking tools Expanded communication
Transfer of knowledge within an organization	Commitment to aggregating and reformatting key data for "intelligence" purposes
Provision for off-site teaming	Structured meetings and socialization outside the office to reinforce bonds between key team members
Provision for off-site training	Development of individuals through education and experiential learning to master new competencies
Use of simple visual models	Simple but compelling frameworks and schematics to clarify core beliefs
Use of the Internet for research	Fluency and access to Web sites (e.g., competitor home pages)

TABLE 6.3 (continued)   Promoting Innovation

Technique	Definition and Examples
Development of processes for implementing new products and ideas	Structured ideation and productization process Clear release criteria Senior management buy-in
Champion products	Identify and prioritize those products that represent the best possible chance for commercial success Personally engage and encourage contributors to strategic initiatives

- Cultural values and institutional commitment
- Allocation of resources
- Linkage with company's business strategy

Creating an "innovation-friendly" environment is time-consuming and will require the manager to forego focusing on the "here and how." As Lyon (2002) explains, when there is constant pressure to "hit the numbers" or "make something happen," it is difficult to be farsighted and build in time for you and your team to "create an environment."

Managing innovation is a bit different from creating an environment that promotes innovation. This refers to the service — or product-specific initiative — whether it is a new car or a streamlined manufacturing process. The big question is: *how do we make this process come together on time and under budget?* There are two main phases to the successful management of innovation.

The first phase seeks to stress-test the proposal with a variety of operational and financial benchmarks, such as the items below.

1. Is the innovation "real?"

Is this "next great thing" dramatic enough to justify the costs, financial and otherwise? Does it clearly and demonstrably distance you from your competitors? And can it be easily duplicated once it becomes public knowledge?

2. Can the innovation actually be done? Does the organization have the resources?

This is where one figures out whether the rubber meets the road. One needs to ask whether one has the capabilities and functional expertise to realize this vision. Many organizations come up with a multitude of ideas. Upon further examination, they often find that they simply do not have the resources to do the vast majority of them. This might lead them to become innovative in a different way as they search for partners. In other words, some organizations try to couple their brains with someone else's brawn.

3. Is the innovation worth it? Does the innovation fit into the organization's mission and strategic plan?

ROI (return on investment) is the most frequently used quantitative measure to help plan and assess new initiatives. Probably more useful, however, is ROM (return on management), which poses a fundamental question: what should the CEO and his or her management team *focus* on? Research extending over a period of ten years led to the concept of *return on management* (Strassman, 1996). This ratio is calculated by first isolating the *Management Value-Added* of a company, and then dividing it by the company's total *Management Costs*:

Return on Management™ =

F(Management Value-Added, Management Costs)

Management Value-Added is that which remains after every contributor to a firm's inputs gets paid. If *Management Value-Added* is greater than *Management Costs,* one can say that managerial efforts are productive because the managerial *outputs* exceed the managerial *inputs.*

Another way of looking at the *Return on Management* ratio (*R-O-M™ Productivity Index*) is to view it as a measure of productivity. It answers the question of how many surplus dollars one gets for every dollar paid for *Management.*

4. The second phase, design, is something examined in greater detail later.

However, for now, the focus is on the process by which these ideas and concepts get distilled into an actual product design (e.g., a Web site map or a prototype). Many mistakes are made by delegating this process to lower-level functional experts, when in fact some of these decisions go a long way toward determining the product's ultimate acceptance in the marketplace.

Lyon (2002) postulates that most of the outward signs of excellence and creativity associated with the most innovative companies are a result of a culture and related values that encourage and support managers who use their specific initiatives to also reinforce and strengthen the company's processes. When these processes become "repeatable," they become the rule instead of the exception, which of course makes it easier for the next manager to "be innovative."

Kuczmarski (2001) points to Capital One as a company that uses a model based on continuous innovation. Capital One utilizes a patented Information-Based Strategy (IBS) that enables the company to expand its mature credit card business by tailoring more than 16,000 different product combinations to customers' needs. It is able to embrace high degrees of risk because it bases its innovations on customer needs. The company tests new ideas against existing customers, or possibly a separate grouping of prospects.

Additional Metrics

A wealth of metrics can be derived from the preceding discussions. Other innovation metrics to consider include:

- *Return on innovation investment:* number of customers who view the brand as innovative, divided by the total number of potential customers.
- *Brand innovation quotient:* number of repeat purchasers, divided by the total number of purchasers.
- *Pipeline process flow:* measures the number of products at every stage of development (i.e., concept development, business analysis, prototype, test, launch).
- *Innovation loyalty:* the number of repeat purchases made before switching to a competitor.

On to Chapter 7

This chapter discussed the customer perspective of the balanced scorecard. Essentially, the goal here was to "get and keep" customers. Whether these customers are internal (i.e., the end users) or external is of little importance as the techniques are the same. Toward this end, this chapter discussed a variety of techniques for measuring customer satisfaction as well as the importance of innovation in attracting and retaining customers.

Chapter 7 discusses the "meat and potatoes" perspective of the balanced scorecard: business process objectives.

References

Aldrich, S. (2001, October 11). Measuring Moments of Truth. Patricia Seybold Group report. Boston, MA: The Patricia Seybold Group. http://www.psgroup.com/doc/products/2001/10/SS10-11-01CC/SS10-11-01CC.asp.

Kuczmarski, T. (2001, Spring). Five Fatal Flaw of Innovation Metrics: Measuring Innovation May Seem Complicated, but It Doesn't Need to Be. *Marketing Management.*

Lyon, S. (2002, July). *Managing Innovation.* Lecture, University of Phoenix.

MacRae, D. (2002, May 10). Welcome to the 'Customer Economy'. *Business Week Online.* http://www.businessweek.com.

Marketing Science Institute. (1996). *Smart Workplace Practices.* http:/www./smart-biz.com/sbs/arts/swp41.htm.

Meyer, C. (1997). *Relentless Growth: How Silicon Valley Innovative Strategies Can Work in Your Business.* New York: Simon & Schuster.

Nelson, B. (2004, May/June). Using Force Field Analysis to Listen to Customers. *productmarketing.com: The Marketing Journal for High-Tech Product Managers.* Volume 2, Issue 3.

Simoudis, E. (1999, October). Creating a Customer-Centric Enterprise. *USBanker.*

Stewart, R.A. and S. Mohamed. (2001, April). Utilizing the Balanced Scorecard for IT/IS Performance Evaluation in Construction. *Construction Innovation,* Vol. 1. pp. 147–163.

Strassmann, P. (1996). Introduction to ROM Analysis: Linking Management Productivity and Information Technology. http://www.strassmann.com/consulting/ROM-intro/Intro_to_ROM.html.

Treacy, M. and Wiersema, F. (1997). *The Discipline of Market Leaders: Choose Your Customers, Narrow Your Focus, Dominate Your Market.* Boulder, CO: Perseus Books Group.

Tucker, R. (2002). *Driving Growth through Innovation.* San Francisco, CA: Berrett-Koehler.

Chapter 7

Aligning IT to Meet Business Process Objectives

What are the processes at which we should excel?

Sample indicators: number of changes, order response time, reduction in cycle time

There is a great story making the rounds lately. It is about a company that used its computer software as part of an analytic customer relationship management project. The company sought to identify unprofitable customers not worth keeping. That it did, but ultimately decided to keep those customers anyway. Why? Because Wall Street analysts use customer turnover as a key metric, and dropping too many customers no matter what the benefit to the bottom line would likely lead to a decrease in market capitalization and a lack of confidence in the company. The story illustrates two points (Burriesci, 2004): (1) metrics are sometimes misguided and (2) coordinating balanced goals with actions can prevent businesses from making critical errors. Ultimately, business performance management is about improving corporate performance in the right direction.

There are literally hundreds of business processes taking place simultaneously in an organization, each creating value in some way. The art of strategy is to identify and excel at the critical few processes that are the most important to the customer value proposition (Kaplan and Norton, 2004).

Both private companies and governmental agencies have outsourced some of their computer processing systems to third parties. Processes commonly outsourced include:

- Asset management
- Help desk
- Infrastructure maintenance
- Systems management and administration
- Network management
- Integration and configuration

These outsourced IT services have come to be known as the "IT utility." The larger IT utilities are typically ISO 9001/9002 certified and offer large pools of IT talent and experience. However, processes must be measured, regardless of whether or not they are outsourced.

The IT Utility

Unisys (2003), a provider of such services, recommends the following metrics:

- Customer satisfaction
- Standardization
- Incident rates
- Security audit
- Incident prevention rates
- Security awareness
- Availability
- Reliability and quality of service
- Call volume
- First-pass yields
- Cycle times
- Architecture accuracy
- IT employee satisfaction
- Root cause analysis
- Change modification cycle times
- Change modification volume by type
- R&D presentation and information flow rate
- Volume of technology pilots
- Business opportunity generate rate
- Strategic IT project counts

Unisys uses these metrics to establish the foundation for management review, trend analysis, and causal analysis. Management review provides insight into current performance and forms the basis for taking corrective action. Trend and root cause analyses identify opportunities for continuous improvement.

Based on its analysis and industry experience, Unisys states that a performance-based environment is anywhere from 10 to 40 percent cost effective than a non-performance-based environment. When deciding how best to optimize the IT infrastructure, organizations need verifiable performance and trend data. While customer satisfaction is usually touted as the key metric for IT improvement, it is actually an outcome metric that depends on several lower-level activities, as shown in Figure 7.1. Understanding the relationship between these co-dependent performance metrics is important in effecting sustainable positive performance.

Essentially, the IT department should consider itself an IT utility for the purposes of aligning itself to the organization's business process objectives. In this way, IT can more effectively track performance using a balanced scorecard and make appropriate performance improvements as a result.

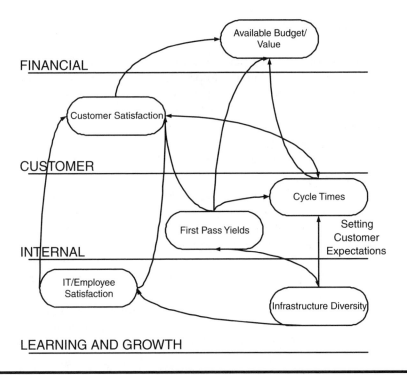

FIGURE 7.1   Cause and effect in the IT utility.

Wright et al. (1999) did an extrapolation of Compaq's (now Hewlett-Packard) balanced scorecard based on research and publicly available information. As a computer company, this case history is interesting from an IT perspective, particularly if a corporate IT department thinks of itself as an IT utility.

Compaq had a number of business process objectives, including:

- Operations cycle:
  - Optimized distribution model
  - JIT manufacturing
  - Outsourcing
  - Build-to-order
  - Reduced cycle times
  - Order process linked to production, supplies
  - Global production optimization
- Innovation cycle:
  - Under $1000 PCs
  - Products preconfigured with SAP and other business software
  - Pricing innovations
  - Design to market requirements: workstations, laptops
  - High-performance desktops

The business process perspective is linked downward to the learning and growth perspective by quality improvements, improved coordination, and integrated information. The business process perspective is linked upward to the customer and financial perspectives by lower operating costs, improved use of resources, reduced waste, new product capabilities, and better service programs.

For Compaq, the chief component of the business process perspective is its operations cycle. This encompasses sourcing parts, components, manufacturing, marketing, distributing, and services products after sale. This cycle had been the major focus of a reengineering effort, the goal of which was to bring them to a higher level of customer focus.

Compaq's reengineering effort required it to change its business processes first and then its information systems to support the reengineered processes. The company relied heavily on enterprise-level information technology and by the late 1990s had begun using SAP R/3 to integrate its business processes and sales information. Compaq also built a global extranet called Compaq On Line to provide customers with a way to automatically configure and order PCs and servers. This was followed by adding an Internet at-home shopping service, allowing customers to order directly online.

The newly enhanced processes and accompanying systems allowed Compaq to achieve the following process efficiencies:

- Linking orders electronically to suppliers. This improved cycle time and facilitated just-in-time (JIT) manufacturing. It also made production status information available to customers so that they could track their own orders.
- Sharing information with suppliers enabled Compaq to anticipate changes in demand and ultimately improve its efficiency. This reduced the cost of supplies and improved on-time delivery.
- Integrating orders with SAP's financial management and production planning modules enabled Compaq to reduce time and cost of orders.
- Capturing customer information after a sale enabled Compaq to provide individualized service and additional marketing opportunities.

Upon implementation of the balanced scorecard in 1997, Compaq did improve its sales volume. According to Wright et al. (1999), this resulted from delivering value, increasing customer service, innovating new products, and reducing time-to-market. This sales spurt more than made up for the decreasing prices of PCs and ultimately generated higher revenue. Improved cycle times and decreasing costs enabled the company to operate far more efficiently, resulting in higher net income levels and, ultimately, higher revenue per employee.

Integrating CMM into Business Process Objectives

The Capability Maturity Model (CMM) devised by the Software Engineering Institute (SEI) of Carnegie Mellon University (http://www.sei.cmu.edu/cmm/) has been used by a wide variety of organizations to increase the maturity level of their software engineering practices. A mature IT organization is one most able to align itself to meet the business process objectives of the organization.

CMM Explained

The CMM model, as shown in Figure 7.2, consists of five levels of maturity that an IT department goes through on its way to becoming completely optimized and productive:

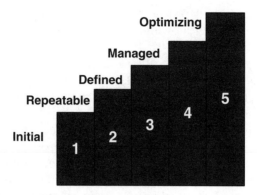

FIGURE 7.2   The Capability Maturity Model.

- Level 1: Initial (i.e., performed) — ad hoc and chaotic.
- Level 2: Repeatable (i.e., managed) — basic project management processes are established to track cost, schedule, and functionality.
- Level 3: Defined — management and engineering activities are documented, standardized, and integrated into the organization.
- Level 4: Quantitatively managed — uses detailed measures.
- Level 5: Optimizing — continuous process improvement is enabled by quantitative feedback and from testing innovative ideas and technologies.

Level 1: Initial

The initial level of CMM is characterized as follows:

- Ad hoc
- Little formalization
- Tools informally applied

The key actions to get to next step include:

- Initiate rigorous project management.
- Initiate management oversight.
- Initiate quality assurance.

This level is characterized by an ad hoc approach to software development. Inputs to the process are not well defined but the outputs are as expected. Preliminary baseline project metrics should be gathered at this level to form a basis for comparison as improvements are made and maturity increases. This can be accomplished by comparing new project measurements with the baseline ones.

Level 2: Repeatable

The repeatable level of the CMM is characterized as follows:

■ Achieved a stable process with a repeatable level of statistical control

Key actions to get to next step include:

■ Establish a process group.
■ Establish a software development process architecture.
■ Introduce software engineering methods and tools.

At this level, the process is repeatable in much the same way that a subroutine is repeatable. The requirements act as input, the code as output, and constraints are such things as budget and schedule. Although proper inputs produce proper outputs, there is no means to discern easily how the outputs are actually produced. Only project-related metrics make sense at this level because the activities within the actual transitions from input to output are not available to be measured. Measures are this level can include:

■ Amount of effort needed to develop the system
■ Overall project cost
■ Software size: non-commented lines of code, function points, object, and method count
■ Personnel effort: actual person-months of effort, report person months of effort
■ Requirements volatility: requirements changes

Level 3: Defined

The defined level of CMM is characterized as follows:

■ Achieved foundation for major and continuing progress

Key actions to get to next step include:

■ Establish a basic set of process management to identify quality and cost parameters.
■ Establish a process database.
■ Gather and maintain process data.
■ Assess relative quality of each product and inform management.

At this level, the activities of the process are clearly defined. This additional structure means that the input to and output from each well-defined functional activity can be examined, which permits a measurement of the intermediate products. Measures include:

- Requirements complexity: number of distinct objects and actions addressed in requirements
- Design complexity: number of design modules
- Code complexity: number of coded modules
- Quality metrics: defects discovered, defects discovered per unit size (defect density), requirements faults discovered, design faults discovered
- Fault density for each product
- Pages of documentation

Level 4: Managed

The managed level of CMM is characterized as follows:

- Substantial quality improvements
- Comprehensive process measurement

Key actions to get to next step include:

- Support automatic gathering of process data.
- Use data to analyze and modify the process.

At this level, feedback from early project activities is used to set priorities for later project activities. At this level, activities are readily compared and contrasted; the effects of changes in one activity can be tracked in the others. At this level, measurements can be made across activities and are used to control and stabilize the process so that productivity and quality can match expectation. Collecting the following types of data is recommended. Metrics at this stage, although derived from the following data, are tailored to the individual organization.

- *Process type.* What process model is used, and how is it correlating to positive or negative consequences?
- *Amount of producer reuse.* How much of the system is designed for reuse? This includes reuse of requirements, design modules, test plans, and code.

- *Amount of consumer reuse.* How much does the project reuse components from other projects? This includes reuse of requirements, design modules, test plans, and code.
- *Defect identification.* How and when are defects discovered?
- *Use of configuration management.* Is a configuration management scheme imposed on the development process? This permits traceability, which can be used to assess the impact of alterations.
- *Module completion over time.* At what rates are modules being completed? This reflects the degree to which the process and development environment facilitate implementation and testing.

Level 5: Optimizing

The optimizing level of CMM is characterized as follows:

- Major quality and quantity improvements

Key actions to get to next step include:

- Continue improvement and optimization of the process.

Getting from CMM to Process Improvements

Process improvements can be thought of in two dimensions. There are those process improvements that are internal to the IT department, and there are process improvements that are quite visible to end users and senior management. For the purposes of this discussion, we refer to the former as *engineering process improvements* and the latter as *business process improvements*. In the following discussion, business process improvements are **bolded** and elaborated upon as these directly relate to the balanced scorecard approach. Readers interested in engineering process improvements are encouraged to refer to the author's books on software engineering and configuration management, both listed in the additional reading section of this chapter.

Table 7.1 redefines the five levels in terms of continuous improvement.

The Systems Engineering Process Office of the U.S. Navy (see Appendix M) has identified a variety of engineering and business process improvements that are relevant to this discussion.

Because CMM level 1, Initial, is characterized by unpredictable processes, the primary area for consideration in process improvement is "people." From a balanced scorecard perspective, this translates to learning and growth (see Chapter 8).

TABLE 7.1 CMM Using a Continuous Improvement Framework

Capability Level	Definition	Critical Distinctions
5: Optimizing	A quantitatively managed process that is improved based on an understanding of the common causes of variation inherent in the process A process that focuses on continually improving the range of process performance through both incremental and innovative improvements	The process is continuously improved by addressing common causes of process variation
4: Quantitatively Managed	A defined process that is controlled using statistical and other quantitative techniques The product quality, service quality, and process performance attributes are measurable and controlled throughout the project	Using appropriate statistical and other quantitative techniques to manage the performance of one or more critical subprocesses of a process so that future performance of the process can be predicted Addresses special causes of variation
3: Defined	A managed process that is tailored from the organization's set of standard processes according to the organization's tailoring guidelines, and contributes work products, measures, and other process-improvement information to the organizational process assets	The scope of application of the process descriptions, standards, and procedures (organizational rather than project-specific). Described in more detail and performed more rigorously. Understanding interrelationships of process activities and details measures or the process, its work products, and its services.

TABLE 7.1 (continued)   CMM Using a Continuous Improvement Framework

Capability Level	Definition	Critical Distinctions
2: Repeatable	A performed process that is also planned and executed in accordance with policy, employs skilled people having adequate resources to produce controlled outputs, involves relevant stakeholders; is monitored, controlled, and reviewed; and is evaluated for adherence to its process description	The extent to which the process is managed The process is planned and the performance of the process is managed against the plan Corrective actions are taken when the actual results and performance deviate significantly from the plan The process achieves the objectives of the plan and is institutionalized for consistent performance
1: Initial	A process that accomplishes the needed work to produce identified output work products using identified input work products The specific goals of the process area are satisfied	All of the specific goals of the process area are satisfied
0: Incomplete	A process that is not performed or is only performed partially One or more of the specific goals of the process area are not satisfied	One or more of the specific goals of the process area are not satisfied

Source: Systems Engineering Process Office. SPAWAR Systems Center. U.S. Navy.

CMM level 2, Repeatable, is characterized by being reactive rather than proactive. Engineering process improvements at this level include implementation of:

- Requirements management
- Project planning
- Project monitoring and control
- Supplier agreement management

- Measurement and analysis
- Process and product quality assurance
- Configuration management

CMM level 3, Defined, is characterized by being proactive. Process improvements at this level include implementation of:

- Requirements development
- Product integration
- Verification
- Validation
- **Organizational process focus**
- **Organizational process definition**
- **Organizational training**
- **Integrated project management**
- **Risk management**
- Integrated teaming
- Decision analysis and resolution
- **Organizational environment for integration**

CMM level 4, Quantitatively Managed, is characterized by measured and controlled processes. Process improvements at this level include:

- **Organizational process performance**
- **Quantitative project management**

CMM level 5, Optimizing, is characterized by a real emphasis on process improvement. Improvements at this level include:

- **Organizational innovation and deployment**
- **Causal analysis and resolution**

Quality and the Balanced Scorecard

Solano et al. (2003) have developed a model for integrating systematic quality—i.e., a balance between product and process effectiveness and efficiency—within systems development organizations through the balanced scorecard. Table 7.2 shows the four balanced scorecard perspectives oriented toward systemic quality integration.

This quality-oriented strategy is a daily, on-going process that needs to be "bought into" by staff members. Solano et al. (2003) provide an

TABLE 7.2 Integrating Quality with the Balanced Scorecard

Perspective	Strategic Topics	Strategic Objectives	Strategic Indicators
Financial	Growth	F1: Increase shareholder value F2: New sources of revenue from outstanding quality products and services F3: Increase customer value through improvements to products and services	Shareholder value Growth rate of volume compared with growth rate of sector Rate of product renewal compared with total customers
	Productivity	F4: Cost leader in the sector F5: Maximize utilization of existing assets	Comparing expenses with the sectors: Free cash flow Operating margin
Customer	Charm the customers	C1: Continually satisfy the customer chosen as the objective C2: Value for money C3: Reliable operations C4: Quality service	Share of selected key markets Comparing value for money with the sector Percentage of errors with customers
Internal Process	Growth	I1: Create and develop innovative products and services I2: Implement a systems product quality model with a systemic approach	Profitability of new product investment Rate of new product acceptance Rate of product quality
	Increase customer value	I3: Technological improvements to products I4: Apply flexible development methodologies I5: Advisory services	Timeliness Product availability

TABLE 7.2 (continued)   Integrating Quality with the Balanced Scorecard

Perspective	Strategic Topics	Strategic Objectives	Strategic Indicators
	Operational excellence	I6: Provide a flexible global infrastructure I7: Meet specifications on time I8: Cost leader in the sector I9: Implement a quality system development model process I10: Develop outstanding relationships with suppliers	Cost reduction Fixed asset production Improved yield Rate of compliance with specifications Rate of process quality
	Good neighborliness	I11: Improve health, safety, and environment	Number of safety incidents Rate of absenteeism
Learning and growth	Motivated and well-prepared staff	L1: Climate for action L2: Fundamental skills and competencies L3: Technology	Employee survey Staff hierarchy table (percent) Availability of strategic information

example of a company, VenSoft C.A., that did just this by relating organizational goals to employee remuneration. Table 7.3 shows employee incentives based on the balanced scorecard. Each perspective and indicator was given a weight that depended on the organization's mission. Yearly bonuses depended on the goals being totally or partially attained.

How is the process (or product) quality index calculated? One of the goals of software engineering is to produce a defect-free product. A module's Quality Profile (STSC, 1999) is the metric used to predict if a module will be defect-free. A Quality Profile is predictive in that its value is known immediately after a module has completed its developer's unit test. It is suggestive in that it can suggest potential quality issues and thus mechanisms to redress those issues. Quality Profiles adhere to software engineering dogmas that design is good, technical reviews are necessary for quality, and that high defect density in a test phase is predictive of

TABLE 7.3   Balanced Scorecard Related Incentives

Category	Indicators	Weighting (%)
Financial (60 percent)	Shareholder value	18
	Return on capital employed (ROCE)	13
	Economic value added (EVA)	13
	Free cash flow	10
	Operating costs	6
Client (10 percent)	Client satisfaction index	7
	Rate of growth of market	3
Internal processes (10 percent)	Process quality index	3
	Product quality index	3
	Productivity	4
Training and growth (20 percent)	Employee quality index	20

TABLE 7.4   A Software Quality Profile

Quality Profile Dimension	Criteria
Design/code time	Design time should be greater than coding time
Design review time	Design review time should be at least half of design time
Code review time	Code review time should be at least half of coding time
Compile defect density	Compile defects should be less than ten defects per thousand lines of code
Unit test defect density	Unit test defects should be less than five defects per thousand lines of code

high defect density in later test phases. Finally, early empirical evidence suggests that Quality Profiles do predict if a module is defect-free. As seen in Table 7.4, a Quality Profile is composed of five dimensions.

The Process Quality Index (PQI) is calculated by multiplying the five dimensions together. The Software Engineering Institute (SEI) has presented preliminary data indicating that PQI values between .4 and 1 predict that the module will have zero subsequent defects.

With this model, Solano et al. (2003) tried to close the gap between software engineering projects and organizational strategy. In their view, the systemic vision of the organization and the balance between the forces of the organization coincide quite nicely with the balanced scorecard approach.

Philips Electronics (Gumbus and Lyons, 2002) implemented a balanced scorecard predicated upon the belief that quality should be a central focus of its performance measurement effort. The Philips Electronics balanced scorecard has three levels. The very highest level is the strategy review card; next is the operations review scorecard; and the third is the business unit card. By the time one has read this book, Philips Electronics will have implemented a fourth level — individual employee card.

The corporate quality department created very specific guidelines for how metrics should link the cascaded scorecards. These guidelines indicate that all top-level scorecard critical success factors (CSFs) for which the department is responsible must link metrically to lower-level cards. Three criteria were established to accomplish this:

1. *Inclusion*. Top-level CSFs must be addressed by lower-level CSFs to achieve top-level metric goals.
2. *Continuity*. CSFs must be connected through all levels. Lower-level measurements should not have longer cycle times than higher-level measurements.
3. *Robustness*. Meeting a lower-level CSF goal must ensure that high-level CSF goals will be met or even surpassed.

As one can see, goals in all card levels align with goals in the next level above, and goals become fewer and less complex as one drills down through the organization.

The CSFs, selected by the departments that had a major controlling responsibility, were the key balanced scorecard indicators. The management team of each business unit selected CSFs that would distinguish the business unit from the competition. They used a value map to assist in determining the customer CSFs and then derived the process CSFs by determining how process improvements can deliver customer requirements. Competence CSFs were identified by figuring out what human resource competencies were required to deliver the other three perspectives of the card. Standard financial reporting metrics were used for the financial perspective.

At this point, each business unit was charged with figuring out what key indicators could best measure the CSFs. The business units had to make some assumptions about the relationships between the processes and results to derive performance drivers and targets. These targets were set based on the gap between current performance and what was desired two and four years into the future. The criteria for these targets were that the targets had to be specific, measurable, realistic, and time-phased. The targets themselves were derived from an analysis of market size, customer base, brand equity, innovation capability, and world-class performance.

Indicators selected included:

- *Financial:* economic profit realized, income from operations, working capital, operational cash flow, inventory turns
- *Customers:* rank in customer survey, market share, repeat order rate, complaints, brand index
- *Processes:* percentage reduction in process cycle time, number of engineering changes, capacity utilization, order response time, process capability
- *Competence:* leadership competence, percentage of patent-protected turnover, training days per employee, quality improvement team participation

In cascading the scorecard throughout its different levels, six indicators were key for all business units:

1. Profitable revenue growth
2. Customer delight
3. Employee satisfaction
4. Drive to operational excellence
5. Organizational development
6. IT support

In one of the business units, Philips Medical Systems North America, results were tracked in real-time. Data was automatically transferred to internal reporting systems and fed into the online balanced scorecard report with the results made immediately accessible to management. The results were then shared with employees using a Lotus Notes-based online reporting system they call Business Balanced Scorecard On-Line. To share metrics with employees, they used an easy-to-understand traffic-light reporting system. Green indicates that the target was met, yellow indicates in-line performance, and red warns that performance is not up to par.

Process Performance Metrics

Some researchers contend that organizations are shooting themselves in the foot by ignoring Web analytics. Swamy (2002) states that without this link, a major portion of the organization's contributions to success or failure is missing. He contends that most online initiatives have a dramatic impact on offline performance. Therefore, excluding Web analytics, as immature as these statistics are, precludes senior executives from seeing the whole picture.

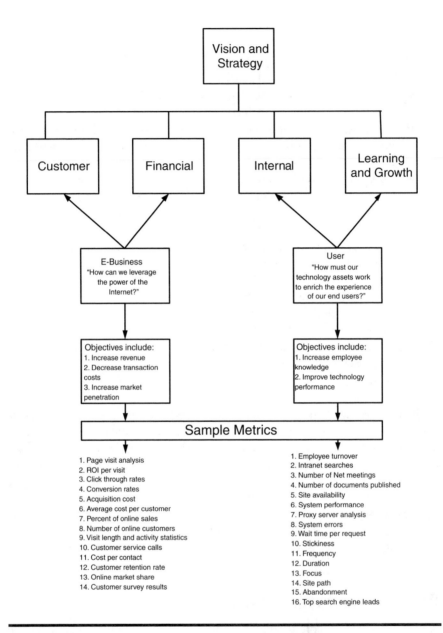

FIGURE 7.3 Web analytics added to the balanced scorecard.

Swamy (2002) recommends adding two new perspectives to the balanced scorecard, as shown in Figure 7.3.

An organization should not randomly select metrics. While the metrics in Figure 7.3 are all generic and would well serve most companies, it is recommended that an "E-business audit" be performed (see Appendix K).

The goal of this audit is to determine holes in performance as well as in business practices and security. The results of the audit should include a recommended set of metrics applicable to the specific organization.

IT processes are project-oriented. Stewart (2001) makes the following metric recommendations when establishing project-specific balanced scorecards:

- Financial:
  - On time
  - Within budget
  - Variance from original baselined budget and final budget
  - Project costs as compared to industry standard and organizational standards for similar projects
  - Earned value
- Customer:
  - Project meeting intended objectives
  - Customer satisfaction (including account payment history)
  - Economic value added (strategic benefits rather than financial benefits achieved — referencibility, increased venture capital support, etc.)
- Project and internal business:
  - Project resource requirements management:
    - Average management time of project manager related to total effort
  - Project portfolio comparatives:
    - Project cancellation rate
    - Project backlog — awaiting start-up
    - Risk management statistics
    - Contingency time allotted and used
  - Change management statistics (number of change records per designated period of time can show whether proper project scope has been set, percent change to customer/vendor environment impact to scope)
  - Quality management statistics (rework, issues, etc.)
  - Project team member satisfaction
- Growth and innovation:
  - Average capabilities per team member and improvement over course of project
  - Development or ongoing improvement of templates, procedures, tools, etc.
  - The rate that innovative ideas are developed (new ways of doing things)
  - Best practices identified

- Lessons learned and applied
- Positive achievements and impacts to the organization
- Evaluate quantitative statistics:
  - Examine true costs of operation, evaluating impact of project slippage and inadequate support and nonsupport infrastructure costs
- Evaluate organizational change:
  - Evaluate how the change has impacted the organization's business
- Reduce to lowest common denominator:
  - Review support costs versus costs of delay per person
  - Review actual project costs versus plans (net present value)
- Review strategic objectives achieved:
  - Review qualitative statistics
  - Identify unanticipated benefits accrued
  - Review attainment or contribution to organizational objectives versus time commitment
- Review overall business value improvement:
  - Revenue increase/decrease
  - Team retention and promotion
  - Increased market share, references

Selected Performance Metrics

There are a wide variety of performance metrics that companies use. Appendix N lists some actual metrics from selected organizations surveyed or researched for this book. The reader is urged to review Appendix C, which lists a wealth of standard IT metrics, and Appendix L, which discusses how to establish a software measure program within an organization.

On to Chapter 8

In this chapter the reader may have finally come to the realization that implementation of the balanced scorecard is much more work than originally thought. It is much more than just dropping a bunch of metrics onto four perspectives (i.e., customer, financial, business process, and learning and growth). In reality, the balanced scorecard provides a framework for reengineering the organization for continuous improvement. Through discussion, examples, and case histories, this chapter delved into the various process improvement techniques, including the Capability Maturity Model (CMM) and quality initiatives. These are the new processes one needs to implement — and then manage and measure using the balanced scorecard.

Chapter 8 discusses the final perspective of the balanced scorecard — learning and growth.

References

Burriesci, J. (2004, June 1). You Say Metric. I Say Distraction. *Intelligent Enterprise,* Vol. 7, Issue 9, p. 4, 2/3p.

Gumbus, A. and B. Lyons. (2002, November). The Balanced Scorecard at Philips Electronics. *Strategic Finance,* pp. 45–49.

Kaplan, R. and D. Norton. (2004, March/April). How Strategy Maps Frame an Organization's Objectives. *Financial Executive.*

Solano, J., M. Perez de Ovalles, T. Rojas, A Griman Padua, and L. Mendoza Morales. (2003, Winter). Integration of Systemic Quality and the Balanced Scorecard. *Information Systems Management,* pp. 66–81.

Stewart, W. (2001, March). Balanced Scorecard for Projects. *Project Management Journal,* pp. 38–52.

STSC. (1999, April 30). Disciplined Software Development. White Paper. Software Technology Support Center. United States Air Force. http://www.stsc.hill.af.mil/resources/tech_docs/PSPv3.DOC.

Swamy. R. (2002, May). Strategic Performance Measurement in the New Millennium: Fitting Web-Based Initiatives into a Company's Balanced Scorecard Is Critical. Here Is a Guide on How to Do It. *CMA Management,* 76(3), 44(4).

Unisys. (2003). Performance-Based Contracting: Measuring the Performance in the Information Technology Utility. White paper.

Wright, W., R. Smith, R. Jesser, and M. Stupeck. (1999, January). Information Technology, Process Reengineering and Performance Measurement: A Balanced Scorecard Analysis of Compaq Computer Corporation. *Communications of AIS,* Vol. 1, Article 8.

Additional Reading

Keyes, J. (2004). *Software Configuration Management.* Boca Raton, FL: Auerbach Publications.

Keyes, J. (2002). *Software Engineering Handbook.* Boca Raton, FL: Auerbach Publications.

Chapter 8

Aligning IT to Promote Learning and Growth

Can we continue to improve and create value?

How do we support, satisfy, and develop our employees into excellence?

Sample indicators: number of training days, number of new products

This chapter is about staff excellence and just how to accomplish it. To start this discussion the right way, the following offers some legendary wisdom about the art of communication — perhaps the most important component of good peopleware:

In the beginning there was the plan.

And then came the assumptions.

And the plan was without form.

And the assumptions without any substance.

And darkness was upon the face of all workers.

And they spake unto their team leaders, saying,

"Lo, this is a pail of dung, and none may abide and the odor thereof."

And the team leaders went unto the supervisors, saying, "This new thing, it is a container of excrement, and it is very strong, such that none may abide by it."

And the supervisors went unto their manager, saying, "This is a vessel of fertilizer, and none may abide its strength."

And the manager went unto the vice president bearing this message:

"Lo, this Plan contains that which aids plant growth, and it is powerful."

And the vice president went unto the senior vice president, saying,

"This new thing promoteth growth, and it is powerful."

And the senior vice president went unto the President and sayeth unto him," This powerful new plan will actively promote the growth and efficiency of all units, even unto the uttermost parts of the organization."

And the president looked upon the plan and saw that it was good.

And "the plan" became "policy."

Liberate Rather than Empower

There is more than one way to manage. There is the way most people do it. And then there is the right way.

If you think that that managing means telling your people specifically what they can do and what they cannot do, keeping tabs on their phone calls, and clocking the time they spend at lunch or at the water cooler, then give back your key to the executive washroom.

If you are like most managers, you are not quite so monstrous. But you are probably still worried that your staff may not be making the "right decisions." What does the right decision mean, anyway? Is it the decision you would have made yourself if you were in your staff's position? Ultimately, the right decision may be different from the one you would have made. So, giving your staff the impression that the right decision is the one you would make is a sure way to diminish motivation, creativity, accountability, and morale. As many executives like to say, "If you've got a yes-person working for you, then one of you is redundant!" Ultimately, because your decision may not be the "right" one anyway, having some real thinkers on your team could only help, not hurt, your own career.

A good manager is not a robotics cop overseeing clones. Instead, a good manager is one who creates an environment in which staff members take on the responsibility to work productively in self-managed, self-starting teams, and then identify and solve complex problems on their own. Think of the benefits of this *modus operandi*. You will be freed to think about the bigger picture. Is this not why you wanted to become a manager in the first place?

Every field has its buzzwords. The latest one among human resources people is "empowerment." Perhaps you have even taken a course on "how to empower your staff." Back to the office you go, full of new ideas. But the moment you get back, you call a meeting of everyone who reports to you. Presumably, these empowered people cannot operate on their own for even a few days and need to report to "momma" or "poppa" every detail of every project they are working on. As management guru Peter Drucker always likes to say, much of what we call management is making it very difficult for people to do their jobs.

The Monster in the Corner Office

The team was bright and well educated. Its total years of experience hovered around 50. But the firm still decided to "look outside" when it came time to replace its retiring senior vice president of technology planning and development.

After months of screening and interviewing, the corporate chieftains made a decision. Of course, the corporate chieftains know little (if anything at all) about technology. So their interviews of candidates probably concentrated on what the candidates looked like, how they presented themselves, and the "gobbledegook" principles of leadership and management, which are difficult to quantify and most certainly impossible to convey in an interview.

The situation was hardly conducive to productivity. But the potentially explosive atmosphere of a work environment could have been eased, maybe even eliminated, had the new "boss" been a good manager.

So began the year that the team came to call "our time in hell." You see, the manager treated his staff like clerks. They were not allowed to make decisions without his input; they could not make a presentation without his seeing it first. Worst of all, they spent their days in endless meetings.

First there were the weekly staff meetings. This took about two hours. Then each staff member had to attend the weekly "one-on-one" with the manager. Sometimes, the one-on-ones were scheduled directly after the weekly staff meeting, so there was little more about which to talk. But each meeting still took an hour. The manager loved to hear himself talk.

Then there was the weekly project meeting with the user department. Although each of the team members was intimately familiar with the users, and in fact was about as knowledgeable as the users and long ago had earned their respect and admiration, the manager still wanted a formal meeting to discuss project progress. The problem was that everybody at the meeting already knew the progress. Again, the manager just wanted to hear himself talk.

Then there was the monthly meeting with the boss' manager. And a meeting with the user department's senior management. All told, each team member spent approximately 16 hours a month attending nonsubstantial meetings. Needless to say, little work got done. Instead of empowering his people, the manager "depowered" them.

Does this story sound familiar? It is a true one. It happened in a Wall Street firm not too long ago, and is offered here because it is representative of the type of manager who seems so prevalent in the industry today. Of course, not all managers are as bad as this one was. Still, there are plenty of people out there who have a psychological need to justify their position at their staff members' expense.

Liberating Your Staff

Oren Harari (1993), a professor at the University of San Francisco and a management consultant, relates an interesting experience with one of his clients. While he was waiting for an appointment with this particular client, he overheard two of the manager's clerical assistants calling customers and asking them how they liked the company's product. Professor Harari reflected that it was no wonder this manager had such a good reputation. When he finally met with her, he offered his congratulations on her ability to delegate the customer service task to her staff. "What are you talking about?" she asked, bewildered. "Why, your secretaries are calling customers on their own," Harari replied. "Oh, really? Is that what they're doing?" she laughed. "You mean you didn't delegate that task to them?" "No," she said. "I didn't even know they were doing it. Listen, Oren, my job is to get everyone on my team to think creatively in pursuit of the same goal. So what I do is talk to people regularly about why we exist as a company and as a team. That means we talk straight about our common purpose and the high standards we want to achieve. I call these our goal lines. Then we talk regularly about some broad constraints we have to work with, like budgets, ethics, policies, and legalities. Those are our sidelines.

"It's like a sport. Once we agree on the goal lines and sidelines, I leave it to my people to figure out how to best get from here to there. I'm available and attentive when they need feedback. Sometimes I praise; sometimes I criticize — but always constructively, I hope. We get together periodically and talk about who's been trying what, and we give constructive feedback to one another. I know that sounds overly simplistic, but I assure you that is my basic management philosophy.

"And that's why I don't know what my assistants are doing, because it's obviously something they decided to try for the first time this week. I happen to think it's a great idea because it's within the playing field and helps keep high standards for being number-one in our industry. I will tell you something else. I don't even know what they intend to do with the data they're collecting, but I know they'll do the right thing.

"Here's my secret: I don't know what my people are doing, but because I work face to face with them as a coach, I know that whatever it is they're doing is exactly what I'd want them to be doing if I knew what they were doing!"

The Challenge of Peopleware

Many say CIOs live by the 10 percent rule. That is, the greatest productivity one can get comes from hiring within the top-10 percentile (see Appendix A for an IT Staff Competency Survey). One of technology's leading gurus, Ed Yourdon, is well known for saying that the easiest approach to developing an efficient technology department is to bring in the better people. Because there is a 25-to-1 differential between the best people and the worst people, and a 4-to-1 differential between the best teams and the worst teams, maybe the best way to improve productivity and quality is just to improve hiring practices.

But who are the people that improved hiring practices would find? For a programming problem, these are the people who were just innately better programmers. If one takes a random group of 100 people and puts them in a room with a complex programming exercise, one of them will finish 25 times faster than the others.

In addition to hiring, other "peopleware" techniques could go a long way toward increasing productivity. Recent studies have shown that the productivity of people with adequate office space is substantially higher than people with traditionally allocated smaller amounts of space. Training also makes a difference, particularly if workers can accrue their training days the way they accrue their vacation time (DeMarco, 1979).

Productivity can also be improved in many other ways: by training managers to develop more skills in handling employee performance reviews, or even by focusing on the psychological makeup of the development team (see Appendix F for a list of behavioral competencies for employees as well as managers). Much work has been done in recent years on team dynamics. For a team to work together successfully, team members must complement each other. Each team needs a distribution of leaders, followers, idea people, testers, problem solvers, etc. Even in an industry where personality profiles are skewed toward introversion, it is still possible to build an effective working team. All it needs is some good management.

Attributes of the Good Tech Manager

The technology manager needs to satisfy his or her managers, end users, and staff members while making sure that projects are delivered on time and on or under budget.

Aside from technical skills, the manager needs to be a "people person." He or she needs to be able to:

- Talk the language of the end users.
- Talk the language of the tech gurus.
- Understand and deal with corporate and departmental politics.
- Cajole reluctant end users into doing something "new."
- Resolve problems.
- Chair meetings.
- Motivate staff and end users.

More specifically, the manager should be able to manage expectations, resolve conflict, overcome fears, facilitate meetings, and motivate team members, as discussed below.

Manage Expectations

Each set of stakeholders will have its own expectations about the outcome of the project:

- End users will have expectations about what the system will be able to do. End users should not be told that features will be implemented in a particular phase if they will not be. This will surely lead to disappointment and possibly even project failure.
- IT staff members will have expectations about what role they will play in the development of the project. IT staff members are usually quite excited to be involved in a new development effort. Promising them a role in the new development effort and then not delivering on that promise will lead to disappointment, a loss of productivity, and sometimes even the loss of the team member.

■ Senior management will have expectations about the project cost and resource utilization. It is critically important that the project manager always provide a complete picture of the status and current costs of the project.

Resolve Conflict

Any time one puts two or more people together, there is room for conflict. The project manager needs to be both cheerleader and referee during the lengthy project development process.

Types of conflict can include:

■ Developer to developer
■ End user to end user
■ Developer to end user
■ Department to department
■ Manager to manager
■ Customer to employee

Overcome Fears

Over time, end users develop a level of comfort with the systems and practices that they already have in place. Some might feel threatened by the aspect of change. If not handled properly, this fear of the unknown can lead to project failure.

This actually happened during the systemization of the U.S. Post Office. When more sophisticated technologies were implemented about a decade ago, the employees were not involved in any of the meetings. Hence, change was foisted upon them suddenly and dramatically. Employees, fueled by the fear of losing their jobs to this new technology, sabotaged the system.

This expensive problem could have been easily avoided if the project manager considered the effect of technological change on these employees and spent some time overcoming their fears. This can easily be done by:

■ Involving end users in the process from the beginning
■ Keeping all employees informed about what is going on. This can be done via newsletter, e-mail, public meetings, systems demonstrations, etc.
■ Actively listening to employees about their fears and acting on those fears

Facilitate Meetings

What does it mean to facilitate a meeting? Meetings do not run well on their own. Instead, a meeting must be "managed." The steps for effective meeting facilitation include:

- The project manager acts as chairperson. He or she schedules the meeting, invites appropriate staff, and sets the agenda.
- The agenda is sent out to attendees in advance.
- The chairperson moderates the meeting, moving through each item on the agenda.
- The chairperson appoints a secretary to take meeting notes.
- The chairperson ensures that all agenda items are covered and that the meeting adjourns on time.
- The chairperson ensures that everyone is permitted to voice his or her opinion.
- The chairperson resolves all disagreements.
- After the meeting, the chairperson makes sure that the meeting notes are distributed to the attendees.
- The chairperson schedules a follow-up meeting, if necessary.

Motivate Team Members

Perhaps the most important of project manager responsibilities is to motivate team members. This means that the project manager must wear many hats:

- The project manager must motivate senior management such that the latter retains interest in funding and supporting the project.
- The project manager must motivate end users and end-user management so that both support the project and cooperate in its development.
- The project manager must motivate development staff so that the effort is completed on time, within budget, and in a quality fashion.

How does one go about motivating people? Some of the methods have already been discussed in this chapter, including managing expectations, resolving conflict, and active listening.

The project manager must be all things to all people. He or she must be a constant presence in the lives of all team members, congratulating their successes as well as supporting and consoling them in the face of failure.

In the end, it is people who control whether there is a productivity paradox. And people in an organization consist of everyone from senior manager to junior clerk.

The art and science of working with people is often referred to as the real technology behind the organization. And motivating them, empowering them, liberating them — and all the buzzwords that apply — make the difference between a successful organization and one and that is not so successful.

Hiring the Best People

Organizations that want to be competitive will simply have to hire the very best people they possibly can — users and technologists.

Of course, in these politically correct times, the concept of the best is being well criticized. The American Management Association (AMA) publishes a newsletter geared to human resources personnel. One issue warned that anyone placing help-wanted ads could be the defendant in a discrimination suit if the advertiser called for "recent graduates" or "college graduates" when the job did not warrant such qualifications.

"Recent graduates" is highly discriminatory against anyone with a bit of mileage, and this author agrees with the AMA's warning. However, this author does not agree with the caution on requesting "college graduates." The AMA's view is that proportionately fewer members of minority groups finish college than do members of non-minority groups. Therefore, indicating college graduates only discriminates against minority candidates. Hogwash!

You cannot help your age, but you can certainly help your educational status. Not all colleges cost $40,000 a year. There are many fine local colleges that are nearly free. The philosophy of my organization is to be the very best. This means that we have to hire the very best. This does not necessarily translate to recruiting at the best colleges (Harvard University as opposed to Podunk U), but translates to finding those people who persevere, who try to make themselves better than what they already are. That is what a college degree means to this author.

In fact, a thorough reading of Dinesh D'Souza's (1992) fine book entitled *Illiberal Education* might just sour you on graduates of some of the better colleges. Basically, the book argues that some of our leading universities have been mandated to common-denominate students. It is his view that, by charging universities with being

> "structurally racist, sexist, and class-biased, a coalition of student activists, junior faculty, and compliant administrators have imposed their own political ideals on admissions, hiring, curriculum, and even personal conduct, while eschewing the goals of liberal education."

Essentially, we can no longer be sure of why a student was accepted at a university or why he got the grades he did. Given an education like the one D'Souza envisions, can we even be sure that future graduates will think on their own (recall the original movie version of *Stepford Wives*) or work well in teams?

Organizations face rough competition every day of their corporate lives. To hobble them for social reasons is to make them lose their competitive edge. That, indeed, may be exactly the course if human resources departments are weighed down with impossible "equal opportunity" hiring requirements.

This author firmly believes in equal opportunity — but only if the candidate has the skills this author is looking for. This author will not hire a woman just because quota dictates a woman. Unfortunately, many American companies have a mind-set of obeying quotas. As a result, instead of getting the very best that money can buy, they wind up with the lowest common denominator — hardly a competitive advantage.

Another interesting phenomenon in today's downsized economy is the sheer number of experienced, dedicated people who have been booted out the door. Many of them are finding it difficult to find new jobs. An acquaintance of mine, a secretary by trade, gets the same brush-off each and every time she goes for an interview: "You're overqualified." Now perhaps this is a euphemism for "you're too old," but think about it. Would you not like to staff up with all overqualified people? I know I would! What benefits a company would reap from all that experience! Personally, this author feels that organizations are shooting themselves in the foot competitively when they decide that Ms. Jones or Mr. Smith is overqualified. The interesting thing is that, because of our wounded economy, all this experience is available on the cheap. A competitor's loss is my gain.

This author belongs to an industry trade association. This group has a lot to grapple with, given the battered economy and the sheer expense of doing business in a large city. However, there is no shortage of seasoned professionals in this city, so I was aghast when one of the association's members spoke enthusiastically about a policy of hiring programmers from abroad. The company's view was that excess staffers — that legion of unemployed technology people — were like so many bad tomatoes. They were not worth salvaging.

While it is true that many excessed tech professionals have rather worn skills, they most definitely can be salvaged with a little training. "Not so," said the marketing chief of this very well-known company. "Better to start from scratch." And the company's idea of starting from scratch was to hire someone young and from another country (cheap, cheap, cheap).

Let us now examine the ramifications. Although it is true that the company following such a policy might get more modern skills for far less money, it would lose out in a number of ways. First of all, remaining personnel are not blind. That is, they are pretty cognizant of the firm's penchant for cutting staff at home and replacing it with what they consider to be "outsiders." Their feelings of firm disloyalty, coupled with the fear of being a victim of downsizing in the next round, lead to lower motivation, dampened enthusiasm, and a marked decrease in productivity and product quality.

Second, for the most part, newly hired labor just does not understand the business. At a time when business and technology are moving closer together, is it wise to throw out all the accumulated business knowledge of the current technical staff?

Today, programmers with a COBOL background seem to be about as employable as chimney sweeps. What the industry tends to forget is that COBOL is merely an attribute of a far greater skill. That skill is being able to develop complex applications. Not only do these people know how to program; they can also look at the big picture and then apportion it into manageable components, each component becoming a program or part of the system. This is a skill far too valuable to throw away.

A Better Workforce

Creating a better workforce means understanding how to work with people. One would be surprised (or maybe not) at how differently bosses look at things than do their staff, as shown in Table 8.1. The object,

TABLE 8.1   What Do Employees Really Want?

What Employees Want	Items	What Employers Think Employees Want
1	Interesting work	5
2	Appreciation of work	8
3	Feeling "in on things"	10
4	Job security	2
5	Good wages	1
6	Promotion and growth	3
7	Good working conditions	4
8	Personal loyalty	6
9	Tactful discipline	7
10	Sympathetic help with problems	9

Source: Kovach, K (1999). Employee Motivation. Addressing a Crucial Factor in Your Organization's Performance. Human Resource Development. Ann Arbor, MI: University of Michigan Press.

clearly, is to narrow the gap. One way to do so is by motivating the workforce. Now, this does not mean taking up the pom-poms and giving the old college cheer. It does mean taking some specific steps.

The first step is to understand your own motivations, your strengths as a manager, as well as your weaknesses. Probably the best approach is to ask your peers and employees to make an anonymous appraisal of your performance as a manager. Have them rate such traits as listening and communications skills, openness, and attitude. Painful as this process may be, it will actually make you seem heroic in your employees' eyes. At the same time, it will give you some food for thought on ways to improve your own performance.

The second step — one that many managers pay only lip service to — can really make the difference between having a motivated employee and one who feels that he or she is just another number. Take the time to learn about your employees and their families. What are their dreams? Then ask yourself how you as a manager can fulfill these dreams from a business perspective.

Perhaps the best way to learn about your employees is in a non-work atmosphere — over lunch or on a company outing. As you learn more about your employees' motives, you can help each one develop a personalized strategic plan and vision. Ultimately, you could convert those horrible yearly performance reviews into goal-setting sessions and progress reports.

Generating a positive attitude is the third step. Studies show that 87 percent of all management feedback is negative, and that traditional management theory has done little to correct the situation. Your goal should be to reverse the trend. Make 87 percent of all feedback good.

Respect for and sensitivity toward others remains essential in developing positive attitudes. Ask employees' opinions regarding problems on the job, and treat their suggestions and ideas like priceless treasures.

The partner of positive attitude in the motivational game is shared goals. A motivated workforce needs well-defined objectives that address both individual and organizational goals. This means that you should include all your employees in the strategic planning process. Getting them involved leads to increased motivation. It also acts as a quality check on whether or not you are doing the right thing. And you will close the communication gap at the same time.

Just setting a goal is insufficient. You have to monitor progress. The goal-setting process should include preparing a detailed roadmap that shows the specific path each person is going to take to meet that goal. One of the things that IT professionals dislike the most is the feeling that they have been left out of the business cycle. In essence, information technology is simply one bullet of a grand strategic plan. IT staffers frequently complain that they rarely get to see the fruits of their labor. Distributing the IT function into the business unit mitigates this problem somewhat, but it is still up to the manager to put technologists into the thick of things — make them feel like part of the entire organization.

Finally, recognizing employees or team achievement is the most powerful tool in the motivating manager's toolbox. Appreciation for a job well done consistently appears at the top of employee "want lists." So hire a band, have a party, send a card, or call in a clown — but thank that person or that team.

Techniques for Motivating Employees

This section provides a wide variety of interesting techniques useful for motivating staff as a part of continuous improvement.

Based on a study at Wichita State University, the top five motivating techniques are:

1. Manager personally congratulates employee who does a good job.
2. Manager writes personal notes about good performance.
3. Organization uses performance as basis for promotion.
4. Manager publicly recognizes employee for good performance.
5. Manager holds morale-building meetings to celebrate successes.

One does not have to actually give an award for recognition to happen. Giving one's attention is just as effective. The Hawthorne Effect says that the act of measuring (paying attention) will itself change behavior.

Nelson and Blanchard (1994) suggest the following low-cost rewards recognition techniques:

- Make a photo collage about a successful project that shows the people who worked on it, its stages of development, and its completion and presentation.
- Create a "yearbook" to be displayed in the lobby that contains each employee's photograph, along with his or her best achievement of the year.
- Establish a place to display memos, posters, photos, etc. recognizing progress toward goals and thanking individual employees for their help.
- Develop a "Behind the Scenes Award" specifically for those whose actions are not usually in the limelight.
- Say thanks to your boss, your peers, and your employees when they have performed a task well or have done something to help you.
- Make a thank-you card by hand.

- Cover the person's desk with balloons.
- Bake a batch of chocolate-chip cookies for the person.
- Make and deliver a fruit basket to the person.
- Tape a candy bar for the typist in the middle of a long report with a note saying, "halfway there."
- Give a person a candle with a note saying, "No one holds a candle to you."
- Give a person a heart sticker with a note saying, "Thanks for caring."
- Purchase a plaque, stuffed animal, anything fun or meaningful, and give it to an employee at a staff meeting with specific praise. That employee displays it for a while, then gives it to another employee at a staff meeting in recognition of an accomplishment.
- Call an employee into your office (or stop by his or her office) just to thank him or her; do not discuss any other issue.
- Post a thank-you note on the employee's office door.
- Send an e-mail thank-you card.
- Praise people immediately. Encourage them to do more of the same.
- Greet employees by name when you pass them in the hall.
- Make sure you give credit to the employee or group that came up with an idea being used.
- Acknowledge individual achievements by using employees' names when preparing status reports.

McCarthy and Allen (2000) suggest that you set up your employees for success. When you give someone a new assignment, tell the employee why you are trusting him or her with this new challenge. "I want you to handle this because I like the way you handled _____last week." They also suggest that you never steal the stage. When an employee tells you about an accomplishment, do not steal her thunder by telling her about a similar accomplishment of your own. They also suggest that you never use sarcasm, even in a teasing way. Resist the temptation to say something like, "It's about time you gave me this report on time." Deal with the "late" problem by setting a specific time the report is due. If it is done on time, make a positive comment about timeliness.

Barbara Glanz (1996) has a more creative approach, suggesting that one:

- Send a handwritten note to at least one customer and one employee per week. This not only keeps your customers coming but builds loyalty internally.
- Keep a bulletin board in your office of pictures of repeat customers and their families. This helps builds relationships and reminds everyone of why they have a job.

- When people in your organization first turn on their computers, have a message of the day such as a quotation on customer service, etc. If a day begins with inspiration, it will lift the interaction level in the workplace.
- Collect company legends and success stories on video or audiotape.
- Create a company mascot that represents the spirit of the company. For example, one company uses a salmon because they are always "swimming upstream."
- Designate one room as the "whine cellar," the place for anyone to go who is having a bad day. Decorate the room with treats, stuffed toys, punching bags, etc.

Nontechnological Issues in Software Engineering

Although much of the emphasis in the current literature is on the technical issues of software engineering, a number of substantive nontechnological problems pose dangers to the effective practice of software engineering. A lack of software engineering productivity can be caused by managerial, organizational, economic, political, legal, behavioral, psychological, and social factors.

To achieve an acceptable level of software engineering productivity, as much emphasis must be placed on "people" issues as on technological issues.

Simmons (1991) focused on the following issues:

- The software engineering profession, for the most part, has not developed a block of capable/competent managers.
- Despite a concerted effort toward making software development an engineering discipline, it is still very much of an individual creative activity rather than a team effort.
- Little has been done to reduce performance differences among individuals or across teams.

Poor management produces:

- Unrealistic project plans due to poor planning, scheduling, and estimation skills
- Unmotivated staff due to the inability of management to manage a creative staff
- Lack of teamwork due to the inability to build and manage effective teams
- Poor project execution due to inadequate organization, delegation, and monitoring

- Technical problems due to lack of management understanding of disciplines such as quality assurance and configuration management
- Inadequately trained staff due to a short-sighted rather than a long-term perspective

Possible solutions to poor management problems include:

- Definition of dual career paths for technical and managerial staff
- Training in managerial skills and techniques
- Active mentoring and supervision by senior managers
- Increased delegation of responsibility and matching authority

Some reasons for lack of teamwork include:

- Desire for autonomy
- A culture that reinforces individual efforts more than team efforts
- Concentration of key application knowledge by a few individuals
- Desire for privacy
- The "not invented here" syndrome translated to the "not invented by me" syndrome
- Large productivity differences from one individual to another
- Political considerations between powerful individuals and managers

Possible solutions to teamwork problems include:

- Objective assessment of team contributions with appropriate rewards
- Development of an organizational culture that condones or rewards group efforts
- Active efforts to disperse crucial application knowledge across project staff
- Improvements in communication and coordination across organizational layers
- Adoption of ego-less programming techniques

Large performance differences between individuals negate productivity increases. Researchers estimate that productivity ranges of 3:1 to 5:1 are typical, with some studies documenting differences as high as 26:1 among experienced programmers. This variability is often due to:

- Misguided staffing practices
- Poor team development
- Inattention to the critical role of motivation
- Poor management

Techniques to increase effective level of productivity include:

- Enhanced training
- Investment in productivity tools (tools, methods)
- Standard practices
- Professional development opportunities
- Recognition
- Effective staffing
- Top talent
- Job matching
- Career progression
- Team balance
- Improved management

Creativity Improvement

The majority of IT organizations use a top-down approach to generating productivity improvements. Couger et al. (1991) suggest a process for generating improvement via a series of bottom-up creativity techniques:

1. Survey participants to obtain perceptions on the environment for creativity and innovation. This same instrument should be used to obtain new perceptions as a measurement of the results.
2. Participants should be asked to keep a "creativity log" in which they keep track of their creativity improvements.
3. Training workshops should be instituted to teach a variety of creativity generation and evaluation techniques.
4. One third of the workshop should be devoted to discussing how to improve the climate for creativity in the IS organization. The methodology used for this assessment is to ask the employees to identify positive and negative contributors to the creativity environment.
5. Creativity generation/evaluation techniques used:
   - *Analogy and metaphor.* An analogy is a statement about how objects, people, situations, or actions are similar in process or relationship. Metaphors, on the other hand, are merely figures of speech. Both of these techniques can be used to create fictional situations for gaining new perspectives on problem definition and resolution.
   - *Brainstorming.* This technique is perhaps the most familiar of all the techniques discussed here. It is used to generate a large quantity of ideas in a short period of time.

- *Blue slip.* Ideas are individually generated and recorded on a 3×5-inch sheet of blue paper. Done anonymously to make people feel more at ease, people readily share ideas. Because each idea is on a separate piece of blue paper, the sorting and grouping of like ideas is facilitated.

- *Extrapolation.* A technique or approach, already used by the organization, is stretched to apply to a new problem.

- *Progressive abstraction technique.* By moving through progressively higher levels of abstraction, it is possible to generate alternative problem definitions from an original problem. When a problem is enlarged in a systematic way, it is possible to generate many new definitions that can then be evaluated for their usefulness and feasibility. Once an appropriate level of abstraction is reached, possible solutions are more easily identified.

- *5Ws and H technique.* This is the traditional, and journalistic, approach of who-what-where-when-why-how. Use of this technique serves to expand a person's view of the problem and to assist in making sure that all related aspects of the problem have been addressed and considered.

- *Force field analysis technique.* The name of this technique comes from its ability to identify forces contributing to or hindering a solution to a problem. This technique stimulates creative thinking in three ways: (1) it defines direction, (2) identifies strengths that can be maximized, and (3) identifies weaknesses that can be minimized

- *Peaceful setting.* This is not so much a technique as an environment. Taking people away from their hectic surroundings enables "a less cluttered, open mental process."

- *Problem reversal.* Reversing a problem statement often provides a different framework for analysis. For example, in attempting to come up with ways to improve productivity, try considering the opposite — how to decrease productivity.

- *Associations/image technique.* Most of us have played the game, at one time or another, where one person names a person, place, or thing and asks for the first thing that pops into the second person's mind. The linking of combining processes is another way of expanding the solution space.

- *Wishful thinking.* This technique enables people to loosen analytical parameters to consider a larger set of alternatives than they might ordinarily consider. By permitting a degree of fantasy into the process, the result just might be a new and unique approach.

6. Follow-up sessions should be scheduled for reinforcement. At these meetings, which are primarily staff meetings, employees should be invited to identify results of creative activity.

Communications and Group Productivity

Simmons (1991) details the many factors that dominate software group productivity. He defines "dominator" as a single factor that causes productivity to decline tenfold. The two dominators he concentrates on are communications and design partition.

- Factors that developers must cope with in developing large systems include:
  - Personnel turnover
  - Hardware and software turnover
  - Major ideas incorporated late
  - Latent bugs
- A Delphi survey performed by Simmons to uncover factors that affect productivity found that the main factors are:
  - External documentation
  - Programming language
  - Programming tools
  - Programmer experience
  - Communications
  - Independent modules for task assignment (design partition)
  - Well-defined programming practices
- Improvement statistics:
  - Any step toward the use of structured techniques, interactive development, inspections, etc. can improve productivity by up to 25 percent.
  - Use of these techniques in combination could yield improvements of between 25 and 50 percent.
  - Change in programming language can, by itself, yield a productivity improvement of more than 50 percent.
  - Gains of between 50 and 75 percent can be achieved by single high achievers or teams of high achievers.
  - Gains of 100 percent can be achieved by database user languages, application generators, and software reuse.
- Dominators are factors that can suppress the effects of other factors and can reduce software group productivity by an order of magnitude.

■ Poor design partition can dominate group productivity. To obtain high productivity in the development of large software systems, the designer must break down the system into chunks that can be developed in parallel. The difference between great and average designers is an order of magnitude.

■ Communications can dominate productivity. Most project problems arise as the result of poor communications between workers. If there are n workers on the team, then there are $n(n - 1)/2$ interfaces across which there may be communications problems.

■ Productivity of individual programmers varies as much as 26 to 1.

■ An individual working alone has no interruptions from fellow group members and, therefore, the productivity can be quite high for a motivated individual. It is estimated that one programmer working 60 hours a week can complete a project in the same calendar time as two others working normal hours, but at three quarters of the cost.

■ Small groups of experienced and productive software developers can create large systems. An example is given of a software consulting company. The company scours the country for the best analytical thinkers. Its senior programmers typically earn $125,000 a year and can be paid bonuses of two to three times that amount. They work in small teams, never more than five to produce large, complex systems. In comparison, most IS departments produce large systems using normal development teams with developers of average ability.

■ In general, the difference between the cost to produce an individual program to be run by the program author and the cost to produce a programming system product developed by a software group is at least nine times more expensive.

■ There is a point where coordination overheads outweigh any benefits that can be obtained by the addition of further staff. Statistics that support this were pioneered during the 19th century in work in military organizations. It was noted that as the number of workers who had to communicate increased arithmetically, from two to three to four to five, etc., the number of communication channels among them increased geometrically, from one to three to six to ten, etc. From this study, it was concluded that the upper limit of effective staff size for cooperative projects is about eight.

■ In studies, it has been shown that when the number of staff increased to 12 or more, the efficiency of the group decreased to less than 30 percent.

- The productive time of a typical software developer during a working day can vary from 51 to 79 percent. It was found that the average duration of work interruption was five minutes for a typical programmer. The average time to regain a train of thought after an interruption was two minutes. Thus, the average total time spent on an interruption was seven minutes. It we assume five productive hours each day, then each interruption takes 2.33 percent of the working day, ten interruptions would take up 23 percent of the day, and twenty interruptions would take approximately 50 percent.
- The optimum group size for a software development team is between five and eight members. The overall design should be partitioned into successively smaller chunks, until the development group has a chunk of software to develop that minimizes intra-group and inter-group communications.

Management Quality Considerations

It comes as no surprise that the majority of software development projects are late, over budget, and out of specification. Redmill (1990) points to a number of technical problems, most of which are related to technical tasks specific to software development.

- The most common reasons given by project managers for failure to meet budget, time scale, and specification are as follows:
  - Incomplete and ambiguous requirements
  - Incomplete and imprecise specifications
  - Difficulties in modeling systems
  - Uncertainties in cost and resource estimation
  - General lack of visibility
  - Difficulties with progress monitoring
  - Complicated error and change control
  - Lack of agreed-upon metrics
  - Difficulties in controlling maintenance
  - Lack of common terminology
  - Uncertainties in software or hardware apportionment
  - Rapid changes in technology
  - Determining suitability of languages
  - Measuring and predicting reliability
  - Problems with interfacing
  - Problems with integration

■ Audits of systems development efforts reveal shortcomings in projects, including:
  − Lack of standards
  − Failure to comply with existing standards
  − Nonadherence to model in use
  − No sign-off at end of stages
  − Lack of project plans
  − No project control statistics recorded or stored
  − No quality assurance (QA) procedures
  − No change control procedures
  − No configuration control procedures
  − Records of test data and results not kept
■ Causes for the lack of control of projects include:
  − Attitude toward quality
  − Attitude toward management
  − Attitude toward project
■ In finding solutions, the principal reasons for project management shortcomings should be reviewed. The project manager:
  − Has no experience working where a quality culture predominates
  − Has not been trained in TQM (Total Quality Management)
  − Has not received adequate management training
  − Has not been managed in accordance with TQM principles by supervisors
  − Has not overcome an inclination toward technical matters and finds that they offer a more friendly environment than the less familiar affairs of management
■ Solutions:
  − Training: project manager and team must be trained in TQM.
  − Management commitment: must always be seen to be 100 percent.
  − Standards: a comprehensive set of standards for all aspects of work should be instituted and used. The project life cycle must be covered, as well as other pertinent issues.
  − Guidelines, procedures, and checklists: assist both workers to meet the standards and QA agents to check the products.
  − Quality assurance: should be carried out at all stages of the life cycle and for all end products.
  − QA team: should be independent of the development team.
  − Audits: should be carried out during the project to ensure that management and QA procedures are being adhered to. The project manager should always initiate a review of the auditors' recommendations and of all resulting corrective action.

- Planning: the project manager should be fastidious in drawing up plans and ensuring their use for control. Plans should include the project plan, stage plans, and a quality plan, which details the quality requirements of the project.
- Reporting: a reporting system — to ensure that problems are quickly escalated to the management level appropriate to the action needed — should be instituted.
- Feedback: statistics that assist in project control and the improvement of quality should be collected, analyzed, and used.
- Continuous review: the whole quality system (components, mode of operation, and quality of results) should be reviewed and improved continuously.
- Project manager: must not be too technically involved.
- Technical duties: should be delegated to a development team manager who reports to the project manager.
- Non-technical support team: should be appointed to assist in nondevelopmental matters, including coordination and interpretation of resource and time statistics, recording all expenditures and tracking against budget, and tracking milestones. This team should report to the project manager.

Training

Training is the key to learning and growth. According to a study by Byrne (2003), the return on investment in training and development was an 8.5 percent increase in productivity compared with a 3.5 percent increase due to spending on capital improvements.

The Hartford uses a balanced approach that links the employee's business opportunity plan to the organization's operating plan. Their developmental approach is centered on employee and supervisor relationships in the development and planning process.

Employees meet annually with their boss to discuss development needs. After the employee's performance review, the employee and supervisor will establish personal goals for the following years. Because the employee's plan is linked to the company's operating plan, it must then be determined which competencies the employee needs to successfully reach corporate business goals. Toward this end, all courses are mapped to a competency profile.

The Hartford corporate strategy is tied to training through what they call Prescriptive Learning Plans and Individual Learning Plans. A Prescriptive Learning Plan is a series of events, not all taking place in the classroom. These may include going to conferences, visiting Web sites, or reading white papers. It may also be reading a book or having a phone conversation with a subject matter expert within the company. Ultimately, Prescriptive Learning Plans are tied to business needs.

The subset of events signed off on by a supervisor for an individual employee is called an Individual Learning Plan.

Hartford uses a balanced scorecard approach to determine its business strategy. Balanced scorecard-derived strategic plans are produced in flow-chart form to ultimately create a strategy map. Ultimately, this business strategy is translated into result-focused training programs by the individual departments.

Upside-Down Training

One of this author's students, who works in a very large, very well-known health insurance company, shares with us a very novel technique for figuring out who and what to train across teams, departments, and organizationally. They call it *upside-down training*.

Figure 8.1 shows the look and feel of the upside-down training scheme. It is divided into four unequal quadrants: (1) company, (2) department,

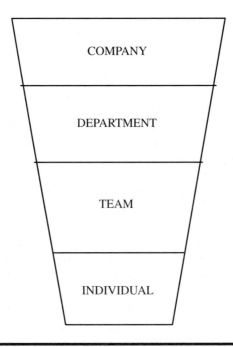

Figure 8.1   Upside-down training sheet.

(3) team, and at the bottom, (4) individual. Employees look at each number and list things that they think each quadrant could use some training on. In other words, each quadrant is filled in as employees ask the questions: "What training do I feel I want as an individual?" "As a team?" "As a department?" and "As a company?" In addition, each employee fills out a form that asks them which way (i.e., learning style) they learn information most effectively — that is, e-mail, online, formal presentation, etc.

On to Chapter 9

This chapter discussed how IT as well as organizational management can "grow" the employee through better management techniques as well as through training and other incentives. This aspect — learning and growth — is fundamental to the success of the balanced scorecard but is generally overlooked. Unless employees are rewarded in some way and unless they feel that they can grow within the organization, balanced scorecard targets will never be met.

Chapter 9 discusses how IT project management fits into the balanced scorecard picture.

References

Byrne, J. (2003, August). How to Lead Now: Getting Extraordinary Performance When You Can't Pay for It. *Fast Company*, pp. 62–70.

Couger, J.D., S.C. McIntyre, L.F. Higgins, and T.A. Snow. (1991, September). Using a Bottom-Up Approach to Creativity Improvement in IS Development. *Journal of Systems Management*, pp. 23–36.

DeMarco, T. (1979). *Structured Analysis and System Application.* Englewood Cliffs, NJ: Prentice Hall.

D'Souza, D. (1992). *Illiberal Education.* New York: Random House.

Glanz, B. (1996). *CARE Packages for the Workplace — Dozens of Little Things You Can Do to Regenerate Spirit at Work.* New York: McGraw-Hill.

Harari, O. (1993, November) Stop Empowering Your People. *Management Review*, pp. 26–29.

McCarthy, M. and J. Allen. (2000). *You Made My Day: Creating Co-Worker Recognition and Relationships.* New York: L-F Books.

Nelson, B. and K. Blanchard. (1994). *1001 Ways to Reward Employees.* New York: Workman Publishing Co.

Redmill, F. J. (1990, January/February). Considering Quality in the Management of Software-Based Development Projects. *Information and Software Technology*, Vol. 32, No. 1.

Simmons, D.B. (1991, November). Communications: A Software Group Productivity Dominator. *Software Engineering Journal*, pp. 454–462.

Chapter 9

Compliance, Awareness, and Assurance

> The difference between failure and success is doing a thing nearly right and doing a thing exactly right.

The four perspectives of a balanced scorecard (BSC) assure the organization that its IT assets are not only aligned with organizational goals, but are well-managed, efficient, and productive. These assets must also be managed in such a way that risk is minimized. This author teaches a course on project management and surveys students on the first day of every new class. From these surveys it is concluded, and the statistics below confirm, that most IT departments utilize ineffective project management techniques.

Over half (53 percent) of IT projects overrun their schedules and budgets, 31 percent are cancelled, and only 16 percent are completed on time. (*Source:* Standish Group; publication date: 2000.)

Of those projects that failed in 2000, 87 percent went more than 50 percent over budget. (*Source:* KPMG Information Technology; publication date: 2000.)

Forty-five percent of failed projects in 2000 did not produce the expected benefits, and 88 to 92 percent went over schedule. (*Source:* KPMG Information Technology; publication date: 2000.)

Half of new software projects in the United states will go significantly over budget. (*Source:* META Group; publication date: 2000.)

The average cost of a development project for a large company is $2,322,000; for a medium company, it is $1,331,000; and for a small company, it is $434,000. (*Source:* Standish Group; publication date: 2000.)

Over half (52.7 percent) of projects were projected to cost over 189 percent of their original estimates. (*Source:* Standish Group; publication date: 2000.)

Eighty-eight percent of all U.S. projects are over schedule, over budget, or both. (*Source:* Standish Group; publication date: 2000.)

The average time overrun on projects is 222 percent of original estimates. (*Source:* Standish Group; publication date: 2000.)

The Proactive Risk Strategy

One should always adopt a proactive risk strategy. It is better to plan for possible risk than have to react to it in a crisis. The first thing that must be done is to identify risks. One method is to create a risk item checklist. A typical project plan might list the following risks:

■ Customer will change or modify requirements.
■ End users lack sophistication.
■ Delivery deadline will be tightened.
■ End users resist system.
■ Server may not be able to handle larger number of users simultaneously.
■ Technology will not meet expectations.
■ There is a larger number of users than planned.
■ End users lack training.
■ The project team is inexperienced.
■ The system (security and firewall) will be hacked.

Keil et al. (1998) developed a framework for identifying software project risks by interviewing experienced software project managers in different parts of the world. The following questions are ordered by their relative importance to the ultimate success of a project:

■ Have top software and customer managers formally committed to support the project?
■ Are end users enthusiastically committed to the project and the system or product to be built?

- Are requirements fully understood by the software engineering team and its customers?
- Have customers been involved fully in the definition of requirements?
- Do end users have realistic expectations?
- Is the project scope stable?
- Does the software engineering team have the right mix of skills?
- Are project requirements stable?
- Does the project team have experience with the technology to be implemented?
- Is the number of people on the project team adequate to do the job?
- Do all customers or user constituencies agree on the importance of the project and on the requirements for the system or product to be built?

Based on the information uncovered from this questionnaire, one can begin to categorize risks. Software risks generally include project risks, technical risks, and business risks:

- **Project risks** can include budgetary, staffing, scheduling, customer, requirement, and resource problems. For example, a key stakeholder may leave the company, taking his knowledge base with him.
- **Technical risks** can include design, implementation, interface, ambiguity, technical obsolescence, and leading-edge problems. An example of this is the development of a project around a leading-edge technology that has not yet been proven.
- **Business risks** include building a product or system no one wants (market risk), losing support of senior management (management risk), building a product that no longer fits into the strategic plan (strategic risk), losing budgetary support (budget risks), and building a product that the sales staff does not know how to sell.

Charette (1989) proposes that risks also be categorized as known, predictable, or unpredictable risks.

- **Known risks** are those that can be uncovered upon careful review of the project plan and the environment in which the project is being developed (e.g., lack of development tools, unrealistic delivery date, or lack of knowledge in the problem domain).
- **Predictable risks** can be extrapolated from past experience. For example, one's past experience with the end users has not been good, so it is reasonable to assume that the current project will suffer from the same problem.
- **Unpredictable risks** are difficult, if not impossible, to identify in advance. For example, no one could have predicted the events of September 11th, but this one event affected computers worldwide.

TABLE 9.1   Typical Risk Table

Risks	Category	Probability (%)	Impact
Risk 1	PS	70	2
Risk 2	CU	60	3

Impact values:
  1 — catastrophic
  2 — critical
  3 — marginal
  4 — negligible

Category abbreviations:
  BU — business impact risk
  CU — customer characteristics risk
  PS — process definition risk
  ST — staff size and experience risk
  TE — technology risk

Once risks have been identified, most managers project these risks in two dimensions: likelihood and consequences. As shown in Table 9.1, a risk table is a simple tool for risk projection. First, based on the risk item checklist, list all risks in the first column of the table. Then in the following columns, fill in each risk's category, probability of occurrence, and assessed impact. Afterward, sort the table by probability and then by impact, study it, and define a cut-off line (i.e., the line demarcating the threshold of acceptable risk). All risks above the cut-off line must be managed and discussed. Factors influencing their probability and impact should be specified.

A risk mitigation, monitoring, and management (RMMM) plan is the tool to help avoid risks. Causes of the risks must be identified and mitigated. Risk monitoring activities take place as the project proceeds and should be planned early.

Sample Risk Plan

An excerpt of a typical risk mitigation, monitoring, and management (RMMM) plan is presented in Table 9.2.

RMMM Strategy

Each risk or group of risks should have a corresponding strategy associated with it. The RMMM strategy discusses how risks will be monitored and

TABLE 9.2   Typical Risk Mitigation, Monitoring, and Management Plan (RMMM)

x.1 Scope and Intent of RMMM Activities

This project will be uploaded to a server and this server will be exposed to the outside world, so we need to develop security protection. We will need to configure a firewall and restrict access to only "authorized users" through the linked Faculty database. We will have to know how to deal with load balance if the amount of visits to the site is very large at one time.

We will need to know how to maintain the database in order to make it more efficient, what type of database we should use, and who should have the responsibility to maintain it and who should be the administrator. Proper training of the aforementioned personnel is very important so that the database and the system contain accurate information.

x.2 Risk Management Organizational Role

The software project manager must maintain track of the efforts and schedules of the team. They must anticipate any "unwelcome" events that may occur during the development or maintenance stages and establish plans to avoid these events or minimize their consequences.

It is the responsibility of everyone on the project team with the regular input of the customer to assess potential risks throughout the project. Communication among everyone involved is very important to the success of the project. In this way, it is possible to mitigate and eliminate possible risks before they occur. This is known as a proactive approach or strategy for risk management.

x.3 Risk Description

This section describes the risks that may occur during this project.

x.3.1 Description of Possible Risks

Business Impact Risk: (BU)

This risk would entail that the software produced does not meet the needs of the client who requested the product. It would also have a business impact if the product no longer fits into the overall business strategy for the company.

Customer Characteristics Risks: (CU)

This risk is the customer's lack of involvement in the project and their non-availability to meet with the developers in a timely manner. Also, the customer's sophistication as to the product being developed and ability to use it is part of this risk.

TABLE 9.2 (continued)   Typical Risk Mitigation, Monitoring, and Management Plan (RMMM)

Development Risks: (DE)

Risks associated with the availability and quality of the tools to be used to build the product. The equipment and software provided by the client on which to run the product must be compatible with the software project being developed.

Process Definition Risks: (PS)

Does the software being developed meet the requirements as originally defined by the developer and client? Did the development team follow the correct design throughout the project? The above are examples of process risks.

Product Size: (PR)

The product size risk involves the overall size of the software being built or modified. Risks involved would include the customer not providing the proper size of the product to be developed, and if the software development team misjudges the size or scope of the project. The latter problem could create a product that is too small (rarely) or too large for the client and could result in a loss of money to the development team because the cost of developing a larger product cannot be recouped from the client.

Staff Size and Experience Risk: (ST)

This would include appropriate and knowledgeable programmers to code the product as well as the cooperation of the entire software project team. It would also mean that the team has enough members who are competent and able to complete the project.

Technology Risk: (TE)

Technology risk could occur if the product being developed is obsolete by the time it is ready to be sold. The opposite effect could also be a factor: if the product is so "new" that the end users would have problems using the system and resisting the changes made. A "new" technological product could also be so new that there may be problems using it. It would also include the complexity of the design of the system being developed.

x.4 Risk Table

The risk table provides a simple technique to view and analyze the risks associated with the project. The risks were listed and then categorized using the description of risks listed in Section x.3.1. The probability of each risk was then estimated and its impact on the development process was then assessed. A key to the impact values and categories appears at the end of the table.

TABLE 9.2 (continued)   Typical Risk Mitigation, Monitoring, and Management Plan (RMMM)

The following is the sorted version of the Table 9.1 by probability and impact:

Risks	Category	Probability (%)	Impact
Customer will change or modify requirements	PS	70	2
Lack of sophistication of end users	CU	60	3
Users will not attend training	CU	50	2
Delivery deadline will be tightened	BU	50	2
End users resist system	BU	40	3
Server may not be able to handle a larger number of users simultaneously	PS	30	1
Technology will not meet expectations	TE	30	1
Larger number of users than planned	PS	30	3
Lack of training of end users	CU	30	3
Inexperienced project team	ST	20	2
System (security and firewall) will be hacked	BU	15	2

Risks Table (sorted first by probability and then by impact value)

Impact values:
   1 — catastrophic
   2 — critical
   3 — marginal
   4 — negligible

Category abbreviations:
   BU — business impact risk
   CU — customer characteristics risk
   PS — process definition risk
   ST — staff size and experience risk
   TE — technology risk

dealt with. Risk plans (i.e., contingency plans) are usually created in tandem with end users and managers. An excerpt of an RMMM strategy is shown in Table 9.3.

Williams et al. (1997) advocate the use of a risk information sheet, an example of which appears in Table 9.4.

Risk is inherent in all projects. The key to project success is to identify risk and then deal with it. Doing this requires the project manager to identify as many risks as possible, categorize those risks, and then develop a contingency plan to deal with each risk. Project plans should always contain a risk analysis.

TABLE 9.3   Sample RMMM Strategy

Project Risk RMMM Strategy

The area of design and development that contributes the largest percentage to the overall project cost is the database subsystem. Our estimate for this portion does provide a small degree of buffer for unexpected difficulties (as do all estimates). This effort will be closely monitored and coordinated with the customer to ensure that any impact, either positive or negative, is quickly identified. Schedules and personnel resources will be adjusted accordingly to minimize the effect or maximize the advantage, as appropriate.

Schedule and milestone progress will be monitored as part of the routine project management with appropriate emphasis on meeting target dates. Adjustments to parallel efforts will be made, as appropriate, should the need arise. Personnel turnover will be managed through the use of internal personnel matrix capacity. Our organization has a large software engineering base with sufficient numbers to support our potential demand.

Technical Risk RMMM Strategy

We are planning for two senior software engineers to be assigned to this project, both of whom have significant experience in designing and developing Web-based applications. The project progress will be monitored as part of the routine project management with appropriate emphasis on meeting target dates, and adjusted as appropriate.

Prior to implementing any core operating software upgrades, full parallel testing will be conducted to ensure compatibility with the system as developed. The application will be developed using only public Application Programming Interfaces (APIs), and no "hidden" hooks. While this does not guarantee compatibility, it should minimize any potential conflicts. Any problems identified will be quantified using cost-benefit and trade-off analyses, then coordinated with the customer prior to implementation.

The database subsystem is expected to be the most complex portion of the application; however, it is still a relatively routine implementation. Efforts to minimize potential problems include the abstraction of the interface from the implementation of the database code to allow for changing the underlying database with minimal impact. Additionally, only industry-standard SQL calls will be used, avoiding all proprietary extensions available.

Business Risk RMMM Strategy

The first business risk, lower than expected success, is beyond the control of the development team. Our only potential impact is to use the current state-of-the-art tools to ensure performance, in particular, database access, meets user expectations; and graphics are designed using industry standard look-and-feel styles.

TABLE 9.3 (continued)   Sample RMMM Strategy

Likewise, the second business risk, loss of senior management support, is really beyond the direct control of the development team. However, to help manage this risk, we will strive to impart a positive attitude during meetings with the customer, as well as present very professional work products throughout the development period.

TABLE 9.4   A Sample Risk Information Sheet

Risk Information Sheet
Risk id: PO2-4-32
Date: March 4, 2004
Probability: 80%
Impact: High

Description:
Over 70 percent of the software components scheduled for reuse will be integrated into the application. The remaining functionality will have to be custom developed.

Refinement/context:
1. Certain reusable components were developed by a third party with no knowledge of internal design standards.
2. Certain reusable components have been implemented in a language that is not supported on the target environment.

Mitigation/monitoring:
1. Contact third party to determine conformance to design standards.
2. Check to see if language support can be acquired.

Management/contingency plan/trigger:
Develop a revised schedule assuming that 18 additional components will have to be built.
Trigger: Mitigation steps unproductive as of March 30, 2004.

Current status:
In process
Originator: Jane Manager

Risk Assessment

Risk avoidance can be accomplished by evaluating the critical success factors (CSFs) of a business or business line. Managers are intimately aware of their missions and goals, but they do not necessarily define the processes required to achieve these goals. That is, "How are you going to get there?" In these instances, technologists must depart from their traditional venue of top-down methodologies and employ a bottom-up approach. They must work with the business units to discover the goal and work their way up through the policies, procedures, and technologies that will be necessary to arrive at that particular goal. For example, the goal of a fictitious business line is to be able to reduce the production or distribution cycle by a factor of ten, providing a customized product at no greater cost than that of the generic product in the past. To achieve this goal, the technology group needs to get the business managers to walk through the critical processes that need to be invented or changed. It is only at this point that any technology solutions are introduced.

One technique, called Process Quality Management (PQM), uses the CSF concept. IBM originated this approach, which combines an array of methodologies to solve a persistent problem: how to get a group to agree on goals and ultimately deliver a complex project efficiently and productively (Hardaker and Ward, 1987).

PQM is initiated by gathering, preferably off site, a team of essential staff. The team's components should represent all facets of the project. Obviously, all teams have leaders and PQM teams are no different. The team leader chosen must have a skill mix closely attuned to the projected outcome of the project. For example, in a PQM team where the assigned goal is to improve plan productivity, the best team leader just might be an expert in process control, albeit the eventual solution might be in the form of enhanced automation.

Assembled at an off-site location, the first task of the team is to develop, in written form, specifically what the team's mission is. With such open-ended goals as "Determine the best method of employing technology for competitive advantage," the determination of the actual mission statement is an arduous task — best tackled by segmenting this rather vague goal into more concrete sub-goals.

In a quick brainstorming session, the team lists the factors that might inhibit the mission from being accomplished. This serves to develop a series of one-word descriptions. Given a ten-minute timeframe, the goal is to get as many of these inhibitors as possible without discussion and without criticism.

It is at this point that the team turns to identifying the critical success factors (CSFs), which are the specific tasks that the team must perform to accomplish its mission. It is vitally important that the entire team reach a consensus on the CSFs.

The next step in the IBM PQM process is to make a list of all tasks necessary in accomplishing the CSF. The description of each of these tasks, called business processes, should be declarative. Start each with an action word such as "study, measure, reduce, negotiate, eliminate."

Table 9.5 and Figure 9.1 show the resulting Project Chart and Priority Graph, respectively, that diagram this PQM technique. The team's mission,

TABLE 9.5   CSF Project Chart

No.	Business Process	\textit{1}	\textit{2}	\textit{3}	\textit{4}	\textit{5}	\textit{6}	Count	Quality
		\multicolumn{6}{l}{Critical Success Factors}		
P1	Measure delivery performance by suppliers	x	x					2	B
P2	Recognize/reward workers					x	x	2	D
P3	Negotiate with suppliers	x	x	x				3	B
P4	Reduce number of parts	x	x	x	x			4	D
P5	Train supervisors					x	x	2	C
P6	Redesign production line	x		x	x			3	A
P7	Move parts inventory	x						1	E
P8	Eliminate excessive inventory build-ups	x	x					2	C
P9	Select suppliers	x	x					2	B
P10	Measure				x	x	x	3	E
P11	Eliminate defective parts		x	x	x			3	D

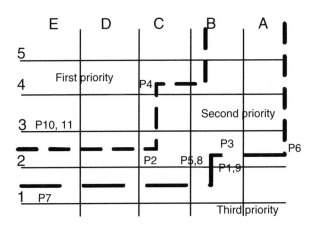

FIGURE 9.1   CSF priority graph.

in this example, is to introduce just-in-time (JIT) inventory control, a manufacturing technique that fosters greater efficiency by promoting stocking inventory only to the level of need. The team, in this example, identified six CSFs and eleven business processes labeled P1 through P11.

The Project Chart (Table 9.5) is filled out by first ranking the business process by importance to the project's success. This is done by comparing each business process to the set of CSFs. A check is made under each CSF that relates significantly to the business process. This procedure is followed until each of the business processes has been analyzed in the same way.

The final column of the Project Chart permits the team to rank each business process relative to current performance, using a scale of A = excellent, to D = bad, and E = not currently performed.

The Priority Graph (Figure 9.1), when completed, will steer the mission to a successful, and prioritized, conclusion. The two axes to this graph are Quality, using the A through E grading scale, and Priority, represented by the number of checks noting each business process received. These can be lifted easily from the Project Chart for the Quality and Count columns, respectively

The final task as a team is to decide how to divide the Priority Graph into different zones representing first priority, second priority, etc. In this example, the team has chosen as a first priority all business processes, such as "negotiate with suppliers" and "reduce number of parts," that are ranked from a quality of "fair," degrading to a quality of "not currently performed," and having a ranking of 3 or greater. Most groups employing this technique will assign priorities in a similar manner.

Determining the right project to pursue is one factor in the push for competitive technology. It is equally as important to "do the project right," which is of paramount importance in the company that aims to run a productive and quality-oriented software factory.

Just What Is Critical to Project Success?

Having the right people on a project team is certainly key to the success of any project. In a large pharmaceutical company, the lead designer walked off a very important project. Obviously, that set the team back quite a bit as no one else had enough experience to do what he did. Even if the IT staff stays put, there is still the possibility that a "people" issue will negatively affect the project. For example, a change in senior management might mean that the project one is working on gets canned or moved to a lower priority. A project manager working for America

Online Time Warner had just started an important new project when a new president was installed. He did what all new presidents do — he engaged in a little housecleaning. Projects got swept away — and so did some people. When the dust settled, the project manager personally had a whole new set of priorities — as well as a bunch of new end users with whom to work. Although the project manager's most important project stayed high on the priority list, unfortunately, some of the end users did not. The departure of a subject matter expert can have disastrous consequences. Lucky for our intrepid project manager, she was able to replace her "domain expert" with someone equally knowledgeable.

Today's dynamically changing business landscape can also play havoc with projects. Mergers and acquisitions can have the effect of changing the key players or adding entirely new sets of stakeholders and stakeholder requirements. Going global adds an entirely new dimension to the importance of being able to speak the end-users' language.

Personnel changes and mergers and acquisitions pale beside the one thing that has the most dramatic effect on the success or failure of our projects: corporate politics. Politics is something that everyone is familiar with and definitely affected by. We cannot change it, so we have to live with it. "Being political" is something one might look down upon. Nonetheless, it is something that we all have to learn to do if we are to shepherd our projects through to successful completion.

Having the right people on a team and being on a team favored by current management are just two critical success factors. There are a wide variety of other factors that will determine the success or failure of a project, as discussed below.

Effective Communications

A project manager must have a variety of important skill sets to be successful. This includes the ability to manage expectations, resolve conflict, overcome fears, facilitate meetings, and motivate team members.

One of the most important skills a project manager can have is interpersonal skills. He or she must be able to effectively communicate with a wide variety of people across the entire organization. The project manager must be equally at ease when working with the CEO as he or she is when working with data entry clerical staff.

The project manager must be able to:

- Make the person being spoken to feel at ease.
- Understand the language of the end user.
- Understand the business of the end user.

- Interpret correctly and completely what the end user is saying.
- Write effectively and use the proper style.
- Be able to make meaningful presentations.
- Be articulate.
- Be able to mediate disputes.
- Understand the politics of the organization.

The Proper Utilization of Standards

There are many methodologies a project manager can employ when doing his or her job. The Software Engineering Institute's (SEI) Capability Maturity Model (CMM) defines five levels of software process maturity. The lowest level, Initial, is typified by little formalization. The highest level, Optimized, is defined by the use of quality standards such as the formal use of a methodology and process measurement. The project manager should strive to utilize the very highest levels of standards of practice such that the Optimized level of CMM can be achieved.

Software engineering (i.e., development) consists of many components: definitions, documentation, testing, quality assurance, metrics, etc. Standards bodies (e.g., ANSI, ISO, and IEEE) have crafted standards for many of these.

Standards enable software developers to develop quality-oriented, cost-effective, and maintainable software in an efficient, cost-productive manner. The goal of each standard is to provide the software developer with a set of benchmarks that enable him or her to complete the task and be assured that it meets at least a minimum level of quality. Indeed, the dictionary definition of standard is: "an acknowledged measure of comparison for quantitative or qualitative value; a criterion." Thus, standards provide the developer with the criteria necessary to build a system. It is the role of the project manager to ensure adherence to the proper standards.

Ethics

One of the very highest standards a project manager can aspire to achieve is a heightened sense of ethics. The newspapers have been filled with stories of the results of a lapse of ethics (e.g., Parmalat, Enron, and Arthur Andersen). When dealing with individuals, the organization as a whole, or society at large, the project manager must be:

- Fair
- Impartial

- Honest
- Forthright

Being Political

A project must be developed from a position of strength. Because the project manager is the one in charge of the project, the he or she must be powerful, know how to get power, or align him- or herself with a powerful sponsor.

What does one do if political gamesmanship is getting in the way of the project's success? Shtub et al. (1994) recommend a series of steps that serve to neutralize opposition to or attacks on a project:

- Identify persons who are opposed to the project.
- Determine why they feel the project is not to their advantage.
- Meet with anyone who directly attacks you or the project, and ask that person what is troubling him or her. Show this person how his or her actions will affect the project and the organization, and then ask for suggestions to get him or her to support the project.
- Place all agreements and progress reports in writing; this provides an audit trail.
- Speak directly and truthfully; never hedge your comments.
- Distribute a memo to stakeholders, including the opposition, to clarify all rumors. Project opponents frequently use the office rumor mill to distribute misinformation about the project.
- Be prepared to defend all actions that you take. Make sure you have a solid rationale for your decisions.

Technical

Technical problems might also jeopardize the success of a system. Having the right technology as well as staff with the right technological skill sets are critically important to all projects. In summary, the project manager needs to make sure that adequate resources to get the job done are provided — that is, hardware, software, and communications

Legal

Legal and regulatory issues will also have an effect on whether or not the system will ultimately be successful. Examples of regulatory and legal changes precluding the successful project completion include:

■ Internet gambling systems built by U.S.-based organizations. Offshore companies currently host Internet gambling systems, as it is illegal to do so in the United States.

■ P2P (peer-to-peer) systems that enable Web surfers to "pirate" music have been deemed illegal.

Organizational

Computer systems can benefit organizations in many ways. However, some changes required by the introduction of a system might be considered disruptive and, thus, undesirable. If, for example, a system will require that the entire company be reorganized, then this system might be deemed infeasible.

The top success factors for projects are as follows:

1. Executive support
2. User involvement
3. Experienced project manager
4. Clear business objectives
5. Minimized scope
6. Standard software infrastructure
7. Firm basic requirements
8. Formal methodology
9. Reliable estimates
10. Other criteria

On to Chapter 10

This chapter discussed the importance of effective project management techniques in a successful balanced scorecard implementation. Interestingly, this author's own research confirms a rather unpleasant fact: few IT organizations are properly managed. If the balanced scorecard implementation is to be successful, this will have to change.

This chapter concludes a whirlwind tour of all things balanced scorecard. As one can see, the implementation process is both easier and more difficult than one thought. It is easier because it should all make sense — particularly after one has read through all of the examples provided. It is more difficult because one probably will have to do much preparatory work to get one's organization and one's department ready to even think about using a balanced scorecard approach.

Chapter 10 presents a few automated balanced scorecard tools that will be of interest.

References

Charette, R.N. (1989). *Software Engineering Risk Analysis and Management.* New York: McGraw-Hill/Intertext.

Hardaker, M. and B. Ward. (1987, November/December). How to Make a Team Work. Harvard Business Review, 65(6), 112.

Keil M. et al. (1998, November). A Framework for Identifying Software Project Risks. *CACM,* 41(11), 76–83.

Shtub A. et al. (1994). *Project Management: Engineering, Technology and Implementation.* Englewood Cliffs, NJ: Prentice Hall.

Williams, R.C., J.A. Walker, and A.J. Dorofee. (1997, May). Putting Risk Management into Practice. *IEEE Software*, pp. 75–81.

Chapter 10

Scorecard and Other Performance Measurement Tools

According to a survey by Lawson, Stratton, and Hatch (2004), 70 percent of organizations using the balanced scorecard use some type of software in their implementation. Of these organizations, 31 percent use off-the-shelf software, 43 percent use software developed in-house (e.g., database, spreadsheet), and 27 percent use a combination of the two.

Many of the business intelligence (BI) and enterprise resource management (ERP) vendors have jumped into the balanced scorecard mix. When one combines these offerings with those of vendors crafting balanced-scorecard only tools, there is quite a selection available.

This chapter previews a few of the available software options available.

Department of Defense Performance Assessment Guide

Company: Government
Web site: http://www.dtic.mil/performance/paguide.html#overview
Cost: Free

The DoD Performance Assessment Guide, as shown in Figure 10.1, is a PC software program designed to help managers assess and improve

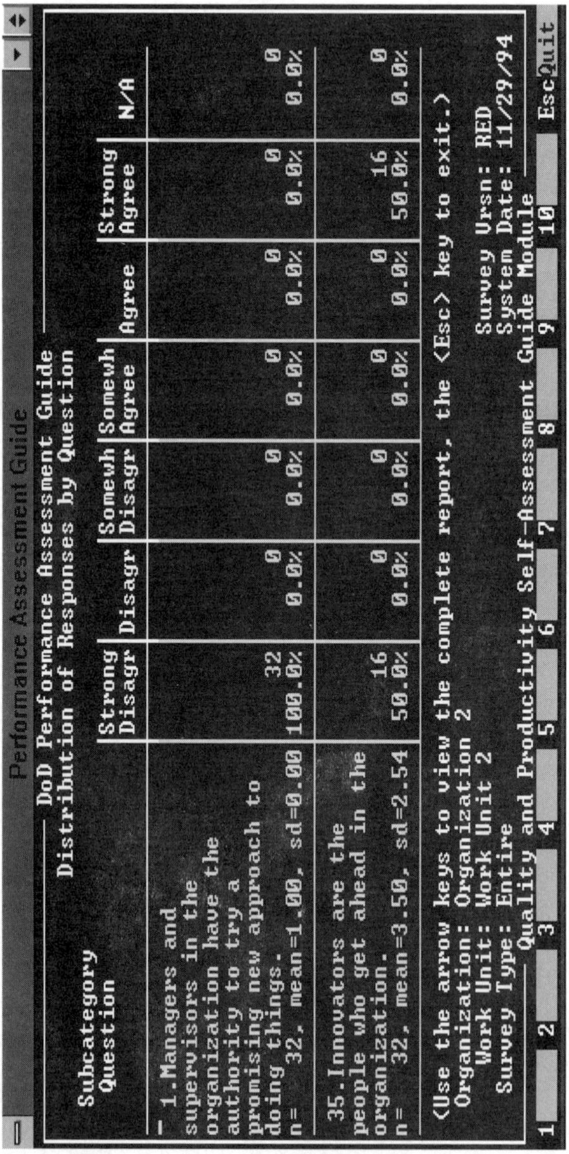

FIGURE 10.1 Sample screen from the DOS-based DoD Performance Assessment Guide.

organizational performance. The DoD Comptroller's Directorate for Performance Measures and Results developed this DOS-based decision support tool with help from more than 1000 government and industry organizations.

The modular design of the guide provides for maximum flexibility by providing the right tools for the right needs. The PC software's interface allows easy access to three modules:

1. Quality and Productivity Self-Assessment Guide for Defense Organizations
2. Guide for Setting Customer Service Standards
3. Guide for Developing Performance Measures

The *Quality and Productivity Self-Assessment Guide for Defense Organizations* is a stand-alone package — printed copy or automated option — that includes questions about performance improvement topics. Immediate confidential scoring and evaluation are provided to respondents and workgroups, along with prescriptive ideas and sources on how to improve. The guide identifies the existing organizational culture and management style, helps target processes for change, and establishes a baseline for judging progress over time. Scores can be compared across an extensive database of government and industry participants — 1900 organizations and 200,000 participants. The guide's diagnostic and educational design include measurement scores and indicators that link to specific ideas and recommendations for improving future scores.

The *Guide for Setting Customer Service Standards* is a PC software program designed to help managers establish a baseline and track what customers think about the services and products they receive. Questions that make up the sample are questions about key service indicators currently in use by government and industry. The guide can be used alone or in combination with any of the other modules. The decision support tool allows managers to:

- Print and duplicate the sample customer survey.
- Create tailored customer surveys.
- Quickly enter and consolidate survey results.
- View results weekly, monthly, quarterly, and annually.
- Receive a printout of customer satisfaction results.

The *Guide for Developing Performance Measures* is an automated tool that links performance measures to specific business areas. This module provides a capability for managers to select or develop their own performance measures, collect data to establish a baseline and track progress, display and print graphs, and receive printouts of performance measurement results. The guide allows managers to:

- Access a library of generic performance measures grouped by performance measurement type and business area.
- Develop their own set of performance measures by either selecting or modifying those contained in a performance measurement library or adding their own.
- Enter period performance measurement values, data, and information.
- Display and print performance measurement graphs and reports.
- After performance measures are selected, the user may designate or assign appropriate units of measures, reporting frequencies, performance goals, and statistics for computing control limits.

Aha! Executive Decision Support System (Balanced Scorecard Application)

Chinook Solutions
Suite U, 1338 36th Ave NE
Calgary, AB
T2E 6T6
Canada
Tel.: 403-219-2222
Web site: http://www.chinooksolutions.com
E-mail: info@chinooksolutions.com

Chinook Solutions provides a complete array of corporate planning and strategy implementation services that apply the balanced scorecard framework and philosophy to clients in Canada, the United states, and Latin America. These services include strategy formulation, strategy mapping, balanced scorecard development, strategic initiative prioritization, project portfolio management, scorecard implementation, scorecard automation, and BSC auditing. Features include:

- Knowledge-driven decisions and assessments
- Leveraging internal lessons learned and external best practices
- Multi-choice Q & A that evaluates characteristics against an "ideal" or "perfect" outcome
- Traffic light scorecard that visualizes fit against "ideal"
- Forced rankings that provide an overall "score" per candidate
- Workshop facilitation screens that help build alignment and consensus

The Aha! Executive Decision Support System (see Figures 10.2 and 10.3) facilitates the key decision points that must be navigated if the implementation of a balanced scorecard is to produce real value. Aha!

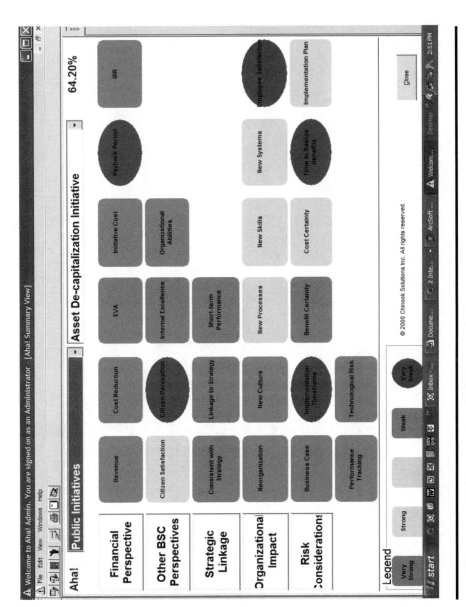

FIGURE 10.2 Aha! asset de-capitalization screen 1.

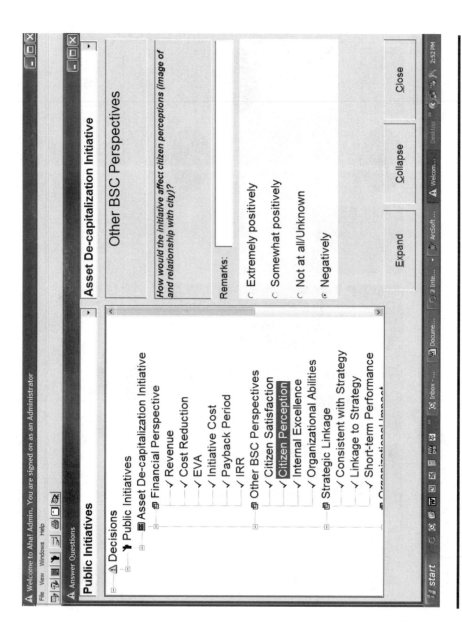

FIGURE 10.3   Aha! decapitalization screen 2.

fosters a consensus-building approach that ensures key decisions and assessments are strong, broadly supported, and which stick once made. Aha!'s BSC Applications assist in decisions that prioritize objectives, measures, and initiatives, evaluate project performance, corporate cultures and resistance to change, and even benchmark implementation progress against industry best practices.

Features include:

- Alignment- and mobilization-focused approach
- Application of scorecard throughout strategy life cycle, from "Vision" to "Results"
- Integration of scorecard into corporate planning processes
- Step-by-step approach, from clarification of objectives through to results feedback
- Independent of scorecard technology vendors such as CorVu, Cognos, and Hyperion
- Personal services provided by senior, experienced people

The Performance Organiser

JIT Software Limited
8 Nadder Road
Tidworth
Wiltshire
SP9 7QA
United Kingdom
U.K. Tel.: 01980 843113
International Tel.: +44 180 843113
Web site: http://www.jit-software.com
E-mail: allenwoods@jit-software.com

The Performance Organiser (Figures 10.4 and 10.5) is a general-purpose business analyst's toolkit designed around principles associated with many best-practice management techniques. The Performance Organiser and its associated KPI Prototyping tool "Scores on the Doors" can be used to design, document, and prototype a structured performance management system based on the balanced scorecard. In short, the Performance Organiser is organization modeling software for quality-driven companies. Anyone, in any organization, or any size, in any country, who needs to describe in a structured and coherent way how their organization works should have a copy of the Performance Organiser.

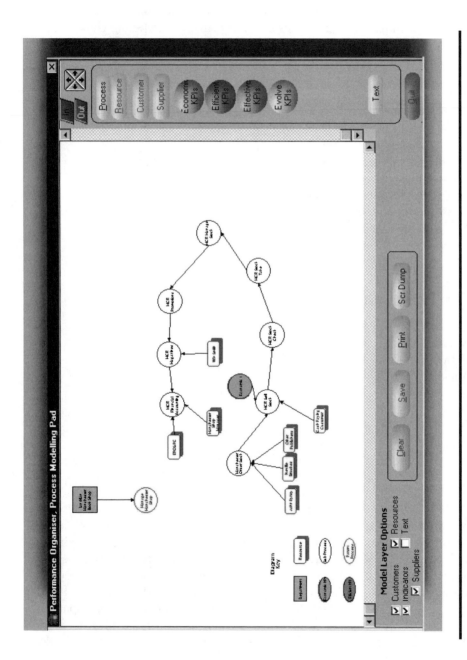

FIGURE 10.4 Process modeling interface.

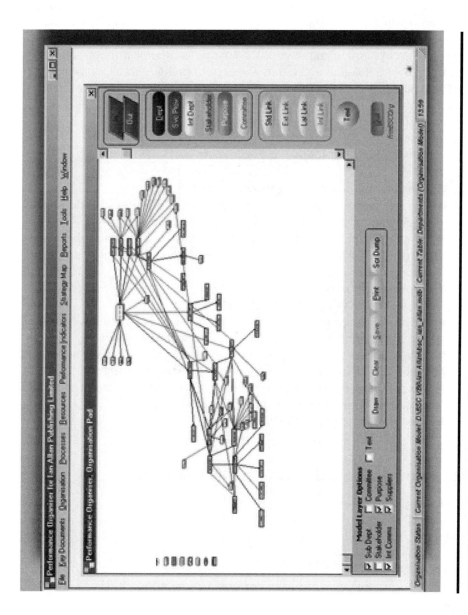

FIGURE 10.5 Organization modeling interface.

The software is built around a series of visual drawing and mapping tools to provide the means to describe organizational structure, scorecards, and process and strategy maps. Supporting the drawing pads are sets of standard data capture screens that provide the means to demonstrate links between organizations, objectives, resources, processes, and all combinations in between. Modular and flexible, the Performance Organiser provides a sound planning framework for anyone contemplating introducing a performance management system. Capable of being used as a full-blown performance management backbone, the Performance Organiser excels as a prototyping and concept tool without breaking the bank. Priced at a very competitive $200, the Performance Organiser represents best practice at best value.

Features include the following:

- Contains full-featured organization charting facilities
- Process mapping tool provides the means to illustrate and describe organization, supplier, and customer interfaces
- Strategy mapping facilities give the means to (say) track the relationships from any model element to any other, where such relationships exist
- Supports a number of best proactive analysis techniques, including the EFQM, Baldrige, ISO 9000, etc.
- Modular, with a growing mix of pick-and-choose modules, including a budget modeling add-on and a document librarian
- Uses desktop technology; no need for additional database licenses
- One year of free technical support from date of purchase
- Complimentary free copy of any new JIT Software products produced in your support year
- Free three-day evaluation license from JIT Software's Web site

Microsoft Balanced Scorecard Framework

Microsoft Corporation
1 Microsoft Way
Redmond, WA 98052
United States
Tel.: 425-882-8080
Web site: http://www.microsoft.com/office/previous/xp/business/intelligence/scorecard/framework.asp

The Microsoft Balanced Scorecard Framework (Figures 10.6 and 10.7) provides a technology environment and an integrated set of tools a

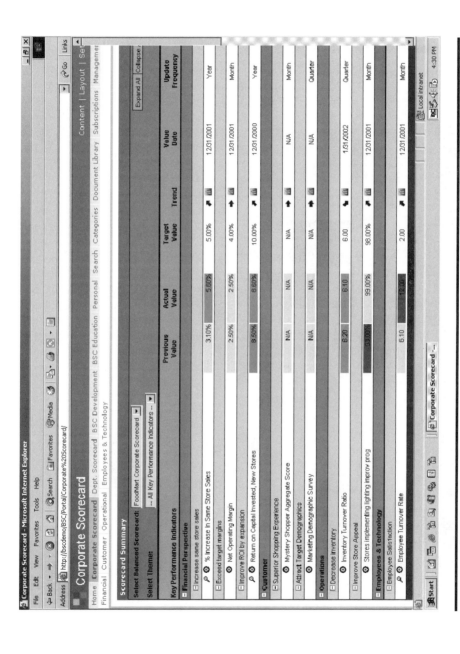

FIGURE 10.6   Microsoft scoreboard.

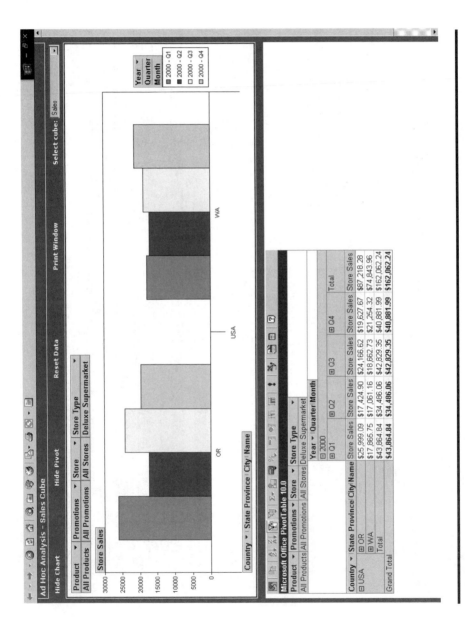

FIGURE 10.7 Microsoft ad-hoc analysis.

company can use to derive maximum value from its balanced scorecard solution. The framework is not a packaged application. Instead, it integrates a variety of Microsoft packaged applications and industry standards to automate a balanced scorecard. It consists of a set of tools and methods to help both business users and developers get to success faster and more reliably so software is no longer a hurdle to overcome in scorecard development, but an asset to speed development.

The Microsoft business intelligence platform includes world-class data collection, data warehousing, and analytical processing technologies that enable flexible balanced scorecard automation. With intuitive, familiar desktop tools and a flexible, open architecture that will meet one's changing needs, these technologies provide the perfect operating environment for delivering a balanced scorecard solution.

Office XP technologies play a key role in bringing business scorecard solutions to the desktop. Knowledge workers can use Office XP analysis tools such as Microsoft Excel and Office Web Components to analyze and explore performance metrics in a familiar, easy-to-use environment. Microsoft SharePoint™ Portal Server provides powerful collaboration features and a personalized information portal.

Features include:

- Personalized portal
- Best practices
- Strategy and metric management
- Business intelligence
- Actionable and operational tools
- Knowledge management

CorVu 5

CorVu Corporation
3400 West 66th Street
Suite 445
Edina, MN 55435
United States
Tel.: 952-944-7777
Tel.: 1-800-610-0769
Web site: www.corvu.com
E-mail: info@corvu.com

CorVu 5 (Figure 10.8) combines the two key technology components necessary for driving breakthrough performance:

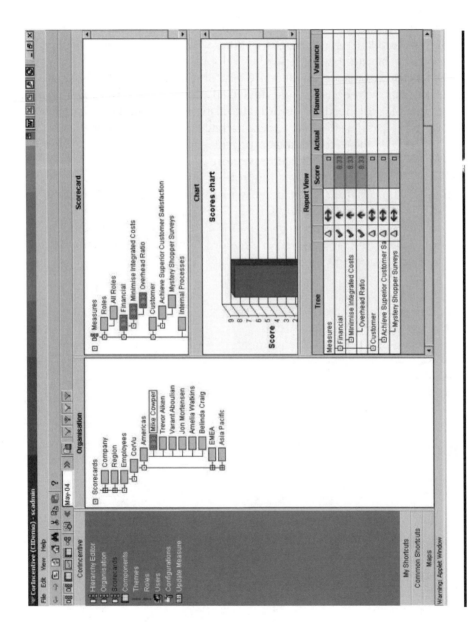

FIGURE 10.8 CorVu5.

1. Strategic management system: a purpose-built application that ties performance metrics to business strategy by managing strategy-related processes, including objective and initiative management, budgeting and planning, risk management, and incentive management.
2. Performance metrics: a robust business intelligence platform for automated data exchange, reporting, and analysis.

Four integrated applications — CorStrategy, CorPlanning, CorRisk, and CorIncentive — form the CorVu strategic management system. CorBusiness, the powerful CorVu business intelligence application, provides enterprise-wide performance metrics.

Features include the following:

- Aligns organizational activities with business objectives, resulting in better strategy execution
- Completely browser-based solution enables CorVu customers to manage strategy for the enterprise entirely over the Web (no client/server administrative connections or additional systems software are required)
- Best ROI (return on investment) for an automated scorecard solution resulting from the lowest total cost of ownership

CorVu supports all of the leading performance management methodologies, including:

- Balanced Scorecard
- Economic value add (EVA)
- European Foundation of Quality Management (EFQM)
- ISO certification
- Malcolm Baldrige Award for Quality
- Management by exception
- President's Award for Quality
- Six Sigma
- Total Quality Management (TQM)
- Value-based management

SAS Strategic Performance Management

SAS Institute Inc.
100 SAS Campus Drive
Cary, NC 27513-2414
United States
Tel.: 1-800-727-0025
Tel.: 1-919-677-8000

Web site: http://www.sas.com/solutions/bsc/
E-mail: citeam@sas.com

SAS Strategic Performance Management (Figure 10.9) helps organizations focus on and monitor key activities, apply sophisticated analytics, and respond proactively. By communicating dependencies clearly and delivering accurate, pertinent information, resources can be deployed for maximum value.

Features include the following:

- Monitor performance using accurate data with combinations of figures, text, traffic lighting, and charts.
- Visualize cause-and-effect impact of results through diagrams and strategy maps.
- Set up and receive personalized alerts.
- Prioritize and identify actions.
- Gather all pertinent information in one place for faster, more accurate decisions.
- Document and articulate corporate and individual strategies, measures, and processes.
- Create custom interfaces so that information can be accessed and navigated in the most appropriate and consistent manner within an organization.
- Provide the centerpiece for an integrated suite of SAS software solutions that deliver business intelligence in activity-based management, customer relationship management, financial management, human capital management, IT management, risk management and corporate compliance, and supply-chain intelligence.

ActiveStrategy Enterprise

ActiveStrategy
190 W. Germantown Pike, Suite 110
East Norriton, PA 19401
United States
Tel.: 610-239-8005
Web site: www.activestrategy.com
E-mail: amingo@activestrategy.com

ActiveStrategy Enterprise™ (Figures 10.10 and 10.11) represents the leading software application suite to automate each individual phase of the strategy execution process, including the balanced scorecard. Offered in three modular editions, ActiveStrategy Enterprise can be quickly implemented to:

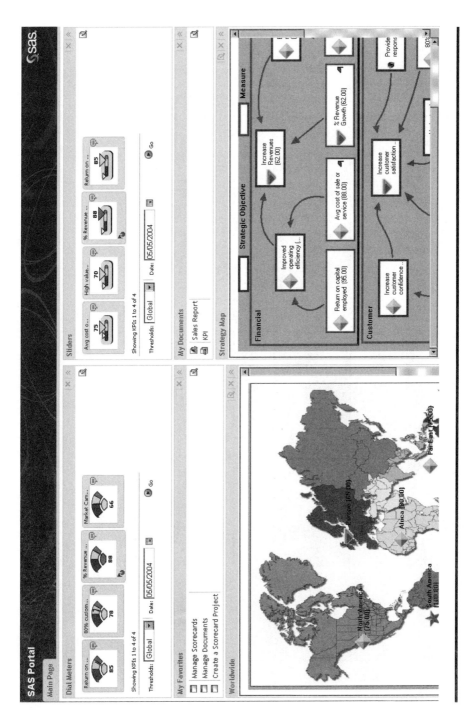

FIGURE 10.9 SAS Strategic Performance Management.

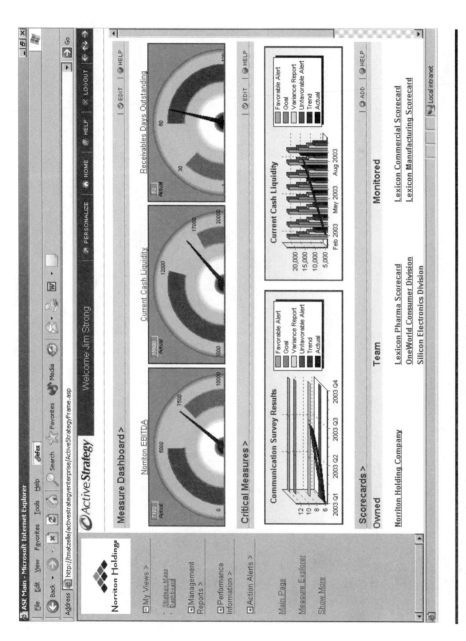

FIGURE 10.10 ActiveStrategy measure dashboard.

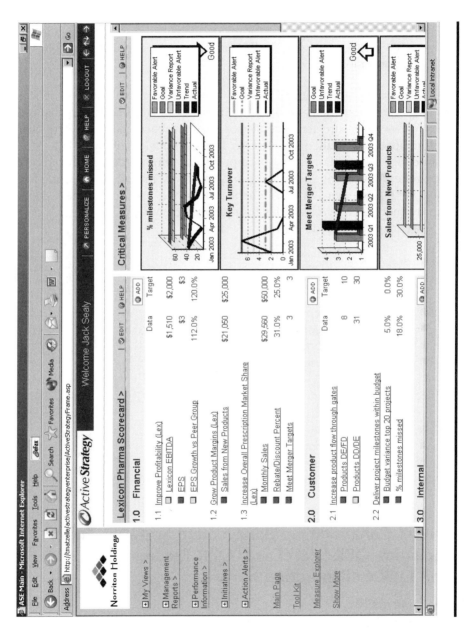

FIGURE 10.11 ActiveStrategy scorecard.

- Help an executive team create and report an initial corporate balanced scorecard
- Enable a distributed management team to deploy balanced scorecards downward and across business units and functions
- Deliver personalized performance information to specific individuals, while managing the key strategy-related activities within the organization

Designed for organizations seeking increased accountability and a focus on aligned improvement actions, the Enterprise Edition adds Personalized User Views to ensure that every user sees the balanced scorecards and performance information relevant to him or her. In addition, Full Alert features are activated to ensure prompt system compliance, variance report capture, early warning indications, and workflow management. Complete Initiative Management is also enabled to drive and focus the proper improvement initiative activities to achieve the strategy.

Core features include:

- Strategy mapping
- Balanced scorecard reporting
- Dashboards
- Measurement reports
- Initiative management
- Personalized portal
- Automatic security

Extended features include:

- Strategic planning
- Risk management
- Process management
- Process improvement management (Six Sigma/DMAIC)

QPR 7 Collaborative Management Software Suite, Including QPR ScoreCard, QPR ProcessGuide, and QPR Collaboration Portal

QPR Software Plc
Sörnäisten Rantatie 27 A
3rd floor
FIN-00500 Helsinki
Finland

Tel.: +358 9 4785 411
Web site: http://www.qpr.com
E-mail: jp.kirton@qpr.com

QPR Collaborative Management Software Suite

QPR 7 (Figures 10.12 and 10.13) enable organizations to successfully plan, implement, communicate, and commit people to collaborative performance management. QPR 7 is the end-to-end solution for performance management, from the strategy down to operational processes. QPR 7 allows organizations to define their strategies and strategic objectives linked to underlying processes, which enables employees to understand and implement process improvements through collaboration. QPR 7 enables people to easily locate under performing areas, responsible people for such areas, historical performance information, processes defined, and existing action plans on how to increase performance and improve supporting processes.

QPR 7 is flexible in its application and supports a multitude of performance and process performance management frameworks, such as Business Activity Monitoring (BAM), Balanced Scorecard (BSC), Scorecarding and Dashboard management, Business Process Management (BPM), Intellectual Capital Management, Quality Management, EFQM, Malcolm Baldrige, ISO 9000/2001, SCOR, and Collaborative Risk Management.

QPR 7 is a very fast way to implement a performance and process performance management solution. The easy-to-use development interface lets you implement your performance management system as you define it. QPR 7 allows you to start communication and collaboration on your performance structure from the planning and development stages.

QPR 7 enables you to leverage your existing systems and build a companywide performance management system. QPR 7 can be integrated with various databases and IT systems, allowing you to automatically update performance data to provide the current status of your organization's performance.

Features include:

■ QPR ScoreCard:
  - Customizable strategy and performance terminology
  - Advanced, multi-level strategy mapping
  - Fast and easy scorecarding with graphical user interface
  - Cascading scorecards
  - Flexible measurement logic and calculations
  - Customizable traffic lights
  - Flexible consolidation rules

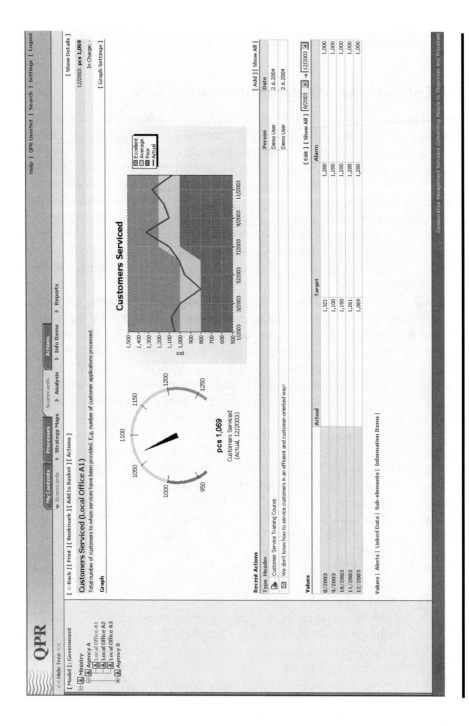

FIGURE 10.12   QPR graphics.

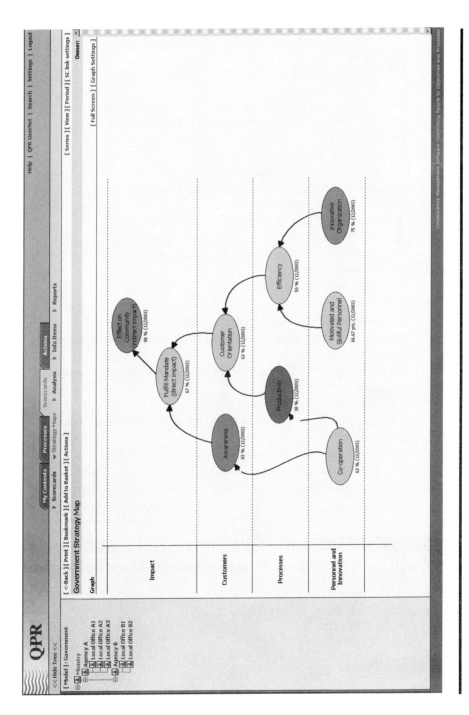

FIGURE 10.13 QPR strategy map.

- Comprehensive security and user rights management
- Automated and scheduled updates from other data sources (e.g., Excel spreadsheets, text files, relational and multidimensional databases)
- API for advanced automation and integration
■ QPR ProcessGuide
- Customizable process terminology and modeling notation
- Fast and easy process modeling with flowcharting
- Hierarchical process models
- Customizable attributes
- Dynamic process simulation
- Comprehensive security and user rights management
- Process performance analysis
- Embedding and linking related documentation
- Open XML-interface for importing and exporting
- API for advanced automation and integration
■ QPR Collaboration Portal
- Fully Web-based dynamic content
- Drill-down capabilities
- Personalized performance information
- Briefing booklets (e.g., for interactive management meeting agendas)
- Advanced commenting, action planning, and collaborative risk management
- E-mail alerts
- Personal and private bookmarks for easy access to relevant information
- Uploading and sharing related documents and links
- Search from all contents
- Seamless integration of performance and process information

QPR ScoreCard Software, QPR ProcessGuide Software, QPR CostControl Software, and Strategy Map Software

Visum Solutions, Inc.
5001 American Blvd. West, Suite 655
Bloomington, MN 55437
United States
Tel.: 952-835-4131
Web site: www.visumsolutions.com
E-mail: sales@visumsolutions.com

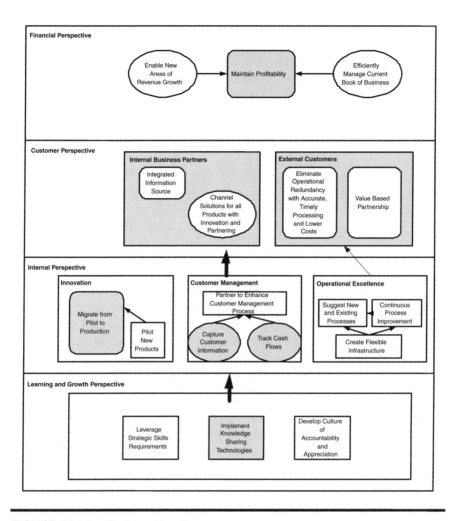

FIGURE 10.14 Strategy Map Pro.

Visum Solutions develops industry-specific applications that provide velocity to the roll-out of performance and process methodologies. Visum Solutions is also the primary reseller and provider of support services for QPR Software in North America. QPR Software is a global provider of enterprise performance management, balanced scorecard, process management, and activity-based costing software.

Strategy Map Pro (Figure 10.14) features:

■ Translates the organization's vision into a business strategy
■ Illustrates the strategy in simple terms so everyone can understand and, more importantly, contribute
■ Defines objectives clearly in simple language

- Clarifies the key projects and processes to support those objectives
- Determines what the targets are for everyone to shoot toward
- Creates cause-and-effect relationship between the external world and the internal operations of the entity
- Transforms intangible assets into definable, measurable outcomes

Healthwise Balanced Scorecard™

PracticingSmarter, Inc.
112 South Duke Street, Suite 3
Durham, NC 27701
United States
Tel.: 919-313-2090 Ext. 3161
Web site: www.practicingsmarter.net
E-mail: ssloate@practicingsmarter.net

PracticingSmarter (Figures 10.15 and 10.16) has implemented Healthwise Balanced Scorecard™ in more than 20 hospitals and health systems, implemented performance improvement initiatives in more than 50, and worked with more than 40 hospitals in a metric design project. PracticingSmarter is the largest implementer of the balanced scorecard in health care. They know what works and what does not work. Leaders can now link strategy to action in ways that accomplish the following features:

- Aligns incentives and addresses key issues by providing a common lexicon for measuring what is important
- Allows the board, physicians, staff, and management to define a set of Key Performance Indicators in a single integrated platform to monitor performance in four interrelated quadrants:
  - Physicians and staff
  - Quality and safety
  - Patients and community
  - Business development and finance
- PracticingSmarter's MAP methodology allows one to *Measure* what matters and *Analyze* the data to determine opportunities for improvement that ultimately lead to improved *Performance.*
- Fosters the aggregation of data such that different levels of an organization can see what they need, when they need it, and then take purposeful action to change behavior consistent with the desired outcomes
- Allows executive management to communicate effectively with the board, external agencies such as JCAHO, physicians, and staff through standard reports populated automatically with Key Performance Indicators and related metrics

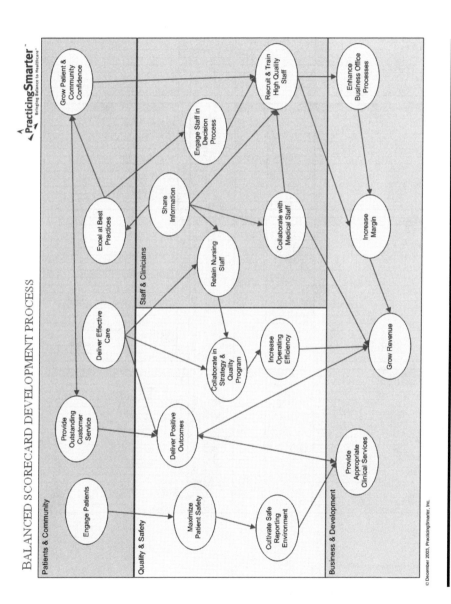

FIGURE 10.15 Balanced Scorecard development process.

Scorecard   CONFIDENTIAL

Healthwise Balanced Scorecard

	Q4 2003	Target	Performance			Comments
			119.87 ▲	⬈		WEIGHTED AVERAGE
Business & Development			128.35 ▲	↑		
Increase Margin			104.50 △	↑		
Operating Profit Margin	-0.40% ↑	-3.68%	200.00 ▲			
Days Cash on Hand	2.26 ↓	25.14	9.00 ▼			
Grow Revenue			145.71 ▲	↑		
Commercial Mix	30.48% ↘	33.34%	91.43 ▽			
Net Revenue Increase	13.97% ↑	0.81%	200.00 ▲			
Increase Ops Efficiency			134.82 ▲	⬈		
Cost per Discharge	$ 2,086.11 ↑	$4,659.62	200.00 ▲			
Salary & Benefits Expense	55.70% ↘	51.51%	92.49 ▽			
Nursing Staff Productivity	11.14 ↘	9.95	111.98 ▲			Hours per Acute Patient Day
Patients & Community			106.92 △	⬈		
Provide Outstanding Customer Service			103.59 △	⬈		
Patient Satisfaction - ER	4.26 ↘	4.00	106.54 △			529 Responses
Patient Satisfaction - Inpatient	4.27 ↘	4.00	106.73 △			21 Responses
Discharge Instructions	4.34 ↘	4.00	108.55 △			550 Responses
Time to Treating Provider - ER	0:32 ⬈	0:30	92.53 ▽			1548 Encounters
Grow Patient & Community Confidence			108.94 △	↘		
Quality of Care Index	4.36 ↘	4.00	108.94 △			550 Responses
Engage Patients			107.71 △	⬈		
Patient Engagement Index	4.31 ⬈	4.00	107.71 △			550 Responses
Provide Appropriate Clinical Services			107.43 △	⬈		
Services Up-to-Date	4.27 ↘	4.00	106.75 △			550 Responses
Access to Care	4.27 ↘	4.00	106.79 △			550 Responses
Average Age of Plant	7.04 ⬈	6.48	108.75 △			
Quality & Safety			118.66 ▲	⬈		
Excel at Best Practices			107.65 △	⬈		
Contractual Allowances	44.10% ⬈	47.47%	107.65 △			
Enhance Business Office Processes			128.54 ▲	⬈		
Bad Debt	9.66% ⬈	13.83%	143.24 ▲			
Net Days in AR	56.31 ⬈	49.46	113.84 ▲			
Deliver Positive Outcomes			80.01 ▼	⬈		
Time to Transfer	1:14 ⬈	0:45	60.02 ▼			1548 Encounters
Unplanned Admit Rate	0.00% ←	0.00%	100.00 △			
Maximize Patient Safety			127.13 ▲	⬈		
Medication Error Rate	2.64 ↑	3.57	135.15 ▲			
Medication Error Reporting	5.41% ↓	2.50%	46.25 ▼			Percent of staff aware of unreported med errors
Patient Falls - Acute	0.88 ↑	1.91	200.00 ▲			
Patient Falls - Swing	- ←	-	100.00 △			
Deliver Effective Care			149.98 ▲	↘		
ER Wait Times	0:01 ↑	0:15	200.00 ▲			1548 Encounters
ALOS for AMI	2.00 ↘	2.73	136.50 ▲			DRG 122
ALOS for CHF	3.17 ⬈	4.73	149.37 ▲			DRG 127
ALOS for Pneumonia	3.20 ↓	3.65	114.06 ▲			DRG 090
Staff & Clinicians			112.63 ▲	⬈		
Collaborate in Strategy & Quality Program			91.72 ▽	⬈		
Staff Engagement Index	3.67 ⬈	4.00	91.72 ▽			185 Responses
Retain Nursing Staff			127.14 ▲	↘		
Nursing Staff Turnover	7.87% ↘	10.00%	127.14 ▲			
Engage Staff in Decision Process			105.93 ▲	⬈		
Staff Satisfaction	4.14 ⬈	4.00	103.48 △			185 Responses
Medical Staff Satisfaction	4.37 ⬈	4.00	109.26 △			9 Responses
Support Goals	4.20 ⬈	4.00	105.06 △			194 Responses
Share Information			100.20 △	⬈		
Aware Goals	4.01 ⬈	4.00	100.20 △			194 Responses
Cultivate Safe Reporting Environment			95.41 ▽	↘		
Medication Error Policy	3.82 ↘	4.00	95.41 △			121 Responses
Recruit & Train High Quality Staff			155.96 ▲	⬈		
Staff Training	$ 177.16 ↑	$ 94.89	186.70 ▲			
Staff Turnover	5.49% ↘	10.00%	182.00 ▲			
Adequate Training	3.97 ⬈	4.00	99.18 △			194 Responses
Collaborate with Medical Staff			112.04 ▲	⬈		
Physician Engagement Index	4.48 ⬈	4.00	112.04 ▲			9 Responses

FIGURE 10.16   Completed Balanced Scorecard.

Reference

Lawson, R., W. Stratton, and T. Hatch. (2004, February). Automating the Balanced Scorecard. *CMA Management*, pp. 39–43.

Appendix A

IT Staff Competency Survey

Directions: Please rate your perception of your abilities on a scale of 1 to 5, with 1 being the lowest and 5 being the highest. In addition, please use the same scale to rate the importance of this trait in your current work environment.

Your Self-Rating:
Low   High

Communications

1. IT professionals must communicate in a variety of settings using oral, written, and multimedia techniques.   1 2 3 4 5

    Importance of this trait to your organization: 1 2 3 4 5

Problem Solving

2. IT professionals must be able to choose from a variety of different problem-solving methodologies to analytically formulate a solution.   1 2 3 4 5

    Importance of this trait to your organization: 1 2 3 4 5

3. IT professionals must think creatively in solving problems.   1 2 3 4 5

   Importance of this trait to your organization: 1 2 3 4 5

4. IT professionals must be able to work on project teams and use group methods to define and solve problems.   1 2 3 4 5

   Importance of this trait to your organization: 1 2 3 4 5

Organization and Systems Theory

5. IT professionals must be grounded in the principles of systems theory.   1 2 3 4 5

   Importance of this trait to your organization: 1 2 3 4 5

6. IT professionals must have sufficient background to understand the functioning of organizations because the information system must be congruent with and supportive of the strategy, principles, goals, and objectives of the organization.   1 2 3 4 5

   Importance of this trait to your organization: 1 2 3 4 5

7. IT professionals must understand and be able to function in the multinational and global context of today's information-dependent organizations.   1 2 3 4 5

   Importance of this trait to your organization: 1 2 3 4 5

Quality

8. IT professionals must understand quality planning steps in the continuous improvement process as it relates to the enterprise, and tools to facilitate quality development.   1 2 3 4 5

   Importance of this trait to your organization: 1 2 3 4 5

9. As the IT field matures, increasing attention is being directed to problem avoidance and to process simplification through reengineering. Error control, risk

management, process measurement, and auditing are areas that IT professionals must understand and apply.   1 2 3 4 5

Importance of this trait to your organization: 1 2 3 4 5

10. IT professionals must possess a tolerance for change and skills for managing the process of change.   1 2 3 4 5

    Importance of this trait to your organization: 1 2 3 4 5

11. Given the advancing technology of the IT field, education must be continuous.   1 2 3 4 5

    Importance of this trait to your organization: 1 2 3 4 5

12. IT professionals must understand mission-directed, principle-centered mechanisms to facilitate aligning group as well as individual missions with organizational missions.   1 2 3 4 5

    Importance of this trait to your organization: 1 2 3 4 5

Groups

13. IT professionals must interact with diverse user groups in team and project activities.   1 2 3 4 5

    Importance of this trait to your organization: 1 2 3 4 5

14. IT professionals must possess communication and facilitation skills with team meetings and other related activities.   1 2 3 4 5

    Importance of this trait to your organization: 1 2 3 4 5

15. IT professionals must understand the concept of empathetic listening and utilize it proactively to solicit synergistic solutions from which all parties to an agreement can benefit.   1 2 3 4 5

    Importance of this trait to your organization: 1 2 3 4 5

16. IT professionals must be able to communicate effectively with a changing workforce.   1 2 3 4 5

    Importance of this trait to your organization: 1 2 3 4 5

Reference

1. McGuire, Eugene G. and Kim A. Randall. (1998). *Process Improvement Competencies for IS Professionals: A Survey of Perceived Needs.* ACM Special Interest Group on Computer Personnel Research. New York: ACM Press.

Appendix B

U.S. Air Force Software Metrics Capability Evaluation Guide

1. Introduction

In its role as an agent for improving software technology use within the U.S. Air Force, the Software Technology Support Center (STSC) is supporting metrics technology improvement activities for its customers. These activities include disseminating information regarding the U.S. Air Force policy on software metrics [AP93M-017], providing metrics information to the public through CrossTalk, conducting customer workshops in software metrics, guiding metrics technology adoption programs at customer locations, researching new and evolving metrics methodologies, etc.

Helping customers become proficient in developing and using software metrics to support their software development and/or management activities is crucial to customer success. The STSC metrics support activities must be tailored to the customer's needs to ensure:

a. That the activities are appropriate to the customer's organization and metrics capability maturity, and[1]

b. That the customer is ready to make improvements based on the support obtained.

Customer support needs include activities based on their apparent metrics capability and those that are particularly focused on dealing with the organizational and cultural issues that often need to be addressed to facilitate change.

This guide covers the following:

    a. It defines a metrics capability evaluation method that deals specifically with defining a customer's metrics capability.

    b. It presents metrics capability questionnaires that help gather metrics capability data.

    c. It outlines a metrics capability evaluation report that provides the basis for developing a metrics customer project plan.

    d. It provides a metrics customer profile form used to determine the initial information required to prepare for a metrics capability evaluation.

    e. It provides a customer organization information form that helps guide the STSC in gathering cultural information about the organization that will help with developing and implementing the metrics customer project plan.

2. Evaluation Approach

2.1 *Background*

The foundation for the evaluation method is "A Method for Assessing Software Measurement Technology."[DASK90][2] Metrics capability maturity consists of five maturity levels that are analogous to the software Capability Maturity Model (CMM) levels defined by the Software Engineering Institute (SEI). [PAUL93] This guide has been designed to cover metrics capability maturity Levels 1 through 3. When metrics capability evaluations show a strong percentage (e.g., 25 percent or more) of organizations at metrics capability maturity Level 3, the scope of the evaluation (and this guide) will be expanded to cover metrics capability maturity Levels 4 and 5.

This guide defines a set of questions to elicit information that will help characterize an organization's metrics capability. The themes used in the questionnaire and their relationships to an organization's metrics capability maturity (for Levels 1 through 3) are shown in Appendix B/A.

The guide contains two metrics capability questionnaires (one for acquisition organizations and one for software development/maintenance organizations). The questions in the questionnaires are used as the basis for interviews with an organization's representative(s) to help determine their metrics capability maturity. After the interviews are complete, the results are collated and reported in an evaluation report that is delivered to the evaluated organization. Additional work with the evaluated organization will depend on the organization's needs. Section 2.2 discusses the evaluation process. Appendix B/B contains a brief metrics customer profile form, which is filled out as a precursor to the metrics capability evaluation. Appendix B/C is an annotated outline of the metrics capability evaluation report, and Appendix B/D contains the customer organization information form.

2.2 Software Metrics Capability Evaluation Process

The software metrics capability evaluation process consists of the three basic parts:

a. An initial contact, which is performed when it is determined that an organization needs and wants assistance with its metrics capability.
b. The evaluation interview, which is the central activity in the software metrics capability evaluation process.
c. Collating and analyzing the results, which are the transition activities that occur between the evaluation interview and evaluation follow-up.

These sets of activities are discussed in Paragraphs 2.2.1 through 2.2.3.

In addition to evaluation, there may be follow-up activities. These include more detailed work with the customer that will provide a metrics capability improvement strategy and plan when applicable. Paragraph 2.3 discusses the follow-up activities.

2.2.1 Initial Contact

The initial contact with a customer generally is set up through an STSC customer consultant. The customer consultant briefs an assigned member of the STSC metrics team regarding a customer's need for a metrics capability evaluation and provides a contact for the metrics team member at the customer's site.

The metrics team member contacts the customer by phone to gain an initial understanding of the customer's organization and to set up the evaluation interview. The metrics customer profile form is used to help gather that information. Information collected during this initial contact will be used to help determine the proper approach for the introduction briefing presented during the evaluation interview visit. Only the point of contact information must be completed at this time; however, it is highly desirable to include the STSC business information. When the profile is not completed during the initial contact, it needs to be completed prior to (or as an introduction to) the evaluation interview at the customer's site.

2.2.2 Evaluation Interview

Two STSC metrics team members conduct the interviews as a metrics evaluation team. On the same day as the evaluation interview, an introduction briefing is provided to key people within the organization (to be determined jointly by the evaluation team members, the customer consultant assigned to the organization, and the organization's primary point of contact). The purpose of the briefing is to manage customer expectations. This is accomplished, in part, by providing education with respect to:

   a. The concepts of metrics maturity
   b. The approach of the metrics evaluation team
   c. What to expect when evaluation results are provided

The interviews are conducted with the manager most closely associated with the software development activities for the program (or project) under question.[3] One other representative from the program (or project) should participate in the interview. (A staff member responsible for metrics analysis and reporting would be most appropriate.) The first part of the interview is to complete the metrics customer profile. When this is completed, the metrics capability questionnaire most related to the organization (either acquirer or development/maintenance organization) is used as the input to the remainder of the evaluation process. The questionnaire sections for both Levels 2 and 3 are used regardless of the customer's perceived metrics capability.

The questions in the metrics capability evaluation questionnaires have been formalized to require answers of yes, no, not applicable (NA), or don't know (?). If an answer is yes, the customer needs to relate examples or otherwise prove performance that fulfills the question. If the answer is no, comments may be helpful but are not required. (If the answer is don't know, a no answer is assumed.) If the answer is NA and it can be shown to be NA, the question is ignored and the answer is not counted as part of the score. The chosen metrics capability evaluation questionnaires need to be completed before the interview is considered complete.

An evaluation interview should not take more than one day for one program (or software project). If an organization is to be assessed, a representative sample of programs (or software projects) needs to be assessed and each requires a separate interview.

2.2.3 Collating and Analyzing the Results

The metrics capability questionnaires completed during the interview(s) and their associated examples (or other evidence of metrics capability maturity, see Paragraph B.1) are collated and returned to STSC for analysis. The metrics capability evaluation team that conducted the interview(s) is responsible for analyzing and reporting the results. An assessed program (or software project) is at Level 2 if at least 80 percent of all Level 2 questions are answered yes. Otherwise, the organization is at Level 1, etc. [DASK90] (Scoring is discussed in more detail in Paragraph B.1. The contents of the metrics capability evaluation report are outlined in Appendix B/C.)

The questions in the metrics capability questionnaires are organized by metrics capability maturity themes to help focus the interviews and the results analysis. (The themes, as defined in [DASK90], and their characteristics at metrics capability maturity Levels 2 and 3 are reported in Appendix B/A.) The customer's strengths and weaknesses can be addressed directly with the information gathered during the interview session(s). In addition, activities for becoming more effective in implementing and using metrics can be highlighted in the metrics capability evaluation report and in the project plan.

2.3 Software Metrics Capability Evaluation Follow-Up

Software metrics capability evaluation follow-up includes two sets of activities:

a. The metrics capability evaluation report
b. The project plan and implementation

The report details the evaluation results and provides recommendations for an initial set of improvement activities.

The project plan consists of a customer-approved, detailed plan to improve the customer's metrics capability (which may include other aspects of support to the customer such as software process definition, project management support, or requirements management workshops, etc.).

The customer's organizational culture is important in developing the content and phasing of the project plan. Issues such as ability to incorporate change into the organization, management commitment to software technology improvement, etc. often need to be addressed in developing a success-oriented plan.[4]

Metrics capability improvement implementation consists of the physical implementation of the project plan and a periodic evaluation of the customer's status to determine the program's improvement and any required modifications to the plan. The project plan and implementation are described in Paragraph 2.3.2.

2.3.1 Metrics Capability Evaluation Report

The metrics capability evaluation report consists of two parts:

a. The analyzed results of the evaluation
b. Recommendations for a set of activities that will help improve the customer's metrics capability

The results portion of the report is organized to discuss the customer's overall software metrics capability and to define the areas of strengths and weaknesses based on each of the measurement themes. The recommendations portion of the report describes an overall improvement strategy that provides a balanced approach toward metrics capability improvement based on the customer's current evaluation results. Appendix B/C contains an annotated outline of the report.

2.3.2 Project Plan and Implementation

If a customer has the interest to proceed with a project plan, the STSC will develop the plan in conjunction with the customer. The contents of the project plan, the estimates for plan implementation, and the schedule will be developed specifically for each customer's needs. Due to the possible variations in customer needs, it is difficult to determine the exact contents of the plan. At a minimum, the project plan contains the following information:

a. An executive overview, which includes a synopsis of the customer's current software metrics capability maturity and a general outline of the plan to be implemented.
b. Organizational responsibilities for the customer, the customer's interfacing organizations (e.g., a contractor), and the STSC. Issues that arise based on organizational information are highlighted.
c. Improvement objectives.
d. A set of activities to support improvement [e.g., a Work Breakdown Structure (WBS)] and a description of the activities' interrelationships.

   e. A schedule for implementation and for periodic evaluation of the customer's progress. (The periodic evaluation may be implemented as additional metrics capability evaluations, as described in this guide.)

   f. Effort and cost estimates for STSC support.

   g. Facility requirements for training and other activities.

   h. Descriptions of STSC products to be delivered as part of the improvement implementation.

After the plan is approved, the metrics capability improvement implementation follows the plan. The periodic evaluations of the customer's products provide feedback regarding the customer's progress and an opportunity to revise the plan if the improvement is not proceeding according to the plan. In this way, the plan and implementation process can be adjusted as necessary to support the customer's ongoing needs.

List of References

AF93M-017Software Metrics Policy — Action Memorandum, February 1994.

DASK90Daskalantonakis, Michael K., Robert H. Yacobellis, and Victor R. Basilli, "A Method for Assessing Software Measurement Technology," *Quality Engineering*, Vol. 3, No. 1, 1990 to 1991, pp. 27–40.

PAUL93Paulk, Mark C. et al. *Capability Maturity Model for Software*, Version 1.1, CMU/SEI-93-TR-24, ESC-TR-93-177, February 1993.

SEI94Software Process Maturity Questionnaire, *CMM*, Version 1.1, April 1994.

Appendix B/A: Measurement Themes and Relationships

Table B-1 shows the six metrics themes and relates the themes to software metrics capability maturity Levels 1 through 3.

Appendix B/B: Software Metrics Capability Questionnaires

This appendix contains scoring information for the software metrics capability evaluations along with copies of the metrics customer profile form and the two software metrics capability evaluation questionnaires.

    The metrics customer profile form helps gather general customer information for choosing the metrics capability evaluation questionnaire

TABLE B.1 Themes and Levels of Software Metrics Capability Maturity.

Theme	Initial (Level 1)	Repeatable (Level 2)	Defined (Level 3)
1. Formalization of development process	Process unpredictable Project depends on seasoned professionals No/poor process focus	Projects repeat previously mastered tasks Process depends on experienced people	Process characterized and reasonably understood
2. Formalization of metrics process	Little or no formalization	Formal procedures established Metrics standards exist	Documented metrics standards Standards applied
3. Scope of metrics	Occasional use on projects with seasoned people or not at all	Used on projects with experienced people Project estimation mechanisms exist Metrics have project focus	Goal/Question/Metric package development and some use Data collection and recording Specific automated tools exist in the environment Metrics have product focus
4. Implementation support	No historical data or database	Data (or database) available on a per-project basis	Product-level database Standardized database used across projects
5. Metrics evolution	Little or no metrics conducted	Project metrics and management in place	Product-level metrics and management in place
6. Metrics support for mgmt control	Management not supported by metrics	Some metrics support for management Basic control of commitments	Product-level metrics and control

The information in this table has been extracted directly from [DASK90].

and for defining the contents of the project plan. The two software metrics capability evaluation questionnaires are as follows:

    a. An acquisition organization questionnaire. The focus of this questionnaire is to determine the metrics capability level of software acquisition organizations.

    b. A software development/maintenance organization questionnaire. The focus of this questionnaire is to determine the metrics capability level of software development or maintenance organizations.

B.1   Use of Questionnaires and Scoring

B.1.1   Use of Questionnaires

These two metrics capability evaluation questionnaires provide the contents of the evaluation interviews described in Paragraph 2.2.2. The questions from the questionnaires are asked as written. The questions for Levels 2 and 3 are used for all interviews. The comments for each question are used to point to examples and other evidence of metrics capability maturity based on the activities referred to in the question. The answers to the questions and the examples and comments are the inputs to the scoring activity presented in Paragraph B.1.2.

B.1.2   Scoring

Scoring from the two metrics capability evaluation questionnaires is relatively simple:

    a. If the answer to a question is yes, then proof of conformance needs to be shown to ensure that the customer has performed the activity(ies) indicated in the question. Proof of conformance includes:

        1. Metrics standards for the organization.
        2. Software acquisition plans, development plans, or contract statements that incorporate metrics requirements.
        3. Meeting minutes or other items that indicate use of metrics.
        4. Examples of database outputs.
        5. Concurrence given by two or more individuals from the same organization who are interviewed separately.
        6. Informal notes.
        7. Briefing charts from management evaluations.
        8. Etc.

b. If the answer is no, or don't know, then the answer is scored as no.
c. If the answer is NA, then the question is subtracted from the total number of questions for that maturity level and the answer is not included in the overall score.
d. When 80 percent or more of the Level 2 questions are answered yes (with proof), then the organization is considered to be a Level 2. Otherwise the organization is considered to be a Level 1.
e. If the organization is a Level 2 and also answers 80 percent or more of the Level 3 questions yes (with proof), then the organization is considered to be a Level 3. Otherwise, the organization is considered to be a Level 1 or 2 as indicated in Item d.

The organization's metrics capability level, as indicated from the scoring process, the proofs of conformance, and comments, are all used as inputs to the metrics capability evaluation report. Appendix B/C contains an annotated outline of a metrics capability evaluation report.

B.2 Metrics Customer Profile Form

1. Point of Contact information:
   a. Name: _____
   b. Position: _____
   c. Office symbol:_____
   d. Location:_____
   e. Phone #:_____ DSN: _____
   f. Fax number: _____
   g. E-mail address: _____
   h. Organization name: _____
   i. Products: _____
2. Environment information:
   a. Hardware platform: _____
   b. Languages used: _____
   c. Tools used for metrics: _____
3. Organization information:
   a. Major command (ACC, AFMC, AETC, AMC, other:_____)
   b. Copy of organization chart (at least name and rank of commanding officer): _____
   c. Type(s) of software (real-time, communication, command & control, MIS, other):_____
   d. Type(s) of activity (development, acquisition, maintenance, combination, other):_____
      _____

    e. Are project teams comprised of members from more than one organization? (If yes, please give examples.)_____

    _____

    f. Typical size of development organization for a particular program (or project) (less than 10, 10–40, more than 40 personnel):

    _____

    g. Typical length of project (<6 mo, 6–18 mo, 18 mo–3 yr, >3 yr):

    _____

4. General background:
    a. What are the organization's strengths? _____

    _____

    b. Can you demonstrate these strengths through measurements or other objective means? (if yes, examples?)_____

    _____

    c. What are the organization's biggest challenges? _____

    _____

    d. Have measurements or other objective means been used to understand or to help manage these challenges? (if yes, examples?)

    _____

    _____

5. Metrics background:
    a. Does your organization require Software Development Plans to be developed and used? _____

    b. Are project management tools used? (examples?)_____

    _____

    c. How is project status reported? (examples?) _____

    _____

    d. How is product quality reported? (examples?) _____

    _____

    e. What forces are driving metrics interest in your organization (SAF/AQ, CO, self, etc.)?_____

6. STSC business information:
    a. Has the organization received STSC information or services?
       CrossTalk? _____
       Technology Reports? _____
       Workshops? _____
       Consulting?_____
    b. Does the organization need help?_____
    c. Does the organization want help?_____
    d. The organization would like help with (describe): _____

    _____

    e. How well is the organization funded for new technology adoption (including training)?

(1) Are there funds to pay for STSC Products and Services?
_____

(2) Is the organization *willing* to pay?_____
f. Are their needs/wants a match to STSC products and services?
_____

B.3 Acquisition Organization Questionnaire[5]

B.3.1 Questions for Metrics Capability Level 2

B.3.1.1 Theme 1: Formalization of Source Selection and Contract Monitoring Process

#	Question	Yes	No	NA	?
1a.	Is a Software Capability Evaluation (SCE) or Software Development Capability Evaluation (SDCE) for developers part of your source selection process?[6]	☐	☐	☐	☐

Comments:_____
_____

| 1b. | Is proof of a specific CMM Level required from developers as part of your source selection process? | ☐ | ☐ | ☐ | ☐ |

Comments:_____
_____

| 2. | Does your organization require and evaluate developers' draft software development plans as part of the source selection process? | ☐ | ☐ | ☐ | ☐ |

Comments:_____
_____

| 3. | Are software metrics required as part of developers' software development plans (or other contractually binding metrics plans)? | ☐ | ☐ | ☐ | ☐ |

Comments:_____
_____

| 4. | Are software cost and schedule estimates required from the developer as part of the source selection process? | ☐ | ☐ | ☐ | ☐ |

Comments:_____
_____

5. Is the developer's project performance monitored based on the cost and schedule estimates? ☐ ☐ ☐ ☐

   Comments:_____

   _____

6. Are the acquirers' management plans developed, used, and maintained as part of managing a program? ☐ ☐ ☐ ☐

   Comments:_____

   _____

B.3.1.2 Theme 2: Formalization of Metrics Process

#	Question	Yes	No	NA	?

1. Is there a written organizational policy for collecting and maintaining software metrics for this program? ☐ ☐ ☐ ☐

   Comments:_____

   _____

2. Is each program required to identify and use metrics to show program performance? ☐ ☐ ☐ ☐

   Comments:_____

   _____

3. Is the use of software metrics documented? ☐ ☐ ☐ ☐

   Comments:_____

   _____

4. Are developers required to report a set of standard metrics? ☐ ☐ ☐ ☐

   Comments:_____

   _____

B.3.1.3 Theme 3: Scope of Metrics

#	Question	Yes	No	NA	?

1. Are internal measurements used to determine the status of the activities performed for planning a new acquisition program? ☐ ☐ ☐ ☐

   Comments:_____

   _____

2. Are measurements used to determine the status of software contract management activities? ☐ ☐ ☐ ☐

   Comments:_____

   _____

3. Do(es) your contract(s) require metrics on the developer's actual results (e.g., schedule, size, and effort) compared to the estimates? ☐ ☐ ☐ ☐

   Comments:_____

   _____

4. Can you determine whether the program is performing according to plan based on measurement data provided by the developer? ☐ ☐ ☐ ☐

   Comments:_____

   _____

5. Are measurements used to determine your organization's planned and actual effort applied to performing acquisition planning and program management? ☐ ☐ ☐ ☐

   Comments:_____

   _____

6. Are measurements used to determine the status of your organization's software configuration management activities? ☐ ☐ ☐ ☐

   Comments:_____

   _____

B.3.1.4 Theme 4: Implementation Support

#	Question	Yes	No	NA	?

1. Does the program (or project) have a database of metrics information? ☐ ☐ ☐ ☐

   Comments:_____

   _____

2. Do you require access to the contractor's metrics data as well as completed metrics reports? ☐ ☐ ☐ ☐

   Comments:_____

   _____

3. Does your database (or collected program data) include both the developer's and acquirer's metrics data? □ □ □ □

   Comments:_____

   _____

B.3.1.5   Theme 5: Metrics Evolution

#	Question	Yes	No	NA	?

1. Is someone from the acquisition organization assigned specific responsibilities for tracking the developer's activity status (e.g., schedule, size, and effort)? □ □ □ □

   Comments:_____

   _____

2. Does the developer regularly report the metrics defined in the developer's software development plan (or other contractually binding metrics plan)? □ □ □ □

   Comments:_____

   _____

3. Do your contracts have clauses that allow the acquirer to request changes to the developer's metrics based on program needs? □ □ □ □

   Comments:_____

   _____

B.3.1.6   Theme 6: Metrics Support for Management Control

#	Question	Yes	No	NA	?

1. Do you track your developer's performance against the developer's commitments? □ □ □ □

   Comments:_____

   _____

2. Are the developer's metrics results used as an indicator of when contract performance should be analyzed in detail? □ □ □ □

   Comments:_____

   _____

3. Are metrics results used to support risk management, particularly with respect to cost and schedule risks? ☐ ☐ ☐ ☐

Comments:_____

_____

4. Are program acquisition and/or program management metrics used to help determine when changes should be made to your plans (e.g., changes to schedules for completion of planning activities and milestones, etc.)? ☐ ☐ ☐ ☐

Comments:_____

_____

5. Are measurements used to determine the status of verification & validation activities for software contracts? ☐ ☐ ☐ ☐

Comments:_____

_____

B.3.2 Questions for Metrics Capability Level 3

B.3.2.1 Theme 1: Formalization of Source Selection and Contract Monitoring Process

#	Question	Yes	No	NA	?

1. Do you require developers to show proof of software development maturity at a minimum of CMM Level 3? ☐ ☐ ☐ ☐

Comments:_____

_____

2. Is your software acquisition process reviewed for improvement periodically? ☐ ☐ ☐ ☐

Comments:_____

_____

3. Does your organization have a standard software acquisition process? ☐ ☐ ☐ ☐

Comments:_____

_____

4. Do one or more individuals have responsibility for maintaining the organization's standard software acquisition processes? □ □ □ □

Comments:_____

_____

5. Does the organization follow a written policy for developing and maintaining the acquisition process and related information (e.g., descriptions of approved tailoring for standards based on program attributes)? □ □ □ □

Comments:_____

_____

B.3.2.2 Theme 2: Formalization of Metrics Process

#	Question	Yes	No	NA	?

1. Do you have documented standards for metrics definitions and for reporting formats you require from developers? □ □ □ □

Comments:_____

_____

2. Are these standards tailorable to the size, scope, and type of the software to be acquired? □ □ □ □

Comments:_____

_____

3. Are specific metrics requested for each new acquisition based on your organization's metrics standards? □ □ □ □

Comments:_____

_____

4. Is someone from your organization assigned specific responsibilities for maintaining and analyzing the contractor's metrics regarding the status of software work products and activities (e.g., effort, schedule, quality)? □ □ □ □

Comments:_____

_____

B.3.2.3 Theme 3: Scope of Metrics

#	Question	Yes	No	NA	?
1.	Do you collect, maintain, and report metrics data for all new (in the last 3 years) contracts?	☐	☐	☐	☐

Comments:_____

_____

#	Question	Yes	No	NA	?
2.	Do you use automated tools that support metrics collection, maintenance, and reporting?	☐	☐	☐	☐

Comments:_____

_____

#	Question	Yes	No	NA	?
3.	Do you and your developer(s) use automated metrics tools that allow you to share contract metrics data?	☐	☐	☐	☐

Comments:_____

_____

#	Question	Yes	No	NA	?
4.	During contract negotiations, do the program goals drive the metrics required for the contract?	☐	☐	☐	☐

Comments:_____

_____

#	Question	Yes	No	NA	?
5.	Do the metrics collected include specific product metrics (e.g., quality, reliability, maintainability)?	☐	☐	☐	☐

Comments:_____

_____

#	Question	Yes	No	NA	?
6.	Do you require metrics summary reports that show general program trends as well as detailed metrics information?	☐	☐	☐	☐

Comments:_____

_____

B.3.2.4 Theme 4: Implementation Support

#	Question	Yes	No	NA	?
1.	Does your program metrics database include information on specific product metrics (e.g., quality, reliability, maintainability)?	☐	☐	☐	☐

Comments:_____

_____

2. Do you share metrics data across programs? ☐ ☐ ☐ ☐

   Comments:_____

   _____

3. Is the metrics data shared through a common organizational database? ☐ ☐ ☐ ☐

   Comments:_____

   _____

4. Does your organization have a standard length of
   time that you retain metrics data? ☐ ☐ ☐ ☐

   Comments:_____

   _____

5. Does the organization verify the metrics data maintained in the metrics database? ☐ ☐ ☐ ☐

   Comments:_____

   _____

6. Does your organization manage and maintain the
   metrics database? ☐ ☐ ☐ ☐

   Comments:_____

   _____

B.3.2.5 Theme 5: Metrics Evolution

#	Question	Yes No NA ?
1.	Do you use product metrics in making management decisions (e.g., a decision is made to delay schedule because of known defects)?	☐ ☐ ☐ ☐
	Comments:_____	
	_____	
2.	Are product metrics reported during program management reviews (e.g., defects by severity, or defects by cause)?	☐ ☐ ☐ ☐
	Comments:_____	
	_____	

3. Are both project and product metrics used in making management decisions regarding contract performance? □ □ □ □

    Comments:_____

    _____

4. Does your organization review the current metrics set periodically for ongoing usefulness? □ □ □ □

    Comments:_____

    _____

5. Does your organization review the current metrics set periodically to determine if new metrics are needed? □ □ □ □

    Comments:_____

    _____

B.3.2.6 Theme 6: Metrics Support for Management Control

#	Question	Yes No NA ?

1. Are measurements used to determine the status of the program office activities performed for managing the software requirements? □ □ □ □

    Comments:_____

    _____

2. Are product metrics used as an indicator for renegotiating the terms of contract(s) when necessary? □ □ □ □

    Comments:_____

    _____

3. Are product metrics used in reports forwarded to higher level management concerning contract performance? □ □ □ □

    Comments:_____

    _____

4. Are measurements used to forecast the status of products during their development? □ □ □ □

    Comments:_____

    _____

5. Are product metrics used as inputs to award fee calculations for cost plus award fee contracts? □ □ □ □

   Comments:_____

   _____

6. Do metrics serve as inputs for determining when activities need to be initiated (or modified) to mitigate technical program risks? □ □ □ □

   Comments:_____

   _____

B.4 Software Development/Maintenance Organization Questionnaire

B.4.1 Questions for Metrics Capability Level 2

B.4.1.1 Theme 1: Formalization of the Development Process

#	Question	Yes	No	NA	?
1a.	Has your organization been assessed via the SEI CMM?[7] (This could be an independent assessment or an internal assessment supported by an SEI authorized source.)	□	□	□	□

Comments:_____

_____

| 1b. | Has your organization been assessed via some vehicle other than the SEI CMM? | □ | □ | □ | □ |

Comments:_____

_____

| 2. | Are software development plans developed, used, and maintained as part of managing software projects? | □ | □ | □ | □ |

Comments:_____

_____

| 3. | Are software metrics included in your software development plans or other contractual binding document(s)? | □ | □ | □ | □ |

Comments:_____

_____

4. Does your organization have an ongoing software process improvement program?   □ □ □ □

   Comments:_____

   _____

B.4.1.2 Theme 2: Formalization of Metrics Process

#	Question	Yes	No	NA	?

1. Is there a written policy for collecting and maintaining project management metrics (e.g., cost, effort, and schedule)?   □ □ □ □

   Comments:_____

   _____

2. Do standards exist for defining, collecting, and reporting metrics?   □ □ □ □

   Comments:_____

   _____

3. Is each project required to identify and use metrics to show project performance?   □ □ □ □

   Comments:_____

   _____

B.4.1.3 Theme 3: Scope of Metrics

#	Question	Yes	No	NA	?

1. Are measurements used to determine the status of activities performed during software planning?   □ □ □ □

   Comments:_____

   _____

2. Are measurements used to determine and track the status of activities performed during project performance?   □ □ □ □

   Comments:_____

   _____

3. Does the project manager establish cost and schedule estimates based on prior experience?   □ □ □ □

Comments:_____

_____

B.4.1.4 Theme 4: Implementation Support

#	Question	Yes	No	NA	?

1. Is there a project database of metrics information? ☐ ☐ ☐ ☐

   Comments:_____

   _____

2. Is the project manager responsible for implementing metrics for the project? ☐ ☐ ☐ ☐

   Comments:_____

   _____

3. Do you keep metrics from project to project (historical data)? ☐ ☐ ☐ ☐

   Comments:_____

   _____

B.4.1.5 Theme 5: Metrics Evolution

#	Question	Yes	No	NA	?

1. Do you report the project's actual results (e.g., schedule and cost) compared to estimates? ☐ ☐ ☐ ☐

   Comments:_____

   _____

2. Is someone on the staff assigned specific responsibilities for tracking software project activity status (e.g., schedule, size, cost)? ☐ ☐ ☐ ☐

   Comments:_____

   _____

3. Do you regularly report the metrics defined in the software development plan or other contractually required document(s)? ☐ ☐ ☐ ☐

   Comments:_____

   _____

B.4.1.6 Theme 6: Metrics Support for Management Control

#	Question	Yes	No	NA	?

1. Do metrics results help the project manager manage deviations in cost and schedule? □ □ □ □

   Comments:_____

   _____

2. Are measurements used to determine the status of software configuration management activities on the project? □ □ □ □

   Comments:_____

   _____

3. Are measurements used to determine the status of software quality assurance activities on the project? □ □ □ □

   Comments:_____

   _____

4. Are measurements used to determine the status of the activities performed for managing the allocated requirements (e.g., total number of requirements changes that are proposed, open, approved, and incorporated into the baseline)? □ □ □ □

   Comments:_____

   _____

5. Are cost and schedule estimates documented and used to refine the estimation process? □ □ □ □

   Comments:_____

   _____

6. Do you report metrics data to the customer based on customer requirements? □ □ □ □

   Comments:_____

   _____

B.4.2 Questions for Metrics Capability Level 3

B.4.2.1 Theme 1: Formalization of the Development Process

#	Question	Yes	No	NA	?

1. Is your software development process reviewed for improvement periodically? □ □ □ □

Comments:_____

_____

2. Does your organization's standard software process include processes that support both software management and software engineering? □ □ □ □

   Comments:_____

   _____

3. Are your processes tailorable to the size/scope of the project? □ □ □ □

   Comments:_____

   _____

B.4.2.2 Theme 2: Formalization of Metrics Process

#	Question	Yes	No	NA	?

1. Do you have documented organizational standards for metrics (e.g., metrics definitions, analysis, reports, and procedures)? □ □ □ □

   Comments:_____

   _____

2. Are these standards tailorable to the size and scope of the software project? □ □ □ □

   Comments:_____

   _____

3. Are there standards established for the retention of metrics? □ □ □ □

   Comments:_____

   _____

4. Are specific project and product metrics proposed for each software project based on the organization's metrics standards? □ □ □ □

   Comments:_____

   _____

5. Is someone assigned specific responsibilities for maintaining and analyzing metrics regarding the

status of software work products and activities (e.g., size, effort, schedule, quality)? ☐ ☐ ☐ ☐

Comments:_____

_____

6. Does the organization collect, review, and make available information related to the use of the organization's standard software process (e.g., estimates and actual data on software size, effort, and cost; productivity data; and quality measurements)? ☐ ☐ ☐ ☐

Comments:_____

_____

B.4.2.3 Theme 3: Scope of Metrics

#	Question	Yes No NA ?
1.	Do the project/organization management and technical goals drive the metrics required? Comments:_____	☐ ☐ ☐ ☐
2.	Do you collect, maintain, and report project and product metrics data for all projects? Comments:_____	☐ ☐ ☐ ☐
3.	Do you use automated tools that support metrics collection, maintenance, and reporting? Comments:_____	☐ ☐ ☐ ☐
4.	Do the metrics collected include specific product metrics (e.g., quality, reliability, maintainability)? Comments:_____	☐ ☐ ☐ ☐
5.	Do you report product metrics (e.g., problem/defect density by product; amount of rework; and/or status of allocated requirements) throughout the development life cycle?	☐ ☐ ☐ ☐

Comments:_____

_____

B.4.2.4   Theme 4: Implementation Support

#	Question	Yes	No	NA	?

1. Does your metrics database include information on specific product metrics (e.g., quality, reliability, maintainability)? ☐ ☐ ☐ ☐

   Comments:_____

   _____

2. Do you share metrics data across software projects? ☐ ☐ ☐ ☐

   Comments:_____

   _____

3. Is the metrics data shared through a common organizational database? ☐ ☐ ☐ ☐

   Comments:_____

   _____

4. Does your organization have a standard length of time that you retain metrics data? ☐ ☐ ☐ ☐

   Comments:_____

   _____

5. Does your organization verify the metrics data maintained in the metrics database? ☐ ☐ ☐ ☐

   Comments:_____

   _____

6. Does your organization manage and maintain the metrics database? ☐ ☐ ☐ ☐

   Comments:_____

   _____

7. Have normal ranges been established for project metrics reported (e.g., the difference between planned and actual schedule commitments)? ☐ ☐ ☐ ☐

   Comments:_____

   _____

B.4.2.5 Theme 5: Metrics Evolution

#	Question	Yes	No	NA	?

1. Do you use product metrics as well as project metrics in making management decisions? ☐ ☐ ☐ ☐

   Comments:_____

   _____

2. Are product metrics as well as project metrics reported during program management reviews (e.g., the number of defects per SLOC)? ☐ ☐ ☐ ☐

   Comments:_____

   _____

3. Do you report metrics to your internal manager? ☐ ☐ ☐ ☐

   Comments:_____

   _____

4. Do you report metrics to your customer? ☐ ☐ ☐ ☐

   Comments:_____

   _____

B.4.2.6 Theme 6: Metrics Support for Management Control

#	Question	Yes	No	NA	?

1. Are product metrics as well as project metrics used as indicators for renegotiating the terms of contract(s) when necessary (e.g., you decide to extend a schedule based on the known number of defects in the product)? ☐ ☐ ☐ ☐

   Comments:_____

   _____

2. Do metric results help isolate technical problems? ☐ ☐ ☐ ☐

   Comments:_____

   _____

3. Are improvements to the metrics process (including metrics standards, procedures, definitions, etc.) based on analysis and lessons learned? ☐ ☐ ☐ ☐

Comments:_____

_____

4. Are measurements used to determine the quality of the software products (i.e., numbers, types, and severity of defects identified)? ☐ ☐ ☐ ☐

   Comments:_____

   _____

5. Do you maintain metrics specifically to help you manage your project? ☐ ☐ ☐ ☐

   Comments:_____

   _____

6. Are management decisions made as a result of metrics reported (e.g., is corrective action taken when actual results deviate significantly from the project's software plans)? ☐ ☐ ☐ ☐

   Comments:_____

   _____

7. Are metrics that are reported to the customer consistent with internally reported metrics? ☐ ☐ ☐ ☐

   Comments:_____

   _____

Appendix B/C: Software Metrics Capability Evaluation Report: Annotated Outline

The goals of the software metrics capability evaluation report are as follows:

a. Report the results of the evaluation. The results have two components:
   1. General results (i.e., metrics capability level and an overview of the organization's metrics-related strengths and weaknesses).
   2. Discussion of the organization's strengths and weaknesses based on each of the six measurement themes identified in Appendix B/A.
b. Discuss recommendations for improvement. These recommendations will be based on the results of the evaluation and may include one or more of several elements, such as:

1. A recommended set of high payback activities that the organization could use to implement metrics capability improvements.
2. Recommendations to implement a metrics improvement program that would be tailored to meet the specific organization's goals based on follow-up consulting and plan preparation. These recommendations would include a brief description of the areas to be covered in the metrics improvement program to help open communication with the organization.
3. Recommendations to implement other management and/or engineering improvement activities that would be tailored to meet the specific organization's objective based on follow-up consulting and plan preparation. These recommendations would include a brief description of the areas to be covered in the program to help open communication with the organization.

Table C-1 is the annotated outline for the software metrics capability evaluation report.

TABLE C-1   Software Metrics Capability Evaluation Results and Recommendations Report: Annotated Outline

1. INTRODUCTION

1.1   Identification

Use the following sentence to identify the evaluation report: "This report provides the results of a software metrics capability evaluation given on (review dates, in mm/dd/yy format) for," then provide the organization's name, office symbol, location, and address. In addition, provide the approximate size of the organization appraised, the names and office symbols for any branches or sections that were represented from within a larger organization, the basic "type" of organization (i.e., acquisition, software development, software maintenance), and the number of individuals interviewed.

1.2   Introduction to the Document

Identify the document's organization and provide a summary of the information contained in each major section.

2. Appraisal Results

2.1   General Results

Give the metrics capability level for the organization, and provide backup for that result.

TABLE C-1 (continued)   Software Metrics Capability Evaluation Results and Recommendations Report: Annotated Outline

2.1.1   General Metrics Strengths

Provide a listing of general areas within the six metrics themes represented in the evaluation where the organization showed strengths, e.g., establishment and general use of a metrics database or general examples of management decision making based on metrics results.

2.1.2   General Metrics Weaknesses

Provide a listing of general areas within the six measurement themes represented in the evaluation where the organization showed weaknesses, e.g., no metrics database or identification of metrics from the Air Force metrics mandate that are not being collected or used.

2.2   Specific Areas for Improvement

2.2.1   Level 2 Areas for Improvement

2.2.1.X   Theme X Areas for Improvement

For each of the six measurement themes, provide a description of the weakness(es) for that theme. Include the following topics in that description:

   a.   Weakness(es)
   b.   Discussion
   c.   Recommended action

2.2.2   Level 3 Areas for Improvement

2.2.2.X   Theme X Areas for Improvement

For each of the six measurement themes, provide a description of the weakness(es) for that theme. Include the following topics in that description:

   a.   Weakness(es)
   b.   Discussion
   c.   Recommended action

3.   RECOMMENDATIONS

Provide any general recommendations that resulted from analyzing the appraisal results, e.g., need to determine general management approach and commitment to change before charting a detailed metrics improvement plan, etc.

TABLE C-1 (continued)   Software Metrics Capability Evaluation Results and Recommendations Report: Annotated Outline

Give the background and rationale for the recommendations, and provide a set of positive steps the organization could take to improve their metrics capabilities. This section should be used as a place to recommend (or propose) possible first steps that the metrics customer and the STSC could explore to determine whether an ongoing relationship would be mutually beneficial. (In the case of metrics capability Level 1 organizations, examples are: to undertake a study of the organization's culture to determine the easy and high payback activities that would give the organization some positive results for minimal effort, to work with the organization's management to determine their commitment to change, etc. Other recommendations could include working with the STSC or another support organization to develop a project plan.)

Appendices

Appendix B/A contains the Measurement Theme and Relationships Table (Table B-1 herein). Also, if necessary, starting with Appendix B/B, provide background information (e.g., the customer profile, etc.) that would be difficult to incorporate in the main body of the report or that would interfere with the readability and understandability of the evaluation results.

Appendix B/D: Organization Information Form

It has been found that the organization's culture often is extremely important in determining how best to work for any type of software process improvement, including establishing a working metrics program. This appendix has been developed to elicit cultural information about the metrics customer that will help STSC develop the project plan and work with the customer for their metrics capability improvement.

Credibility

1. How would you characterize the organization's customer satisfaction?
    ☐ Excellent   ☐ Good   ☐ Fair   ☐ Poor
    Please explain: _____

2. How would you characterize the organization's ability to meet schedule commitments?

   ☐ Excellent ☐ Good ☐ Fair ☐ Poor

   Please explain: _____

3. How would you characterize the organization's ability to meet budget commitments?

   ☐ Excellent ☐ Good ☐ Fair ☐ Poor

   Please explain: _____

4. How would you characterize the organization's product quality?

   ☐ Excellent ☐ Good ☐ Fair ☐ Poor

   Please explain: _____

5. How would you characterize the organization's staff productivity?

   ☐ Excellent ☐ Good ☐ Fair ☐ Poor

   Please explain: _____

6. How would you characterize the organization's staff morale/job satisfaction?

   ☐ Excellent ☐ Good ☐ Fair ☐ Poor

   Please explain: _____

7. How frequently do the development projects have to deal with changes in customer requirements?

   ☐ Weekly or Daily ☐ Monthly ☐ Less Often ☐ Rarely if Ever

   Please explain: _____

Motivation

1. To what extent are there tangible incentives or rewards for successful metrics use?

   ☐ Substantial ☐ Moderate ☐ Some ☐ Little if any ☐ Don't know

   Please explain: _____

2. To what extent do technical staff members feel that metrics get in the way of their real work?

   ☐ Substantial ☐ Moderate ☐ Some ☐ Little if any ☐ Don't know

   Please explain: _____

3. To what extent have managers demonstrated their support for rather than compliance to organizational initiatives or programs?

☐ Substantial   ☐ Moderate   ☐ Some   ☐ Little if any   ☐ Don't know

Please explain: _____

4. To what extent do personnel feel genuinely involved in decision making?

☐ Substantial   ☐ Moderate   ☐ Some   ☐ Little if any   ☐ Don't know

Please explain: _____

5. What does management expect from implementing metrics?

Please explain: _____

Culture/Change History

1. To what extent has the organization used task forces, committees, and special teams to implement projects?

☐ Substantial   ☐ Moderate   ☐ Some   ☐ Little if any   ☐ Don't know

Please explain: _____

2. To what extent does "turf guarding" inhibit the operation of the organization?

☐ Substantial   ☐ Moderate   ☐ Some   ☐ Little if any   ☐ Don't know

Please explain: _____

3. To what extent has the organization been effective in implementing organization initiatives (or improvement programs)?

☐ Substantial   ☐ Moderate   ☐ Some   ☐ Little if any   ☐ Don't know

Please explain: _____

4. To what extent has previous experience led to much discouragement or cynicism about metrics?

☐ Substantial   ☐ Moderate   ☐ Some   ☐ Little if any   ☐ Don't know

Please explain: _____

5. To what extent are lines of authority and responsibility clearly defined?

☐ Substantial   ☐ Moderate   ☐ Some   ☐ Little if any   ☐ Don't know

Please explain: _____

Organization Stability

1. To what extent has there been turnover in key senior management?
    ☐ Substantial ☐ Moderate ☐ Some ☐ Little if any ☐ Don't know
    Please explain: _____

2. To what extent has there been a major reorganization(s) or staff downsizing?
    ☐ Substantial ☐ Moderate ☐ Some ☐ Little if any ☐ Don't know
    Please explain: _____

3. To what extent has there been growth in staff size?
    ☐ Substantial ☐ Moderate ☐ Some ☐ Little if any ☐ Don't know
    Please explain: _____

4. How much turnover has there been among middle management?
    ☐ Substantial ☐ Moderate ☐ Some ☐ Little if any ☐ Don't know
    Please explain: _____

5. How much turnover has there been among the technical staff?
    ☐ Substantial ☐ Moderate ☐ Some ☐ Little if any ☐ Don't know
    Please explain: _____

Organizational Buy-In

1. To what extent are organizational goals clearly stated and well understood?
    ☐ Substantial ☐ Moderate ☐ Some ☐ Little if any ☐ Don't know
    Please explain: _____

2. What level of management participated in the goal setting?
    ☐ Senior ☐ Middle ☐ First Line Mgmt ☐ Don't know
    Please explain: _____

3. What is the level of buy-in to the goals within the organization?
    ☐ Senior Mgmt ☐ Middle Mgmt ☐ First Line Mgmt
    ☐ Individual Contributor ☐ Don't know
    Please explain: _____

4. To what extent does management understand the issues faced by the practitioners?

   ☐ Substantial ☐ Moderate ☐ Some ☐ Little if any ☐ Don't know

   Please explain: _____

5. To what extent have metrics been used for improving processes?

   ☐ Substantial ☐ Moderate ☐ Some ☐ Little if any ☐ Don't know

   Please explain: _____

6. To what extent has there been involvement of the technical staff in metrics?

   ☐ Substantial ☐ Moderate ☐ Some ☐ Little if any ☐ Don't know

   Please explain: _____

7. To what extent do individuals whose work is being measured understand how the metrics are/will be used in the management process?

   ☐ Substantial ☐ Moderate ☐ Some ☐ Little if any ☐ Don't know

   Please explain: _____

Measurement Knowledge/Skills

1. How widespread is metrics knowledge/training?

   ☐ Substantial ☐ Moderate ☐ Some ☐ Little if any ☐ Don't know

   Please explain: _____

2. What type of metrics training have members of the organization participated in?

   ☐ Statistical Process Control ☐ Data Analysis

   ☐ Metrics Application ☐ Basics ☐ Don't know

   Other: _____

Notes

1. Metrics capability maturity (or metrics capability) refers how well an organization uses metrics to help manage and control project performance, product quality, and process implementation and improvement. This concept is discussed in more detail in [DASK90].

2. The assessment method defined in [DASK90] was based on the Software Engineering Institute (SEI) process assessment methodology, which is currently exemplified in the *Capability Maturity Model (CMM) for Software*, Version 1.1 [PAUL93].

3. In the case of the acquirer, this will be the individual responsible for overseeing the software development organization. In the case of a development or maintenance organization, this will be the software project manager.

4. Appendix B/D contains an organization information form the STSC uses to help define cultural issues that need to be addressed in the project plan.

5. Throughout these questionnaires, acquirer refers to an organization that acquires software or systems. Developer refers to an organization that develops or maintains software or systems for an acquirer. (For example, a developer could refer to a non-military organization (e.g., a defense contractor, a university, etc.) that works under the terms of a legal contract; an external Government or Military organization that works under the terms of a Memorandum of Agreement (MOA); or an organic organization tasked with developing or maintaining software under an informal agreement, etc.) Contract refers to an agreement between the acquirer and the contractor, regardless of its actual form (e.g., an MOA).

6. Score only one correct for a yes response to either 1a or 1b. If neither is a yes answer, score only one no.

Appendix C

Traditional IT Metrics Reference

That metrics are an absolute requirement are proven by the following dismal statistics:

- Over half (53 percent) of IT projects overrun their schedules and budgets, 31 percent are cancelled, and only 16 percent are completed on time. [Source: Standish Group, publication date: 2000]
- Of those projects that failed in 2000, 87 percent went more than 50 percent over budget. [Source: KPMG Information Technology, publication date: 2000]
- Forty-five percent of failed projects in 2000 did not produce the expected benefits, and 88 to 92 percent went over schedule. [Source: KPMG Information Technology, publication date: 2000]
- Half of new software projects in the United States will go significantly over budget. [Source: META Group, publication date: 2000]
- The average cost of a development project for a large company is $2,322,000; for a medium company it is $1,331,000; and for a small company, it is $434,000. [Source: Standish Group, publication date: 2000]
- $81 billion was the estimated cost for cancelled projects in 1995. [Source: Standish Group, publication date: 1995]
- Over half (52.7 percent) of projects were projected to cost over 189 percent of their original estimates. [Source: Standish Group, publication date: 2000]

- Eighty-eight percent of all U.S. projects are overschedule, overbudget, or both. [Source: Standish Group, publication date: 2000]
- The average time overrun on projects is 222 percent of original estimates. [Source: Standish Group, publication date: 2000]

Why should we care about productivity and quality? There are several reasons for this. The first and foremost reason is that our customers and end users require a working, quality product. Measuring the process as well as the product tells us whether we have achieved our goal. However, there are other, more subtle reasons why we need to measure productivity and quality:

The development of systems is becoming increasing complex. Unless we measure, we will never know whether or not our efforts have been successful.

On occasion, technology is used just for the sake of using a new technology. This is not an effective use of a technology. Measuring the effectiveness of an implementation assures us that our decision has been cost effective.

We measure productivity and quality to quantify the project's progress as well as to quantify the attributes of the product. A metric enables us to understand and manage the process as well as to measure the impact of change to the process — that is, new methods, training, etc. The use of metrics also enables us to know when we have met our goals — that is, usability, performance, and test coverage.

In measuring software systems we can create metrics based on the different parts of a system — for example, requirements, specifications, code, documentation, tests, and training. For each of these components, we can measure its attributes, which include usability, maintainability, extendibility, size, defect level, performance, and completeness.

While the majority of organizations will use metrics found in books such as this one, it is possible to generate metrics specific to a particular task. Characteristics of metrics dictate that they should be:

1. Collectable
2. Reproducible
3. Pertinent
4. System independent

Typical IT Metrics

Sample product metrics include:

1. *Size:* lines of code, pages of documentation, number and size of test, token count, function count
2. *Complexity:* decision count, variable count, number of modules, size/volume, depth of nesting
3. *Reliability:* count of changes required by phase, count of discovered defects, defect density = number of defects/size, count of changed lines of code

Sample process metrics include:

1. *Complexity:* time to design, code, and test, defect discovery rate by phase, cost to develop, number of external interfaces, defect fix rate
2. *Methods and tool use:* number of tools used and why, project infrastructure tools, tools not used and why
3. *Resource metrics:* years experience with team, years of experience with language, years experience with type of software, MIPS per person, support personnel to engineering personnel ratio, non-project time to project time ratio
4. *Productivity:* percent time to redesign, percent time to redo, variance of schedule, variance of effort

Once the organization determines the slate of metrics to be implemented, it must develop a methodology for reviewing the results of the metrics program. Metrics are useless if they do not result in improved quality or productivity. At a minimum, the organization should:

1. Determine the metric and measuring technique.
2. Measure to understand where you are.
3. Establish worst and best planned cases.
4. Modify the process or product, depending on results of measurement.
5. Remeasure to see what has changed.
6. Reiterate.

Developing an IT Assessment Program

A four-step procedure (Linkman and Walker, 1991) is outlined for establishing targets and means for IT system development assessment. The procedure does not focus on any particular set of metrics; rather, it believes that metrics should be selected on the basis of goals. This procedure is suitable for setting up goals for either the entire project deliverables or for any partial product created in the software life cycle.

1. *Define measurable goals.* The project goals establishment process is similar to the development process for project deliverables. Software projects usually start with abstract problem concepts and the final project deliverables are obtained by continuously partitioning and refining the problem into tangible and manageable pieces. Final quantified goals can be transformed from initial intangible goals by following the same divide-and-conquer method for software deliverables. Three sources of information are helpful in establishing the targets:
   a. Historical data under the assumptions that data are available, development environment is stable, and projects are similar in terms of type, size, and complexity
   b. Synthetic data such as modeling results is useful if models used are calibrated to specific development environment
   c. Expert opinions
2. *Maintain balanced goals.* The measurable goals are usually established on the basis of the following four factors: cost, schedule, effort, and quality. It is feasible to achieve just a single goal but it is always a challenge to deliver a project with the minimum staff and resources, on time, and within budget. It must be kept in mind that trade-offs are always involved and all issues should be addressed to reach a set of balanced goals.
3. *Set up intermediate goals.* A project should never be measured only at its end point. Checkpoints should be set up to provide confidence that the project is running on course. The common practice involves setting up quantifiable targets for each phase, measuring the actual values against the targets, and establishing a plan to make corrections for any deviations. All four aforementioned factors should be broken down into phase or activity for setting up intermediate targets. Measurements for cost and effort can be divided into machine and human resources according to software life-cycle phase so that expenditures can be monitored to ensure that the project is running within budget. The schedule should always be defined in terms of milestones or checkpoints to ensure that intermediate products can be evaluated and the final product will be delivered on time. The quality of intermediate products should always be measured to guarantee that the final deliverable will meet its target goal.
4. *Establish means of assessment.* Two aspects are involved in this activity:
   a. *Data collection.* Based on the project characteristics such as size, complexity, level of control, etc., a decision should be made in terms of whether a manual data collection process or

an automated data collection process should be used. If a nonautomated way is applied, then the availability of the collection medium at the right time should be emphasized.

  b. *Data analysis.* The following two types of analyses should be considered:

  i.   Project analysis consists of checkpoint analysis and continuous analysis (trend analysis), and is concerned with verifying that the intermediate targets are met to ensure that the project is on the right track.

  ii. Component analysis concentrates on the finer level of details of the end product, and is concerned with identifying those components in the product that may require special attention and action. The complete process includes deciding on the set of measures to be analyzed, identifying the components detected as anomalous using measured data, finding out the root cause of the anomalies, and taking actions to make correction.

Traditional Configuration Management Metrics

The following metrics are typically used by those measuring the configuration management (CM) process:

1. Average rate of variance from scheduled time
2. Rate of first-pass approvals
3. Volume of deviation requests by cause
4. The number of scheduled, performed, and completed configuration management audits by each phase of the life cycle
5. The rate of new changes being released and the rate that changes are being verified as completed; history compiled from successive deliveries is used to refine the scope of the expected rate
6. The number of completed versus scheduled (stratified by type and priority) actions
7. Man-hours per project
8. Schedule variances
9. Tests per requirement
10. Change category count
11. Changes by source
12. Cost variances
13. Errors per thousand lines of code (KSLOC)
14. Requirements volatility

IEEE Process for Measurement

Using the IEEE methodology (IEEE, 1989), the measurement process can be described in nine stages. These stages can overlap or occur in different sequences, depending on an organization's needs. Each of these stages in the measurement process influences the production of a delivered product with the potential for high reliability. Other factors influencing the measurement process include the following:

1. A firm management commitment to continually assess product and process maturity, or stability, or both during the project
2. Use of trained personnel in applying measures to the project in a useful way
3. Software support tools
4. A clear understanding of the distinctions among errors, faults, and failures

Product measures include:

1. *Errors, faults, and failures* is the count of defects with respect to human cause, program bugs, and observed system malfunctions.
2. *Mean time to failure or failure rate* is a derivative measure of defect occurrence and time.
3. *Reliability growth and projection* is the assessment of change in failure-freeness of the product under testing or operation.
4. *Remaining product faults* is the assessment of fault-freeness of the product in development, test, or maintenance.
5. *Completeness and consistency* is the assessment of the presence and agreement of all necessary software system parts.
6. *Complexity* is the assessment of complicating factors in a system.

Process measures include:

1. *Management control* measures address the quantity and distribution of error and faults and the trend of cost necessary for defect removal.
2. *Coverage measures* allow one to monitor the ability of developers and managers to guarantee the required completeness in all the activities of the life cycle and support the definition of corrective actions.
3. *Risk, benefit, cost evaluation measures* support delivery decisions based both on technical and cost criteria.
4. *Risk* can be assessed based on residual faults present in the product at delivery and the cost with the resulting support activity.

The nine stages are described below.

Stage 1: Plan Organizational Strategy

Initiate a planning process. Form a planning group and review reliability constraints and objectives, giving consideration to user needs and requirements. Identify the reliability characteristics of a software product necessary to achieve these objectives. Establish a strategy for measuring and managing software reliability. Document practices for conducting measurements.

Stage 2: Determine Software Reliability Goals

Define the reliability goals for the software being developed in order to optimize reliability in light of realistic assessments of project constraints, including size scope, cost, and schedule.

Review the requirements for the specific development effort to determine the desired characteristics of the delivered software. For each characteristic, identify specific reliability goals that can be demonstrated by the software or measured against a particular value or condition. Establish an acceptable range of values. Give consideration to user needs and requirements.

Establish intermediate reliability goals at various points in the development effort.

Stage 3: Implement Measurement Process

Establish a software reliability measurement process that best fits an organization's needs. Review the rest of the process and select those stages that best lead to optimum reliability. Add to or enhance these stages as needed. Consider the following suggestions:

1. Select appropriate data collection and measurement practices designed to optimize software reliability.
2. Document the measures required, the intermediate and final milestones when measurements are taken, the data collection requirements, and the acceptable values for each measure.
3. Assign responsibilities for performing and monitoring measurements, and provide the necessary support for these activities from across the internal organization.
4. Initiate a measure selection and evaluation process.
5. Prepare educational material for training personnel in concepts, principles, and practices of software reliability and reliability measures.

Stage 4: Select Potential Measures

Identify potential measures that would be helpful in achieving the reliability goals established in Stage 2.

Stage 5: Prepare Data Collection and Measurement Plan

Prepare a data collection and measurement plan for the development and support effort. For each potential measure, determine the primitives needed to perform the measurement. Data should be organized so that information related to events during the development effort can be properly recorded in a database and retained for historical purposes.

For each intermediate reliability goal identified in Stage 2, identify the measures needed to achieve this goal. Identify the points during development when the measurements are to be taken. Establish acceptable values or a range of values to assess whether the intermediate reliability goals are achieved.

Include in the plan an approach for monitoring the measurement effort itself. The responsibility for collecting and reporting data, verifying its accuracy, computing measures, and interpreting the results should be described.

Stage 6: Monitor the Measurements

Monitor measurements. Once the data collection and reporting begins, monitor the measurements and the progress made during development, so as to manage the reliability and thereby achieve the goals for the delivered product. The measurements assist in determining whether the intermediate reliability goals are achieved and whether the final goal is achievable. Analyze the measure and determine if the results are sufficient to satisfy the reliability goals. Decide whether a measured result assists in affirming the reliability of the product or process being measured. Take corrective action.

Stage 7: Assess Reliability

Analyze measurements to ensure that the reliability of the delivered software satisfies the reliability objectives and that the reliability as measured is acceptable.

Identify assessment steps that are consistent with the reliability objectives documented in the data collection and measurement plan. Check the consistency of acceptance criteria and the sufficiency of tests to satisfactorily demonstrate that the reliability objectives have been achieved.

Identify the organization responsible for determining final acceptance of the reliability of the software. Document the steps in assessing the reliability of the software.

Stage 8: Use Software

Assess the effectiveness of the measurement effort and perform necessary corrective action. Conduct a follow-up analysis of the measurement effort to evaluate reliability assessment and development practices, record lessons learned, and evaluate user satisfaction with the software's reliability.

Stage 9: Retain Software Measurement Data

Retain measurement data on the software throughout the development and operation phases for use in future projects. This data provides a baseline for reliability improvement and an opportunity to compare the same measures across completed projects. This information can assist in developing future guidelines and standards.

Metrics as a Component of the Process Maturity Framework

Pfleeger (1990) has suggested a set of metrics for which data can be collected and analyzed for the improvement of software engineering productivity. This set of metrics is based on a process maturity framework developed at the Software Engineering Institute (SEI) at Carnegie Mellon University. The SEI framework divides organizations into five levels based on how mature (i.e., organized, professional, aligned to software tenets) the organization is. The five levels range from initial, or ad hoc, to an optimizing environment. Pfleeger recommends that metrics be divided into five levels as well. Each level is based on the amount of information made available to the development process. As the development process matures and improves, additional metrics can be collected and analyzed.

Level 1: Initial Process

This level is characterized by an ad hoc approach to software development. Inputs to the process are not well defined but the outputs are as expected. Preliminary baseline project metrics should be gathered at this level to form a basis for comparison as improvements are made and maturity increases. This can be accomplished by comparing new project measurements with the baseline ones.

Level 2: Repeatable Process

At this level, the process is repeatable in much the same way that a subroutine is repeatable. The requirements act as input, the code as output, and constraints are such things as budget and schedule. Although proper inputs produce proper outputs, there is no means to discern easily how the outputs are actually produced. Only project-related metrics make sense at this level because the activities within the actual transitions from input to output are not available for measurement. Measures at this level can include:

1. Amount of effort needed to develop the system
2. Overall project cost
3. Software size: non-commented lines of code, function points, object and method count
4. Personnel effort: actual person-months of effort, report
5. Person-months of effort
6. Requirements volatility: requirements changes

Level 3: Defined Process

At this level, the activities of the process are clearly defined. This additional structured means that the input to and output from each well-defined functional activity can be examined, which permits a measurement of the intermediate products. Measures include:

1. *Requirements complexity:* number of distinct objects and actions addressed in requirements
2. *Design complexity:* number of design modules, cyclomatic complexity, McCabe design complexity
3. *Code complexity:* number of code modules, cyclomatic complexity
4. *Test complexity:* number of paths to test, of object-oriented development, then number of object interfaces to test
5. *Quality metrics:* defects discovered, defects discovered per unit size (defect density), requirements faults discovered, design faults discovered, fault density for each product
6. Pages of documentation

Level 4: Managed Process

At this level, feedback from early project activities are used to set priorities for later project activities. At this level, activities are readily compared and contrasted; the effects of changes in one activity can be tracked in the others. At this level, measurements can be made across activities and are used to control and stabilize the process so that productivity and quality can match expectations. The following types of data are recommended to be collected. Metrics at this stage, although derived from the following data, are tailored to the individual organization.

1. *Process type:* What process model is used and how is it correlating to positive or negative consequences?
2. *Amount of producer reuse:* How much of the system is designed for reuse? This includes reuse of requirements, design modules, test plans, and code.
3. *Amount of consumer reuse:* How much does the project reuse components from other projects? This includes reuse of requirements, design modules, test plans, and code. (By reusing tested, proven components, effort can be minimized and quality can be improved.)
4. *Defect identification:* How and when are defects discovered? Knowing this will indicate whether those process activities are effective.
5. *Use of defect density model for testing:* To what extent does the number of defects determine when testing is complete? This controls and focuses testing as well as increases the quality of the final product.
6. *Use of configuration management:* Is a configuration management scheme imposed on the development process? This permits traceability, which can be used to assess the impact of alterations.
7. *Module completion over time:* At what rates are modules being completed? This reflects the degree to which the process and development environment facilitate implementation and testing.

Level 5: Optimizing Process

At this level, measures from activities are used to change and improve the process. This process change can affect the organization and the project as well. Studies by the SEI report that 85 percent of organizations are at Level 1, 14 percent are at Level 2, and 1 percent is at Level 3. None of the firms surveyed had reached Levels 4 or 5. Therefore, the authors have not recommended a set of metrics for Level 5.

Steps to Take in Using Metrics

1. Assess the process: determine the level of process maturity.
2. Determine the appropriate metrics to collect.

3. Recommend metrics, tools, and techniques.
4. Estimate project cost and schedule.
5. Collect appropriate level of metrics.
6. Construct project database of metrics data, which can be used for analysis and to track value of metrics over time.
7. Cost and schedule evaluation: when the project is complete, evaluate the initial estimates of cost and schedule for accuracy. Determine which of the factors may account for discrepancies between predicted and actual values.
8. Form a basis for future estimates.

Standard Software Engineering Metrics

Software engineering practitioners utilize defined measures as indicators of reliability. By emphasizing early reliability assessment, this standard supports methods through measurement to improve product reliability.

This section presents the most popular of these metrics.

1. Fault Density

This measure can be used to predict remaining faults by comparison with expected fault density, determine if sufficient testing has been completed, and establish standard fault densities for comparison and prediction.

$$F_d = F/KSLOC$$

where:

F = total number of unique faults found in a given interval resulting in failures of a specified severity level

$KSLOC$ = number of source lines of executable code and nonexecutable data declarations in thousands

2. Defect Density

This measure can be used after design and code inspections of new development or large block modifications. If the defect density is outside the norm after several inspections, it is an indication of a problem.

$$DD = \frac{\sum_{i=1}^{I} D_i}{KSLOD}$$

where:

D_i = total number of unique defects detected during the ith design or code inspection process

I = total number of inspections

KSLOD = in the design phase, this is the number of source lines of executable code and nonexecutable data declarations, in thousands

3. Cumulative Failure Profile

This is a graphical method used to predict reliability, estimate additional testing time to reach an acceptable reliable system, and identify modules and subsystems that require additional testing. A plot is drawn of cumulative failures versus a suitable time base.

4. Fault-Days Number

This measure represents the number of days that faults spend in the system from their creation to their removal. For each fault detected and removed, during any phase, the number of days from its creation to its removal is determined (fault-days). The fault-days are then summed for all faults detected and removed, to get the fault-days number at system level, including all faults detected and removed up to the delivery date. In those cases where the creation date of the fault is not known, the fault is assumed to have been created in the middle of the phase in which it was introduced.

5. Functional or Modular Test Coverage

This measure is used to quantify a software test coverage index for a software delivery. From the system's functional requirements, a cross-referenced listing of associated modules must first be created.

$$\frac{\text{Functional (Modular) Test}}{\text{Coverage Index}} = \frac{\text{FE}}{\text{FT}}$$

where:

FE = number of the software functional (modular) requirements for which all test cases have been satisfactorily completed

FT = total number of software functional (modular) requirements

6. Requirements Traceability

This measure aids in identifying requirements that are either missing from, or in addition to, the original requirements.

$$TM = \frac{R1}{R2} \times 100\%$$

where:

$R1$ = number of requirements met by the architecture
$R2$ = number of original requirements

7. Software maturity index

This measure is used to quantify the readiness of a software product. Changes from previous baselines to current baselines are an indication of the current product stability.

$$SMI = \frac{M_T - (F_a + F_c + F_{del})}{M_T}$$

where:

SMI = Software Maturity Index
MT = number of software functions (modules) in the current delivery
F_a = number of software functions (modules) in the current delivery that are additions to the previous delivery
F_c = number of software functions (modules) in the current delivery that include internal changes from a previous delivery
F_{del} = number of software functions (modules) in the previous delivery that are deleted in the current delivery

The Software Maturity Index (SMI) can be *estimated* as:

$$SMI = \frac{M_T - F_c}{M_T}$$

8. Number of Conflicting Requirements

This measure is used to determine the reliability of a software system resulting from the software architecture under consideration, as represented by a specification based on the entity-relationship-attribute model. What is required is a list of the system's inputs, outputs, and the functions performed by each program. The mappings from the software architecture to the requirements are identified. Mappings from the same specification item to more than one differing requirement are examined for requirements inconsistency. Additionally, mappings from more than one specification item to a single requirement are examined for specification inconsistency.

9. Cyclomatic Complexity

This measure is used to determine the structured complexity of a coded module. The use of this measure is designed to limit the complexity of the module, thereby promoting understandability of the module.

$$C = E - N + 1$$

where:

C = complexity
N = number of nodes (sequential groups of program statements)
E = number of edges (program flows between nodes)

10. Design Structure

This measure is used to determine the simplicity of the detailed design of a software program. The values determined can be used to identify problem areas within the software design.

$$DSM = \frac{6}{i=1} W_i D_i$$

where:

DSM = Design Structure Measure
P1 = total number of modules in program
P2 = number of modules dependent on input or output
P3 = number of modules dependent on prior processing (state)
P4 = number of database elements
P5 = number of nonunique database elements
P6 = number of database segments
P7 = number of modules not single entrance/single exit

The design structure is the weighted sum of six derivatives determined by using the primitives given above.

D1 = designed organized top-down
D2 = module dependence (P2/P1)
D3 = module dependent on prior processing (P3/P1)
D4 = database size (P5/P4)
D5 = database compartmentalization (P6/P4)
D6 = module single entrance/exit (P7/P1)

The weights (Wi) are assigned by the user based on the priority of each associated derivative. Each Wi has a value between 0 and 1.

11. Test Coverage

This is a measure of the completeness of the testing process from both a developer and user perspective. The measure relates directly to the development, integration, and operational test stages of product development.

$$TC(\%) = \frac{(\text{implemented capabilities})}{(\text{required capabilities})} \times \frac{(\text{program primitives tested})}{(\text{total program primitives})} \times 100\%$$

where:
   Program functional primitives = either modules, segments, statements, branches, or paths
   Data functional primitives = classes of data requirement primitives are test cases or functional capabilities

12. Data or Information Flow Complexity

This is a structural complexity or procedural complexity measure that can be used to evaluate the information flow structure of large-scale systems, the procedure and module information flow structure, the complexity of the interconnections between modules, and the degree of simplicity of relationships between subsystems, and to correlate total observed failures and software reliability with data complexity.

$$\text{Weighted IFC} = \text{Length} \times (\text{Fanin} \times \text{Fanout})^2$$

where:
      IFC = Information Flow Complexity
   Fanin = local flows into a procedure + number of data structures from which the procedure retrieves data
   Fanout = local flows from a procedure + number of data structures that the procedure updates
   Length = number of source statements in a procedure (excluding comments)

The flow of information between modules or subsystems must be determined either through the use of automated techniques or charting mechanisms. A local flow from module A to B exists if one of the following occurs:

1. A calls B.
2. B calls A and A returns a value to B that is passed by B.
3. Both A and B are called by another module that passes a value from A to B.

13. Mean Time to Failure

This measure is the basic parameter required by most software reliability models. Detailed record keeping of failure occurrences that accurately track time (calendar or execution) at which the faults manifest themselves is essential.

14. Software Documentation and Source Listings

The objective of this measure is to collect information to identify the parts of the software maintenance products that may be inadequate for use in a software maintenance environment. Questionnaires are used to examine the format and content of the documentation and source code attributes from a maintainability perspective.

The questionnaires examine the following product characteristics:

1. Modularity
2. Descriptiveness
3. Consistency
4. Simplicity
5. Expandability
6. Testability

Two questionnaires — the Software Documentation Questionnaire and the Software Source Listing Questionnaire — are used to evaluate the software products in a desk audit.

For the software documentation evaluation, the resource documents should include those that contain the program design specifications, program testing information and procedures, program maintenance information, and guidelines used in preparation of the documentation. Typical questions from the questionnaire include:

1. The documentation indicates that data storage locations are not used for more than one type of data structure.
2. Parameter inputs and outputs for each module are explained in the documentation.
3. Programming conventions for I/O processing have been established and followed.
4. The documentation indicates that the resource (storage, timing, tape drives, disks, etc.) allocation is fixed throughout program execution.
5. The documentation indicates that there is a reasonable time margin for each major time-critical program function.
6. The documentation indicates that the program has been designed to accommodate software test probes to aid in identifying processing performance.

The software source listings evaluation reviews either high-order language or assembler source code. Multiple evaluations using the questionnaire are conducted for the unit level of the program (module). The modules selected should represent a sample size of at least 10 percent of the total source code. Typical questions include:

1. Each function of this module is an easily recognizable block of code.
2. The quantity of comments does not detract from the legibility of the source listings.
3. Mathematical models as described or derived in the documentation correspond to the mathematical equations used in the source listing.
4. Esoteric (clever) programming is avoided in this module.
5. The size of any data structure that affects the processing logic of this module is parameterized.
6. Intermediate results within this module can be selectively collected for display without code modification.

IT Developer's List of Metrics

McCabe's Complexity Metric (1976)

McCabe's proposal for a cyclomatic complexity number was the first attempt to objectively quantify the "flow of control" complexity of software. This metric is computed by decomposing the program into a directed graph that represents its flow of control. The cyclomatic complexity number is then calculated using the following formula:

$$V(g) = Edges - Nodes + 2$$

In its shortened form, the cyclomatic complexity number is a count of decision points within a program with a single entry and a single exit plus one.

Halstead Effort Metric (1976)

In the 1970s, Maurice Halstead developed a theory regarding the behavior of software. Some of his findings evolved into software metrics. One of these is referred to as "Effort" or just "E," and is a well-known complexity metric.

The Effort measure is calculated as:

$$E = Volume/Level$$

where Volume is a measure of the size of a piece of code and Level is a measure of how "abstract" the program is. The level of abstracting varies from almost zero (0) for programs with low abstraction to almost one (1) for programs that are highly abstract.

References

Halstead, M. (1977). *Elements of Software Science.* New York: Elsevier.

McCabe, T. (1976, December). A Complexity Measure. *IEEE Transactions on Software Engineering*, pp. 308–320.

Pfleeger, S.L. and C. McGowan. (1990). Software Metrics in the Process Maturity Framework. *Journal of Systems Software,* Vol. 12, pp. 255–261.

Appendix D

---

eBay Balanced Scorecard Analysis

My MBA students at the University of Phoenix did a thorough analysis of eBay from a balanced scorecard perspective. Their goal was to do a thorough literature search concerning eBay, assess the eBay "experience," and then debate eBay's pros and cons. With their permission, their analysis is reproduced here in its entirety. The authors of this study include Sue Allan, Wayne Botha, Michael Lewitz, Krista Lilley, and Chris Yanko.

The eBay Debate

One of the most visible icons of the ever-evolving E-business revolution is eBay, the online auction pioneer. Almost single-handedly, it has transformed the Internet from a research tool into a vibrant marketplace for buyers and sellers exchanging all types of merchandise. For the first time in history, it is possible for individual buyers and sellers to reach a global market for their offerings. The original business model endures after several years of maturity, and eBay continues to grow exponentially. The question is: how well is eBay really doing in terms of fulfilling its promise, both from a business perspective and from the public's?

This chapter presents a balanced scorecard approach to analysis of this question, where key areas of relevant measurement are identified and quantified. A pro and con format is used to debate the fulfillment of each particular measurement as identified in the balanced scorecard, which follows in the appendix.

eBay and the Balanced Scorecard

The balanced scorecard is an analytical tool for use in setting goals, setting priorities, and aligning a business' strategy by defining the metrics that will be used for evaluation. It is here within the scorecard that we define that which is really important to our success. The benchmark it provides, in such key areas of the business as Finance, Accounting, Sales, Customer Service, and others, serves as the basis for our ongoing continuous improvement plan (CI) for the future. Incremental improvements can always be qualified through the scorecard to determine real progress in those areas that are formally identified with the company's success.

This appendix presents a balanced scorecard, broken down into four key areas, which have been previously identified as critical to eBay as it moves forward with its online auction model. To highlight the thought process that led to the scorecard, this writing takes an interesting pro and con approach to each item. We proceed through the items in the same order in which they are presented in the scorecard included in Appendix D/A:

- ■ Financial
- ■ External/customer
- ■ Internal business processes
- ■ Learning and growth

For each category, we identify two objectives and two measurements, which we will use to evaluate progress. For each category we also identify the target output we wish to achieve, and finally, we suggest ways to initiate the action.

Financial

Objective	Measurement	Target	Initiative
Increase shareholder wealth	Gross profits	50% per year	Aggressive marketing to attract new small business sellers to eBay
Grow revenues from international markets	Growth from international transaction revenues	35% growth per quarter	Offer promotions to customers in foreign countries to shop at eBay

Objective 1: Increase Shareholder Wealth

Pro

eBay has become a tremendous force, with some likening it to an economy in and of itself. More success indicators include the fact that this year alone, more than 30 million people will buy and sell over $20 billion in merchandise. Over 150,000 entrepreneurs earn a full-time living by buying and selling goods on eBay (Hof, 2003, p. 1). eBay shows strong financial progress toward stated objective 1, having achieved the following financial milestones:

- eBay's management is credited for eBay's profits increasing by 176 percent last year.
- Shares rose 47 percent from the beginning of the year 2003.
- Larger players are entering the eBay marketplace, such as Sears and Disney.
- eBay will easily exceed a forecast from two years ago of $3 billion in net revenues by 2005 (Hof, 2003, p. 1).

Pro

Consider these numbers: there are nearly 95 million eBay users who spend $894 per second! Most eBay sellers are individuals and small businesses that sell everything from porcelain dolls to DVD players to Mercedes convertibles. Every day, more than two million new items are added to the eBay marketplace, more than ten million bids are placed, and more than 100,000 new people register to buy and sell on eBay.

At any given moment, eBay is conducting some 19 million auctions, divided into more than 45,000 different categories. About two million new items are offered for sale every day. One company is grossing more than $5 million per year selling brand-new pool tables on eBay. Their eBay store is so profitable that they have closed their retail location and now sell solely online. That is right, they are making $5 million by selling pool tables — proof that you can sell just about anything on eBay if you know how to do it.

Con

The financial success that eBay has had is unquestionable, and it is difficult to debate that. However, it would be remiss to point out that some concern lies with the speed with which it has happened. eBay will likely run into some managerial issues while trying to meet the needs of its smallest players with the new entries into the market that are large corporations

(Hof, 2003). Disney and Sears and Roebuck are examples of new, large players in the eBay market.

There is also concern over the dramatic rise in share prices. It is possible that this fast and wild growth trend has caused shares to become overvalued. A value adjustment may be around the corner. "The company is not just a wildly successful start-up. It has invented a whole new business world." (Hof, 2003, p. 1)

Con

With the expectations for revenue and profit, eBay has set a standard for dot.com companies that will be difficult to beat. The glowing accolades of financial success have come back to bite eBay in the stock price. While eBay has continued to turn a healthy profit, the stockholders are now accustomed to rates of return and growth that may no longer be sustained. As a result, the Q4 numbers for 2003 have been released and even though the return was positive, it was under the expectations posted earlier in the year by the company and analysts alike.

With the continued push to grow the business and remain the market leader in online auctions, both domestic and international, it might be wiser for eBay to retain a larger portion of its earnings in order to build a more robust server farm. The cost of this undertaking would be significant, but the long-run return is stronger than the short-term boost to the profit numbers in regard to customer satisfaction and stockholder expectations (Baertlein, 2003, p. 1).

Pro

In June 2003, eBay totally changed its technology to a Sun J2EE platform for all its servers. It has invested in new hardware, and holding back returns now in order to save for later does not seem to make sense. eBay has $1.3 billion in cash. That is $200 million more than it had a year ago!

In terms of setting a standard that other companies will find difficult to measure up against, this might not hold water either. Investors will self-correct the stock price at some point if it is inflated. The same argument could be made for Berkshire-Hathaway, which has sustained high returns and growth under Warren Buffet.

Objective 2: Grow Revenues from International Markets

Pro

eBay is on track to meet its targets for growth in the International market. Its preliminary estimates for 2003 year-end show a 36 percent growth in international transaction revenues relative to the previous quarter and 96 percent growth versus the same quarter one year earlier. International advertising revenue also represents almost 14 percent of total advertising revenues (eBay Press Release, 2004, p. 12). Overall international net revenue represents 38 percent of total revenue, which is a 97 percent increase on a quarter-to-quarter comparison versus last year.

eBay has recently invested in Korean and German endeavors to grow international business. The United Kingdom and Germany represent eBay's top two international sites, based on revenue. As of June 30, 2003, it has 800 employees based outside the United States, and currently has job positions available in Austria, Belgium, China, France, Germany, Italy, the Netherlands, Spain, Switzerland, and the United Kingdom. eBay's own mission statement, "to provide a global trading platform where practically anyone can trade practically anything," targets global business (eBay Press Release, 2004). In a September 2003 interview with eBay CEO Meg Whitman, she explains that eBay is the number-one online auction trading space in every country but Japan, where Yahoo! auctions dominates (Gardner and Gardner, 2003). She goes on to explain that they foresee international revenues surpassing U.S. domestic revenues in the future. Based on these facts and the CEO's outlook, international growth is not only on track, but may exceed our scorecard targets.

Con

To get a toehold in Korea, the world's sixth largest auction market, eBay shelled out $120 million to buy the national market leader. The Korean foray has been troublesome for eBay as well — in documents filed with the Securities and Exchange Commission in March, eBay disclosed that Korean credit card companies providing payment services to Internet Auction, eBay's Korean subsidiary, had "experienced higher-than-anticipated delinquency rates on transactions carried out on (its) platform." As a result, the credit card companies had withheld $2.6 million as "collateral" against certain auction accounts and threatened to terminate their agreements with Internet Auction (Knowledge@Wharton, 2002, p. 1).

eBay also had to withdraw from Japan, where it lost to Yahoo! In an interview with *Business Week,* Meg Whitman provided insight into this venture:

Q: What about Japan? What went wrong there?

A: {Meg}We didn't have the first-mover advantage in Japan. Yahoo Japan launched its auction product six to eight months before us. It was able to leverage its incredibly strong position with its portal. With 20/20 hindsight, I don't think we executed as well as we might have. In terms of the management team and support to them in the U.S., we were a much less experienced company in early 2000 than we are today. Probably the biggest factor is that we were late to the market.

—Harbrecht, 2002, p. 1

This information indicates that eBay is facing challenges in some international markets, and is not doing very well on the scorecard.

Con

eBay's recent decision (eBay Investor Relations, 2004) to purchase mobile.de, the German classified ad marketplace for vehicles, appears on the surface to work toward the goal of increasing overseas revenue. However, at a purchase price of $152 million (U.S.), the price is too high. eBay already runs a successful eBay Germany, with current International net revenues of $212 million in the fourth quarter of 2003. This was a significant increase from the third quarter of 2003, which was $156 million.

eBay's international growth is already on a fast track without the additional investment; $152 million represents approximately 25 percent of international annual revenues — a pretty high price to pay, particularly given that it is estimated to have a "nominal impact on 2004 net revenues."

While the purchase of mobile.de does bring in approximately 0.8 million listings and 22 million visitors, additional monies will be needed to transition those ads and visitors over to the eBay brand and to consolidate mobile.de's Hamburg facility. eBay Germany was already one of the top two International eBay sites (along with eBay U.K.) according to an October 29, 2003 press release. eBay's focus on expansion should have been on other geographic areas with more growth potential.

Conclusion: Objectives 1 and 2:

Score

Objective	Did Not Meet Goal	Met Goal	Exceeded Goal
1			Profits increased by 176% last year
2			Increased growth by 36% in international transaction revenues over previous quarter

External/Customer

Customer Satisfaction/Customer Service

Objective	Measurement	Target	Initiative
Achieve high levels of customer loyalty	Ranking in SatMetrix: Best Customer Satisfaction Award	Ranked in the top 10% of participating companies	Provide excellent customer service
Mitigate effects of disputes on customer satisfaction	Length of time taken to resolve disputes	Resolve all disputes within four hours	Implement method for customer to interact with eBay in real-time

Objective 1: Achieve High Levels of Customer Loyalty

Pro

In the same way car manufacturers rely on the J.D. Powers and Associates survey to rank how well customers like their Toyota or Honda, some retailers look forward to customer satisfaction surveys from online companies like Mountain View-based SatMetrix to gauge consumer loyalty.

> The latest ranking released Tuesday found that some Internet firms have achieved the same high customer satisfaction levels as brick and mortar companies. Case in point: Online auction giant eBay (Nasdaq: EBAY) and Amazon.com (Nasdaq: AMZN) are joint winners of the SatMetrix Best Customer Satisfaction award for the Internet category. The two were in a "dead-heat" with virtually identical high customer loyalty index scores.

—Singer, 2001, p. 1

Pro

There are several positive aspects to eBay's customer service. First of all, eBay is accessible 24 hours a day. This is a tremendous convenience to buyers and sellers throughout the world who live and work in differing time zones.

One of the tremendous sources of good customer service is in the buyer/seller rating system that has been developed. This feedback system allows buyers and sellers to rate each other on how transactions are handled. Buyers and sellers work hard to gain positive reputations. A seller that has a positive customer rating will perform better in the eBay marketplace. The users who build these reputations set the standard for customer service.

eBay takes a proactive approach to customer service by actively listening to its users. eBay has developed a program called Voice of the Customer. As a part of this program, as many as a dozen buyers and sellers are brought in to communicate how they work and identify what else eBay can do for them. eBay also holds teleconferences at least two times per week to poll users on new features and policies (Hof, 2003, p. 1).

Objective 2: Mitigate Effects of Disputes on Customer Satisfaction

Pro

Since the implementation of eBay's live chat service capabilities with Customer Service, the number of customer resolutions has begun to show signs of improvement. In 2002, eBay joined forces with LivePerson, Inc., in an effort to improve the service level agreement of having all inquiries resolved within four hours. eBay now can support an instant messenger-like program where customers can write to the customer service center in a real-time fashion and work toward issue resolutions quickly and efficiently.

In addition, LivePerson's technology will provide greater support to sellers in an effort to market special promotions in conjunction with eBay. Programs such as free shipping, reduced commission, and add-on sales will foster greater registered user activity as well an increase the current 46 million users to even higher numbers (LivePerson, Inc., 2002, p. 1).

Con

However, not all users are as satisfied. One user posted a scathing letter on Complaints.com (read the letter in its entirety in Appendix D/B). Basically, it reveals a darker side of the customer satisfaction equation, detailing what can happen if you get lost within the customer service hierarchy. It can be difficult to find a real person to address your concerns.

Con

Another problem with auctions is sniping. Sniping is when a buyer slips in at the final minutes of an auction with only a slightly higher bid to win the auction. One customer trying to buy photo equipment experienced this. He discovered that the "sniper" had done this on more than 25 different auctions and then never followed through on payment for any of them. Although the buyer had several poor ratings, eBay allowed him to continue this practice and the sellers were not aware!

According to one user:

> The main problem with eBay is its own ultra-liberal policy toward deadbeats and mischief-makers. It took me two months and numerous e-mails to get one buyer's membership suspended after he was the high bidder on 25 different photography-related auctions (mine was one of them) — and failed to pay on any of them. His technique was to bid in the final seconds of the auction with a bid high enough to top the existing top bid by the minimum. It was only after the auction closed that the seller discovered all the negative feedback for "the winning bidder." There they were, over a period of months, for all to see, yet eBay hadn't pulled his membership. Although eBay eventually refunded all commission fees to those who went through the convoluted application process, we all lost about a month's time in re-listing the item for sale once again.

—Gormly, 2001, p. 1

Sniping is a behavior that has obtained its own market. There are now tools that enable users to snipe auctions. One of these tools can be found at www.bidnapper.com. This product is specifically designed to allow users to win auctions without allowing time for other bidders to respond.

Conclusion: Objectives 1 and 2:

Score

Objective	Did Not Meet Goal	Met Goal	Exceeded Goal
1			Profits increased by 176% last year
2			Increased growth by 36% in international transaction revenues over previous quarter

Internal Business Process

Technology Offerings

Objective	Measurement	Target	Initiative
Keep Web site accessible at all times	Amount of time that customer cannot access Web site	Less than 3 minutes delay in accessing site	Implement redundant hardware for real-time failover
Provide easy-to-use buying and selling interfaces	Level of technology skills required to buy and sell	Minimal levels of skill required	Make processes easy to use Offer online and offline training courses to buyers and sellers

Objective1: Keep Web Site Accessible at All Times

Con

Because the eBay economy is completely driven by technology, downtime can cost eBay and its customers millions of dollars. With gross revenue of over $20 billion last year, that equates to $ 2,283,105 per hour — or $38,051 per minute. Any amount of downtime can be a significant loss.

In January 2001, eBay was down for 11 hours when its primary and backup systems failed. The systems failed because the company made a decision to delay replacing some of its hardware during the holiday season. eBay's connectivity was interment for a four-hour time period again in June 2001. Another outage of 90 minutes occurred in March 2002 (Wolverton, 2002, p. 1).

Most recently, a power outage in August 2003 in California caused eBay services to be inaccessible for nearly three hours. Although the power outage only lasted 10 minutes, eBay technicians were forced to shut down and reboot their local systems, causing them to be unavailable.

Pro

eBay's availability is continually improving. eBay is learning from the technical failures that have occurred.

The company has strengthened its back-end systems to prevent lengthy outages. eBay is also in the process of upgrading its

Web hosting functions by spreading its facilities across multiple geographic regions.

—Hu, 2003, p. 1

Pro

The technology skills required to buy and sell on eBay are minimal. The skills required are Web navigation, e-mail, and digital photography or scanning and file attachment. Because few skills are needed, the benefits of eBay are open to most households. The search utility allows buyers to pull up hundreds of potential products at the same time.

The acquisition of PayPal (www.paypal.com) helps level the playing field for individual sellers. PayPal provides a tool for sellers to collect payment for goods. Many sellers cannot afford the expense of becoming credit card merchants. The availability of PayPal allows the individual user the freedom to collect payment without great expense.

Con

The search utility allows buyers to pull up hundreds of potential products at the same time (this is a pro and a con). With so many sellers providing similar products or even different products with the same keyword, it can be overwhelming to wade through the hundreds of hits for each search. It may take several searches to narrow down the returns; and then, by narrowing down the product list, the potential is there to exclude something you wanted to see.

This can also be difficult for the seller. If there are 500 Mickey Mouse stuffed toys for sale, how can I make my ad stand out? We have also seen the rating profiles that are generated for sellers. If I am a new seller with no selling history, it may be difficult to get buyers to bid on my product.

Pro

eBay provides online learning courses for both buyers and sellers. Buyers can learn how to bid and buy, perform successful searches, pay for items, and track progress with My eBay. Sellers can learn how to sell, accept online payments, and track sales with My eBay. Advanced Selling shows sellers various tools, how to open an eBay store, and how to become a trading assistant. Classroom instruction is also available through eBay University in various cities throughout the United States.

Conclusion: Objectives 1 and 2:

Score

Objective	Did Not Meet Goal	Met Goal	Exceeded Goal
1	January 2001: eBay was down for 10 hours Intermittent response in June 2001 for 4 hours 90-minute outage in March 2002		
2		Yes, minimal skills are required Online training and offline training courses are available in major cities	

Growth

Retail customers

Objective	Measurement	Target	Initiative
Expand and capture foreign markets	Successfully lead the industry in targeted countries	Become top auction site in Japan and Korea	Purchase existing auction sites in Japan and Korea
Increase variety of items for sale	Number of new items added each day to the marketplace	2 million per day	Provide incentives to list new items

Objective 1: Expand and Capture Foreign Markets

Pro

Expand and capture foreign markets. eBay needs to expand to foreign markets to stabilize revenues through diversification. The majority of the business is based on the U.S. and European divisions. eBay needs to establish a stable presence in the Middle East and Asia to provide stability should the U.S. and European economies suffer any setbacks.

eBay can enter into these markets easily, and at fairly low cost initially. The eBay brand is known worldwide, and the proprietary software can be installed on any new servers in a matter of days. In addition, the Web site uses a "template" technology that allows for easy translation of sites to local languages. If eBay is going to succeed in providing a marketplace for anyone to sell anything, then strategic initiatives for eBay must include expansion to foreign markets.

Con

One of the downsides to performing business transactions with users across the world is fraud. Reports of fraud on auction sites continue to increase. These reports have risen sharply although eBay continues to hire more virtual cops. Because eBay still accounts for about 80 percent of the online auction market, much of this fraud is on eBay (Hof, 2003, p. 1).

Objective 2: Increase Variety of Items for Sale

Pro

eBay is completely committed to growing sales via retail customers. Several new enhancements are specifically targeting the retailer in order to make the selling process easier. In an effort to draw in new retailers, eBay recently ran a three-day "free" listing day for store sellers allowing them to place items for sale at no cost (eBay GAB, 2004). The free listing allowed 30-day store-inventory listings, a longer type of sale offering that allows stores to place items up for sale for long periods of time.

In addition, in February 2004, eBay introduced enhanced billing for its fees to assist high-volume sellers, such as retailers, with a more detailed billing that itemized products more logically (eBay GAB, 2004). eBay has shown that it is committed to attracting retailers and their sales to the site. In an October 2003 bicycle-focused trade show, eBay offered free seminars to teach cycling retailers how to get started selling their products on eBay. Collateral specifically targeting "how" to place an item for sale and the benefits, including expanded geographical reach and using brand-name items as loss leaders to draw consumers into an eBay storefront or other Web site, were also discussed.

eBay is not only attracting retailers as buyers. In a February 2004 promotion, eBay encouraged businesses to buy office supplies and equipment via eBay by "giving visitors a chance to win weekly prizes, receive discounts, and access a wide array of resource, including business workshops, articles, and tips" and ultimately the chance to win a $50,000 grand-prize shopping spree (eBay GAB, 2004).

In summary, eBay is taking clear and decisive action to attract retailers to the site as both buyers and sellers in order to meet their corporate objectives.

Con

eBay's objective of increasing the presence of retail sales is hitting a rough road. While the company is expending efforts to woo retailers at trade show seminars and has created category managers within the eBay organization to focus on specific industries and products, not all retailers have met with success.

The Wall Street Journal reports (Wingfield, 2004) that eBay disappoints larger retailers looking to move volumes of product. Basic economics are against the eBay auction model. "Because of limited demand for any particular item from users of the eBay auction site, merchants that offer a big supply of identical items often drive the price way down" (Wingfield, 2004). Driving the price down cuts into profitability and many large corporations are pulling out of the eBay channel. Accenture, the consulting firm, decided to end an initiative to offer its clients the ability to move large volumes of product through eBay. ReturnBuy and Callaway Golf Pre-Owned have both tried the eBay model and were disappointed with results. Initial test sales showed good results; but as more products were moved onto eBay, prices plummeted.

If eBay is serious about increasing their customer base beyond consumers and mom-and-pop retailers, they are going to have to have to change their strategy. eBay cites 95 percent of their $24 billion in sales come from smaller merchants or retailers (Wingfield, 2004), so there is plenty of growth opportunity in luring larger retailers. But in the current state, eBay is not positioning itself to grow in the important large vendor section.

Conclusion: Objectives 1 and 2:

Score

Objective	Did Not Meet Goal	Met Goal	Exceeded Goal
1	Lost Japan market to Yahoo! Closed Korean operation due to credit card fraud		
2		Yes, research validates that two new items were listed each day	

Conclusion

In summary, we conclude that within the four areas of Finance, External Customer, Internal Business Process, and Learning/Self-Growth on the Balanced Scorecard, there were successes and failures. Successes came in the financial and customer service categories although the latter was hotly debated. In terms of failures we at least have a framework with which to judge future progress as we initiate the changes that will lead to success in the future. What we take away from our deliberations is a high-level view of the road ahead.

References

Baertlein, L. (2003). UPDATE 3-Ebay Profit Up, but Stock Falls on Outlook. *Forbes.com*. Retrieved on February 18, 2004, from the World Wide Web: http://www.forbes.com/newswire/2003/10/16/rtr1112771.html.

eBay GAB, eBay General Announcement Board. (2004). General Announcement Board: 3 Day Penny Listing Designer Sale. Retrieved on March 1, 2004, from the World Wide Web: http://www2.eBay.com/aw/marketing.shtml.

eBay Investor Relations. (2004). eBay to Acquire Germany's Mobile.de. eBay press release dated January 26, 2004. Retrieved from the World Wide Web on March 1, 2004: http://investor.eBay.com/releasedetail.cfm?releaseid=127383.

eBay Press Release. (January 21, 2004). Unaudited fourth quarter and full year 2003 financial results. Retrieved March 1, 2004, from the World Wide Web at http://www.ebay.com.

Gardner, D. and Gardner, T. (September 17, 2003). Motley Fool: eBay's international future. Retrieved March 6, 2004, from the World Wide Web at http://www.fool.com/specials/2003/03091700ceo.htm.

Gifford, M. (2001). Ebay's Lack of Customer Service. Message posted to Complaints.com. Retrieved February 18, 2004, from the World Wide Web: http://www.complaints.com/nov2001/complaintoftheday.november28.18.htm.

Gormly, William. (2001). What's Wrong with eBay?. Photo.net message board as retrieved from the World Wide Web on March 6, 2004: http://www.photo.net/bboard/q-and-a-fetch-msg?msg_id=001bXk.

Harbrecht, D. (2002). Meg Whitman's Bid for Growth. *BusinessWeek Online*. Retrieved on February 18, 2004, from the World Wide Web: http://www.businessweek.com/technology/content/oct2002/tc2002101_8728.htm.

Hof, R.D. (2003). The eBay Economy. *BusinessWeek Online*. August 25, 2003. Retrieved from the World Wide Web on March 6, 2004: http://www.businessweek.com/magazine/content/03_34/b3846650.htm.

Hu, J. (2003). eBay Blacks Out for Three Hours. *News.com*. Retrieved from the World Wide Web on March 4, 2004: http://news.com.com/2100-1017-5066669.html.

Knowledge@Wharton. (2002). eBay: Last Man Standing. *News.com*. Retrieved on February 18, 2004, from the World Wide Web: http://news.com.com/2009-1017-887630.html.

LivePerson, Inc. (2002). eBay Selects LivePerson to Enhance Real-Time Sales, Marketing and Support for eBay Community. Retrieved on February 18, 2004, from the World Wide Web: http://www.liveperson.com/pressroom/pr/060602.htm.

Singer, M. (2001). Survey Ranks eBay, Amazon.com Highest in Customer Satisfaction. *Silicon Valley Internet.com*. Retrieved on February 18, 2004, from the World Wide Web: http://siliconvalley.internet.com/news/article.php/588061.

Wolverton, T. (2002). Problems Plague eBay a Third Day. *News.com*. Retrieved from the World Wide Web on March 4, 2004: http://news.com.com/2100-1017-879240.html.

Wingfield, N. (February 26, 2004). Overstocked: as eBay Grows, Site Disappoints Some Big Vendors. *Wall Street Journal*, 243(39), 1.

Appendix D/A: The Balanced Scorecard

Objective	Measurement	Target	Initiative	Score		
				Did Not Meet Goal	Met Goal	Exceeded Goal
Financial						
Increase shareholder wealth	Gross profits	50 percent per year	Aggressive marketing to attract new small business sellers			Profits increased by 176 percent last year
Grow revenues from international markets	Growth from international transaction revenues	35 percent growth per quarter	Offer promotions to customers in foreign countries to shop at local eBays			Increased growth by 36 percent in international transaction revenues over previous quarter
External/Customer						
Achieve high levels of customer loyalty	Ranking in SatMetrix Best Customer Satisfaction Award	Ranked in the top 10 percent of participating companies	Provide excellent customer service			Joint winner with Amazon in Internet Category

Objective	Measurement	Target	Initiative	Score		
				Did Not Meet Goal	Met Goal	Exceeded Goal
Mitigate effects of disputes on customer satisfaction	Length of time taken to resolve disputes	Resolve all disputes within four hours	Implement method for customer to interact with eBay in real-time			Yes (Implemented LivePerson's technology); also used to market special promotions
Internal Business Process						
Keep Web site accessible at all times	Amount of time that customer cannot access Web site	Less than three minutes delay in accessing site	Implement redundant hardware for real-time failover	January 2001: eBay was down for ten hours Intermittent response in June 2001 for four hours 90-minute outage in March 2002		
Provide easy-to-use buying and selling interfaces	Level of technology skills required to buy and sell	Minimal levels of skill required	Make processes easy to use. Offer online and offline training courses to buyer and seller		Yes. Minimal skills are required Online training and offline training courses are available in major cities	

Objective	Measurement	Target	Initiative	Did Not Meet Goal	Score Met Goal	Exceeded Goal
Learning and Growth						
Expand and capture foreign markets	Successfully lead the industry in targeted countries	Become top auction site in Japan and Korea	Purchase existing auction sites in Japan and Korea	Lost Japan market to Yahoo! Closed Korean operation due to credit card fraud		
Increase variety of items for sale	Number of new items added each day to marketplace	2 million per day	Provide incentives to list new items		Yes. Research validates that two new items were listed each day	

Appendix D/B: Customer Letter

Topic: eBay's Lack of Customer Service
Conf: eBay
From: Mark Gifford moonlightcruiser@aol.com
Date: Tuesday, November 27, 2001, 10:01 PM

Dear Business: a consumer posted the following e-message at Complaints.com. Please respond directly to the consumer, using the consumer's name and e-mail address (as per the From: field above). You may also wish to respond publicly on the Complaints.com site. Just locate this e-message posted in your business's conference and click on the "Reply to" link. (Note: a user registration is required before posting e-messages to the Complaints.com site.)

To whom it may concern,

I have resorted to posting a complaint here because no one from eBay.com would address my concerns. After three attempts at contacting them, all I received was a generic letter, which did not apply to my situation at all.

My first bad experience with eBay was after I was the winning bidder of an item where the seller demanded I pay a shipping charge, which was over twice the actual cost of the shipping. The item listing clearly stated "winning bidder to pay actual shipping charge." When I questioned the seller about the astronomical shipping charge, she invited me to price the shipping myself. She furnished the weight, size, and shipping information of the package. Upon pricing the shipping with the same carrier that she was using …I was told what the shipping price would be.

The price I was quoted was less than half of the price that the seller was demanding. When I mentioned this to the seller, she responded that she can charge any amount she wants for shipping. Upon hearing this I had no choice but to contact eBay and ask them to investigate this seller's fraudulent activity. Well, eBay's only response was to send me a letter demanding that I pay the seller. They refused to look into the situation. I refused to pay for the item and allow myself to be the victim of a scam.

My second bad experience with eBay was after I had won an auction where the seller demanded that I pay a handling charge, which was more than the price of the item!!! The handling fee was mentioned nowhere in the ad. The seller demanded I pay the fee or I would be turned into eBay as a non-paying bidder. I once again took the offensive and asked eBay to investigate the inflated charges this customer was requiring. eBay once again refused to investigate the seller.

The last straw with eBay occurred when I won an auction and asked the seller where I should mail the money order to complete the sale, and was informed that I was only allowed to pay by Pay Pal. I explained to the seller that I had recently been the victim of an identity theft, and had been instructed by a police detective handling my case to avoid using my credit cards online until the identity theft case was straightened out. The seller replied that either I pay by Pay Pal, or she would turn me into eBay as a non-paying bidder. For the third time I contacted eBay requesting that they help resolve the situation, and for the third straight time EBAY REFUSED TO DO ANYTHING.

eBay recently suspended me for non-payment ...even though I had on several occasions tried to pay the seller with a money order or cashiers check, and asked them to help me resolve this situation. They in fact are preventing me from completing a couple auctions, which I won.

I had an excellent rating as an eBay trading partner, I received excellent ratings from 147 eBay users, 0 neutral ratings, and only 3 negative ratings (for the situations mentioned above). It is obvious that eBay lacks a professional customer service oriented team.

Their policies apparently are only for show, since even the company refuses to abide by them. When they refuse to investigate anything three times in a row, you really begin to lose your confidence in their organization.

Their policies should state that "If you are a seller on eBay .... you can charge any amount you wish .... and we will back you 100%." "If you are a bidder on eBay you are required to do whatever the seller wants .... pay whatever they ask .... if you don't like it ...don't ask us for help."

My advice to all online auction buyers is WATCH OUT!!! What happened to me on eBay will continue to happen to many people, until someone finally exposes what eBay is all about!

– Mark Gifford (2001)

Appendix E

Benchmarking Data Collection from a Software Engineering Requirements Elicitation Perspective

Without proper information, it is difficult — if not impossible — to initiate a proper benchmarking effort. Information gathered in this process — called data collection by planners and requirements elicitation by software developers — will enable the organization to develop valid measures against which it should be measured.

Interviewing

The most common method of gathering information is by interviewing people. Interviewing can serve two purposes at the same time. The first is a fact-finding mission to discover what each person's goals and objectives are with respect to the project; and the second is to begin a communications process that enables one to set realistic expectations for the project.

334 ■ *Implementing the IT Balanced Scorecard*

There are a wide variety of stakeholders who can and should be interviewed. Stakeholders are those who have an interest in seeing the project successfully completed — that is, they have a "stake" in the project. Stakeholders include employees, management, clients, and benchmarking partners.

Employees

Interviews have some major obstacles to overcome. The interviewee may resist giving information out of fear, they may relate their perception of how things should be done rather than how they really do them, or they may have difficulty in expressing themselves. On the other hand, the analyst's own mindset may also act as a filter. Interviewers sometimes have to set aside their own technical orientations and make the best effort they can to put themselves in the position that the interviewee is in. This requires analysts to develop a certain amount of empathy.

An interview outline should contain the following information:

- Name of interviewee
- Name of interviewer
- Date and time
- Objectives of interview (i.e., what areas you are going to explore and what data you are going to collect)
- General observations
- Unresolved issues and topics not covered
- Agenda (i.e., introduction, questions, summary of major points, closing)

Recommended guidelines for handling the employee interview process include:

- Determine the process type to be analyzed (e.g., tactical, strategic, hybrid).
- Make a list of departments involved in the process.
- For each department, either request or develop an organization chart that shows the departmental breakdown, along with the name, extension, and a list of responsibilities for each employee.
- Meet with the department head to request recommendations and then formulate a plan that details which employees are the best interview prospects. The "best" employees to interview are those who:

- Are very experienced (i.e., senior) in performing their job function
- May have come from a competing company and thus have a unique perspective
- Have held a variety of positions within the department or company

■ Plan to meet with employees from all units of the department. In some cases, one may find that interviewing several employees at a time is more effective than dealing with a single employee because interviewing a group of employees permits them to bounce ideas off each other.

■ If there are many employees within a departmental unit, it is not optimal to interview each one. It would be wrong to assume that the more people in a department, the higher the number of interviewees. Instead, sampling should be used. Sampling is used to:

- Contain costs
- Improve effectiveness
- Speed up the data-gathering process
- Reduce bias

Systems analysts often use a random sample. However, calculating a sample size based on population size and a desired confidence interval is more accurate. Rather than provide a formula and instructions on how to calculate sample size, the reader is referred to the sample size calculator located at http://www.surveysystem.com/sscalc.htm.

■ Carefully plan the interview sessions. Prepare interview questions in advance. Be familiar with any technical vocabulary the interview subjects might use.

■ No meeting should last longer than an hour. A half-hour is optimal. There is a point of diminishing returns with the interview process. The interviewees are busy and usually easily distracted. Keep in mind that some interviewees may be doing this against their will.

Customers

Customers often have experiences with other vendors or suppliers and can offer insight into the processes that other companies use or that they have experienced.

Guidelines for interviewing customers include:

- Work with the sales or marketing departments to select knowledgeable and cooperative customers.
- Prepare an adequate sample size, as discussed in the previous section.
- Carefully plan the interview sessions. Prepare the interview questions in advance.

Companies and Consultants

Another source of potentially valuable information emanates from other companies in the industry and consultants who specialize in the process areas being examined. While consultants can be easily located and paid for their expert advice, it is wise to tread slowly when working with other companies that are current or potential competitors.

Guidelines for interviewing other companies include:

- Work with senior management and marketing to create a list of potential companies to interview. This list should contain the names of trading partners, vendors (companies that your companies buys from), and competitors.
- Attend industry trade shows to meet and mingle with competitor employees and listen to speeches made by competitive companies.
- Attend trade association meetings; sit on policy and standards committees.

Suppliers

Suppliers of the products one is considering are also an important source of ideas. These suppliers know a great deal about how their products are being used in the processes one is examining.

Types of Questions

When interviewing anyone, it is important to be aware of how to ask questions properly. Open-ended questions are best for gaining the most information because they do not limit the individuals to predefined answers. Other benefits of using open-ended questions are: (1) it puts the interviewee at ease, (2) it provides more detail, (3) it induces spontaneity, and (4) it is far more interesting for the interviewee. Open-ended questions require more than a yes or no answer (Yate, 1993). An example of an open-ended question is: What types of problems to you see on a daily basis with the current process? These types of questions allow individuals to elaborate on the topics and potentially uncover the hidden problems at hand that might not be discoverable with a question that requires a yes or no answer.

One disadvantage of open-ended questions is that they create lengthier interviews. Another disadvantage is that it is easy for the interview to get off track and it takes an interviewer with skill to maintain the interview in an efficient manner.

Closed-ended questions are, by far, the most common questions in interviewing. They are questions that have yes and no answers and are utilized to elicit definitive responses.

Past-performance questions can be useful to determine past experiences with similar problems and issues. An example of how a past-performance question is used is: In your previous job, how did you deal with these processes?

Reflexive questions are appropriate for closing a conversation or moving forward to a new topic. Reflexive questions are created with a statement of confirmation and adding a phrase such as: Don't you? Couldn't you? Or wouldn't you?

Mirror questions form a subtle form of probing and are useful in obtaining additional detail on a subject. After the interviewee makes a statement, pause and repeat that statement with an additional or leading question such as: So, when this problem occurs, you simply move on to more pressing issues?

Often, answers do not give the interviewer enough detail, so one follows the question with additional questions to prod the interviewee to divulge more details on the subject. For example:

- Can you provide some more details on that?
- What did you learn from that experience?

Another, more subtle, prodding technique can be used by merely sitting back and saying nothing. The silence will feel uncomfortable, causing the interviewee to expand on his or her previous statement.

Questionnaires/Surveys

If there are large numbers of people to interview, one might start with a questionnaire and then follow up with certain individuals who present unusual ideas or issues in the questionnaires. Survey development and implementation is composed of the following tasks, according to Creative Research Systems, makers of a software solution for survey creation (surveysolutions.com):

1. *Establish the goals of the project:* what you want to learn.
2. *Determine your sample:* whom you will interview.
3. *Choose interviewing methodology:* how you will interview.
4. *Create your questionnaire:* what you will ask.
5. *Pre-test the questionnaire, if practical:* test the questions.
6. *Conduct interviews and enter data:* ask the questions.
7. *Analyze the data:* produce the reports.

Similar to interviews, questionnaires may contain closed-end or open-ended questions, or a hybrid (i.e., a combination of the two).

Survey creation is quite an art form. Guidelines for the creation of a survey include:

■ Provide an introduction to the survey. Explain why it is important they respond to it. Thank them for their time and effort.
■ Put all important questions first. It is rare that the respondent will answer all the questions. Those filling out the survey often become tired or bored of the process.
■ Use plenty of "white space." Use an appropriate-sized font (e.g., Arial), font size (i.e., at least 12), and do skip lines.
■ Use nominal scales if you wish to classify things (e.g., What make is your computer? 1 = Dell, 2 = Gateway, 3 = IBM, etc.).
■ Use ordinal scales to imply rank (e.g., How helpful was this class? 3 = not helpful at all, 2 = moderately helpful, 1 = very helpful).
■ Use interval scales when you want to perform some mathematical calculations on the results (e.g., How helpful was this class?):

Not useful at all   *Very useful*

1   2   3   4   5

Survey questions must be carefully worded. Ask yourself the following questions when reviewing each question:

■ *Will the words be uniformly understood?* In general, use words that are part of the commonly shared vocabulary of the customers. For example:
 – (poor) Rate the proficiencies of the personnel.
 – (better) Personnel are knowledgeable.
■ *Do the questions contain abbreviations or unconventional phrases?* Avoid these to the extent possible, unless they are understood by everyone and are the common way of referring to something. For example:
 – (poor) Rate our walk-in desk.
 – (better) Personnel at our front desk are friendly.

- *Are the questions too vague?* Survey items should be clear and unambiguous. If they are not, the outcome is difficult to interpret. Make sure you ask something that can truly be measured. For example:
  - (poor) This library should change its procedures.
  - (better) Did you receive the information you needed?
- *Are the questions too precise?* Sometimes, the attempt to avoid vagueness results in items being too precise and customers may be unable to answer them. For example:
  - (poor) Each time I visit the library, the waiting line is long.
  - (better) Generally, the waiting line in the library is long.
- *Are the questions biased?* Biased questions influence the customer to respond in a manner that does not correctly reflect his or her opinion. For example:
  - (poor) How much do you like our library?
  - (better) Would you recommend our library to a friend?
- *Are the questions objectionable?* Usually, this problem can be overcome by asking the question in a less direct way. For example:
  - (poor) Are you living with someone?
  - (better) How many people, including yourself, are in your household?
- *Are the questions double-barreled?* Two separate questions are sometimes combined into one. The customer is forced to give a single response and this, of course, would be ambiguous. For example:
  - (poor) The library is attractive and well-maintained.
  - (better) The library is attractive.
- *Are the answer choices mutually exclusive?* The answer categories must be mutually exclusive, and the respondent should not feel forced to choose more than one. For example:
  - (poor) Scale range: 1, 2–5, 5–9, 9–13, 13 or over
  - (better) Scale range: 0, 1–5, 6–10, 11–15, 16 or over
- *Are the answer choices mutually exhaustive?* The response categories provided should be exhaustive. They should include all the possible responses that might be expected. For example:
  - (poor) Scale range: 1–5, 6–10, 11–15, 16–20
  - (better) Scale range: 0, 1–5, 6–10, 11–15, 16 or over

Tallying the responses will provide a "score" that assists in making a decision that requires the use of quantifiable information. When using interval scales, keep in mind that not all questions will carry the same weight. Hence, it is a good idea to use a weighted average formula during calculation. To do this, assign a "weight" or level of importance to each question. For example, the question above might be assigned a weight of 5 on a scale of 1 to 5, meaning that this is a very important question. On the other hand, a question such as "Was the training center comfortable?" might carry a weight of only 3. The weighted average is calculated by multiplying the weight (w) by the score (s) (that is, w * s) to get the final score. Thus, the formula is s_{new} = w * s.

There are several problems that might result in a poorly constructed questionnaire. Leniency is caused by respondents who grade nonsubjectively — in other words, too easily. Central tendency occurs when respondents rate everything as average. The halo effect occurs when the respondent carries his good or bad impression from one question to the next.

There are several methods that can be used to successfully deploy a survey. The easiest and most accurate is to gather all respondents in a conference room and hand out the survey. For the most part, this is not realistic, so other approaches would be more appropriate. E-mail and traditional mail are two methodologies that work well, although you often have to supply an incentive (e.g., a prize) to get respondents to fill out those surveys on a timely basis. Web-based surveys (Internet and intranet) are becoming increasingly popular as they enable the inclusion of demos, audio, and video. For example, a Web-based survey on what type of user interface is preferable could have hyperlinks to demos or screen shots of the choices.

Observation

Observation is an important tool that can provide a wealth of information. There are several forms of observation, including silent and directed. In silent observation, the analyst merely sits on the sidelines, pen and pad in hand, and observes what is happening. If it is suitable, a tape recorder or video recorder can record what is being observed. However, this is not recommended if the net result will be several hours of random footage.

Silent observation is best used to capture the spontaneous nature of a particular process or procedure. For example:

- When customers will be interacting with staff
- During group meetings
- On the manufacturing floor
- In the field

Directed observation provides the analyst with a chance to micro-control a process or procedure so that it is broken down into its observable parts. At one accounting firm, a tax system was being developed. The analysts requested that several senior tax accountants be coupled with a junior staff member. The group was given a problem as well as all of the manuals and materials they needed. The junior accountant sat at one end of the table with the pile of manuals and forms, while the senior tax accountants sat at the other end. A tough tax problem was posed. The senior tax accountants were directed to think through the process and then direct the junior member to follow through on their directions to solve this problem. The catch was that the senior members could neither walk over to the junior person nor touch any of the reference guides. This entire exercise had to be verbal and use just their memories and expertise. The entire process was videotaped. The net result was that the analyst had a complete record of how to perform one of the critical functions of the new system.

Participation

The flip side of observation is participation. Actually becoming a member of the staff — and thereby learning exactly what it is that the staff does so that it might be automated — is an invaluable experience.

Documentation

It is logical to assume that there will be a wide variety of documentation available to the analyst. This includes, but is not limited to, the following:

- Documentation from existing systems. This includes requirements and design specifications, program documentation, user manuals, and help files. This also includes whatever "wish" lists have been developed for the existing system.
- Archival information
- Policies and procedures manuals
- Reports
- Memos
- Standards
- E-mail
- Minutes from meetings
- Government and other regulatory guidelines and regulations
- Industry or association manuals, guidelines, and standards (e.g., accountants are guided not only by in-house "rules and regulations," but by industry and other rules and regulations)

Brainstorming

In a brainstorming session, one gathers together a group of people, creates a stimulating and focused atmosphere, and lets people come up with ideas without any risk of being ridiculed. Even seemingly stupid ideas may turn out to be "golden."

Focus Groups

Focus groups are derived from marketing. These are structured sessions wherein a group of stakeholders are presented with a solution to a problem and then are closely questioned on their views about that solution.

Reference

Yate, M. (1997). *Hiring the Best,* 4th ed. Avon, MA: Adams Media Corporation.

Appendix F

Behavioral Competencies

Companies interested in stimulating learning and growth among employees will be interested in this list of behavioral competencies for employees and managers.

For Employees

Communicates Effectively

1. Listens to others in a patient, empathetic, and nonjudgmental way; acknowledges their ideas in a respectful manner; questions appropriately
2. Is straightforward and direct; behavior is consistent with words
3. Discusses concerns and conflict directly and constructively
4. Communicates in a timely fashion

Promotes Teamwork

1. Networks with other employees within and outside of one's area; makes internal referrals to connect people with each other
2. Readily volunteers to be on teams
3. Is a participating and equal partner on teams; has the same purpose as the team; encourages cohesion and trust
4. Is receptive to and solicits other team members' advice and ideas

5. Keeps supervisor and team informed of status of work so that surprises are minimized
6. Verbally and nonverbally supports established decisions and actions; represents the collective stance

Presents Effectively

1. Understands the makeup of the audience and is sensitive to their values, backgrounds, and needs
2. Presents ideas clearly so that others can easily understand their meaning
3. Delivers presentations with the appropriate level of expression and confidence
4. Incorporates humor when appropriate and in good taste

Makes Sound Decisions

1. Knows when a decision is necessary and makes decisions in a timely manner
2. Connects decisions to strategic plans; separates essential from nonessential information, considering all logical alternatives when generating conclusions
3. Seeks and considers input from others who are close to the situation before establishing a course of action
4. Considers the relevance and impact of decisions on others prior to making decisions

Uses Resources Wisely

1. Considers need and cost prior to making resource-related requests and decisions
2. Makes maximum use of available resources through the efficient and creative use of people, time, material, and equipment
3. Reduces waste, reuses materials, and recycles appropriate materials
4. Functions within the budget

Takes Initiative and Accepts Accountability

1. Is proactive; plans ahead; sees things that need to be done and accomplishes them on one's own initiative and on time
2. Accepts responsibility and consequences for one's decisions and actions

3. Follows through on commitments; does what one says one will do — the first time
4. Acknowledges, accepts, and learns from mistakes

Lives Company's Values

1. Demonstrates the organizational and professional code of ethics, including honesty, respect, dignity, caring, and confidentiality
2. Demonstrates and consistently applies organizational principles, policies, and values to all employees and situations
3. Respects and operates within the boundaries established for one's job and personal boundaries set by others
4. Promotes a positive work environment

Demonstrates a Customer-First Approach (Internal Partners and External Customers)

1. Anticipates customers' needs; facilitates customers to express their needs; listens to customer and hears what they say
2. Promptly attends to customers' needs (e.g., answers phone and returns phone calls within a reasonable amount of time)
3. Treats customers with respect, politeness, and dignity while maintaining appropriate boundaries
4. When appropriate, provides customers with options for action in response to their needs

Generates New Ideas

1. Generates imaginative and original ideas that will bring about positive change
2. Seizes opportunities to expand on other people's ideas to create something new and add value
3. Encourages others to create new ideas, products, and solutions that will add value to the organization

Demonstrates Flexibility

1. Adapts to and accepts changing work schedules, priorities, challenges, and unpredictable events in a positive manner
2. Is visible and accessible; is approachable even when interruptions are inconvenient

3. Is receptive to new ideas that are different from one's own ideas
4. Offers to help others when circumstances necessitate sharing the workload

Demonstrates a Professional Demeanor

1. Demonstrates acceptable hygiene and grooming; dresses appropriately for one's job
2. Uses proper verbal and nonverbal communications and tone with internal partners and external customers and patients
3. Places work responsibilities and priorities before personal needs while at work
4. Maximizes positive and professional communication with internal partners and external customers and patients; minimizes complaining and nonfactual communication

Stimulates and Adapts to Change

1. Stimulates positive attitudes about change; pushes the change process along
2. Takes personal responsibility for adapting to and coping with change
3. Commits quickly when change reshapes one's area of work
4. Accepts ambiguity and uncertainty; is able to improvise and still add value

Continually Improves Processes

1. Anticipates and looks for opportunities to improve steps in the development and delivery of one's products or services; takes logical risks that may lead to improvement and change
2. Examines one's work for conformance to predetermined plans, specifications, and standards
3. Freely shares and promotes new ideas that may lead to improvement and positive change, even when the idea may be unpopular
4. Seeks input from others who are closest to the situation in making improvements

For Managers
Organizational Acumen

1. Demonstrates a thorough knowledge of the company model, organizational history, and values
2. Applies knowledge of services, products, and processes to understand key issues within one's own division and work unit
3. Demonstrates understanding of and ability to influence organizational culture, norms, and expectations.
4. Contributes to, fosters, and supports changes resulting from organizational decisions and initiatives

Strategic Direction

1. Integrates own work and that of one's work unit with the organization's mission, values, and objectives
2. Analyzes and utilizes customer, industry, and stakeholder inputs in strategic and operating plan processes
3. Establishes workgroup priorities to support strategic objectives
4. Gathers input from internal and external resources to analyze business unit needs
5. Promotes and embraces innovation and creativity to achieve organizational and work unit goals
6. Develops work unit plans and measures that are aligned with division and organization strategic objectives
7. Defines operational goals for work unit
8. Integrates strategies and plans with other areas
9. Promotes and supports the use of corporate and cross-functional teams
10. Ensures customer and employee confidentiality through monitoring access to information to individuals who have need, reason, and permission for such access

Systems Improvement

1. Demonstrates understanding of the "big picture" — interrelationships of divisions, departments, and work units
2. Incorporates a broad range of internal and external factors in problem solving and decision making

3. Solicits and incorporates customer and stakeholder needs and expectations into work unit planning
4. Applies and encourages the use of process improvement methods and tools
5. Encourages and supports innovative and creative problem solving by others
6. Integrates process thinking into management of daily operations to enhance quality, efficiency, and ethical standards
7. Utilizes data in decision making and managing work units

Communication

1. Communicates the mission, values, structure, and systems to individuals, groups, and larger audiences
2. Provides leadership in communicating "up," "down," and "across" the organization
3. Reinforces organization's key messages
4. Creates a work environment for and models open expression of ideas and diverse opinions
5. Routinely includes a communications plan in work and project planning
6. Applies, communicates, and educates others about organizational policies and procedures
7. Keeps employees informed of industry trends and implications
8. Understands, communicates, and administers compensation and benefits to employees

Employee and Team Direction

1. Anticipates and assesses staffing needs
2. Maintains and updates staff job descriptions, linking employee job descriptions and projects to unit, division, and corporate strategies
3. Recruits, selects, and retains high-performing individuals
4. Provides information, resources, and coaching to support individual and team professional and career development
5. Applies knowledge of team dynamics to enhance group communication, synergy, creativity, conflict resolution, and decision making
6. Assures staff has training to fully utilize technological tools necessary for job performance
7. Delegates responsibilities to, coaches, and mentors employees to develop their capabilities

8. Involves staff in planning and reporting to assure integration with operational activities and priorities
9. Coaches employees by providing both positive and constructive feedback and an overall realistic picture of their performance
10. Ensures that core functions in areas of responsibility can be continued in the absence of staff members — either short-term or long-term
11. Recognizes and acknowledges successes and achievements of others

Financial Literacy

1. Partners with financial specialists in planning and problem solving
2. Develops and meets financial goals using standard budgeting and reporting processes
3. Continually finds ways to improve revenue, reduce costs, and leverage assets in keeping with the organization's strategic direction and objectives
4. Uses financial and quantitative information in work unit management
5. Communicates unit budget expectations and status to employees
6. Coaches employees on financial implications of work processes

Professional Development

1. Keeps up-to-date with the external environment through professional associations, conferences, journals, etc.
2. Nurtures and maintains working relationships with colleagues across the organization
3. Demonstrates commitment to professional development, aligning that development with current and future needs of the organization whenever possible
4. Models self-development and healthy work:life balance for employees

Appendix G

The Malcolm Baldrige National Quality Award Program

For 16 years, the Baldrige Criteria have been used by thousands of U.S. organizations to stay abreast of ever-increasing competition and to improve performance. For today's business environment, the Criteria help organizations respond to current challenges: openness and transparency in governance and ethics, the need to create value for customers and the business, and the challenges of rapid innovation and capitalizing on your knowledge assets. Whether your business is small or large, is involved in service or manufacturing, or has one office or multiple sites across the globe, the Criteria provide a valuable framework that can help you plan in an uncertain environment. Use the Criteria to assess performance on a wide range of key business indicators: customer, product and service, financial, human resource, and operational. The Criteria can help you align resources and approaches such as ISO 9000, Lean Enterprise, Balanced Scorecard, and Six Sigma; improve communication, productivity, and effectiveness; and achieve strategic goals.

Criteria

The Criteria are the basis for organizational self-assessments, for making awards, and for giving feedback to applicants. In addition, the Criteria have three important roles in strengthening U.S. competitiveness:

1. To help improve organizational performance practices, capabilities, and results
2. To facilitate communication and sharing of best practices information among U.S. organizations of all types
3. To serve as a working tool for understanding and managing performance and for guiding organizational planning and opportunities for learning

Core Values and Concepts

The Criteria are built upon the following set of interrelated Core Values and Concepts:

- Visionary leadership
- Customer-driven excellence
- Organizational and personal learning
- Valuing employees and partners
- Agility
- Focus on the future
- Managing for innovation
- Management by fact
- Social responsibility
- Focus on results and creating value
- Systems perspective

These values and concepts, described below, are embedded beliefs and behaviors found in high-performing organizations. They are the foundation for integrating key business requirements within a results-oriented framework that creates a basis for action and feedback.

Visionary Leadership

Your organization's senior leaders should set directions and create a customer focus, clear and visible values, and high expectations. The directions, values, and expectations should balance the needs of all your stakeholders. Your leaders should ensure the creation of strategies, systems, and methods for achieving excellence, stimulating innovation, and building knowledge and capabilities. The values and strategies should help guide all activities and decisions of your organization. Senior leaders should inspire and motivate your entire workforce and should encourage all employees to contribute, to develop and learn, to be innovative, and to be creative. Senior leaders should be responsible to your organization's governance body for their actions and performance. The governance body should be responsible ultimately to all your stakeholders for the ethics, vision, actions, and performance of your organization and its senior leaders.

Senior leaders should serve as role models through their ethical behavior and their personal involvement in planning, communications, coaching, development of future leaders, review of organizational performance, and employee recognition. As role models, they can reinforce ethics, values, and expectations while building leadership, commitment, and initiative throughout your organization.

Customer-Driven Excellence

Quality and performance are judged by an organization's customers. Thus, your organization must take into account all product and service features and characteristics and all modes of customer access that contribute value to your customers. Such behavior leads to customer acquisition, satisfaction, preference, referral, retention and loyalty, and business expansion. Customer-driven excellence has both current and future components: understanding today's customer desires and anticipating future customer desires and marketplace potential.

Value and satisfaction may be influenced by many factors throughout your customers' overall purchase, ownership, and service experiences. These factors include your organization's relationships with customers, which help to build trust, confidence, and loyalty.

Customer-driven excellence means much more than reducing defects and errors, merely meeting specifications, or reducing complaints. Nevertheless, reducing defects and errors and eliminating causes of dissatisfaction contribute to your customers' view of your organization and thus also are important parts of customer-driven excellence. In addition, your organization's success in recovering from defects and mistakes ("making things right for your customer") is crucial to retaining customers and building customer relationships.

Customer-driven organizations address not only the product and service characteristics that meet basic customer requirements, but also those features and characteristics that differentiate products and services from competing offerings. Such differentiation may be based upon new or modified offerings, combinations of product and service offerings, customization of offerings, multiple access mechanisms, rapid response, or special relationships.

Customer-driven excellence is thus a strategic concept. It is directed toward customer retention and loyalty, market share gain, and growth. It demands constant sensitivity to changing and emerging customer and market requirements and to the factors that drive customer satisfaction and loyalty. It demands listening to your customers. It demands anticipating changes in the marketplace. Therefore, customer-driven excellence demands awareness of developments in technology and competitors' offerings, as well as rapid and flexible response to customer and market changes.

Organizational and Personal Learning

Achieving the highest levels of business performance requires a well-executed approach to organizational and personal learning. Organizational learning includes both continuous improvement of existing approaches and adaptation to change, leading to new goals and/or approaches. Learning needs to be embedded in the way your organization operates. This means that learning (1) is a regular part of daily work; (2) is practiced at personal, work unit, and organizational levels; (3) results in solving problems at their source ("root cause"); (4) is focused on building and sharing knowledge throughout your organization; and (5) is driven by opportunities to effect significant, meaningful change. Sources for learning include employees' ideas, research and development (R&D), customer input, best practice sharing, and benchmarking.

Organizational learning can result in (1) enhancing value to customers through new and improved products and services; (2) developing new business opportunities; (3) reducing errors, defects, waste, and related costs; (4) improving responsiveness and cycle time performance; (5) increasing productivity and effectiveness in the use of all resources throughout your organization; and (6) enhancing your organization's performance in fulfilling its societal responsibilities and its service to your community as a good citizen.

Employees' success depends increasingly on having opportunities for personal learning and practicing new skills. Organizations invest in employees' personal learning through education, training, and other opportunities for continuing growth. Such opportunities might include job rotation and increased pay for demonstrated knowledge and skills. On-the-job training offers a cost-effective way to train and to better link training to your organizational needs and priorities. Education and training programs may benefit from advanced technologies, such as computer- and Internet-based learning and satellite broadcasts.

Personal learning can result in (1) more satisfied and versatile employees who stay with your organization, (2) organizational cross-functional learning, (3) building the knowledge assets of your organization, and (4) an improved environment for innovation. Thus, learning is directed not only toward better products and services, but also toward being more responsive, adaptive, innovative, and efficient — giving your organization marketplace sustainability and performance advantages and giving your employees satisfaction and motivation to excel.

Valuing Employees and Partners

An organization's success depends increasingly on the diverse knowledge, skills, creativity, and motivation of all its employees and partners. Valuing employees means committing to their satisfaction, development, and well-being. Increasingly, this involves more flexible, high-performance work practices tailored to employees with diverse workplace and home life needs. Major challenges in the area of valuing employees include: (1) demonstrating your leaders' commitment to your employees' success, (2) recognition that goes beyond the regular compensation system, (3) development and progression within your organization, (4) sharing your organization's knowledge so your employees can better serve your customers and contribute to achieving your strategic objectives, and (5) creating an environment that encourages risk taking and innovation.

Organizations need to build internal and external partnerships to better accomplish overall goals. Internal partnerships might include labor-management cooperation, such as agreements with unions. Partnerships with employees might entail employee development, cross-training, or new work organizations, such as high-performance work teams. Internal partnerships also might involve creating network relationships among your work units to improve flexibility, responsiveness, and knowledge sharing.

External partnerships might be with customers, suppliers, and education organizations. Strategic partnerships or alliances are increasingly important kinds of external partnerships. Such partnerships might offer entry into new markets or a basis for new products or services. Also, partnerships might permit the blending of your organization's core competencies or leadership capabilities with the complementary strengths and capabilities of partners.

Successful internal and external partnerships develop longer-term objectives, thereby creating a basis for mutual investments and respect. Partners should address the key requirements for success, means for regular communication, approaches to evaluating progress, and means for adapting to changing conditions. In some cases, joint education and training could offer a cost-effective method for employee development.

Agility

Success in globally competitive markets demands agility — a capacity for rapid change and flexibility. E-business requires and enables more rapid, flexible, and customized responses. Businesses face ever-shorter cycles for the introduction of new/improved products and services, as well as for faster and more flexible response to customers. Major improvements in response time often require simplification of work units and processes and/or the ability for rapid changeover from one process to another. Cross-trained and empowered employees are vital assets in such a demanding environment.

A major success factor in meeting competitive challenges is the design-to-introduction (product or service initiation) or innovation cycle time. To meet the demands of rapidly changing global markets, organizations need to carry out stage-to-stage integration (such as concurrent engineering) of activities from research or concept to commercialization.

All aspects of time performance now are more critical, and cycle time has become a key process measure. Other important benefits can be derived from this focus on time; time improvements often drive simultaneous improvements in organization, quality, cost, and productivity.

Focus on the Future

In today's competitive environment, a focus on the future requires understanding the short- and longer-term factors that affect your business and marketplace. Pursuit of sustainable growth and market leadership requires a strong future orientation and a willingness to make long-term commitments to key stakeholders — your customers, employees, suppliers and partners, stockholders, the public, and your community. Your organization's planning should anticipate many factors, such as customers' expectations, new business and partnering opportunities, employee development and hiring needs, the increasingly global marketplace, technological developments, the evolving E-business environment, new customer and market segments, evolving regulatory requirements, community and societal expectations, and strategic moves by competitors. Strategic objectives and resource allocations need to accommodate these influences. A focus on the future includes developing employees and suppliers, doing effective succession planning, creating opportunities for innovation, and anticipating public responsibilities.

Managing for Innovation

Innovation means making meaningful changes to improve an organization's products, services, and processes and to create new value for the organization's stakeholders. Innovation should lead your organization to new dimensions of performance. Innovation is no longer strictly the purview of research and development departments; innovation is important for all aspects of your business and all processes. Organizations should be led and managed so that innovation becomes part of the learning culture and is integrated into daily work.

Innovation builds on the accumulated knowledge of your organization and its employees. Therefore, the ability to capitalize on this knowledge is critical to managing for innovation.

Management by Fact

Organizations depend on the measurement and analysis of performance. Such measurements should derive from business needs and strategy, and they should provide critical data and information about key processes, outputs, and results. Many types of data and information are needed for performance management. Performance measurement should include customer, product, and service performance; comparisons of operational, market, and competitive performance; and supplier, employee, and cost and financial performance. Data should be segmented by, for example, markets, product lines, and employee groups to facilitate analysis.

Analysis refers to extracting larger meaning from data and information to support evaluation, decision making, and improvement. Analysis entails using data to determine trends, projections, and cause and effect that might not otherwise be evident. Analysis supports a variety of purposes, such as planning, reviewing your overall performance, improving operations, change management, and comparing your performance with competitors' or with "best practices" benchmarks.

A major consideration in performance improvement and change management involves the selection and use of performance measures or indicators. *The measures or indicators you select should best represent the factors that lead to improved customer, operational, and financial performance. A comprehensive set of measures or indicators tied to customer and/or organizational performance requirements represents a clear basis for aligning all processes with your organization's goals.*

Through the analysis of data from your tracking processes, your measures or indicators themselves may be evaluated and changed to better support your goals.

Social Responsibility

An organization's leaders should stress responsibilities to the public, ethical behavior, and the need to practice good citizenship. Leaders should be role models for your organization in focusing on business ethics and protection of public health, safety, and the environment. Protection of health, safety, and the environment includes your organization's operations, as well as the life cycles of your products and services. Also, organizations should emphasize resource conservation and waste reduction at the source. Planning should anticipate adverse impacts from production, distribution, transportation, use, and disposal of your products. Effective planning should prevent problems, provide for a forthright response if problems occur, and make available information and support needed to maintain public awareness, safety, and confidence.

For many organizations, the product design stage is critical from the point of view of public responsibility. Design decisions impact your production processes and often the content of municipal and industrial waste. Effective design strategies should anticipate growing environmental concerns and responsibilities.

Organizations should not only meet all local, state, and federal laws and regulatory requirements, but they should treat these and related requirements as opportunities for improvement "beyond mere compliance." Organizations should stress ethical behavior in all stakeholder transactions and interactions. Highly ethical conduct should be a requirement of and should be monitored by the organization's governance body.

Practicing good citizenship refers to leadership and support — within the limits of an organization's resources — of publicly important purposes. Such purposes might include improving education and health care in your community, environmental excellence, resource conservation, community service, improving industry and business practices, and sharing nonproprietary information. Leadership as a corporate citizen also entails influencing other organizations, private and public, to partner for these purposes. For example, your organization might lead or participate in efforts to help define the obligations of your industry to its communities. Managing social responsibility requires the use of appropriate measures and leadership responsibility for those measures.

Focus on Results and Creating Value

An organization's performance measurements need to focus on key results. Results should be used to create and balance value for your key stakeholders — customers, employees, stockholders, suppliers and partners, the public, and the community. By creating value for your key stakeholders, your organization builds loyalty and contributes to growing the economy. To meet the sometimes conflicting and changing aims that balancing value implies, organizational strategy should explicitly include key stakeholder requirements. This will help ensure that plans and actions meet differing stakeholder needs and avoid adverse impacts on any stakeholders. The use of a balanced composite of leading and lagging performance measures offers an effective means to communicate short- and longer-term priorities, monitor actual performance, and provide a clear basis for improving results.

Systems Perspective

The Baldrige Criteria provide a systems perspective for managing your organization and its key processes to achieve results — performance excellence. The seven Baldrige Categories and the Core Values form the building blocks and the integrating mechanism for the system. However, successful management of overall performance requires organization-specific synthesis, alignment, and integration. Synthesis means looking at your organization as a whole and builds upon key business requirements, including your strategic objectives and action plans. Alignment means using the key linkages among requirements given in the Baldrige Categories to ensure consistency of plans, processes, measures, and actions. Integration builds on alignment so that the individual components of your performance management system operate in a fully interconnected manner.

A systems perspective includes your senior leaders' focus on strategic directions and on your customers. It means that your senior leaders monitor, respond to, and manage performance based on your business results. A systems perspective also includes using your measures, indicators, and organizational knowledge to build your key strategies. It means linking these strategies with your key processes and aligning resources to improve overall performance and satisfy customers. Thus, a systems perspective means managing your whole organization, as well as its components, to achieve success.

Criteria for Performance Excellence Framework

The Core Values and Concepts are embodied in seven categories, as follows:

1. Leadership
2. Strategic Planning
3. Customer and Market Focus
4. Measurement, Analysis, and Knowledge Management

5. Human Resource Focus
6. Process Management
7. Business Results

The criteria can be thought of within the context of a framework consisting of:

Organizational Profile

Your Organizational Profile sets the context for the way your organization operates. Your environment, key working relationships, and strategic challenges serve as an overarching guide for your organizational performance management system.

System Operations

The system operations are composed of the six Baldrige Categories in the center of the figure that define your operations and the results you achieve.

Leadership (Category 1), Strategic Planning (Category 2), and Customer and Market Focus (Category 3) represent the leadership triad. These Categories are placed together to emphasize the importance of a leadership focus on strategy and customers. Senior leaders set your organizational direction and seek future opportunities for your organization.

Human Resource Focus (Category 5), Process Management (Category 6), and Business Results (Category 7) represent the results triad. Your organization's employees and key processes accomplish the work of the organization that yields your business results.

All actions point toward Business Results — a composite of customer, product and service, financial, and internal operational performance results, including human resource, governance, and social responsibility results.

The horizontal arrow in the center of the framework links the leadership triad to the results triad, a linkage critical to organizational success. Furthermore, the arrow indicates the central relationship between Leadership (Category 1) and Business Results (Category 7). The two-headed arrows indicate the importance of feedback in an effective performance management system.

System Foundation

Measurement, Analysis, and Knowledge Management (Category 4) are critical to the effective management of your organization and to a fact-based, knowledge-driven system for improving performance and competitiveness. Measurement, analysis, and knowledge management serve as a foundation for the performance management system.

Criteria Structure

The seven Criteria Categories are subdivided into Items and Areas to Address. There are 19 Items, each focusing on a major requirement. Items consist of one or more Areas to Address (Areas). Organizations should address their responses to the specific requirements of these Areas.

1. The Criteria focus on business results.
2. The Criteria support a systems perspective to maintaining organizationwide goal alignment.
3. The Criteria are nonprescriptive and adaptable. The Criteria are made up of results-oriented requirements. However, the Criteria *do not* prescribe that your organization should or should not have departments for quality, planning, or other functions; how your organization should be structured; or that different units in your organization should be managed in the same way.
   (1) The focus is on results, not on procedures, tools, or organizational structure. Organizations are encouraged to develop and demonstrate creative, adaptive, and flexible approaches for meeting requirements. Nonprescriptive requirements are intended to foster incremental and major ("breakthrough") improvements, as well as basic change.
   (2) The selection of tools, techniques, systems, and organizational structure usually depends on factors such as business type and size, organizational relationships, your organization's stage of development, and employee capabilities and responsibilities.
   (3) A focus on common requirements, rather than on common procedures, fosters understanding, communication, sharing, and alignment, while supporting innovation and diversity in approaches.
   Alignment in the Criteria is built around connecting and reinforcing measures derived from your organization's processes and strategy. These measures tie directly to customer value and to overall performance. The use of measures thus channels different activities in consistent directions with less need for detailed procedures, centralized decision making, or overly complex process management. Measures thereby serve both as a communications tool and a basis for deploying consistent overall performance requirements.

Such alignment ensures consistency of purpose while also supporting agility, innovation, and decentralized decision making.

A systems perspective to goal alignment, particularly when strategy and goals change over time, requires dynamic linkages among Criteria Items. In the Criteria, action-oriented cycles of learning take place via feedback between processes and results.

The learning cycles have four, clearly defined stages:
(1) Planning, including design of processes, selection of measures, and deployment of requirements
(2) Executing plans
(3) Assessing progress and capturing new knowledge, taking into account internal and external results
(4) Revising plans based upon assessment findings, learning, new inputs, and new requirements

4. The Criteria support goal-based diagnosis. The Criteria and the Scoring Guidelines make up a two-part diagnostic (assessment) system. The Criteria are a set of 19 performance-oriented requirements. The Scoring Guidelines spell out the assessment dimensions — Process and Results — and the key factors used to assess each dimension. An assessment thus provides a profile of strengths and opportunities for improvement relative to the 19 performance-oriented requirements. In this way, assessment leads to actions that contribute to performance improvement in all areas, as described in the shaded box above. This diagnostic assessment is a useful management tool that goes beyond most performance reviews and is applicable to a wide range of strategies and management systems.

P. Preface: Organizational Profile

The *Organizational Profile* is a snapshot of your organization, the key influences on how you operate, and the key challenges you face.

P.1 Organizational Description

Describe your organization's business environment and your key relationships with customers, suppliers, and other partners.

Within your response, include answers to the following questions:

(a) Organizational Environment
(1) What are your organization's main products and services? What are the delivery mechanisms used to provide your products and services to your customers?

(2) What is your organizational culture? What are your stated purpose, vision, mission, and values?

(3) What is your employee profile? What are their educational levels? What are your organization's workforce and job diversity, organized bargaining units, use of contract employees, and special health and safety requirements?

(4) What are your major technologies, equipment, and facilities?

(5) What is the regulatory environment under which your organization operates? What are the applicable occupational health and safety regulations; accreditation, certification, or registration requirements; and environmental, financial, and product regulations?

b. Organizational Relationships

(1) What is your organizational structure and governance system? What are the reporting relationships among your board of directors, senior leaders, and your parent organization, as appropriate?

(2) What are your key customer groups and market segments, as appropriate? What are their key requirements and expectations for your products and services? What are the differences in these requirements and expectations among customers groups and market segments?

(3) What role do suppliers and distributors play in your value creation processes? What are your most important types of suppliers and distributors? What are your most important supply chain requirements?

(4) What are your key supplier and customers partnering relationships and communication mechanisms?

P.2   Organizational Challenges

Describe your organization's competitive environment, your key strategic challenges, and your system for performance improvement.

Within your response, include answers to the following questions:

a. Competitive Environment

(1) What is your competitive position? What is your relative size and growth in your industry or markets served? What are the numbers and types of competitors for your organization?

(2) What are the principal factors that determine your success relative to your competitors? What are any key changes taking place that affect your competitive situation?

(3) What are your key available sources of comparative and competitive data from within your industry? What are your key available sources of comparative data for analogous processes outside your industry? What limitations, if any, are there in your ability to obtain these data?

b. Strategic Challenges
   (1) What are your key business, operational, and human resource strategic challenges?
   (2) What is the overall approach you use to maintain an organizational focus on performance improvement and to guide systematic evaluation and improvement of key processes?
   (3) What is your overall approach to organizational learning and sharing your knowledge assets within the organization?

1. Leadership (120 pts.)

The *Leadership* Category examines how your organization's senior leaders address values, directions, and performance expectations, as well as a focus on customers and other stakeholders, empowerment, innovation, and learning. Also examined are your organization's governance and how your organization addresses its public and community responsibilities.

1.1 Organizational Leadership (70 pts.)

Describe how senior leaders guide your organization. Describe your organization's governance system. Describe how senior leaders review organizational performance.

Within your response, include answers to the following questions:

a. Senior Leadership Direction
   (1) How do senior leaders set and deploy organizational values, short- and longer-term directions, and performance expectations? How do senior leaders include a focus on creating and balancing value for customers and other stakeholders in their performance expectations? How do senior leaders communicate organizational values, directions, and expectations through your leadership system, to all employees, and to key suppliers and partners? How do senior leaders ensure two-way communication on these topics?
   (2) How do senior leaders create an environment for empowerment, innovation, and organizational agility? How do they create an environment for organizational and employee learning?

How do they create an environment that fosters and requires legal and ethical behavior?

b. Organizational Governance

(1) How does your organization address the following key factors in your governance system?

1. Management accountability for the organization's actions
2. Fiscal accountability
3. Independence in internal and external audits
4. Protection of stockholder and stakeholder interests, as appropriate

c. Organizational Performance Review

(1) How do senior leaders review organizational performance and capabilities? How do they use these reviews to assess organizational success, competitive performance, and progress relative to short- and longer-term goals? How do they use these reviews to assess your organizational ability to address changing organizational needs?

(2) What are the key performance measures regularly reviewed by your senior leaders? What are your key recent performance review findings?

(3) How do senior leaders translate organizational performance review findings into priorities for continuous and breakthrough improvement of key business results and into opportunities for innovation? How are these priorities and opportunities deployed throughout your organization? When appropriate, how are they deployed to your suppliers and partners to ensure organizational alignment?

(4) How do you evaluate the performance of your senior leaders, including the chief executive? How do you evaluate the performance of members of the board of directors, as appropriate? How do senior leaders use organizational performance review findings to improve both their own leadership effectiveness and that of your board and leadership system, as appropriate?

1.2 Social Responsibility (50 pts.)

Describe how your organization addresses its responsibilities to the public, ensures ethical behavior, and practices good citizenship.

Within your response, include answers to the following questions:

a. Responsibilities to the Public

(1) How do you address the impacts on society of your products, services, and operations? What are your key compliance

processes, measures, and goals for achieving and surpassing regulatory and legal requirements, as appropriate? What are your key processes, measures, and goals for addressing risks associated with your products, services, and operations?

(2) How do you anticipate public concerns with current and future products, services, and operations? How do you prepare for these concerns in a proactive manner?

b. Ethical Behavior

(1) How do you ensure ethical behavior in all stakeholder transactions and interactions? What are your key processes and measures or indicators for monitoring ethical behavior throughout your organization, with key partners, and in your governance structure?

c. Support of Key Communities

(1) How does your organization actively support and strengthen your key communities? How do you identify key communities and determine areas of emphasis for organizational involvement and support? What are your key communities? How do your senior leaders and your employees contribute to improving these communities?

2. Strategic Planning (85 pts.)

The *Strategic Planning* Category examines how your organization develops strategic objectives and action plans. Also examined are how your chosen strategic objectives and action plans are deployed and how progress is measured.

2.1 Strategy Development (40 pts.)

Describe how your organization establishes its strategic objectives, including how it enhances its competitive position, overall performance, and future success.

Within your response, include answers to the following questions:

(a) Strategy Development Process

(1) What is your overall strategic planning process? What are the key steps? Who are the key participants? What are your short- and longer-term planning time horizons? How are these time horizons set? How does your strategic planning process address these time horizons?

(2) How do you ensure that strategic planning addresses the key factors listed below? How do you collect and analyze relevant data and information to address these factors as they relate to your strategic planning?

- Your customers and market needs, expectations, and opportunities
- Your competitive environment and your capabilities relative to competitors
- Technological and other key innovations or changes that might affect your products and services and how you operate
- Your strengths and weaknesses, including human and other resources
- Your opportunities to redirect resources to higher priority products, services, or areas
- Financial, societal and ethical, regulatory, and other potential risks
- Changes in the national or global economy
- Factors unique to your organization, including partner and supply chain needs, strengths, and weaknesses

b. Strategic Objectives

(1) What are your key strategic objectives and your timetable for accomplishing them? What are your most important goals for these strategic objectives?

(2) How do your strategic objectives address the challenges identified in response to P.2 in your Organizational Profile? How do you ensure that your strategic objectives balance short- and longer-term challenges and opportunities? How do you ensure that your strategic objectives balance the needs of all key stakeholders?

2.2 *Strategy Deployment (45 pts.)*

Describe how your organization converts its strategic objectives into action plans. Summarize your organization's action plans and related key performance measures or indicators. Project your organization's future performance on these key performance measures or indicators.

Within your response, include answers to the following questions:

a. Action Plan Development and Deployment

(1) How do you develop and deploy action plans to achieve your key strategic objectives? How do you allocate resources to ensure accomplishment of your action plans? How do you

ensure that the key changes resulting from action plans can be sustained?

(2) What are your key short- and longer-term action plans? What are the key changes, if any, in your products and services, your customers and markets, and how you will operate?

(3) What are your key human resource plans that derive from your short- and longer-term strategic objectives and action plans?

(4) What are your key performance measures or indicators for tracking progress on your action plans? How do you ensure that your overall action plan measurement system reinforces organizational alignment? How do you ensure that the measurement system covers all key deployment areas and stakeholders?

b. Performance Projection

(1) For the key performance measures or indicators identified in 2.2a(4), what are your performance projections for both your short- and longer-term planning time horizons? How does your projected performance compare with competitors' projected performance? How does it compare with key benchmarks, goals, and past performance, as appropriate?

3 Customer and Market Focus (85 pts.)

The *Customer and Market Focus* Category examines how your organization determines requirements, expectations, and preferences of customers and markets. Also examined is how your organization builds relationships with customers and determines the key factors that lead to customer acquisition, satisfaction, loyalty and retention, and to business expansion.

3.1 Customer and Market Knowledge (40 pts.)

Describe how your organization determines requirements, expectations, and preferences of customers and markets to ensure the continuing relevance of your products and services and to develop new opportunities.

Within your response, include answers to the following questions:

a. Customer and Market Knowledge

(1) How do you determine or target customers, customer groups, and market segments? How do you include customers of competitors and other potential customers and markets in this determination?

(2) How do you listen and learn to determine key customer requirements and expectations (including product and service features) and their relative importance to customers' purchasing decisions?

How do determination methods vary for different customers or customer groups? How do you use relevant information from current and former customers, including marketing and sales information, customer loyalty and retention data, win/loss analysis, and complaints? How do you use this information for purposes of product and service planning, marketing, process improvements, and other business development?

(3) How do you keep your listening and learning methods current with business needs and directions?

3.2 Customer Relationships and Satisfaction (45 pts.)

Describe how your organization builds relationships to acquire, satisfy, and retain customers, to increase customer loyalty, and to develop new opportunities. Describe also how your organization determines customer satisfaction.

Within your response, include answers to the following questions:

a. Customer Relationship Building
   (1) How do you build relationships to acquire customers, to meet and exceed their expectations, to increase loyalty and repeat business, and to gain positive referrals?
   (2) What are your key access mechanisms for customers to seek information, conduct business, and make complaints? How do you determine key customer contact requirements for each mode of customer access? How do you ensure that these contact requirements are deployed to all people and processes involved in the customer response chain?
   (3) What is your complaint management process? How do you ensure that complaints are resolved effectively and promptly? How are complaints aggregated and analyzed for use in improvement throughout your organization and by your partners?
   (4) How do you keep your approaches to building relationships and providing customers access current with business needs and directions?
b. Customer Satisfaction Determination
   (1) How do you determine customer satisfaction and dissatisfaction? How do these determination methods differ among customer groups? How do you ensure that your measurements capture actionable information for use in exceeding your customers' expectations, securing their future business, and gaining positive referrals? How do you use customer satisfaction and dissatisfaction information for improvement?

(2) How do you follow up with customers on products, services, and transaction quality to receive prompt and actionable feedback?

(3) How do you obtain and use information on your customers' satisfaction relative to customers' satisfaction with your competitors and/or industry benchmarks?

(4) How do you keep your approaches to determining satisfaction current with business needs and directions?

4 Measurement, Analysis, and Knowledge Management (90 pts.)

The *Measurement, Analysis, and Knowledge Management* Category examines how your organization selects, gathers, analyzes, manages, and improves its data, information, and knowledge assets.

4.1 Measurement and Analysis of Organizational Performance (45 pts.)

Describe how your organization measures, analyzes, aligns, and improves its performance data and information at all levels and in all parts of your organization.

Within your response, include answers to the following questions:

a. Performance Measurement
   (1) How do you select, collect, align, and integrate data and information for tracking daily operations and for tracking overall organizational performance? How do you use these data and information to support organizational decision making and innovation?
   (2) How do you select and ensure the effective use of key comparative data and information to support operational and strategic decision making and innovation?
   (3) How do you keep your performance measurement system current with business needs and directions? How do you ensure that your performance measurement system is sensitive to rapid or unexpected organizational or external changes?

b. Performance Analysis
   (1) What analyses do you perform to support your senior leaders' organizational performance review? What analyses do you perform to support your organization's strategic planning?

(2) How do you communicate the results of organizational-level analyses to workgroup and functional-level operations to enable effective support for their decision making?

4.2 Information and Knowledge Management (45 pts.)

Describe how your organization ensures the quality and availability of needed data and information for employees, suppliers and partners, and customers. Describe how your organization builds and manages its knowledge assets.

Within your response, include answers to the following questions:

a. Data and Information Availability
   (1) How do you make needed data and information available? How do you make them accessible to employees, suppliers and partners, and customers, as appropriate?
   (2) How do you ensure that hardware and software are reliable, secure, and user friendly?
   (3) How do you keep your data and information availability mechanisms, including your software and hardware systems, current with business needs and directions?
b. Organizational Knowledge
   (1) How do you manage organizational knowledge to accomplish:
      ■ The collection and transfer of employee knowledge
      ■ The transfer of relevant knowledge from customers, suppliers, and partners
      ■ The identification and sharing of best practices
   (2) How do you ensure the following properties of your data, information, and organizational knowledge:
      ■ Integrity
      ■ Timeliness
      ■ Reliability
      ■ Security
      ■ Accuracy
      ■ Confidentiality

5   Human Resource Focus (85 pts.)

The *Human Resource Focus* Category examines how your organization's work systems and employee learning and motivation enable employees to develop and utilize their full potential in alignment with your organization's overall objectives and action plans. Also examined are your organization's efforts to build and maintain a work environment and employee support climate conducive to performance excellence and to personal and organizational growth.

5.1 Work Systems (35 pts.)

Describe how your organization's work and jobs enable employees and the organization to achieve high performance. Describe how compensation, career progression, and related workforce practices enable employees and the organization to achieve high performance.

Within your response, include answers to the following questions:

a. Organization and Management of Work
   (1) How do you organize and manage work and jobs to promote cooperation, initiative, empowerment, innovation, and your organizational culture? How do you organize and manage work and jobs to achieve the agility to keep current with business needs?
   (2) How do your work systems capitalize on the diverse ideas, cultures, and thinking of your employees and the communities with which you interact (your employee hiring and your customer communities)?
   (3) How do you achieve effective communication and skill sharing across work units, jobs, and locations?
b. Employee Performance Management System
   (1) How does your employee performance management system, including feedback to employees, support high-performance work? How does your employee performance management system support a customer and business focus? How do your compensation, recognition, and related reward and incentive practices reinforce high-performance work and a customer and business focus?
c. Hiring and Career Progression
   (1) How do you identify characteristics and skills needed by potential employees?
   (2) How do you recruit, hire, and retain new employees? How do you ensure that the employees represent the diverse ideas, cultures, and thinking of your employee hiring community?
   (3) How do you accomplish effective succession planning for leadership and management positions, including senior leadership? How do you manage effective career progression for all employees throughout the organization?

5.2 Employee Learning and Motivation (25 pts.)

Describe how your organization's employee education, training, and career development support the achievement of your overall objectives and contribute to high performance. Describe how your organization's education, training, and career development build employee knowledge, skills, and capabilities.

Within your response, include answers to the following questions:

a. Employee Education, Training, and Development
   (1) How do employee education and training contribute to the achievement of your action plans? How do your employee education, training, and development address your key needs associated with organizational performance measurement, performance improvement, and technological change? How does your education and training approach balance short- and longer-term organizational objectives with employee needs for development, learning, and career progression?
   (2) How do employee education, training, and development address your key organizational needs associated with new employee orientation, diversity, ethical business practices, and management and leadership development? How do employee education, training, and development address your key organizational needs associated with employee, workplace, and environmental safety?
   (3) How do you seek and use input from employees and their supervisors and managers on education and training needs? How do you incorporate your organizational learning and knowledge assets into your education and training?
   (4) How do you deliver education and training? How do you seek and use input from employees and their supervisors and managers on options for the delivery of education and training? How do you use both formal and informal delivery approaches, including mentoring and other approaches, as appropriate?
   (5) How do you reinforce the use of new knowledge and skills on the job?
   (6) How do you evaluate the effectiveness of education and training, taking into account individual and organizational performance?
b. Motivation and Career Development
   (1) How do you motivate employees to develop and utilize their full potential? How does your organization use formal and informal mechanisms to help employees attain job- and career-related development and learning objectives? How do managers and supervisors help employees attain job- and career-related development and learning objectives?

5.3 Employee Well-Being and Satisfaction (25 pts.)

Describe how your organization maintains a work environment and an employee support climate that contribute to the well-being, satisfaction, and motivation of all employees.

Within your response, include answers to the following questions:

a. Work Environment
   (1) How do you improve workplace health, safety, security, and ergonomics? How do employees take part in improving them? What are your performance measures or targets for each of these key workplace factors? What are the significant differences in workplace factors and performance measures or targets if different employee groups and work units have different work environments?
   (2) How do you ensure workplace preparedness for emergencies or disasters? How do you seek to ensure business continuity for the benefit of your employees and customers?

b. Employee Support and Satisfaction
   (1) How do you determine the key factors that affect employee well-being, satisfaction, and motivation? How are these factors segmented for a diverse workforce and for different categories and types of employees?
   (2) How do you support your employees via services, benefits, and policies? How are these tailored to the needs of a diverse workforce and different categories and types of employees?
   (3) What formal and informal assessment methods and measures do you use to determine employee well-being, satisfaction, and motivation? How do these methods and measures differ across a diverse workforce and different categories and types of employees? How do you use other indicators, such as employee retention, absenteeism, grievances, safety, and productivity, to assess and improve employee well-being, satisfaction, and motivation?
   (4) How do you relate assessment findings to key business results to identify priorities for improving the work environment and employee support climate?

6 Process Management (85 pts.)

The *Process Management* Category examines the key aspects of your organization's process management, including key product, service, and business processes for creating customers and organizational value and key support processes. This Category encompasses all key processes and all work units.

6.1 Value Creation Processes (50 pts.)

Describe how your organization identifies and manages its key processes for creating customer value and achieving business success and growth.
Within your response, include answers to the following questions:

a. Value Creation Processes
   (1) How does your organization determine its key value creation processes? What are your organization's key product, service, and business processes for creating or adding value? How do these processes create value for the organization, your customers, and your other key stakeholders? How do they contribute to profitability and business success?
   (2) How do you determine key value creation process requirements, incorporating input from customers, suppliers, and partners, as appropriate? What are the key requirements for these processes?
   (3) How do you design these processes to meet all the key requirements? How do you incorporate new technology and organizational knowledge into the design of these processes? How do you incorporate cycle time, productivity, cost control, and other efficiency and effectiveness factors into the design of these processes? How do you implement these processes to ensure they meet design requirements?
   (4) What are your key performance measures or indicators used for the control and improvement of your value creation processes? How does your day-to-day operation of these processes ensure meeting key process requirements? How are in-process measures used in managing these processes? How is customer, supplier, and partner input used in managing these processes, as appropriate?
   (5) How do you minimize overall costs associated with inspections, tests, and process or performance audits, as appropriate? How do you prevent defects and rework, and minimize warranty costs, as appropriate?
   (6) How do you improve your value creation processes to achieve better performance, to reduce variability, to improve products and services, and to keep the processes current with business needs and directions? How are improvements shared with other organizational units and processes?

6.2 Support Processes (35 pts.)

Describe how your organization manages its key processes that support your value creation processes.

Within your response, include answers to the following questions:

a. Support Processes
   (1) How does your organization determine its key support processes? What are your key processes for supporting your value creation processes?
   (2) How do you determine key support process requirements, incorporating input from internal and external customers, and suppliers and partners, as appropriate? What are the key requirements for these processes?
   (3) How do you design these processes to meet all the key requirements? How do you incorporate new technology and organizational knowledge into the design of these processes? How do you incorporate cycle time, productivity, cost control, and other efficiency and effectiveness factors into the design of the processes? How do you implement these processes to ensure they meet design requirements?
   (4) What are your key performance measures or indicators used for the control and improvement of your support processes? How does your day-to-day operation of key support processes ensure meeting key performance requirements? How are in-process measures used in managing these processes? How is customer, supplier, and partner input used in managing these processes, as appropriate?
   (5) How do you minimize overall costs associated with inspections, tests, and process or performance audits, as appropriate? How do you prevent defects and rework?
   (6) How do you improve your support processes to achieve better performance, to reduce variability, and to keep the processes current with business needs and directions? How are improvements shared with other organizational units and processes?

7 Business Results (450 pts.)

The *Business Results* Category examines your organization's performance and improvement in key business areas — customer satisfaction, product and service performance, financial and marketplace performance, human resource results, operational performance, and governance and social responsibility. Also examined are performance levels relative to those of competitors.

7.1   Customer-Focused Results (75 pts.)

Summarize your organization's key customer-focused results, including customer satisfaction and customer-perceived value. Segment your results by customer groups and market segments, as appropriate. Include appropriate comparative data.

Provide data and information to answer the following questions:

a. Customer-Focused Results

(1) What are your current levels and trends in key measures or indicators of customer satisfaction and dissatisfaction? How do these compare with competitors' levels of customer satisfaction?

(2) What are your current levels and trends in key measures or indicators of customer-perceived value, including customer loyalty and retention, positive referral, and other aspects of building relationships with customers, as appropriate?

7.2   Product and Service Results (75 pts.)

Summarize your organization's key product and service performance results. Segment your results by product groups, customer groups, and market segments, as appropriate. Include appropriate comparative data.

Provide data and information to answer the following question:

a. Product and Service Results

(1) What are your current levels and trends in key measures or indicators of product and service performance that are important to your customers? How do these results compare with your competitors' performance?

7.3   Financial and Market Results (75 pts.)

Summarize your organization's key financial and marketplace performance results by market segments, as appropriate. Include appropriate comparative data.

Provide data and information to answer the following questions:

a. Financial and Market Results

(1) What are your current levels and trends in key measures or indicators of financial performance, including aggregate measures of financial return and economic value, as appropriate?

(2) What are your current levels and trends in key measures or indicators of marketplace performance, including market share or position, business growth, and new markets entered, as appropriate?

7.4   Human Resource Results (75 pts.)

Summarize your organization's key human resource results, including work system performance and employee learning, development, well-being, and satisfaction. Segment your results to address the diversity of your workforce and the different types and categories of employees, as appropriate. Include appropriate comparative data.

Provide data and information to answer the following questions:

a.   Human Resource Results
   (1) What are your current levels and trends in key measures or indicators of work system performance and effectiveness?
   (2) What are your current levels and trends in key measures of employee learning and development?
   (3) What are your current levels and trends in key measures or indicators of employee well-being, satisfaction, and dissatisfaction?

7.5   Organizational Effectiveness Results (75 pts.)

Summarize your organization's key operational performance results that contribute to the achievement of organizational effectiveness. Segment your results by product groups and market segments, as appropriate. Include appropriate comparative data.

Provide data and information to answer the following questions:

a.   Organizational Effectiveness Results
   (1) What are your current levels and trends in key measures or indicators of the operational performance of your key value creation processes? Include productivity, cycle time, supplier and partner performance, and other appropriate measures of effectiveness and efficiency.
   (2) What are your current levels and trends in key measures or indicators of the operational performance of your key support processes? Include productivity, cycle time, supplier and partner performance, and other appropriate measures of effectiveness and efficiency.
   (3) What are your results for key measures or indicators of accomplishment of organizational strategy and action plans?

7.6 Governance and Social Responsibility Results (75 pts.)

Summarize your organization's key governance and social responsibility results, including evidence of fiscal accountability, ethical behavior, legal compliance, and organizational citizenship. Segment your results by business units, as appropriate. Include appropriate comparative data.

Provide data and information to answer the following questions:

a. Governance and Social Responsibility Results
   (1) What are your key current findings and trends in key measures or indicators of fiscal accountability, both internal and external, as appropriate?
   (2) What are your results for key measures or indicators of ethical behavior and of stakeholder trust in the governance of your organization?
   (3) What are your results for key measures or indicators of regulatory and legal compliance?
   (4) What are your results for key measures or indicators of organizational citizenship in support of your key communities?

Author Note

This appendix is based on and excerpted from *Criteria for Performance Excellence for Business*, National Institute of Standards and Technology, Baldrige National Quality Program; http://www.baldrige.nist.gov/Business _Criteria.htm.

Appendix H

Value Measuring Methodology

The purpose of the Value Measuring Methodology (VMM) is to define, capture, and measure value associated with electronic services unaccounted for in traditional Return-on-Investment (ROI) calculations, to fully account for costs, and to identify and consider risk. Developed in response to the changing definition of value brought on by the advent of the Internet and advanced software technology, VMM incorporates aspects of numerous traditional business analysis theories and methodologies, as well as newer hybrid approaches.

VMM was designed to be used by organizations across the Federal Government to steer the development of an E-Government initiative, assist decision makers in choosing among investment alternatives, provide the information required to manage effectively, and to maximize the benefit of an investment to the Government.

VMM is based on public and private sector business and economic analysis theories and best practices. It provides the structure, tools, and techniques for comprehensive quantitative analysis and comparison of value (benefits), cost, and risk at the appropriate level of detail.

This appendix provides a high-level overview of the four steps that form the VMM framework. The terminology used to describe the steps should be familiar to those involved in developing, selecting, justifying, and managing an IT investment:

Step 1: Develop a decision framework
Step 2: Alternatives analysis
Step 3: Pull the information together
Step 4: Communicate and document

Step 1: Develop a Decision Framework

A decision framework provides a structure for defining the objectives of an initiative, analyzing alternatives, and managing and evaluating ongoing performance. Just as an outline defines a paper's organization before it is written, a decision framework creates an outline for designing, analyzing, and selecting an initiative for investment, and then managing the investment. The framework can be a tool that management uses to communicate its agency, government-wide, or focus-area priorities.

The framework facilitates establishing consistent measures for evaluating current and/or proposed initiatives. Program managers may use the decision framework as a tool to understand and prioritize the needs of customers and the organization's business goals. In addition, it encourages early consideration of risk and thorough planning practices directly related to effective E-government initiative implementation.

The decision framework should be developed as early as possible in the development of a technology initiative. Employing the framework at the earliest phase of development makes it an effective tool for defining the benefits that an initiative will deliver, the risks that are likely to jeopardize its success, and the anticipated costs that must be secured and managed.

The decision framework is also helpful later in the development process as a tool to validate the direction of an initiative, or to evaluate an initiative that has already been implemented.

The decision framework consists of value (benefits), cost, and risk structures, as shown in Figure H.1. Each of these three elements must be understood to plan, justify, implement, evaluate, and manage an investment.

The tasks and outputs involved with creating a sound decision framework include:

- Tasks:
  - Identify and define value structure
  - Identify and define risk structure
  - Identify and define cost structure
  - Begin documentation

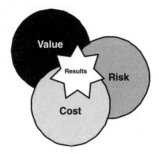

FIGURE H.1 The decision framework.

- Outputs:
  - Prioritized value factors
  - Defined and prioritized measures within each value factor
  - Risk factor inventory (initial)
  - Risk tolerance boundary
  - Tailored cost structure
  - Initial documentation of basis of estimate of cost, value, and risk

Task 1: Identify and Define the Value Structure

The Value Structure describes and prioritizes benefits in two layers. The first considers an initiative's ability to deliver value within each of the five Value Factors (User Value, Social Value, Financial Value, Operational and Foundational Value, and Strategic Value). The second layer delineates the measures to define those values.

By defining the Value Structure, managers gain a prioritized understanding of the needs of stakeholders. This task also requires the definition of metrics and targets critical to the comparison of alternatives and performance evaluation.

The Value Factors consist of five separate, but related, perspectives on value. As defined in Table H.1, each Factor contributes to the full breath and depth of the value offered by the initiative.

Because the Value Factors are usually not equal in importance, they must be "weighted" in accordance with their importance to executive management.

Identification, definition, and prioritization of measures of success must be performed within each Value Factor, as shown in Table H.2. Valid results depend on project staff working directly with representatives of user communities to define and array the measures in order of importance.

TABLE H.1 Value Factors

Value Factor	Definitions	Examples
Direct customer (user)	Benefits to users or groups associated with providing a service through an electronic channel	Convenient access
Social (non-user/public)	Benefits to society as a whole	Trust in government
Gov't/operational foundational	Improvements in government operations and enablement of future initiatives	Cycle time Improved infrastructure
Strategic/political	Contributions to achieving strategic goals, priorities, and mandates	Fulfilling the organizational mission
Government financial	Financial benefits to both sponsoring and other agencies	Reduced cost of correcting errors

TABLE H.2 A Value Factor with Associated Metrics

24/7 Access to Real-Time Information and Services, Anytime and Anywhere
Brief Description: Are customers able to access real-time electronic travel services and policy information from any location 24 hours a day?

Metrics and Scales
Percent of remote access attempts that are successful (10 points for every 10 percent)
Percent of travel services available electronically
10 points = 25 percent
90 points = 75 percent (threshold requirement)
100 points = 100 percent

Is data updated in the system in real-time?
No = 0   Yes = 100

These measures are used to define alternatives, and also serve as a basis for alternatives analysis, comparison, and selection, as well as ongoing performance evaluation.

In some instances, measures may be defined at a higher level to be applied across a related group of initiatives, such as organization-wide or across a focus-area portfolio. These standardized measures then facilitate "apples-to-apples" comparison across multiple initiatives. This provides a standard management "yardstick" against which to judge investments.

Whether a measure has been defined by project staff or at a higher level of management, it must include the identification of a metric, a target, and a normalized scale. The normalized scale provides a method for integrating objective and subjective measures of value into a single decision metric. The scale used is not important; what is important is that the scale remains consistent.

The measures within the Value Factors are prioritized by representatives from the user and stakeholder communities during facilitated group sessions.

Task 2: Identify and Define Risk Structure

The risk associated with an investment in a technology initiative may degrade performance, impede implementation, and/or increase costs. Risk that is not identified cannot be mitigated or managed causing a project to fail either in the pursuit of funding or, more dramatically, during implementation. The greater the attention paid to mitigating and managing risk, the greater the probability of success.

The Risk Structure serves a dual purpose. First, the structure provides the starting point for identifying and inventorying potential risks factors that may jeopardize an initiative's success and ensures that plans for mitigating their impact are developed and incorporated into each viable alternative solution.

Second, the structure provides management the information it needs to communicate the organization's tolerance for risk. Risk tolerance is expressed in terms of cost (what is the maximum acceptable cost "creep" beyond projected cost) and value (what is the maximum tolerable performance slippage).

Risks are identified and documented during working sessions with stakeholders. Issues raised during preliminary planning sessions are discovered, defined, and documented. The result is an initial risk inventory.

To map risk tolerance boundaries, selected knowledgeable staff are polled to identify at least five data points that will define the highest acceptable level of risk for cost and value.

Task 3: Identify and Define the Cost Structure

A Cost Structure is a hierarchy of elements created specifically to accomplish the development of a cost estimate, and is also called a Cost Element Structure (CES).

The most significant objective in the development of a Cost Structure is to ensure a complete, comprehensive cost estimate and to reduce the risk of missing costs or double counting. An accurate and complete cost estimate is critical for an initiative's success. Incomplete or inaccurate estimates can result in exceeding the budget for implementation requiring justification for additional funding or a reduction in scope. The Cost Structure developed in this step will be used during Step 2 to estimate the cost for each alternative.

Ideally, a Cost Structure will be produced early in development, prior to defining alternatives. However, a Cost Structure can be developed after an alternative has been selected or, in some cases, in the early stage of implementation. Early structuring of costs guides refinement and improvement of the estimate during the progress of planning and implementation.

Task 4: Begin Documentation

Documentation of the elements leading to the selection of a particular alternative above all others is the "audit trail" for the decision. The documentation of assumptions, the analysis, the data, the decisions, and the rationale behind them are the foundation for the business case and the record of information required to defend a cost estimate or value analysis.

Early documentation will capture the conceptual solution, desired benefits, and attendant global assumptions (e.g., economic factors such as the discount and inflation rates). The documentation also includes project-specific drivers and assumptions, derived from tailoring the structures.

The basis for the estimate, including assumptions and business rules, should be organized in an easy-to-follow manner that links to all other analysis processes and requirements. This will provide easy access to information supporting the course of action, and will also ease the burden associated with preparing investment justification documents. As an initiative evolves through the life cycle, becoming better defined and more specific, the documentation will also mature in specificity and definition.

Step 2: Alternative Analysis — Estimate Value, Costs, and Risk

An alternatives analysis is an estimation and evaluation of all value, cost, and risk factors (Table H.3) leading to the selection of the most effective plan of action to address a specific business issue (e.g., service, policy, regulation, business process, or system). An alternative that must be considered is the "base case." The base case is the alternative where no change is made to current practices or systems. All other alternatives are compared against the base case, as well as to each other.

TABLE H.3   Risk Can Bundled across Categories

Selected E-Travel Initiative Risks by Risk Category	*C*	*T*	*S*	*O*	*L*
Different agencies have different levels and quality of security mechanisms, which may leave government data vulnerable.	X	X			
Web-enabled system will have increased points of entry for unauthorized internal or external users and pose greater security risks.					
The E-travel concept relies heavily on technology.	X	X	X	X	
Although the private sector has reduced travel fees and operational costs by implementing E-travel services, the commercial sector has not yet widely adopted/developed end-to-end solutions that meet the broad needs articulated by the E-Travel initiative.					
The technology and applications may not be mature enough to provide all of the functionality sought by the E-travel initiative managers.					
Resistance to change may be partially due to fear of job loss, which may lead to challenges from unions.			X	X	X

Note: C = Cost; T = Technology; S = Schedule; O = Operations; L = Legal

Defining Risk

In the assessment of an E-travel initiative, risks were bundled into five categories: cost, technical, schedule, operational, and legal.

The sample table above demonstrates how a single "risk" factor is likely to impact multiple risk categories. Note the level of detail provided in the description. Specificity is critical to distinguish among risks and avoid double counting.

An alternatives analysis requires a disciplined process to consider the range of possible actions to achieve the desired benefits. The rigor of the process to develop the information on which to base the alternatives evaluation yields the data required to justify an investment or course of action. It also provides the information required to support the completion of the budget justification documents. The process also produces a baseline of anticipated value, costs, and risks to guide the management and ongoing evaluation of an investment.

An alternatives analysis must consistently assess the value, cost, and risk associated with more than one alternative for a specific initiative. Alternatives must include the base case and accommodate specific parameters of the decision framework. VMM, properly used, is designed to avoid "analysis paralysis."

The estimation of cost and projection of value uses ranges to define the individual elements of each structure. Those ranges are then subject

Example 1: This measure was established for an e-Travel initiative in the Direct User Value Factor

Value	10	20	30	40	50	60	70	80	90	100
Average # hours from receipt of customer feedback message to response	48.00	44.67	41.33	38.00	34.67	31.33	28.00	24.67	21.33	18.00

Analysts projected the low, expected, and high performance for that measure.

	Low	Expected	High
Average # hours from receipt of customer feedback message to response	38	24	18

The model translated those projections onto the normalized scale.

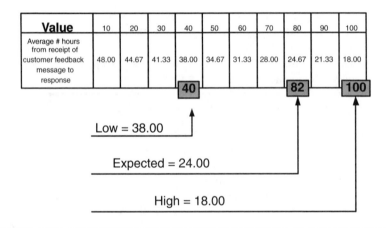

FIGURE H.2   Predicting performance.

to an uncertainty analysis (see Note 1). The result is a range of expected values and cost. Next, a sensitivity analysis (see Note 2) identifies the variables that have a significant impact on this expected value and cost. The analyses will increase confidence in the accuracy of the cost and predicted performance estimates (Figure H.2). However, a risk analysis is critical to determine the degree to which other factors may drive up expected costs or degrade predicted performance.

An alternatives analysis must be carried out periodically throughout the life cycle of an initiative. The following list provides an overview of how the business value resulting from an alternatives analysis changes depending on where in the life cycle the analysis is conducted.

- Strategic Planning (pre-decisional)
  - How well will each alternative perform against the defined value measures?
  - What will each alternative cost?
  - What is the risk associated with each alternative?
  - What will happen if no investment is made at all (base case)?
  - What assumptions were used to produce the cost estimates and value projections?
- Business Modeling and Pilots
  - What value is delivered by the initiative?
  - What are the actual costs to date? Do estimated costs need to be reexamined?
  - Have all risks been addressed and managed?
- Implementation and Evaluation
  - Is the initiative delivering the predicted value? What is the level of value delivered?
  - What are the actual costs to date?
  - Which risks have been realized, how are they affecting costs and performance, and how are they being managed?

The tasks and outputs involved with conducting an alternative analysis include:

- Tasks:
  1. Identify and define alternatives
  2. Estimate value and cost
  3. Conduct risk analysis
  4. Ongoing documentation
- Outputs:
  - Viable alternatives
  - Cost and value analyses
  - Risk analyses
  - Tailored basis of estimate documenting value, cost, and risk economic factors and assumptions

Task 1: Identify and Define Alternatives

The challenge of this task is to identify viable alternatives that have the potential to deliver an optimum mix of both value and cost efficiency. Decision makers must be given, at a minimum, two alternatives plus the base case to make an informed investment decision.

The starting point for developing alternatives should be the information in the Value Structure and preliminary drivers identified in the initial basis of estimate (see Step 1).

Using this information will help to ensure that the alternatives and, ultimately, the solution chosen accurately reflect a balance of performance, priorities, and business imperatives. Successfully identifying and defining alternatives requires cross-functional collaboration and discussion among the stakeholders.

The base case explores the impact of identified drivers on value and cost if an alternative solution is not implemented. That may mean that current processes and systems are kept in place or that organizations will build a patchwork of incompatible, disparate solutions. There should always be a base case included in the analysis of alternatives.

Task 2: Estimate Value and Cost

Comparison of alternatives, justification for funding, creation of a baseline against which ongoing performance may be compared, and development of a foundation for more detailed planning require an accurate estimate of an initiative's cost and value. The more reliable the estimated value and cost of the alternatives, the greater confidence one can have in the investment decision.

The first activity to pursue when estimating value and cost is the collection of data. Data sources and detail will vary based on an initiative's stage of development. Organizations should recognize that more detailed information may be available at a later stage in the process and should provide best estimates in the early stages rather than delaying the process by continuing to search for information that is likely not available.

To capture cost and performance data, and conduct the VMM analyses, a VMM model should be constructed. The model facilitates the normalization and aggregation of cost and value, as well as the performance of uncertainty, sensitivity, and risk analyses.

Analysts populate the model with the dollar amounts for each cost element and projected performance for each measure. These predicted values, or the underlying drivers, will be expressed in ranges (e.g., low, expected, or high). The range between the low and high values will be determined based on the amount of uncertainty associated with the projection.

Initial cost and value estimates are rarely accurate. Uncertainty and sensitivity analyses increase confidence that likely cost and value have been identified for each alternative.

Task 3: Conduct Risk Analysis

The only risks that can be managed are those that have been identified and assessed. A risk analysis considers the probability and potential negative impact of specific factors on an organization's ability to realize projected benefits or estimated cost, as shown in Figure H.3.

Even after diligent and comprehensive risk mitigation during the planning stage, some level of residual risk will remain that may lead to increased costs and decreased performance. A rigorous risk analysis will help an organization better understand the probability that a risk will occur and the level of impact the occurrence of the risk will have on both cost and value. Additionally, risk analysis provides a foundation for building a comprehensive risk management plan.

Task 4: Ongoing Documentation

Inherent in these activities is the need to document the assumptions and research that compensate for gaps in information or understanding. For each alternative, the initial documentation of the high-level assumptions and risks will be expanded to include a general description of the alternative being analyzed, a comprehensive list of cost and value assumptions, and assumptions regarding the risks associated with a specific alternative. This often expands the initial risk inventory.

Step 3: Pull Together the Information

As shown in Figure H.4, the estimations of cost, value, and risk provide important data points for investment decision making. However, when analyzing an alternative and making an investment decision, it is critical to understand the relationships among them.

- ▪ Tasks:
  1. Aggregate the cost estimate
  2. Calculate the return on investment
  3. Calculate the value score
  4. Calculate the risk scores (cost and value)
  5. Compare value, cost, and risk
- ▪ Outputs:
  - – Cost estimate
  - – Return on investment metrics
  - – Value score
  - – Risk scores (cost and value)
  - – Comparison of cost, value, and risk

Alternative 1: Discrete e-Authentication			
Risk	**Probability**	**Cost Impacted**	**Impact**
Cost Overruns			
	Medium		
		1.0 System Planning & Development 2.0 System Acquisition & Implementation 3.0 System Maintenance & Operations	Low Medium High
Cost of Lost Information/Data			
	High		
		1.0 System Planning & Development 2.0 System Acquisition & Implementation 3.0 System Maintenance & Operations	Medium Medium Low

Alternative 1: Discrete e-Authentication			
Risk	**Probability**	**Value Impacted**	**Impact**
Cost Overruns			
	Medium		
		Total Cost Savings to Investment Total Cost Avoidance to Investment	Low Low
Cost of Lost Information/Data			
	High		
		Total Cost Savings to Investment Total Cost Avoidance to Investment	Low Low

These two tables were developed for the risk analysis of an e-Authentication initiative. Note that the impact and probability of risk were assessed for both cost and value.

The probability of a specific risk occurring remains constant throughout the analysis of a specific alternative, regardless of where it impacts the value or cost of a particular impact.

The impact of a single risk factor may differ in magnitude at each point where it interacts with cost and value.

FIGURE H.3   Assessing probability and impact.

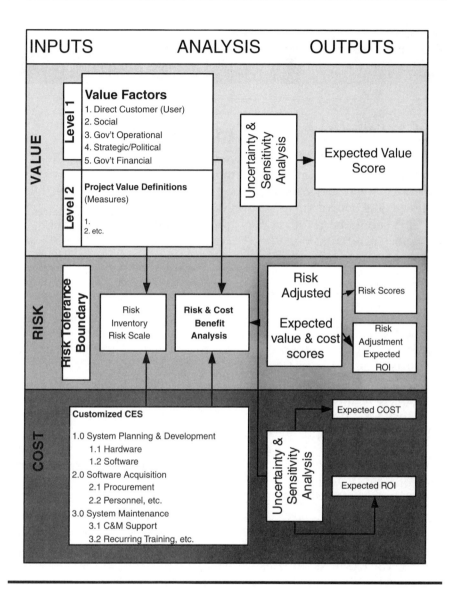

FIGURE H.4 Risk- and cost-benefit analysis.

Task 1: Aggregate the Cost Estimate

A complete and valid cost estimate is critical to determining whether or not a specific alternative should be selected. It also is used to assess how much funding must be requested. Understating cost estimates to gain approval, or not considering all costs, may create doubt as to the veracity of the entire analysis. An inaccurate cost estimate might lead to cost overruns, create the need to request additional funding, or reduce scope.

The total cost estimate is calculated by aggregating expected values for each cost element.

Task 2: Calculate the Return on Investment

Return-on-investment (ROI) metrics express the relationship between the funds invested in an initiative and the financial benefits the initiative will generate. Simply stated, it expresses the financial "bang for the buck." Although it is not considered the only measure upon which an investment decision should be made, ROI is, and will continue to be, a critical data point for decision making.

Task 3: Calculate the Value Score

The value score quantifies the full range of value that will be delivered across the five value factors as defined against the prioritized measures within the decision framework. The interpretation of a value score will vary based on the level from which it is being viewed. At the program level, the value score will be viewed as a representation of how alternatives performed against a specific set of measures. They will be used to make an "apples-to-apples" comparison of the value delivered by multiple alternatives for a single initiative.

For example, the alternative that has a value score of 80 will be preferred over the alternative with a value score of 20, if no other factors are considered. At the organizational or portfolio level, value scores are used as data points in the selection of initiatives to be included in an investment portfolio. Since the objectives and measures associated with each initiative will vary, decision makers at the senior level use value scores to determine what percentage of identified value an initiative will deliver. For example, an initiative with a value score of 75 is providing 75 percent of the possible value the initiative has the potential to deliver. In order to understand what exactly is being delivered, the decision maker will have to look at the measures of the Value Structure.

Consider the value score as a simple math problem. The scores projected for each of the measures within a value factor should be aggregated according to their established weights. The weighted sum of these scores is a factor's value score. The sum of the factors' value scores, aggregated according to their weights, is the total value score.

Task 4: Calculate the Risk Scores

After considering the probability and potential impact of risks, risk scores are calculated to represent a percentage of overall performance slippage or cost increase.

Risk scores provide decision makers with a mechanism to determine the degree to which value and cost will be negatively affected and whether that degree of risk is acceptable based on the risk tolerance boundaries defined by senior staff. If a selected alternative has a high cost and/or high value risk score, program management is alerted to the need for additional risk mitigation, project definition, or more detailed risk management planning. Actions to mitigate the risk may include establishment of a reserve fund, a reduction of scope, or refinement of the alternative's definition. Reactions to excessive risk may also include reconsideration of whether it is prudent to invest in the project at all, given the potential risks, the probability of their occurrence, and the actions required to mitigate them.

Task 5: Compare Value, Cost, and Risk

Tasks 1 through 4 of this step analyze and estimate the value, cost, and risk associated with an alternative. In isolation, each data point does not provide the depth of information required to ensure sound investment decisions.

Previous to the advent of VMM, only financial benefits could be compared to investment costs through the development of an ROI metric. When comparing alternatives, the consistency of the decision framework allows the determination of how much value will be received for the funds invested. Additionally, the use of risk scores provides insight into how all cost and value estimates are affected by risk.

By performing straightforward calculations, it is possible to model the relationships among value, cost, and risk:

- ■ The effect risk will have on estimated value and cost
- ■ The financial ROI
- ■ If comparing alternatives, the value "bang for the buck" (total value returned compared to total required investment)
- ■ If comparing initiatives to be included in the investment portfolio, senior managers can look deeper into the decision framework, moving beyond overall scores to determine the scope of benefits through an examination of the measures and their associated targets

Step 4: Communicate and Document

Regardless of the projected merits of an initiative, its success will depend heavily on the ability of its proponents to generate internal support, to gain buy-in from targeted users, and to foster the development of active leadership supporters (champions). Success or failure may depend as much on the utility and efficacy of an initiative as it does on the ability to communicate its value in a manner that is meaningful to stakeholders with diverse definitions of value. The value of an initiative can be expressed to address the diverse definitions of stakeholder value in funding justification documents and in materials designed to inform and enlist support.

Using VMM, the value of a project is decomposed according to the different Value Factors. This gives project-level managers the tools to customize their value proposition according to the perspective of their particular audience. Additionally, the structure provides the flexibility to respond accurately and quickly to project changes requiring analysis and justification.

The tasks and outputs associated with Step 4 are:

- Tasks:
    1. Communicate value to customers and stakeholders
    2. Prepare budget justification documents
    3. Satisfy ad hoc reporting requirements
    4. Use lessons learned to improve processes
- Outputs:
    - Documentation, insight, and support
    - To develop results-based management controls
    - For communicating initiatives value
    - For improving decision making and performance measurement through "Lessons Learned"
    - Change and ad hoc reporting requirements

Task 1: Communicate Value to Customers and Stakeholders

Leveraging the results of VMM analysis can facilitate relations with customers and stakeholders. VMM makes communication to diverse audiences easier by incorporating the perspectives of all potential audience members from the outset of analysis. Since VMM calculates the potential value that an investment could realize for all stakeholders, it provides data pertinent to each of those stakeholder perspectives that can be used to bolster support for the project. It also fosters substantive discussion with customers regarding the priorities and detailed plans of the investment. These stronger relationships not only prove critical to the long-term success of the project, but can also lay the foundation for future improvements and innovation.

Task 2: Prepare Budget Justification Documents

Many organizations require comprehensive analysis and justification to support funding requests. IT initiatives that have not been proven may not be funded:

- Their applicability to executive missions
- Sound planning
- Significant benefits
- Clear calculations and logic justifying the amount of funding requested
- Adequate risk identification and mitigation efforts
- A system for measuring effectiveness
- Full consideration of alternatives
- Full consideration of how the project fits within the confines of other government entities and current law

After completion of the VMM, one will have the data required to complete or support completion of budget justification documents.

Task 3: Satisfy ad hoc Reporting Requirements

Once a VMM model is built to assimilate and analyze a set of investment alternatives, it can easily be tailored to support ad hoc requests for information or other reporting requirements. In the current, rapidly changing political and technological environment, there are many instances when project managers need to be able to perform rapid analysis. For example, funding authorities, agency partners, market pricing fluctuations, or portfolio managers might impose modifications on the details (e.g., the weighting factors) of a project investment plan; many of these parties are also likely to request additional investment-related information later in the project life cycle. VMM's customized decision framework makes such adjustments and reporting feasible under short time constraints.

Task 4: Use Lessons Learned to Improve Processes

Lessons learned through the use of VMM can be a powerful tool when used to improve overall organizational decision-making and management processes. For example, in the process of identifying metrics, one might discover that adequate mechanisms are not in place to collect critical performance information. Using this lesson to improve measurement mechanisms would give an organization better capabilities for (1) gauging the project's success and mission fulfillment, (2) demonstrating progress to stakeholders and funding authorities, and (3) identifying shortfalls in performance that could be remedied.

Note 1: Uncertainty Analysis

Conducting an uncertainty analysis requires the following:

1. *Identify the variables.* Develop a range of value for each variable. This range expresses the level of uncertainty about the projection. For example, an analyst may be unsure whether an Internet application will serve a population of 100 or 100,000. It is important to be aware of and express this uncertainty in developing the model in order to define the reliability of the model in predicting results accurately.
2. *Identify the probability distribution for the selected variables.* For each variable identified, assign a probability distribution. There are several types of probability distributions (see "Definitions"). A triangular probability distribution is frequently used for this type of analysis. In addition to establishing the probability distribution for each variable, the analyst must also determine whether the actual amount is likely to be high or low.
3. *Run the simulation.* Once the variables' level of uncertainty is identified and each one has been assigned a probability distribution, run the Monte Carlo simulation. The simulation provides the analyst with the information required to determine the range (low to high) and "expected" results for both the value projection and cost estimate. As shown in Figure H.5, the output of the Monte Carlo simulation produces a range of possible results and defines the "mean," the point at which there is an equal chance that the actual value or cost will be higher or lower. The analyst then surveys the range and selects the expected value.

Note 2: Sensitivity Analysis

Sensitivity analysis is used to identify the business drivers that have the greatest impact on potential variations of an alternative's cost and its returned value. Many of the assumptions made at the beginning of a

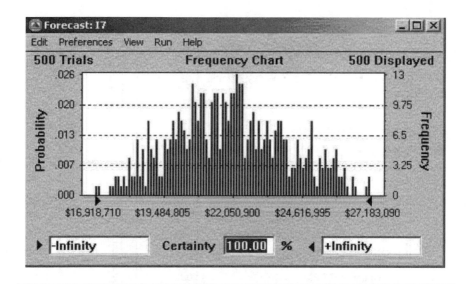

FIGURE H.5 Output of Monte Carlo simulation.

project's definition phase will be found inaccurate later in the analysis. Therefore, one must consider how sensitive a total cost estimate or value projection is to changes in the data used to produce the result. Insight from this analysis allows stakeholders not only to identify variables that require additional research to reduce uncertainty, but also to justify the cost of that research.

The information required to conduct a sensitivity analysis is derived from the same Monte Carlo simulation used for the uncertainty analysis.

Figure H.6 is a sample sensitivity chart. Based on this chart, it is clear that "Build 5/6 Schedule Slip" is the most sensitive variable.

Definitions

Analytic Hierarchy Process (AHP): A proven methodology that uses comparisons of paired elements (comparing one against the other) to determine the relative importance of criteria mathematically.

Benchmark: A measurement or standard that serves as a point of reference by which process performance is measured.

Benefit: A term used to indicate an advantage, profit, or gain attained by an individual or organization.

Benefit to Cost Ratio (BCR): The computation of the financial benefit/cost ratio is done within the construct of the following formula: Benefits ÷ Cost.

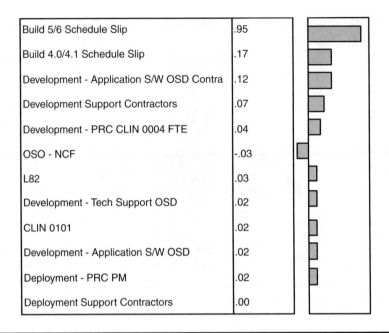

Build 5/6 Schedule Slip	.95
Build 4.0/4.1 Schedule Slip	.17
Development - Application S/W OSD Contra	.12
Development Support Contractors	.07
Development - PRC CLIN 0004 FTE	.04
OSO - NCF	-.03
L82	.03
Development - Tech Support OSD	.02
CLIN 0101	.02
Development - Application S/W OSD	.02
Deployment - PRC PM	.02
Deployment Support Contractors	.00

FIGURE H.6   Sensitivity chart.

Cost Element Structure (CES): A hierarchical structure created to facilitate the development of a cost estimate. May include elements that are not strictly products to be developed or produced (e.g., Travel, Risk, Program Management Reserve, Life-Cycle Phases, etc.). Samples include:

1. System planning and development
   1.1 Hardware
   1.2 Software
       1.2.1 Licensing fees
   1.3 Development support
       1.3.1 Program management oversight
       1.3.2 System engineering architecture design
       1.3.3 Change management and risk assessment
       1.3.4 Requirement definition and data architecture
       1.3.5 Test and evaluation
   1.4 Studies
       1.4.1 Security
       1.4.2 Accessibility
       1.4.3 Data architecture
       1.4.4 Network architecture

      1.5 Other
          1.5.1 Facilities
          1.5.2 Travel
2. System acquisition and implementation
      2.1 Procurement
          2.1.1 Hardware
          2.1.2 Software
          2.1.3 Customized software
      2.2 Personnel
      2.3 Training
3. System maintenance and operations
      3.1 Hardware
          3.1.1 Maintenance
          3.1.2 Upgrades
          3.1.3 Life-cycle replacement
      3.2 Software
          3.2.1 Maintenance
          3.2.2 Upgrades
          3.2.3 License fees
      3.3 Support
          3.3.1 Helpdesk
          3.3.2 Security
          3.3.3 Training

Cost Estimate: The estimation of a project's life-cycle costs, time-phased by fiscal year, based on the description of a project or system's technical, programmatic, and operational parameters. A cost estimate may also include related analyses such as cost-risk analyses, cost-benefit analyses, schedule analyses, and trade studies.

Commercial Cost Estimating Tools:

- PRICE S: A parametric model used to estimate software size, development cost, and schedules, along with software operations and support costs. Software size estimates can be generated for source lines of code, function points, or predictive objective points. Software development costs are estimated based on input parameters reflecting the difficulty, reliability, productivity, and size of the project. These same parameters are used to generate operations and support costs. Monte Carlo risk simulation can be generated as part of the model output. Government Agencies (e.g., NASA, IRS, U.S. Air Force, U.S. Army, U.S. Navy, etc.) as well as private companies have used PRICE S.

- PRICE H, HL, M: A suite of hardware parametric cost models used to estimate hardware development, production, and operations and support costs. These hardware models provide the capability to generate a total ownership cost to support program management decisions. Monte Carlo risk simulation can be generated as part of the model output. Government Agencies (e.g., NASA, U.S. Air Force, U.S. Army, U.S. Navy, etc.) as well as private companies have used the PRICE suite of hardware models.

▪ SEER-SEM (System Evaluations and Estimation of Resources-Software Estimating Model): A parametric modeling tool used to estimate software development costs, schedules, and manpower resource requirements. Based on the input parameters provided, SEER-SEM develops cost, schedule, and resource requirement estimates for a given software development project.

▪ SEER-H (System Evaluations and Estimation of Resources-Hybrid): A hybrid cost estimating tool that combines analogous and parametric cost estimating techniques to produce models that accurately estimate hardware development, production, and operations and maintenance cost. SEER-H can be used to support a program manager's hardware Life-Cycle Cost estimate or provide an independent check of vendor quotes or estimates developed by third parties. SEER-H is part of a family of models from Galorath Associates, including SEER SEM (which estimates the development and production costs of software) and SEER-DFM (used to support design for manufacturability analyses).

▪ Data Sources (by phase of development):

1. Strategic planning
   1.1 Strategic and performance plans
   1.2 Subject matter expert input
   1.3 New and existing user surveys
   1.4 Private/public sector best practices, lessons learned, and benchmarks
   1.5 Enterprise architecture
   1.6 Modeling and simulation
   1.7 Vendor market survey
2. Business modeling and pilots
   2.1 Subject matter expert input
   2.2 New and existing user surveys
   2.3 Best practices, lessons learned, and benchmarks
   2.4 Refinement of modeling and simulation
3. Implementation and evaluation
   3.1 Data from phased implementation
   3.2 Actual spending/cost data
   3.3 User group/stakeholder focus groups
   3.4 Other performance measurement

Internal Rate of Return (IRR): The internal rate of return is the discount rate that sets the net present value of the program or project to zero. While the internal rate of return does not generally provide an acceptable decision criterion, it does provide useful information, particularly when budgets are constrained or there is uncertainty about the appropriate discount rate.

Life-Cycle Costs: The overall estimated cost for a particular program alternative over the time period corresponding to the life of the program, including direct and indirect initial costs plus any periodic or continuing costs of operation and maintenance.

Monte Carlo Simulation: A simulation is any analytical method that is meant to imitate a real-life system, especially when other analyses are too mathematically complex or too difficult to reproduce. Spreadsheet risk analysis uses both a spreadsheet model and simulation to analyze the effect of varying inputs on outputs of the modeled system. One type of spreadsheet simulation is Monte Carlo simulation, which randomly generates values for uncertain variables over and over to simulate a model. (Monte Carlo simulation was named for Monte Carlo, Monaco, where the primary attractions are casinos containing games of chance.) Analysts identify all key assumptions for which the outcome was uncertain. For the life cycle, numerous inputs are each assigned one of several probability distributions. The type of distribution selected depended on the conditions surrounding the variable. During simulation, the value used in the cost model is selected randomly from the defined possibilities.

Net Present Value (NPV): The difference between the present value of benefits and the present value of costs. The benefits referred to in this calculation must be quantified in cost or financial terms in order to be included.

$$\text{Net present value} = \big[\text{PV (internal project cost savings, operational)}$$
$$+ \text{PV (mission cost savings)}\big] - \text{PV (initial investment)}$$

Polling Tools:

■ Option finder: A real-time polling device that permits participants, using handheld remotes, to vote on questions and have the results displayed immediately, with statistical information such as "degree of variance," and discussed.

■ Group systems: A tool that allows participants to answer questions using individual laptops. The answers to these questions are then displayed to all participants anonymously, in order to spur discussion and the free flowing exchange of ideas. Group Systems also has a polling device.

Return-on-Investment (ROI): A financial management approach used to explain how well a project delivers benefits in relation to its cost. Several methods are used to calculate a return on investment. Refer to Internal Rate of Return (IRR), Net Present Value (NPV), and Savings to Investment Ratio (SIR).

Risk: A term used to define the class of factors that (1) have a measurable probability of occurring during an investment's life cycle, (2) have an associated cost or effect on the investment's output or outcome (typically an adverse effect that jeopardizes the success of an investment), and (3) have alternatives from which the organization may choose.

Risk Categories:

■ Project Resources/Financial: Risk associated with "cost creep," misestimation of life-cycle costs, reliance on a small number of vendors without cost controls, and (poor) acquisition planning.

■ Technical/Technology: Risk associated with immaturity of commercially available technology; reliance on a small number of vendors; risk of technical problems/failures with applications and its ability to provide planned and desired technical functionality.

■ Business/Operational: Risk associated with business goals; risk that the proposed alternative fails to result in process efficiencies and streamlining; risk that business goals of the program or initiative will not be achieved; risk that the program effectiveness targeted by the project will not be achieved.

■ Organizational and Change Management: Risk associated with organizational/agency/government-wide cultural resistance to change and standardization; risk associated with bypassing, lack of use, or improper use or adherence to new systems and processes due to organizational structure and culture; inadequate training planning.

■ Data/Information: Risk associated with the loss/misuse of data or information, risk of increased burdens on citizens and businesses due to data collection requirements if the associated business processes or the project requires access to data from other sources (federal, state, and/or local agencies).

■ Security: Risk associated with the security/vulnerability of systems, Web sites, information and networks; risk of intrusions and connectivity to other (vulnerable) systems; risk associated with the misuse (criminal/fraudulent) of information; must include level of risk (hi, med, basic) and what aspect of security determines the level of risk (e.g., need for confidentiality of information associated with the project/system, availability of the information or system, or reliability of the information or system).

■ Strategic: Risk that the proposed alternative fails to result in the achievement of those goals or in making contributions to them.

- ▪ Privacy: Risk associated with the vulnerability of information collected on individuals, or risk of vulnerability of proprietary information on businesses.

Risk Analysis: A technique to identify and assess factors that may jeopardize the success of a project or achieving a goal. This technique also helps define preventive measures to reduce the probability of these factors from occurring and identify countermeasures to successfully deal with these constraints when they develop.

Savings to Investment Ratio (SIR): SIR represents the ratio of savings to investment. The "savings" in the SIR computation are generated by Internal Operational Savings and Mission Cost Savings. The flow of costs and cost savings into the SIR formula is as shown in Figure H.7.

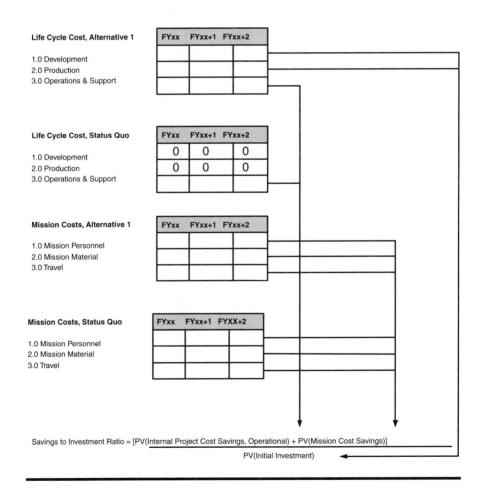

FIGURE H.7   Savings to investment ratio.

Sensitivity Analysis: Analysis of how sensitive outcomes are to changes in the assumptions. The assumptions that deserve the most attention should depend largely on the dominant benefit and cost elements and the areas of greatest uncertainty of the program or process being analyzed.

Stakeholder: An individual or group with an interest in the success of an organization in delivering intended results and maintaining the viability of the organization's products and services. Stakeholders influence programs, products, and services.

Author Note:

This appendix is based on and excerpted from the *Value Measuring Methodology — How-To-Guide,* The U.S. Chief Information Officers Council; http://www.cio.gov/archive/ValueMeasuring_Methodology_HowToGuide _Oct_2002.pdf.

Appendix I

Balanced Scorecard Samples

Southwest Airlines

| | | Strategic Theme: | | |
Operating Efficiency	Objectives	Management	Target	Initiative
Financial	Profitability	Market value	30 percent CAGR[a]	
	More customers	Seat revenue	20 percent CAGR	
	Fewer planes	Plane least cost	5 percent CAGR	
Customer	Flight is on time	FAA on time arrival rating	#1	Quality mgmt
	Lowest prices	Customer ranking	#1	Customer loyalty program
Internal	Fast ground turnaround	On ground time	30 minutes	Cycle time optimization
		On time departure	90 percent	
Learning	Ground crew alignment	Percent ground crew trained	Year 1, 70 percent	ESOP
		Percent ground crew stockholders	Year 3, 90 percent Year 5, 100 percent	Ground crew training

[a] CAGR = compound annual growth rate.

Assisted Living

Objectives	Measure	Target	Initiatives
Financial			
Increase sales	Sales data and reports	15 percent increase in sales	Reward and recognition program
Increase profits	Net earnings	Increase revenue	Improve sales volume efforts
Internal Business Processes			
Decrease time spent on manual processes	Actual time per day spent on manual functions	Decrease time by 75 percent	Technology options
Learning and Growth			
Increase employee involvement	Employee surveys and questionnaires	30 percent increase in employee involvement in specific programs	Team participation programs and individual involvement programs
Increase employee knowledge and productivity	Employee testing and data analysis	20 percent increase in productivity	Continual training programs
Customer Relations			
Improve customer service	Customer surveys and questionnaires	Improve service ratings by 20 percent	Implement plan to open communications with customers

School

Objective	Measurement	Target	Initiative
Customer			
Increase Web site user activity	Data gathered regarding number of hits and number of return visits	15 percent increase per year	Improve content management functionality and provide relevant and timely data

Objective	Measurement	Target	Initiative
Improve parent/student/ teacher communication	Data gathered from students, specific Web data recorded by student/ parent log-in	75 percent parent/student participation for secondary grade levels	Provide timely entry of grades, assignment and attendance information
Improve district communication to community members	Online survey data collected periodically	85 percent satisfactory or above responses to survey	Provide daily school bulletins, weekly news updates, and current district calendar of events

Internal

Increase staff participation in online content	Number of staff and classroom Web sites maintained	30 percent participation at each grade level, year one	Provide training and early adapter incentives
Improve data collection methods for tests/quizzes	Number of assessments given online	5 percent increase in participation for each content area	Identify existing assessments performed on paper that meet online criteria

Financial

Reduce the amount of dollars spent on paper communication	Copy and mailing costs by building/ department	20 percent decrease in paper communications	Identify unnecessary paper communications and encourage online alternatives

Learning and Growth

Provide online learning opportunities	Instructional guides and training resources	Increase online training content available by 10 percent	Convert existing training materials to electronic format

Billing Service

Objective	Measurement	Target	Initiative
Internal Process			
Increase the number of suppliers working on a summary billing format	Year over year number of suppliers is increasing	5 percent increase in supplier participation	Any supplier that submits a monthly invoice or existing supplier that submits an invoice greater than ten lines
Increase the number of suppliers that offer a discount for early payment	Year over year number of suppliers is increasing	Average of 3.5 percent for all suppliers that provide products or services in excess of $50,000	
Shorten cycle time for payment processing	Year over year days to process payments decreases	20 days from date of submission to date of funds transfer	Improve the cycle time for invoice process from the current cycle of 46 days to 10 days for all suppliers greater than $50,000
Learning Process			
Identify the business relationship between families of suppliers	Strategically source from parent supplier organizations for volume discounts	Rationalize supply base according to parent/child relationships by 2 percent or supplier rationalization of 2 percent	Use analytics tools bench and SEC codes from D&B to maintain clean AP vendor files

Warranty Registration System

Objective	Measurement	Target	Initiative	Did Not Meet Goal	Met Goal	Exceeded Goal
					Score	

Financial

Objective	Measurement	Target	Initiative	Did Not Meet Goal	Met Goal	Exceeded Goal
Reduction of printing costs	Actual printing costs of warranty card	Eliminate all printing costs	Remove printed card, publicize new registration process			

External/Customer

Objective	Measurement	Target	Initiative	Did Not Meet Goal	Met Goal	Exceeded Goal
Increase customer registration by making the process easier and fee free (no mailing cost)	Number of registered products via new online method	Currently get 15 cards per day via mail New target for first year is 25 registrations per day by year end	Make obvious sticker to draw attention to new registration process on product, promote registration on other areas of Web site, run promotion with retailers with random giveaway each month to all those who register online			

Objective	Measurement	Target	Initiative	Score		
				Did Not Meet Goal	Met Goal	Exceeded Goal
Get customer onto our Web site so we can expose them to other products they may not know	Measure pages visited and session time on site via Webtrends software if they start on registra-tion page	Get 20 percent of people coming for registration to go to other pages	Cross promotions on registration page			

Internal Business Process

Save time and cost by eliminating manual sorting and processing of cards	Employee hours	35 minutes/ day reduction, which is current time spent	Create online registration process			
Give marketing the ability to mine a database of consumers for more targeted campaigns	Mailing costs by focusing mailings on interested consumers	50 percent reduction in mailing costs for at least three campaigns per year	Teach marketing how to use database, what fields are available, add target audience to marketing plan form			

Objective	Measurement	Target	Initiative	Score		
				Did Not Meet Goal	Met Goal	Exceeded Goal

Learning and Growth

Objective	Measurement	Target	Initiative	Did Not Meet Goal	Met Goal	Exceeded Goal
Allow marketing to learn about consumers that are purchasing our products through surveys	Survey response completion by consumers that are registering product	15 percent of consumers who register are willing to answer optional survey questions	Targeted short surveys — survey design, possible giveaway each month for those who answer survey questions			

Web Store

Objective	Measure	Target	Initiative
Increase Web site visits	Number of hits	Increase by 10 percent monthly	Track hits using a counter
Increase sales	Number of individual sales	Increase monthly by 15 percent	Track using internal accounting system
Increase repeat sales	Number of repeat customers	Increase monthly by 5 percent	Track using internal CRM program
Increase dollar amount of each sale	Average dollar amount of each sale	Increase monthly by 10 percent	Track using internal accounting system
Increase specific products sales	Number of sales by product	Increase each by 10 percent	Track using internal inventory program

Vendor Registration

Objectives	Measures	Target	Initiative
Financial			
Reduce the cost spent to purchase transactions	Percent of purchasing operating expense to purchasing dollars	3.3 percent	Use Web site to reduce labor and administrative purchasing costs
Reduce the cost of goods purchased	Costs for goods and services purchased	Reduce by 5 percent	Increase competition through Web site
Internal Business Processes			
Reduce cycle time to process bids	The number of days from initiation to contract award	Process in an average of 9.5 days	Post all bids and quotations on Web site
Increase percent of invoices paid within 30 days	The number of invoices paid under 30 days as compared to total number of invoices processed	Achieve 99 percent paid on time every month	Process as many invoices as possible electronically
Learning and Growth			
Increase training for purchasing staff	Annual hours of training received per purchasing employee	Achieve 31 hours per year per employee	Use train the trainer as well as formal training programs
Increase number of active suppliers per purchasing employee	Number of active suppliers	Increase to 550 active suppliers	Aggressively market new E-business initiative

Objectives	Measures	Target	Initiative
Stakeholder Relations			
Improve communication of project to external stakeholders	External stakeholder satisfaction with project, measured by surveys	Increase satisfaction by 5 percent	Weekly or monthly electronic newsletter updating external stakeholders on developments with the project
Increase the number of purchasing transactions through e-commerce	Number of transactions occurring through website	Increase to 7.5% of all transactions	Continually seek quotations that can be transacted through Web site instead of manually

Purchasing Systems

Objectives	Measures	Target	Initiative
Financial			
Reduce administrative costs	Cost to spend ratio	Reduce administrative costs by 10 percent	Implement plan to improve efficiencies
Increase profits	Net earnings	Increase revenue	Improve volume and collection efforts
Internal Business Processes			
Decrease the number of fraudulent transactions	The number of fraud instances reported	Reduce the number by 10 percent	Implement stronger policies to penalize dishonest sellers
Reduce system downtime	Downtime, in minutes per month	Achieve 99 percent online per month	Schedule system maintenance during low customer use times
Learning and Growth			
Improve Internet marketing	Number of hits and site visits from Internet ads	Increase by 15 percent	Assess target market for effectiveness of current ad placements
Increase number of buyers and sellers by regions	Number of auctions and bids per auction	Increase by 5 percent per region	Form region-specific auctions
Increase participants in B2C auctions	Number of businesses selling surplus via auctions	Increase by 10 percent	Market push to businesses
Customer Relations			
Improve response time to respond to questions	Time from receipt of question to response	Decrease to four hours for 99 percent of responses	Empower first-level CSRs to respond to questions
Decrease the number of disputes	Number of resolved and unresolved disputes	Decrease unresolved disputes by 5 percent	Implement plan to intervene earlier and faster in disputes

General Business

Objective	Measure	Target
Financial Perspective		
Provide excellent return for our stockholders	Return on equity	15 percent
Be a growing and profitable company	Annual sales	$2.0 billion
	Net income	450 million
	Net profit margin	20 percent
	Net revenue growth	50 percent
Maintain low risk on investment	Debt/equity ratio	0.02 percent
Customer Perspective		
Increase customer satisfaction	Customer satisfaction rate	95 percent
Increase number of registered users	Number of registered users	50 million users by 2005
Customer retention	Customer retention rate	80 percent
Internal Perspective		
Provide technology and technology support	Upgrade software and hardware on quarterly basis or at equipment failure	Increase server efficiency 15 percent per quarter and decrease dead time 25 percent per quarter
Increase management support	Annual review of management actions	Remove management not meeting 10 percent company objectives yearly
Increase services offered	Use surveys and call centers for customer preferences every six months	5 percent addition of auction houses and new niches
Learning and Growth Perspective		
Continue to be the leader in the industry	Compare quarterly results to that of our competitors	Be in the top 5 percent with a difference of at least −1.5 percent between us and our competitors

Objective	Measure	Target
Adapt and change to demands in the industry	Conduct customer survey to identify if we are meeting the demands of a changing market	95 percent satisfaction rating for keeping up with changing trends
Recruit and obtain the best employees	Employee turnover rate	10 percent

Appendix J

Resources

http://www.balancedscorecard.org/ — The Balanced Scorecard Institute is an independent educational institute that provides training and guidance to assist government agencies and companies in applying best practices in balanced scorecard (BSC) and performance measurement for strategic management and transformation.

http://www.bscol.com/ — BSCol offers a wide variety of services for organizations at any stage of developing and using the balanced scorecard. Its advisory, educational, online, and training services can be extensively customized to develop solutions for organizations small and large throughout the world. This is the Kaplan and Norton site.

http://www.bscnews.com/ — The Balanced Scorecard Newswire aims to keep you updated on every aspect of the scorecard. Join its more than 3,000 (free) subscribers and discover the balanced scorecard — the most compelling and innovative strategic performance management tool available.

http://www.performance-measurement.net/ — A portal for people specifically interested in performance measurement and management. A resource for articles, case studies, books, events, and links. Visitors have the opportunity to share knowledge, ask questions of the experts, and exchange experiences through the online forum.

http://www.valuebasedmanagement.net/ — This is the number-one source on the Internet on value-based management and corporate performance management. It offers articles, magazines, news sites, books, communities, thought leaders, best practices, research, training, methods, tools, etc.

http://www.aspanet.org/bscorecard/index.html — The purpose of the Balanced Scorecard Interest Group is twofold: (1) to provide an opportunity for federal agencies contemplating the use of balanced scorecard techniques to learn from the experiences of others and to consequently make a more informed decision; and (2) to prove an ongoing opportunity for federal agencies engaged in the application of balanced scorecard techniques to share their experiences and learn from each other.

http://www.som.cranfield.ac.uk/som/cbp/pma/ — The Performance Measurement Association, a global network for those interested in the theory and practice of performance measurement and management.

http://www.acq.osd.mil/pm/ — Information on earned value project management for government, industry, and academic users.

http://www.themanager.org/Knowledgebase/Management/BSC.htm — Balanced scorecard management portal.

http://www.uspto.gov/web/offices/com/oqm-old/balanced_scorecards.htm — Complete list of balanced scorecard indicators and metrics for 16 different departments of the United States Patent and Trademark Office. Makes for interesting reading.

http://www.ohr.sc.gov/orgperformance/hrmeasures.htm — Human resources performance measures.

http://www.baselinemag.com/category2/0,1426,655835,00.asp — Various downloadable calculators, including internal rate of return, EVA, and ROI.

http://www.balancedscorecard.org/webbbs/ — Balanced Scorecard Institute's public message forum.

Appendix K

The E-Business Audit

There are four components of an E-business audit:

1. Systemic audit
2. Security and quality
3. Ergonomics
4. Customer service

1   Systemic Audit

It is surprising that many companies spend millions of dollars on advertising budgets to draw more "eyeballs" to their sites but never factor in whether or not the projected additional load can be supported by the current system configuration.

A systemic audit looks at such things as response time, network architecture, and linkages.

1.1   Response Time

Measurables in this section include actual response time versus projected response time. Despite the advances in supplying high-bandwidth connections to consumers, the vast majority of PCs are connected to the Web with little more than a 56 Kb modem and good intentions. This means that sites that are highly graphical or use add-ons such as Macromedia Flash will appear slow to download.

Given the wide variety of modem types, auditors should test the response time of the site using different scenarios, such as:

- Using a DSL or cable modem connection
- Using a 56 Kb connection
- Using a 28 Kb connection
- At random times during the day, particularly at 9 a.m. (start of work day) and 4 p.m. (kids home from school)

Web sites such as netmechanic.com, a subscription service, can assist in this endeavor by checking for slow response time directly from their Web sites.

1.2   Broken Links

One of the top five irritants that Web surfers report is clicking on a link and getting a "nonexistent page" error message. This is often the result of system maintenance where Web programmers move the actual page but neglect to modify the link to that page. Unfortunately, this is a frequent occurrence. One of a number of tools, including netmechanic.com, can assist in tracking down these broken links. Metrics in this section include the number of broken links.

1.3   Database Audit

Originally, the Web was a simple place. It consisted of mostly text and there was nary a database in sight. Today, the Web is filled to the brim with databases. The addition of databases makes the audit process even more complex. Because programming code is used to query — and perhaps even calculate — against that database, it is imperative that random checks be performed in an effort to pinpoint database query and calculation errors.

Essentially, auditing database access is similar to the traditional IT (information technology) QA (quality assurance) process. One or more scripts must be written that will take that database through its paces. For example, if a database program calculates insurance rates based on a zip code, then that calculation should be duplicated either manually or in a different parallel automated fashion to ensure that the result is correct.

The same can be said for information that visitors to the site enter via a form. Is the information being entered the same that is being sent to the database?

Metrics include wait time per database request, number of database error messages, and number of incorrect results.

1.4 Network Audit

The network itself, including node servers, should be tested to see if it is effectively configured to provide optimum response. It is not uncommon to find the Web development group separated from the traditional IT development group. This means that one frequently finds network configurations architected inappropriately for the task at hand. For example, a site attracting tens of thousands of hits a day would do well to run a multitude of Web servers rather than just one.

Most organizations use one or more ISPs (Internet service providers) to host their sites. The auditor should carefully gauge the level of service provided by these ISPs as well.

Metrics include network response time and network downtime.

2 Security and Quality

There is no one topic that is discussed more in the press than Internet security. From sasser worms to wily hackers breaking into Western Union, security is an important component of the E-business audit.

It is worthwhile to keep in mind that the auditor is not a security auditor, nor should he be. His role is to do a top-level assessment of the security of the E-business and, if warranted, recommend the services of a security firm well-versed in penetration and intrusion testing.

The entire issue of security is wrapped up within the more comprehensive issue of quality. This section will address both issues.

2.1 Review the Security Plan

All organizations must possess a security plan — in writing. If they do not have this, then they are severely deficient. The plan, at a minimum, should address:

2.1.1 *Authentication.* Is the person who he or she says he is?

2.1.2 *Authorization.* What users have what privileges? That is, who can do what?

2.1.3 *Information integrity.* Can the end user maliciously modify the information?

2.1.4 *Detection.* Once a problem is identified, how is it handled?

2.2 Passwords

Passwords are the first shield of protection against malicious attacks upon your E-business. Questions to ask in this section include:

2.2.1   Is anonymous log-in permitted? Under what conditions?

2.2.2   Is a password scanner periodically used to determine if passwords used can be hacked? Examples of this sort of utility include L0phtcrack.com for NT and www.users.dircon.co.uk/~crypto for UNIX.

2.2.3   How often are passwords changed?

2.2.4   How often are administrative accounts used to log on to systems? Passwords are difficult to remember. This means that to quickly gain entrance to systems, administrative and programming systems people often create easy-to-remember passwords such as admin. These are the first passwords that hackers use to try to gain entrance into a system.

2.3 Staff Background

Administrative network staff must have a security background as well as a technical background. Those wishing to train their staff members would do well to look into the Security Skills Certification Program provided by www.sans.org.

2.4 Connectivity

Today's organization may have many external connections (i.e., partners, EDI, etc.). For each company connected to, the auditor should examine:

2.4.1   *The data being passed between organizations.* Is what the company sent being received correctly?

2.4.2   *The security of the connection.* How is the data being transmitted? Is it required to be secure? Is encryption being used?

2.4.3   *Encryption algorithm.* If encryption is indeed being used, it must be determined whether an appropriate algorithm is being deployed.

2.5 The Product Base

All organizations invest and then use a great deal of third-party software. As publicized by the press, much of this software, particularly browsers and e-mail packages but word processing packages as well, contain security holes that, left unpatched, put the organization at risk. Therefore, for each software package (for Net purposes) being used:

2.5.1 Check for publicized security holes.
2.5.2 Check for availability of software patches. Always upgrade to the latest version of software and apply the latest patches.
2.5.3 Check to see if patches have been successfully applied.
2.5.4 Check security software for security holes. Security software, such as a firewall, can contain security holes just like any other type of software. Check for updates.

2.6 In-House Development

The vast majority of E-business software is written by in-house programming staff. When writing for the Web, it is important to ensure that your own staff does not leave gaping holes through which malicious outsiders can gain entrance. There are a variety of programming "loopholes," so to speak, that open the door wide to hackers:

2.6.1 In programming parlance, a "GET" sends data from the browser (client) to the server. For example, look at the query string below:

```
http://www.site.com/process_card.asp?cardnum-
ber=123456789
```

All HTTP (Hypertext Transport Protocol) requests get logged into the server log as straight text as shown below:

```
2000-09-15 00:12:30 - W3SVC1
GET/process_card.asp
cardnumber=123456789 200 0 623 360 570
80 HTTP/1.1 Mozilla/4.0+(compati-
ble;+5.01;+Windows+NT)
```

Not only is the credit card number clearly visible in the log but it might also be stored in the browser's history file, thus exposing this sensitive information to someone else using the same machine later on.

Security organizations recommend the utilization of the POST method rather than the GET method for this reason.

2.6.2 Are the programmers using "hidden" fields to pass sensitive information? An example of this is relying on hidden form fields used with shopping carts. The hidden fields are sometimes used to send the item price when the customer submits the form. It is rather easy for a malicious user to save the Web page to his or her own PC, change the hidden field to reflect any price he or she wants, and then submit it.

2.6.3 One way to combat the problem discussed in 2.6.2 is to use a hash methodology. A hash is a function that processes a variable-length input and produces a fixed-length output. Because it is difficult to reverse the process, the sensitive data transmitted in this matter is secured. The auditor is required to assess the utilization of this methodology given any problems he or she might find in assessing 2.6.2.

2.6.4 Is sensitive data being stored in ASP or JSP pages? Microsoft's Internet Information Server (IIS) contains a number of security flaws that, under certain circumstances, allow the source of an ASP or JSP page to be displayed rather than executed. That is, the source code is visible to anyone browsing that particular Web site. If sensitive data, such as passwords, is being stored in the code, then this sensitive data will be displayed as well. The rule here is to not hardcode any security credentials into the page itself.

2.6.5 Are application-specific accounts with rights identified early in the development cycle? There are two types of security. One is referred to as "declarative" and takes place when access control is set from the outset the application program. "Programmatic" security occurs when the program itself checks the rights of the person accessing the system. When developing code for E-business, it is imperative that the rights issued be addressed early on in the development cycle. Questions to ask include:

- How many groups will be accessing the data?
- Will each group have the same rights?
- Will you need to distinguish between different users within a group?
- Will some pages permit anonymous access while others enforce authentication?

2.6.6 How are you dealing with cross-site scripting? When sites accept user-provided data (e.g., registration information, bulletin boards), which is then used to build dynamic pages (i.e., pages created on the spur of the moment), the potential for security problems increases a hundred-fold. No longer is the Web content created entirely by the Web designers — some of it now comes from other users. The risk comes from the existence of a number of ways in which text can be entered to simulate code. This code can then be executed as any other code written by the Web designers — except that it was written by a malicious user instead.

Both JavaScript and html can be manipulated to contain malicious code. The malicious code can perform a number of activities such as redirecting users to other sites, modifying cookies, etc. More information on this topic can be obtained from the CERT Web site at http://www.cert.org/advisories/CA-2000-02.html and http://www.cert.org/tech_tips/malicious_code_mitigation.html.

2.6.7   Have you checked wizard-generated/sample code? Often, programmers "reuse" sample code they find on the Web or make use of generated code from Web development tools. And the sample or generated code frequently contains hardcoded credentials to access databases, directories, etc. The auditor will want to make sure that this is not the case in the code being audited.

2.6.8   Are code reviews being performed? There is nothing worse than the lone programmer. Many of the problems discussed in the sections above can be negated if the code all programmers write is subject to peer review. Code reviews, a mainstay of traditional quality-oriented programming methodology, are rarely done in today's fast-paced E-business environment. This is one of the reasons why there are so many security break-ins.

2.6.9   Web server review. To run programs on the Web, many organizations use the CGI (common gateway interface) to enable programs (i.e., scripts) to run on their servers. A CGI is not only a gateway for your programming code (i.e., via data collections forms), but is also a gateway for hackers to gain access to your systems. Vulnerable CGI programs present an attractive target to intruders because they are easy to locate, and usually operate with the privileges and power of the Web server software itself. The replacement of Janet Reno's picture with that of Hitler on the Department of Justice Web site is an example of just this sort of CGI hole. The following questions must be asked of developers using a CGI:

■ Are CGI interpreters located in bin directories? This should not be the case because you are providing the hacker with all the capabilities he or she needs to insert malicious code and then run it directly from your server.

■ Is CGI support configured when not needed?

■ Are you using remote procedure calls (RPCs)? Remote procedure calls allow programs on one computer to execute programs on a second computer. There is much evidence that the majority of distributed denial-of-service attacks launched during 1999 and early 2000 were executed by systems that had RPC vulnerabilities. It is recommended that, wherever possible, one should turn off or remove these services on machines directly accessible from the Internet. If this is not possible, then at least ensure that the latest patches to the software are installed because these mitigate some of the known security holes.

■ Is IIS (Internet Information Server) being used? This is the software used on most Web sites deployed on Windows NT and Windows 2000 servers. Programming flaws in IIS Remote Data Services (RDS) are being used by hackers to run remote commands with administrator privileges. Microsoft's own Web site discusses methodologies to use to combat these flaws.

2.7 Testing

Pre-PC testing was a slow and meticulous process. Today's faster pace means that inadequate testing is being performed by most organizations. In addition, many organizations forego security testing entirely. In this section of the audit we determine whether adequate security is being performed.

2.7.1 Has penetration testing been done? Penetration testing is used to assess the type and extent of security-related vulnerabilities in systems and networks, testing network security perimeters, and empirically verifying the resistance of applications to misuse and exploitation. While it is possible that system administrators are sophisticated enough to be able to utilize the toolsets available to scan the systems for vulnerabilities, a whole host of "white-hat" hacker security consulting firms has sprung up over the past several years and it is these that are recommended.

2.7.2 Has intrusion testing been done? There is a whole host of software tools available on the market today that "monitor" systems and report on possible intrusions. These are referred to as intrusion detection systems (IDSs). In this section of the audit we determine whether an IDS is being used and how effectively it is being used.

2.7.3 Is there a QA (quality assurance) function? While QA departments have been a traditional part of the IT function for decades, many newer pure-play Internet companies seem to ignore this function. In this section, the auditor will determine if the QA function is present. If it is present, then it will be reviewed.

2.8 Reporting

Logging of all log-ins, attempted intrusions, etc. must be maintained for a reasonable period of time. In this section, the auditor will determine if these logs are maintained and for how long.

2.9 Backup

In the event of failure, it is usual that the last backup be used to restore the system. In this section, the auditor will determine the frequency of backups and the reasonableness of this schedule.

Metrics for this section include the number of logged break-in attempts, frequency of passwords changed, number of encrypted messages, number of security patches applied, number of security patches available, number of critical updates applied, number of critical updates available, number of programming audits for security purposes, number of systems implemented without security audits, number of server reviews, number of penetration tests, number of intrusion tests, and number of backups.

3   Ergonomics

At this stage, the auditor becomes involved in more abstract issues. In the last section on security we could be very specific about what a system exhibiting good E-business health requires. In the section on Ergonomics, we need to be more subjective.

To achieve this end will require the auditor to meet not only with the system developers, but also with the end users. At times, these end users will be current customers of the system or potential customers of the system. To this end, it might be necessary to develop surveys and establish focus groups.

The goal here is nothing less than determining a "thumbs up" or "thumbs down" on the E-business vis-à-vis other E-businesses.

3.1 Navigability

Navigation means the determination of whether or not the site makes sense in terms of browsing it.

3.1.1   How easy is it to find something on this site? If looking for a specific product, how many pages does one have to surf through to find it?

3.1.2   Is there a search engine? If so, review for correctness and completeness. Many sites do not have search engines (in this instance, we are talking about a search engine to search the site only rather than the Internet). If the E-business site exhibits depth (i.e., many pages), it becomes rather difficult to navigate around it to find what you are looking for. If a search engine is available, the auditor must check to see if what is being searched for can be correctly found.

3.1.3 Is there a site map? If so, review for correctness and completeness. While not required and not often found, site maps are one of the most useful site navigation tools. If available, the auditor will determine the correctness of this tool.

3.1.4 Are back/forward (or other) buttons provided? What tools are provided the end user for moving backward and forward within the site. Are the browser's Back/Forward buttons the only navigation tools — or did the Web designers provide fully functional toolbars? If so, do these toolbars work on all pages? We have found that, of those firms audited, 10 percent of the pages pointed to by the toolbars cannot be found.

3.1.5 Are frames used? If so, do toolbars and other navigation tools still work?

3.2 Usability

In the end, it really comes down to one question: How usable is the Web site? In this section, we ask:

3.2.1 How easy is it to use this site? While the auditor might have an opinion that might well be valid, in this section we resort to surveys and focus groups to determine the answer.

3.2.2 How useful is this site?

3.3 Content

In this section, we assess the value of the information contained within the site as compared to competitive sites.

3.3.1 Is content updated regularly?

3.3.2 Is content relevant?

3.3.3 Do visitors consider content worthwhile? The auditor will use survey techniques to determine the answer to this question.

3.3.4 How does content compare with competitors? The auditor will use survey techniques to determine the answer to this question.

3.4 Search Engine

While the use of search engines has declined in popularity as a way to find a site, it is still an important marketing vehicle on the Web. In this section, the auditor will determine where the site places when performing a search using the top-ten search engines.

Metrics for this section include the number of clicks to find something on the Web site, frequency of content update, survey to compare site to competitors, and failure rate to find Web site in the first three pages of a search engine.

4   Customer Service

The Web is a doorway to the company's business. However, it is just one part of the business. Tangential services must be audited as well. Customer service is one of the biggest problem areas for Net firms. There have been many well-publicized instances of shoddy customer service. It is in the company's best interests, therefore, to assess customer service within the firm vis-à-vis its Web presence.

4.1   Accessibility

How easy is it for your customers to reach you?

4.1.1   Review e-mail response. How long does it take you to respond to a customer e-mail.
4.1.2   Review telephone response. How long does a customer have to wait on hold before a person answers his or her query?

4.2   E-Commerce

If your site doubles as an E-commerce site (i.e., you sell goods or services from your site), you need to assess the quality of this customer experience.

4.2.1   Check shopping experience. Using a "mystery shopper" approach, the auditor will endeavor to make routine purchases using the Web site. Determine:
    4.2.1.1   Is the shopping cart correct (i.e., are the goods you purchased in the shopping cart)?
    4.2.1.2   Does the E-commerce software calculate taxes properly?
    4.2.1.3   Does the E-commerce software calculate shipping charges properly?
4.2.2   Check the fulfillment experience.
    4.2.2.1   Is a confirmation e-mail sent to the purchaser?
    4.2.2.2   Is the return policy carefully explained?
    4.2.2.3   How quickly does the company refund money on returns?

4.3 Privacy

At a minimum, the auditor must review the company's privacy policy statement. He or she should then review the data flow to determine if the privacy policy is being adhered to.

5 Legality

The digital age makes it easy to perform illegal or potentially litigious acts. From a corporate perspective, this can be anything from a Web designer illegally copying a copyrighted piece of art to employees downloading pornography.

5.1 Copyright

5.1.1   Check the content ownership of text on your site. It is quite easy to copy text from one site to another. Ensure that your copy is completely original or that you have the correct permissions to reprint the data.

5.1.2   In the same way, check image ownership.

5.2 Employee Web Usage

There have been a number of court cases where employees claimed harassment when other employees within the organization downloaded or e-mailed pornography. The company is responsible for the actions of its employees; therefore, it is highly recommended that the company do the following:

5.2.1   Create a policy memo detailing what can and cannot be done on the Internet (include e-mail). Make sure all employees sign and return this memo. Use tools such as those on surfcontrol.com to monitor employee Net usage.

5.2.2   Determine whether any e-mail monitoring software is used and determine its effectiveness.

Metrics include customer e-mail response time, number of shopping cart errors, number of confirmation e-mails sent, and length of time it takes for customer refunds.

Appendix L

Establishing a Software Measurement Program

This appendix provides an overview of software measurement and an infrastructure for establishing a software measurement program. It is recommended to start small and build on success. It is also recommended to combine a software measurement program with a software process improvement initiative so the measurement program is sustainable. As far as possible, establish automated mechanisms for measurement data collection and analysis. Automated methods should be a support resource of the measurement process rather than a definition of the process. Regularly collect the core measurements and additional measurements specific to the local goals in the organization. Plan and schedule the resources that will be required to collect and analyze the measurement data within the organization's overall software process improvement efforts and the specific organization's projects. Evolve the measurement program according to the organization's goals and objectives. Provide a mechanism for projects and the organization's software process improvement group to consolidate software project measurements.

The following four steps illustrate a comprehensive process for establishing a software measurement program.

Step 1: Adopt a software measurement program model:
- Identify resources, processes, and products.
- Derive core measurement views.

Step 2: Use a software process improvement model:
- Establish a baseline assessment of the project or organization.
- Set and prioritize measurable goals for improvement.
- Establish action plan with measures.
- Accomplish actions and analyze results.
- Leverage improvements through measurement.

Step 3: Identify a goal-question-metric (GQM) structure:
- Link software goals with corporate goals.
- Derive measures from attribute questions.
- Establish success criteria for measurement.

Step 4: Develop a software measurement plan and case:
- Plan: what, why, who, how, and when.
- Case: measurement evidence and analysis results.

An organization may decide to implement a subset of these activities. Organizations should tailor their use of the activities as necessary to meet organization and project goals and objectives. Each of these four major activities is described in the following subsections.

An organization or a project must understand what to measure, who is interested in the results, and why. To assist this understanding, it is recommended that a software measurement program model be adopted, such as illustrated in Figure L.1.

The measurement program model provides a simple framework for specifically identifying what software attributes are of potential interest to measure, who the various customers of measurement results might be, and why such measurement results are of interest to those customers. The measurement program model includes the general software objects of

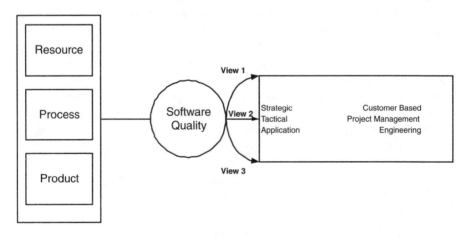

FIGURE L.1   Software measurement program model.

measurement interest, such as resources, processes, and products. The measurement customers include the end-use customer, software organization and project management, and software application personnel. These customers need software measures for different reasons. Their viewpoints drive the eventual measurement selection priorities and must be integrated and consistent to be most effective.

To establish a successful measurement program (e.g., one that is used for organization or project decision making and lasts more than two years), it is necessary to have a basic understanding of measurement. The following subsections provide an introduction to attributes of resources, processes, and products that might be useful to measure and some software measurement terminology that relates to the software measurement program.

Resources, Products, and Processes

Software objects such as resources, products, and processes have attributes that characterize software projects and are therefore of interest to measure. A software measure is an objective assignment of a number (or symbol) to a software object to characterize a specific attribute (Fenton, 1991).

Resources are inputs to processes. Such inputs specifically include personnel, materials, tools, and methods. Resources for some processes are products of other processes. An attribute of great interest that is relevant to all of these types of resources is *cost*. Cost is dependent on the number of resources and the market price of each resource. For personnel, the cost is dependent upon the effort expended during the process and the market price value of each person assigned to the process.

Processes are any software-related activities such as requirements analysis, design activity, testing, formal inspections, and project management. Processes normally have *time* and *effort* as attributes of interest, as well as the number of incidents of a specified type arising during the process. Certain incidents may be considered to be *defects in the process* and may result in *defects* or *faults in products*.

Products are any artifacts, deliverables, or documents that are produced by software processes. Products include specifications, design documentation, source code, test results, and unit development folders. Products normally have *size* and *inherent defects* as attributes of interest.

Direct and Indirect Software Measurement

Direct measurement of a software attribute does not depend on the measurement of any other attribute. Measures that involve counting, such as number of SLOC and number of staff hours expended on a process, are examples of a direct measure.

Indirect or derived measurement involves more than one attribute. Rates are typically indirect measures because they involve the computation of a ratio of two other measures. For example, software failure rate is computed by dividing the count of the failures observed during execution by the execution time of the software. Productivity is also an indirect measure because it depends on the amount of product produced divided by the amount of effort or time expended.

Two other very important aspects of the measurement assignment are preservation of attribute properties and mapping uniqueness. The mapping should preserve natural attribute properties (e.g., such as order and interval size). If another assignment mapping of the attribute is identified, there should be a unique relationship between the first mapping and the second mapping. It is very difficult to ensure that measures satisfy these preservation and uniqueness properties. This document will not consider these issues in any detail.

Views of Core Measures

The three views (strategic, tactical, application) of the core measures illustrated in Figure L.1 identify important attributes from the viewpoints of the customer, project management, or applications engineers, respectively. It is extremely important for the measurement program to be consistent across the three views of core measures. There must be agreement and consistency on what measures mean, what measures are important, and how measures across the three views relate to and support each other.

- *Strategic view.* This view is concerned with measurement for the long-term needs of the organization and its customers. Important measures include product cost (effort), time to market (schedule), and the trade-offs among such quality measures as functionality, reliability, usability, and product support. It may be critical to an organization to establish new customers and solidify old customers through new product capabilities — with limited reliability and usability, but with a well-planned support program. Time to market is usually a critical measure and may become one of upper management's most important measures.
- *Tactical view.* This view is concerned with short- and long-term needs of each individual project's management goals. The project measures that support the tactical view should be able to be

aggregated to show a relationship to the organization's strategic goals. If not, then individual projects will appear to be "out of sync" with the organization. The primary measures of interest to project management are schedule progress and labor cost.

■ *Application view.* This view is concerned with the immediate resource, process, and product engineering needs of the project. Resources (e.g., personnel and support equipment) are of some interest in this view, but the engineer is primarily interested in the process activities to produce a high-quality product. The engineering definitions of process and product quality should be consistent with project management or upper-level organization management understanding. Product size, complexity, reliability, and inherent defect measures are important to the engineers because they indicate achievement of functional and performance requirements.

Use a Software Process Improvement Model

For a software measurement program to be successful, the measurement activities should be conducted within the environment of continuous software process improvement. Without such an environment, measures will not be seen as value-added and the measurement program will not be sustainable. Two models are important to a software process improvement initiative and the integration of software measurement, as illustrated in Figure L.2. The IDEAL model (McFeeley, 1996) provides an organization with an approach to continuous improvement. The Capability Maturity Model (Paulk et al., 1993) can be used to establish a measurement baseline.

The IDEAL model (McFeeley, 1996) provides a framework for conducting process improvement activities at the organization level and the project level. The IDEAL model is similar to the Plan/Do/Check/Act model identified by Deming (1986).

■ *Organization software measurement.* During the Initiate stage, the organization's goals and measures for the improvement are defined along with success criteria. The Diagnose stage includes baselining the organization's current process capability (e.g., using the SEI CMM during a software process assessment) in accordance with the measures inherent in the assessment process. The Establish stage provides focus on identifying specific improvements that will be accomplished by action teams and the measures for those improvements. Prioritized improvement actions are determined and action teams are formed to develop specific plans that address the high-priority improvements. The Act stage includes implementation

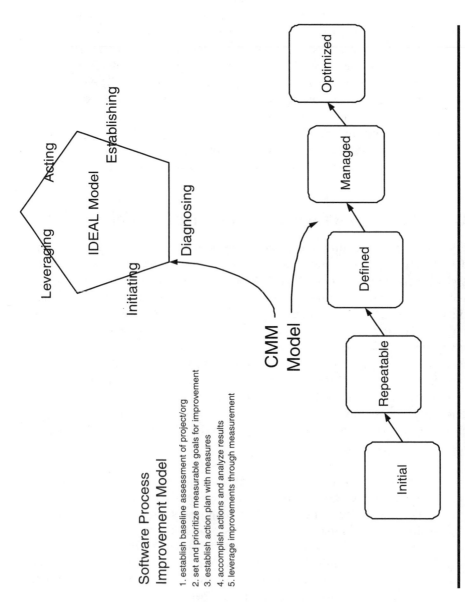

Software Process
Improvement Model

1. establish baseline assessment of project/org
2. set and prioritize measurable goals for improvement
3. establish action plan with measures
4. accomplish actions and analyze results
5. leverage improvements through measurement

FIGURE L.2 Software process improvement models.

of the action team plan, including collection of measurements to determine if the improvement has been (or can be) accomplished. The Leverage stage includes documenting the results of the improvement effort and leveraging the improvement across all applicable organization projects.

■ *Project Software Measurement.* During the Initiate stage, the project goals and measures for success are defined along with success criteria. A project Software Measurement Plan should be developed or included as part of the software project management information (e.g., referenced as an appendix to a Software Development Plan). The Diagnose stage includes documenting and analyzing the project's measures as a Measurement Case during the project life cycle in accordance with the measures in the Measurement Plan. The Establish stage provides focus on identifying specific project or organization improvements that might be accomplished. Prioritized improvement actions are determined and assigned to a project or organization level, as appropriate. For more mature organizations, project teams can accomplish the improvements during the project. For less mature organizations, the identified improvements will serve as lessons learned for future projects. Action teams are formed (by the project or organization) and a plan developed to address the high-priority improvements. The Act and Leverage stages for the project are limited to making mid-course project corrections based on the measurement information. Such measurement data and the actions taken are recorded in the Measurement Case. The project's Measurement Case then becomes the complete documentation of the project management and engineering measures, any changes to project direction based on measurement analysis, and lessons learned for future projects.

SEI CMM

The SEI CMM serves as a guide for determining what to measure first and how to plan an increasingly comprehensive improvement program. The measures suggested for different levels of the CMM are illustrated in Table L.1. The set of core measures described in this document primarily address Level 1, 2, and 3 issues.

Level 1 measures provide baselines for comparison as an organization seeks to start improving. Measurement occurs at a project level without good organization control, or perhaps on a pilot project with better controls.

TABLE L.1 Relationship of Software Measures to Process Maturity

Maturity Level	Measurement Focus	Applicable Core Measures
1	Establish baselines for planning and estimating project resources and tasks	Effort, schedule progress (pilot or selected projects)
2	Track and control project resources and tasks	Effort, schedule progress (project by project basis)
3	Define and quantify products and processes within and across projects	Products: size, defects processes: effort, schedule (compare above across projects)
4	Define, quantify, and control sub-processes and elements	Set upper and lower statistical control boundaries for core measures Use estimated versus actual comparisons for projects and compare across projects
5	Dynamically optimize at the project level and improve across projects	Use statistical control results dynamically within the project to adjust processes and products for improved success

Level 2 measures focus on project planning and tracking. Applicable core measures are the staff effort and schedule progress. Size and defect data are necessary to understand measurement needs for Level 3 and Level 4 and to provide a database for future evaluations. Individual projects can use the measurement data to set process entry and exit criteria.

Level 3 measures become increasingly directed toward measuring and comparing the intermediate and final products produced across multiple projects. The measurement data for all core measures are collected for each project and compared to organization project standards.

Level 4 measures capture characteristics of the development process to allow control of the individual activities of the process. This is usually done through techniques such as statistical process control where upper and lower bounds are set for all core measures (and any useful derived measures). Actual measure deviation from the estimated values is tracked to determine whether the attributes being measured are within the statistically allowed control bounds. A decision process is put into place to react to projects that do not meet the statistical control boundaries. Process improvements can be identified based on the decision process.

Level 5 processes are mature enough and managed carefully enough that the statistical control process measurements from Level 4 provide immediate feedback to individual projects based on an integrated decisions across multiple projects. Decisions concerning dynamically changing processes across multiple projects can then be optimized while the projects are being conducted.

Identify a Goal-Question-Metric (GQM) Structure

One of the organization's or project's most difficult tasks is to decide what to measure. The key is to relate any measurement to organization and project goals. One method for doing this is to use Basili's (1984) Goal-Question-Metric (GQM) paradigm, illustrated in Figure L.3 with a partial example related to software reliability.

This method links software goals to corporate goals and derives the specific software measures that provide evidence of whether the goals are met. Because such measures are linked directly to organization goals, it is much easier to show the value of the measurement activity and establish success criteria for measurement.

The GQM method to software measurement uses a top-down approach with the following steps:

1. Determine the goals of the organization or project in terms of what is wanted, who wants it, why it is wanted, and when it is wanted.
2. Refine the goals into a set of questions that require quantifiable answers.
3. Refine the questions into a set of measurable attributes (measures for data collection) that attempt to answer the question.
4. Develop models relating each goal to its associated set of measurable attributes.

Some attributes of software development, such as productivity, are dependent on many factors that are specific to a particular environment. The GQM method does not rely on any standard measures and the method can cope with any environment.

This activity may be conducted concurrently with any other software measurement activities and may be used to iteratively refine the software measurement program model, core measurement views, and process improvement efforts.

Develop a Software Measurement Plan and Case

The software measurement program activities provide organization and project-specific planning information and a variety of measurement data

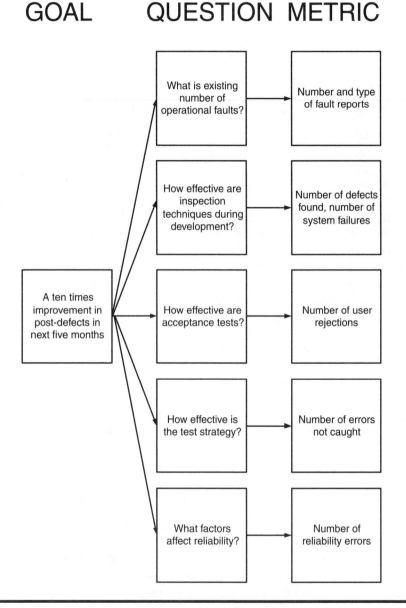

FIGURE L.3 Goal-question-metric (GQM) paradigm.

and analysis results. These plans, data, and results should be documented through use of a software measurement plan and software measurement case.

A software measurement plan defines:

- What measurement data are to be collected
- How the data are to be analyzed to provide the desired measures
- The representation forms that will describe the measurement results

Such a plan also provides information as to who is responsible for the measurement activities and when the measurement activities are to be conducted. A software measurement plan should be developed at an organization level to direct all measurement activity and at a project level to direct specific project activity. In most cases, a project's software measurement plan can be a simple tailoring of the organizational plan. The organization's software measurement plan can be a separate document or might be an integrated part of the organization's Software Management Plan or Software Quality Plan.

A software measurement plan at either the organization or project level should relate goals to specific measures of the resource, process, and product attributes that are to be measured. The GQM method can be used to identify such measures. Improvement in accordance with the SEI CMM key process areas should be an integrated part of the derivation. The identified measures may be a core measure or derived from one or more core measures.

The following activities are key to developing a software measurement plan:

1. *Establish program commitment.* Define why the program is needed, obtain management approval, and identify ownership.
2. *Determine goals and expected results.* Use software process assessment results to set the improvement context.
3. *Select project measurements.* Apply the GQM method to derive project measures.
4. *Develop measurement plan.* Document the measures to be collected, data collection, analysis and presentation methods, and relationship to an overall improvement program.

The software measurement case documents the actual data, analysis results, lessons learned, and presentations of information identified in an associated software measurement plan. The following activities are key to developing a Software Measurement Case:

1. *Implement measurement plan.* Collect and analyze data, provide project feedback, and modify project/program as necessary.
2. *Analyze measurement results.* Store project measurement results and analyze results against historical project results.

3. *Provide measurement feedback.* Report results of analysis as project lessons learned, update measurement and process improvement programs, and repeat the process of developing/updating a Measurement Plan and Case.

Summary of Recommendations

Specific software measurement actions on individual projects and within organizations will depend on existing software capability and initiatives. The following recommendations summarize the guidelines in this appendix.

1. Software Measurement Program

Adopt a measurement model appropriate to the organization. Identify core measures of product, process, and resource attributes as a baseline model. Integrate measurement as a part of a process improvement program. Baseline current process and measurement practices using a model such as the SEI CMM. Initiate process improvement activities following a model such as the SEI IDEAL. Use the Goal-Question-Metric approach to link organization goals to software measures. Use the CMM and the core measures to link the software measures to process improvement. Develop organization and project measurement plans and document measurement evidence as standard activities. Use the measurement evidence to influence organization and project decision making.

2. Core Measures

Define and collect the four core measures of size, effort, progress to schedule, and defects for all projects.

Size

Some of the more popular and effective measures of software size are physical source lines of code (noncomment, nonblank source statements); logical source statement (instructions); function points (or feature points); and counts of logical functions or computer software units (i.e., modules). Size measurements can be used to track the status of code from each production process and to capture important trends. It is recommended that projects adopt physical source lines of code or function points as the principal measure for size.

Effort

Reliable measures for effort are prerequisites to dependable measures of software cost. By tracking human resources assigned to individual tasks and activities, effort measures provide the principal means for managing and controlling costs and schedules. It is recommended that projects adopt staff hours as the principal measure for effort.

Progress to Schedule

Schedule and progress are primary project management concerns. Accordingly, it is important for managers to monitor adherence to intermediate milestone dates. Early schedule slips often foreshadow future problems. It is also important to have objective and timely measures of progress that accurately indicate status and that can be used to project completion dates for future milestones.

At a minimum, the following information should be planned for and tracked:

- Major milestone completion progress — estimates and actuals: requirements, design, implementation, test, delivery
- Intermediate milestone completion progress — estimates and actuals: modules coded, modules integrated
- Estimated size progress — estimates and actuals by date completed
- Exit or completion criteria associated with each milestone date

Defects

The number of problems and defects associated with a software product varies inversely with perceived quality. Counts of software problems and defects are among the few direct measures for software processes and products. These counts allow qualitative description of trends in detection and repair activities. They also allow the tracking of progress in identifying and fixing process and product imperfections. In addition, problem and defect measures are the basis for quantifying other software quality attributes such as reliability, correctness, completeness, efficiency, and usability.

3. Automated Methods

To make the software measurement program as efficient as possible, it is recommended to establish automated mechanisms for measurement data collection and analysis. Automated methods should be a support resource of the measurement process rather than a definition of the process. Regularly collect the core measurements and additional measurements specific to the local goals in your organization.

Example Measurement Plan Standard

Abstract

This document contains an example of a standard defining the contents and structure of a Software Measurement Plan for each project of an organization. The term "Measurement Plan" will be used throughout.

Table of Contents

1. Introduction
2. Policy
3. Responsibility and Authorities
4. General Information
5. Thematic Outline of Measurement Plan

1. Introduction

This standard provides guidance on the production of a Measurement Plan for individual software projects.

1.1 Scope

This standard is mandatory for all projects. Assistance in applying it to existing projects will be given by the Organization Measures Coordinator.

2. Policy

It is policy to collect measures to assist in the improvement of:

■ The accuracy of cost estimates
■ Project productivity
■ Product quality
■ Project monitoring and control

In particular, each project will be responsible for identifying and planning all activities associated with the collection of these measures. The project is responsible for the definition of the project's objectives for collecting measures, analyzing the measures to provide the required presentation results, and documenting the approach in an internally approved Measurement Plan. The project is also responsible for capturing the actual measurement information and analysis results. The form of this actual measurement information could be appended to the Measurement Plan or put in a separate document called a Measurement Case.

3. Responsibility and Authorities

The Project Leader/Manager shall be responsible for the production of the project Measurement Plan at the start of the project. Advice and assistance from the Organization Measures Coordinator shall be sought when needed.

The Measurement Plan shall be approved by the Project Leader/Manager (if not the author), Product Manager, Organization Measures Coordinator, and Project Quality Manager.

4. General Information

4.1 Overview of Project Measures Activities

The collection and use of measures must be defined and planned into a project during the start-up phase. The haphazard collection of measures is more likely to result in the collection of a large amount of inconsistent data that will provide little useful information to the project management team, or for future projects.

The following activities shall be carried out at the start of the project:

- Define the project's objectives for collecting measures.
- Identify the users of the measures-derived information, as well as any particular requirements they may have.
- Identify the measures to meet these objectives or provide the information. Most, if not all, of these should be defined at the Organization level.
- Define the project task structure (e.g., Work Breakdown Structure [WBS]).
- Define when each measure is to be collected, in terms of the project task structure.
- Define how each measure is to be collected, in terms of preprinted forms/tools, who will collect it, and where and how it will be stored.
- Define how the data will be analyzed to provide the required information, including the specification of any necessary algorithms and the frequency with which this will be done.

- Define the organization, including the information flow, within the project required to support the measures collection and analyses activities.
- Identify the standards and procedures to be used.
- Define which measures will be supplied to the Organization.

4.2 Purpose of the Measurement Plan

The project's Measurement Plan is produced as one of the start-up documents to record the project's objectives for measures collection and how it intends to carry out the program. The plan also:

- Ensures that activities pertinent to the collection of project measures are considered early in the project and are resolved in a clear and consistent manner.
- Ensures that project staff are aware of the measures activities and provides an easy reference to them.

The Measurement Plan complements the project's Quality and Project Plans, highlighting matters specifically relating to measures. The Measurement Plan information can be incorporated into the Quality and Project Plans. Information and instructions shall not be duplicated in these plans.

4.3 Format

Section 5 defines a format for the Measurement Plan in terms of a set of headings that are to be used, and the information required to be given under each heading. The front pages shall be the minimum requirements for a standard configurable document.

4.4 Document Control

4.5 Filing

The Measurement Plan shall be held in the project filing system.

4.6 Updating

The Measurement Plan may require updating during the course of the project. Updates shall follow any changes in requirements for collecting measures or any change to the project that results in change to the project

WBS. The Project Leader or Manager shall be responsible for such updates or revisions.

5. Contents of Measurement Plan

This section details what is to be included in the project's Measurement Plan (Table L.2). Wherever possible, the Measurement Plan should point to existing Organization standards, etc., rather than duplicating the information. The information required in the Plan is detailed below under appropriate headings.

For small projects, the amount of information supplied under each topic may amount to only a paragraph or so and may not justify the production of the Measurement Plan as a separate document. Instead, the information may form a separate chapter in the Quality plan, with the topic headings forming the sections or paragraphs in that chapter. On larger projects, a separate document will be produced, with each topic heading becoming a section in its own right.

TABLE L.2   Thematic Outline for a Measurement Plan

Section 1. Objectives for Collecting Measures
The project's objectives for collecting measures shall be described here. These will also include the relevant Organization objectives. Where the author of the Measurement Plan is not the Project Leader or Manager, Project Management agreement to these objectives will be demonstrated by the fact that the Project Manager is a signatory to the Plan.

Section 2. Use and Users of Information
Provide information that includes:

- Who will be the users of the information to be derived from the measures
- Why the information is needed
- Required frequency of the information

Section 3. Measures To Be Collected
This section describes the measures to be collected by the project. As far as possible, the measures to be collected should be a derivative of the Core Measures. If Organization standards are not followed, justification for the deviation should be provided. Project-specific measures shall be defined in full here in terms of the project tasks.

A Goal-Question-Metric (GQM) approach should be used to identify the measures from the stated project objectives. The results of the GQM approach should also be documented.

TABLE L.2 (continued)   Thematic Outline for a Measurement Plan

Section 4. Collection of Measures
Provide information that includes:

- Who will collect each measure
- The level within the project task against which each measure is to be collected
- When each measure is to be collected in terms of initial estimate, re-estimates, and actual measurement
- How the measures are to be collected, with reference to proformas, tools, and procedures as appropriate
- Validation to be carried out, including details of the project specific techniques if necessary, and by whom
- How and where the measures are to be stored — including details of electronic database, spreadsheet, filing cabinet as appropriate; how the data is amalgamated and when it is archived; who is responsible for setting up the storage process; and who is responsible for inserting the data into the database
- When, how, and which data is provided to the Organization Measures database

Section 5. Analysis of Measures
Provide information that includes:

- How the data is to be analyzed, giving details of project-specific techniques if necessary, any tools required, and how frequently it is to be carried out
- The information to be provided by the analysis
- Who will carry out the analysis
- Details of project-specific reports, frequency of generation, and how they are generated and by whom

Section 6. Project Organization
Describe the organization within the project that is required to support the measurement activities. Identify roles and the associated tasks and responsibilities. These roles may be combined with other roles within the project to form complete jobs for individual people.

The information flow between these roles and the rest of the project should also be described.

Section 7. Project Task Structure
Describe or reference the project's the project task structure. It should be noted that the project's measurement activities should be included in the project task structure.

TABLE L.2 (continued)   Thematic Outline for a Measurement Plan

Section 8. Standards

Describe the measurement standards and procedures to be used by the project that must be given, indicating which are Organization standards and which are project specific. These standards will have been referenced throughout the plan, as necessary. If it is intended not to follow any of the Organization standards in full, this must be clearly indicated in the relevant section of the Measurement Plan, and a note made in this section.

Example Project Core Measures

This section provides examples, summarized in Table L.3, that illustrate the use of the recommended core measures (with some minor variations) for a variety of software projects.

Author Note

This appendix has been adapted from Software Quality Assurance Subcommittee of the Nuclear Weapons Complex Quality Managers, United States Department of Energy Albuquerque Operations Office. (1997, April). *Guidelines for Software Measurement, Quality Report SAQS97-001.* http://cio.doe.gov/ITReform/sqse/download/sqas971.doc.

TABLE L.3 Core Measures for Example Projects

Core Measures	Project A: Large Embedded Development	Project B: Commercial Purchase	Project C: Information System Development	Project D: Simulation Analysis Code Support	Project E: Graphical User Interface Small Development
Size	SLOC (reused and new)	Disk space (utilized)	Function points (reused and new)	SLOC (total, new, and modified for each release)	Function points (reused and new)
Effort	Staff hours (development)	Staff hours (installation and updates)	Staff hours (development)	Staff hours (total, change request for each release)	Staff hours (development)
Progress to schedule	Total months (estimated and actual)	Installation time (estimated and actual for initial release and updates)	Total months (estimated and actual)	Total months (estimated and actual for each release)	Total months (estimated and actual)
	Task months (estimated and actual)		Task months (estimated and actual)	Task months (estimated and actual for each release)	Task months (estimated and actual)
	Task completion ratio per reporting period		Task completion ratio per reporting period	Task completion ratio per reporting period	Task completion ratio per reporting period
Defects	Inspection defects (major and minor)	Operational failures (all)	Inspection defects (major and minor)	Inspection defects (major and minor)	Test failures (major and minor)
	Test failures (major and minor)	Operational problem reports (all)	Test failures (major and minor)	Test failures (major and minor total and in modified code)	Operational problem reports (all)
	Operational problem reports (all)		Operational problem reports (all)	Operational problem reports (all and for modified code)	

References

Basili, V. and D.M. Weiss. (1984, November). A Methodology for Collecting Valid Software Engineering Data, *IEEE Transactions on Software Engineering*, Vol. SE-10, No. 6.

Deming, W.E. (1986). *Out of the Crisis,* Cambridge, MA: MIT Press.

Fenton, N.E. (1991). *Software Metrics: A Rigorous Approach*, London, England: Chapman & Hall.

McFeeley, B. (1996, February). *IDEAL: A User's Guide for Software Process Improvement* (CMU/SEI-96-HB-001), Pittsburgh, PA: Software Engineering Institute.

Paulk, M.C., B. Curtis, M.B. Chrissis, and C.V. Weber. (1993). *Capability Maturity Model for Software, Version 1.1* (CMU/SEI-93-TR-024), Pittsburgh, PA: Software Engineering Institute.

Appendix M

Process Assets by CMM Level: Focus on Process Improvement

[**Source:** The Systems Engineering Process Office of the Navy. Process Assets. (2004). Systems Engineering Process Office. Space and Naval Warfare Systems Center San Diego. Office of the Navy. http://sepo.spawar.navy.mil/sepo/index2.html.]

The Navy's office of systems engineering has meticulously put together a series of guidelines that tie CMM (Capability Maturity Model) to systems development process improvements ("Process Assets," 2004). This appendix is an excerpt of these guidelines but focuses only on the process improvements most appropriate for our balanced scorecard approach.

Organizational Process Focus (CMM Level 3 Defined)

The purpose of Organizational Process Focus is to plan and implement organizational process improvement based on a thorough understanding of the current strengths and weaknesses of the organization's processes and process assets.

Specific Goals (SG) and Practices (SP)

SG 1   Strengths, weaknesses, and improvement opportunities for the organization's processes are identified periodically and as needed.

SP 1.1   Establish and maintain the description of the process needs and objectives for the organization.

SP 1.2   Appraise the processes of the organization periodically and as needed to maintain an understanding of their strengths and weaknesses.

SP 1.3   Identify improvements to the organization's processes and process assets.

SG 2   Improvements are planned and implemented, organizational process assets are deployed, and process-related experiences are incorporated into the organizational process assets.

SP 2.1   Establish and maintain process action plans to address improvements to the organization's processes and process assets.

SP 2.2   Implement process action plans across the organization.

SP 2.3   Deploy organizational process assets across the organization.

SP 2.4   Incorporate process-related work products, measures, and improvement information derived from planning and performing the process into the organizational process assets.

Generic Goals (GG) and Practices (GP)

GG 3   The process is institutionalized as a defined process.

GP 2.1   Establish and maintain an organizational policy for planning and performing the organizational process focus process.

GP 3.1   Establish and maintain the description of a defined organizational process focus process.

GP 2.2   Establish and maintain the plan for performing the organizational process focus process.

GP 2.3   Provide adequate resources for performing the organizational process focus process, developing the work products, and providing the services of the process.

GP 2.4   Assign responsibility and authority for performing the process, developing the work products, and providing the services of the organizational process focus process.

GP 2.5   Train the people performing or supporting the organizational process focus process as needed.

GP 2.6   Place designated work products of the organizational process focus process under appropriate levels of configuration management.

GP 2.7   Identify and involve the relevant stakeholders of the organizational process focus process as planned.

GP 2.8 Monitor and control the organizational process focus process against the plan for performing the process and take appropriate corrective action.

GP 3.2 Collect work products, measures, measurement results, and improvement information derived from planning and performing the organizational process focus process to support the future use and improvement of the organization's processes and process assets.

GP 2.9 Objectively evaluate adherence of the organizational process focus process against its process description, standards, and procedures, and address noncompliance.

GP 2.10 Review the activities, status, and results of the organizational process focus process with higher level management and resolve issues.

Organizational Process Definition (CMM Level 3 Defined)

The purpose of Organizational Process Definition is to establish and maintain a usable set of organizational process assets.

Specific Goals (SG) and Practices (SP)

SG 1 A set of organizational process assets is established and maintained.

SP 1.1 Establish and maintain the organization's set of standard processes.

SP 1.2 Establish and maintain descriptions of the life-cycle models approved for use in the organization.

SP 1.3 Establish and maintain the tailoring criteria and guidelines for the organization's set of standard processes.

SP 1.4 Establish and maintain the organization's measurement repository.

SP 1.5 Establish and maintain the organization's process asset library.

Generic Goals (GG) and Practices (GP)

GG 3 The process is institutionalized as a defined process.

GP 2.1 Establish and maintain an organizational policy for planning and performing the organizational process definition process.

GP 3.1 Establish and maintain the description of a defined organizational process definition process.

GP 2.2 Establish and maintain the plan for performing the organizational process definition process.

GP 2.3   Provide adequate resources for performing the organizational process definition process, developing the work products, and providing the services of the process.

GP 2.4   Assign responsibility and authority for performing the process, developing the work products, and providing the services of the organizational process definition process.

GP 2.5   Train the people performing or supporting the organizational process definition process as needed.

GP 2.6   Place designated work products of the organizational process definition process under appropriate levels of configuration management.

GP 2.7   Identify and involve the relevant stakeholders of the organizational process definition process as planned.

GP 2.8   Monitor and control the organizational process definition process against the plan for performing the process and take appropriate corrective action.

GP 3.2   Collect work products, measures, measurement results, and improvement information derived from planning and performing the organizational process definition process to support the future use and improvement of the organization's processes and process assets.

GP 2.9   Objectively evaluate adherence of the organizational process definition process against its process description, standards, and procedures, and address noncompliance.

GP 2.10 Review the activities, status, and results of the organizational process definition process with higher level management and resolve issues.

Organizational Training (CMM Level 3 Defined)

The purpose of Organizational Training is to develop the skills and knowledge of people so they can perform their roles effectively and efficiently.

Specific Goals (SG) and Practices (SP)

SG 1   A training capability that supports the organization's management and technical roles is established and maintained.

SP 1.1   Establish and maintain the strategic training needs of the organization.

SP 1.2   Determine which training needs are the responsibility of the organization and which will be left to the individual project or support group.

SP 1.3   Establish and maintain an organizational training tactical plan.
SP 1.4   Establish and maintain training capability to address organizational training needs.
SG 2   Training necessary for individuals to perform their roles effectively is provided.
SP 2.1   Deliver the training following the organizational training tactical plan.
SP 2.2   Establish and maintain records of the organizational training.
SP 2.3   Assess the effectiveness of the organization's training program.

Generic Goals (GG) and Practices (GP)

GG 3   The process is institutionalized as a defined process.
GP 2.1   Establish and maintain an organizational policy for planning and performing the organizational training process.
GP 3.1   Establish and maintain the description of a defined organizational training process.
GP 2.2   Establish and maintain the plan for performing the organizational training process.
GP 2.3   Provide adequate resources for performing the organizational training process, developing the work products, and providing the services of the process.
GP 2.4   Assign responsibility and authority for performing the process, developing the work products, and providing the services of the organizational training process.
GP 2.5   Train the people performing or supporting the organizational training process as needed.
GP 2.6   Place designated work products of the organizational training process under appropriate levels of configuration management.
GP 2.7   Identify and involve the relevant stakeholders of the organizational training process as planned.
GP 2.8   Monitor and control the organizational training process against the plan for performing the process and take appropriate corrective action.
GP 3.2   Collect work products, measures, measurement results, and improvement information derived from planning and performing the organizational training process to support the future use and improvement of the organization's processes and process assets.
GP 2.9   Objectively evaluate adherence of the organizational training process against its process description, standards, and procedures, and address noncompliance.
GP 2.10 Review the activities, status, and results of the organizational training process with higher level management and resolve issues.

Integrated Project Management (CMM Level 3 Defined)

The purpose of Integrated Project Management is to establish and manage the project and the involvement of the relevant stakeholders according to an integrated and defined process that is tailored from the organization's set of standard processes.

For Integrated Product and Process Development, Integrated Project Management also covers the establishment of a shared vision for the project and a team structure for integrated teams that will carry out the objectives of the project.

Specific Goals (SG) and Practices (SP)

SG 1   The project is conducted using a defined process that is tailored from the organization's set of standard processes.

SP 1.1   Establish and maintain the project's defined process.

SP 1.2   Use the organizational process assets and measurement repository for estimating and planning the project's activities.

SP 1.3   Integrate the project plan and the other plans that affect the project to describe the project's defined process.

SP 1.4   Manage the project using the project plan, the other plans that affect the project, and the project's defined process.

SP 1.5   Contribute work products, measures, and documented experiences to the organizational process assets.

SG 2   Coordination and collaboration of the project with relevant stakeholders is conducted.

SP 2.1   Manage the involvement of the relevant stakeholders in the project.

SP 2.2   Participate with relevant stakeholders to identify, negotiate, and track critical dependencies.

SP 2.3   Resolve issues with relevant stakeholders.

SG 3   The project is conducted using the project's shared vision[2].

SP 3.1   Identify expectations, constraints, interfaces, and operational conditions applicable to the project's shared vision.

SP 3.2   Establish and maintain a shared vision for the project.

SG 4   The integrated teams needed to execute the project are identified, defined, structured, and tasked[1].

SP 4.1   Determine the integrated team structure that will best meet the project objectives and constraints.

SP 4.2   Develop a preliminary distribution of requirements, responsibilities, authorities, tasks, and interfaces to teams in the selected integrated team structure.

SP 4.3   Establish and maintain teams in the integrated team structure.

Generic Goals (GG) and Practices (GP)

GG 3   The process is institutionalized as a defined process.

GP 2.1   Establish and maintain an organizational policy for planning and performing the integrated project management process.

GP 3.1   Establish and maintain the description of a defined integrated project management process.

GP 2.2   Establish and maintain the plan for performing the integrated project management process.

GP 2.3   Provide adequate resources for performing the integrated project management process, developing the work products, and providing the services of the process.

GP 2.4   Assign responsibility and authority for performing the process, developing the work products, and providing the services of the integrated project management process.

GP 2.5   Train the people performing or supporting the integrated project management process as needed.

GP 2.6   Place designated work products of the integrated project management process under appropriate levels of configuration management.

GP 2.7   Identify and involve the relevant stakeholders of the integrated project management process as planned.

GP 2.8   Monitor and control the integrated project management process against the plan for performing the process and take appropriate corrective action.

GP 3.2   Collect work products, measures, measurement results, and improvement information derived from planning and performing the integrated project management process to support the future use and improvement of the organization's processes and process assets.

GP 2.9   Objectively evaluate adherence of the integrated project management process against its process description, standards, and procedures, and address noncompliance.

GP 2.10 Review the activities, status, and results of the integrated project management process with higher level management and resolve issues.

Risk Management (CMM Level 3 Defined)

The purpose of Risk Management is to identify potential problems before they occur, so that risk-handling activities may be planned and invoked as needed across the life of the product or project to mitigate adverse impacts on achieving objectives. Readers are also directed to Chapter 9, which covers the subject of risk in more detail.

Specific Goals (SG) and Practices (SP)

SG 1   Preparation for risk management is conducted.

SP 1.1   Determine risk sources and categories.

SP 1.2   Define the parameters used to analyze and categorize risks, and the parameters used to control the risk management effort.

SP 1.3   Establish and maintain the strategy to be used for risk management.

SG 2   Risks are identified and analyzed to determine their relative importance.

SP 2.1   Identify and document the risks.

SP 2.2   Evaluate and categorize each identified risk using the defined risk categories and parameters, and determine its relative priority.

SG 3   Risks are handled and mitigated, where appropriate, to reduce adverse impacts on achieving objectives.

SP 3.1   Develop a risk mitigation plan for the most important risks to the project, as defined by the risk management strategy.

SP 3.2   Monitor the status of each risk periodically and implement the risk mitigation plan as appropriate.

Generic Goals (GG) and Practices (GP)

GG 3   The process is institutionalized as a defined process.

GP 2.1   Establish and maintain an organizational policy for planning and performing the risk management process.

GP 3.1   Establish and maintain the description of a defined risk management process.

GP 2.2   Establish and maintain the plan for performing the risk management process.

GP 2.3   Provide adequate resources for performing the risk management process, developing the work products, and providing the services of the process.

GP 2.4   Assign responsibility and authority for performing the process, developing the work products, and providing the services of the risk management process.

GP 2.5   Train the people performing or supporting the risk management process as needed.

GP 2.6   Place designated work products of the risk management process under appropriate levels of configuration management.

GP 2.7   Identify and involve the relevant stakeholders of the risk management process as planned.

GP 2.8   Monitor and control the risk management process against the plan for performing the process and take appropriate corrective action.

GP 3.2   Collect work products, measures, measurement results, and improvement information derived from planning and performing the risk management process to support the future use and improvement of the organization's processes and process assets.

GP 2.9   Objectively evaluate adherence of the risk management process against its process description, standards, and procedures, and address noncompliance.

GP 2.10 Review the activities, status, and results of the risk management process with higher level management and resolve issues.

Organizational Environment for Integration (CMM Level 3 Defined)

The purpose of Organizational Environment for Integration is to provide an Integrated Product and Process Development (IPPD) infrastructure and manage people for integration.

Specific Goals (SG) and Practices (SP)

SG 1   An infrastructure that maximizes the productivity of people and affects the collaboration necessary for integration is provided.

SP 1.1   Establish and maintain a shared vision for the organization.

SP 1.2   Establish and maintain an integrated work environment that supports IPPD by enabling collaboration and concurrent development.

SP 1.3   Identify the unique skills needed to support the IPPD environment.

SG 2   People are managed to nurture the integrative and collaborative behaviors of an IPPD environment.

SP 2.1   Establish and maintain leadership mechanisms to enable timely collaboration.

SP 2.2   Establish and maintain incentives for adopting and demonstrating integrative and collaborative behaviors at all levels of the organization.

SP 2.3   Establish and maintain organizational guidelines to balance team and home organization responsibilities.

Generic Goals (GG) and Practices (GP)

GG 3   The process is institutionalized as a defined process.

GP 2.1   Establish and maintain an organizational policy for planning and performing the organizational environment for integration process.

GP 3.1   Establish and maintain the description of a defined organizational environment for integration process.

GP 2.2   Establish and maintain the plan for performing the organizational environment for integration process.

GP 2.3   Provide adequate resources for performing the organizational environment for integration process, developing the work products, and providing the services of the process.

GP 2.4   Assign responsibility and authority for performing the process, developing the work products, and providing the services of the organizational environment for integration process.

GP 2.5   Train the people performing or supporting the organizational environment for integration process as needed.

GP 2.6   Place designated work products of the organizational environment for integration process under appropriate levels of configuration management.

GP 2.7   Identify and involve the relevant stakeholders of the organizational environment for integration process as planned.

GP 2.8   Monitor and control the organizational environment for integration process against the plan for performing the process and take appropriate corrective action.

GP 3.2   Collect work products, measures, measurement results, and improvement information derived from planning and performing the organizational environment for integration process to support the future use and improvement of the organization's processes and process assets.

GP 2.9   Objectively evaluate adherence of the organizational environment for integration process against its process description, standards, and procedures, and address noncompliance.

GP 2.10 Review the activities, status, and results of the organizational environment for integration process with higher level management and resolve issues

Organizational Process Performance (CMM Level 4 Quantitatively Managed)

The purpose of Organizational Process Performance is to establish and maintain a quantitative understanding of the performance of the organization's set of standard processes in support of quality and process-performance objectives, and to provide the process performance data, baselines, and models to quantitatively manage the organization's projects.

Specific Goals (SG) and Practices (SP)

SG 1   Baselines and models that characterize the expected process performance of the organization's set of standard processes are established and maintained.

SP 1.1   Select the processes or process elements in the organization's set of standard processes that are to be included in the organization's process performance analyses.

SP 1.2   Establish and maintain definitions of the measures that are to be included in the organization's process performance analyses.

SP 1.3   Establish and maintain quantitative objectives for quality and process performance for the organization.

SP 1.4   Establish and maintain the organization's process performance baselines.

SP 1.5   Establish and maintain the process performance models for the organization's set of standard processes.

Generic Goals (GG) and Practices (GP)

GG 3   The process is institutionalized as a defined process.

GP 2.1   Establish and maintain an organizational policy for planning and performing the organizational process performance process.

GP 3.1   Establish and maintain the description of a defined organizational process performance process.

GP 2.2   Establish and maintain the plan for performing the organizational process performance process.

GP 2.3   Provide adequate resources for performing the organizational process performance process, developing the work products, and providing the services of the process.

GP 2.4   Assign responsibility and authority for performing the process, developing the work products, and providing the services of the organizational process performance process.

GP 2.5   Train the people performing or supporting the organizational process performance process as needed.

GP 2.6   Place designated work products of the organizational process performance process under appropriate levels of configuration management.

GP 2.7   Identify and involve the relevant stakeholders of the organizational process performance process as planned.

GP 2.8   Monitor and control the organizational process performance process against the plan for performing the process and take appropriate corrective action.

GP 3.2   Collect work products, measures, measurement results, and improvement information derived from planning and performing the organizational process performance process to support the future use and improvement of the organization's processes and process assets.

GP 2.9   Objectively evaluate adherence of the organizational process performance process against its process description, standards, and procedures, and address noncompliance.

GP 2.10 Review the activities, status, and results of the organizational process performance process with higher level management and resolve issues.

Quantitative Project Management (CMM Level 4 Quantitatively Managed)

The purpose of the Quantitative Project Management process area is to quantitatively manage the project's defined process to achieve the project's established quality and process performance objectives.

Specific Goals (SG) and Practices (SP)

SG 1   The project is quantitatively managed using quality and process performance objectives.

SP 1.1   Establish and maintain the project's quality and process performance objectives.

SP 1.2   Select the sub-processes that compose the project's defined process based on historical stability and capability data.

SP 1.3   Select the sub-processes of the project's defined process that will be statistically managed.

SP 1.4   Monitor the project to determine whether the project's objectives for quality and process performance will be satisfied, and identify corrective action as appropriate.

SG 2   The performance of selected sub-processes within the project's defined process is statistically managed.

SP 2.1   Select the measures and analytic techniques to be used in statistically managing the selected sub-processes.

SP 2.2   Establish and maintain an understanding of the variation of the selected sub-processes using the selected measures and analytic techniques.

SP 2.3   Monitor the performance of the selected sub-processes to determine their capability to satisfy their quality and process-performance objectives, and identify corrective action as necessary.

SP 2.4   Record statistical and quality management data in the organization's measurement repository.

Generic Goals (GG) and Practices (GP)

GG 3   The process is institutionalized as a defined process.

GP 2.1   Establish and maintain an organizational policy for planning and
performing the quantitative project management process.

GP 3.1   Establish and maintain the description of a defined quantitative
project management process.

GP 2.2   Establish and maintain the plan for performing the quantitative
project management process.

GP 2.3   Provide adequate resources for performing the quantitative
project management process, developing the work products, and
providing the services of the process.

GP 2.4   Assign responsibility and authority for performing the process,
developing the work products, and providing the services of the
quantitative project management process.

GP 2.5   Train the people performing or supporting the quantitative
project management process as needed.

GP 2.6   Place designated work products of the quantitative project management process under appropriate levels of configuration management.

GP 2.7   Identify and involve the relevant stakeholders of the quantitative
project management process as planned.

GP 2.8   Monitor and control the quantitative project management process
against the plan for performing the process and take appropriate
corrective action.

GP 3.2   Collect work products, measures, measurement results, and
improvement information derived from planning and performing
the quantitative project management process to support the future
use and improvement of the organization's processes and process
assets.

GP 2.9   Objectively evaluate adherence of the quantitative project management process against its process description, standards, and
procedures, and address noncompliance.

GP 2.10   Review the activities, status, and results of the quantitative project
management process with higher level management and resolve
issues.

Organizational Innovation and Deployment (CMM Level 5 Optimizing)

The purpose of Organizational Innovation and Deployment is to select and deploy incremental and innovative improvements that measurably improve the organization's processes and technologies. The improvements support the organization's quality and process performance objectives as derived from the organization's business objectives.

Specific Goals (SG) and Practices (SP)

SG 1   Process and technology improvements that contribute to meeting quality and process-performance objectives are selected.
SP 1.1   Collect and analyze process- and technology-improvement proposals.
SP 1.2   Identify and analyze innovative improvements that could increase the organization's quality and process performance.
SP 1.3   Pilot process and technology improvements to select which ones to implement.
SP 1.4   Select process- and technology-improvement proposals for deployment across the organization.
SG 2   Measurable improvements to the organization's processes and technologies are continually and systematically deployed.
SP 2.1   Establish and maintain the plans for deploying the selected process and technology improvements.
SP 2.2   Manage the deployment of the selected process and technology improvements.
SP 2.3   Measure the effects of the deployed process and technology improvements.

Generic Goals (GG) and Practices (GP)

GG 3   The process is institutionalized as a defined process.
GP 2.1   Establish and maintain an organizational policy for planning and performing the organizational innovation and deployment process.
GP 2.2   Establish and maintain the description of a defined organizational innovation and deployment process.
GP 2.3   Provide adequate resources for performing the organizational innovation and deployment process, developing the work products, and providing the services of the process.
GP 2.4   Assign responsibility and authority for performing the process, developing the work products, and providing the services of the organizational innovation and deployment process.

GP 2.5   Train the people performing or supporting the organizational innovation and deployment process as needed.

GP 2.6   Place designated work products of the organizational innovation and deployment process under appropriate levels of configuration management

GP 2.7   Identify and involve the relevant stakeholders of the organizational innovation and deployment process as planned.

GP 2.8   Monitor and control the organizational innovation and deployment process against the plan for performing the process and take appropriate corrective action.

GP 3.2   Collect work products, measures, measurement results, and improvement information derived from planning and performing the organizational innovation and deployment process to support the future use and improvement of the organization's processes and process assets.

GP 2.9   Objectively evaluate adherence of the organizational innovation and deployment process against its process description, standards, and procedures, and address noncompliance.

GP 2.10 Review the activities, status, and results of the organizational innovation and deployment process with higher level management and resolve issues.

Causal Analysis and Resolution (CMM Level 5 Optimizing)

The purpose of Causal Analysis and Resolution is to identify causes of defects and other problems and take action to prevent them from occurring in the future.

Specific Goals (SG) and Practices (SP)

SG 1   Root causes of defects and other problems are systematically determined.

SP 1.1   Select the defects and other problems for analysis.

SP 1.2   Perform causal analysis of selected defects and other problems and propose actions to address them.

SG 2   Root causes of defects and other problems are systematically addressed to prevent their future occurrence.

SP 2.1   Implement the selected action proposals that were developed in causal analysis.

SP 2.2   Evaluate the effect of changes on process performance.

SP 2.3   Record causal analysis and resolution data for use across the project and organization.

Generic Goals (GG) and Practices (GP)

GG 3 The process is institutionalized as a defined process.

GP 2.1 Establish and maintain an organizational policy for planning and performing the causal analysis and resolution process.

GP 3.1 Establish and maintain the description of a defined causal analysis and resolution process.

GP 2.2 Establish and maintain the plan for performing the causal analysis and resolution process.

GP 2.3 Provide adequate resources for performing the causal analysis and resolution process, developing the work products, and providing the services of the process.

GP 2.4 Assign responsibility and authority for performing the process, developing the work products, and providing the services of the causal analysis and resolution process.

GP 2.5 Train the people performing or supporting the causal analysis and resolution process as needed.

GP 2.6 Place designated work products of the causal analysis and resolution process under appropriate levels of configuration management.

GP 2.7 Identify and involve the relevant stakeholders of the causal analysis and resolution process as planned.

GP 2.8 Monitor and control the causal analysis and resolution process against the plan for performing the process and take appropriate corrective action.

GP 3.2 Collect work products, measures, measurement results, and improvement information derived from planning and performing the causal analysis and resolution process to support the future use and improvement of the organization's processes and process assets.

GP 2.9 Objectively evaluate adherence of the causal analysis and resolution process against its process description, standards, and procedures, and address noncompliance.

GP 2.10 Review the activities, status, and results of the causal analysis and resolution process with higher level management and resolve issues.

Appendix N

Selected Performance Metrics

Distribution Center

- Average number of orders per day
- Average number of lines (SKUs) per order
- Picking rate by employee (order lines/hour) by storage zone (picking off some of the automated equipment is different than off shelves)
- Average freight cost
- Number of errors by employee

On a monthly basis:

- Volume of inbound freight (SKUs and $ cost) by week
- Volume of outbound freight (SKUs and $ cost) by week
- Volume of repackaged goods (work orders) by week
- Comparison of in-house repackaged goods versus outsourced to compare efficiencies
- Cycle count $ cost variance (to check if things are disappearing at a higher rate than normal)
- Average shipping time to customer (these reports are provided by trucking carriers)

- Number of returns versus shipments
- Transcontinental shipments (we have two warehouses, and California should ship to western customers and East coast to eastern customers — this tells us when inventory is not balanced)

For bonuses, employees track (monthly):

- Expense control
- Revenue
- Accounts receivable turns
- Inventory turns

Software Testing

- Number of projects completed.
- Number of projects cancelled during testing.
- Number of defects found. This is further broken down into categories of defects, such as major defects (software will not install or causes blue screen) and minor or cosmetic defects (e.g., text in message box is missing). These numbers are put into a calculation that shows how much money we saved the company by catching defects before they were found in production.
- Number of new projects started. (Shows expected workload for next month.)
- Number of projects not completed or carried over to next month. (This shows if we are staying current with work. For example, if we started 50 new projects this month, and completed 20, we are carrying 30 projects to next month. Typically, this number is constant each month, but will increase if we encounter a number of difficult projects. The value of this metric is only meaningful compared to the number of new requests, number of projects completed, and number of requests carried forward in previous months.)

Product Marketing

- New customers over multiple periods
- Lost customers over multiple periods
- Customer retention percent
- Product quality: total defects

- Technical support: number of calls per product
- Product life cycle: time from requirements to finished product, percent original requirements implemented, number of out-of-scope requirements
- Sales support: number of non-sales resources supporting the channel, number of resources time hours per week
- Product revenue: actual versus planned revenue by channel, region, market segment
- Product profit: revenue and expense by product, net profit, or contribution
- Market share: graph trends over multiple years, market share by key players in your segment
- Marketing programs: lead quality (leads to close ratio), ROI for marketing programs, cost per lead closed

Enterprise Resource Planning

Reduction of operational problems:

- Number of problems with customer order processing
- Percent of problems with customer order processing
- Number of problems with warehouse processes
- Number of problems with standard reports
- Number of problems with reports on demand

Availability of the ERP system:

- Average system availability
- Average downtime
- Maximum downtime

Avoidance of operational bottlenecks:

- Average response time in order processing
- Average response time in order processing during peak time
- Average number of OLTP transactions
- Maximum number of OLTP transactions

Actuality of the system:

- Average time to upgrade the system release levels behind the actual level

Improvement in system development:

- Punctuality index of system delivery
- Quality index

Avoidance of developer bottlenecks:

- Average workload per developer
- Rate of sick leave per developer
- Percent of modules covered by more than two developers

Project Management

Category	Measurement (How)	Metric (What)
Costs	Actual versus budget	Labor (costs) Materials (hardware/software) Other (office space, telcom)
Schedule	Actual versus planned	Key deliverables completed Key deliverables not completed Milestones met Milestones not met
Risks	Anticipated versus actual	Event (actual occurrence) Impact (effect on project)
Quality	Actual versus planned activities	Number of reviews (peer, structured walkthrough) Number of defects (code, documentation) Type defect (major/minor) Origin of defect (coding, testing, documentation)

Software Maintenance

	Factors	Metrics
Problem Identification Stage	Correctness Maintainability	Number of omissions on Modification Request (MR) Number of MR submittals Number of duplicate MRs Time expended for problem validation
Analysis Stage	Flexibility Traceability Usability Reusability Maintainability Comprehensibility	Requirement changes Documentation error rates Effort per function area (e.g., SQA) Elapsed time (schedule) Error rates, by priority and type
Design Stage	Flexibility Traceability Reusability Testability Maintainability Comprehensibility Reliability	Software complexity design changes Effort per function area Elapsed time Test plans and procedure changes Error rates, by priority and type Number of lines of code, added, deleted, modified, tested
Programming Stage	Flexibility Traceability Maintainability Comprehensibility Reliability	Volume/functionality (function points or lines of code) Error rates, by priority and type
System Test Stage	Flexibility Traceability Verifiability Testability Interoperability Comprehensibility Reliability	Error rates, by priority and type Generated Corrected
Acceptance Stage	Flexibility Traceability Interoperability Testability Comprehensibility Reliability	Error rates, by priority and type Generated Corrected
Delivery Stage	Completeness Reliability	Documentation changes (i.e., version description documents, training manuals, operation guidelines)

General IT Measures

Focus	Purpose	Measure of Success
Schedule Performance		
Tasks completed versus tasks planned at a point in time	Assess project progress Apply project resources	100 percent completion of tasks on critical path; 90 percent all others
Major milestones met versus planned	Measure time efficiency	90 percent of major milestones met
Revisions to approved plan	Understand and control project "churn"	All revisions reviewed and approved
Changes to customer requirements	Understand and manage scope and schedule	All changes managed through approved change process
Project completion date	Award/penalize (depending on contract type)	Project completed on schedule (per approved plan)
Budget Performance		
Revisions to cost estimates	Assess and manage project cost	100 percent of revisions are reviewed and approved
Dollars spent versus dollars budgeted	Measure cost efficiency	Project completed within approved cost parameters
Return on investment (ROI)	Track and assess performance of project investment portfolio	ROI (positive cash flow) begins according to plan
Acquisition cost control	Assess and manage acquisition dollars	All applicable acquisition guidelines followed
Product Quality		
Defects identified through quality activities	Track progress in, and effectiveness of, defect removal	90 percent of expected defects identified (e.g., via peer reviews, inspections)
Test case failures versus number of cases planned	Assess product functionality and absence of defects	100 percent of planned test cases execute successfully
Number of service calls	Track customer problems	75 percent reduction after three months of operation

Focus	Purpose	Measure of Success
Customer satisfaction index	Identify trends	95 percent positive rating
Customer satisfaction trend	Improve customer satisfaction	5 percent improvement each quarter
Number of repeat customers	Determine if customers are using the product multiple times (could indicate satisfaction with the product)	"X" percent of customers use the product "X" times during a specified time period
Number of problems reported by customers	Assess quality of project deliverables	100 percent of reported problems addressed within 72 hours

Compliance

Compliance with Enterprise Architecture model requirements	Track progress toward department-wide architecture model	Zero deviations without proper approvals
Compliance with Interoperability requirements.	Track progress toward system interoperability	Product works effectively within system portfolio
Compliance with standard	Alignment, interoperability, consistency	No significant negative findings during architect assessments
For Web site projects, compliance with Style Guide	To ensure standardization of Web site	All Web sites have the same "look and feel"
Compliance with Section 508	To meet regulatory requirements	Persons with disabilities may access and utilize the functionality of the system

Redundancy

Elimination of duplicate or overlapping systems	Ensure return on investment	Retirement of 100 percent of identified systems
Decreased number of duplicate data elements	Reduce input redundancy and increase data integrity	Data elements are entered once and stored in one database
Consolidate help desk functions	Reduce $ spent on help desk support	Approved consolidation plan by fill-in-date

Focus	Purpose	Measure of Success
Cost Avoidance		
System is easily upgraded	Take advantage of e.g., COTS upgrades	Subsequent releases do not require major "glue code" project to upgrade
Avoid costs of maintaining duplicate systems	Reduce IT costs	100 percent of duplicate systems have been identified and eliminated
System is maintainable	Reduce maintenance costs	New version (of COTS) does not require "glue code"
Customer Satisfaction		
System availability (uptime)	Measure system availability	100 percent of requirement is met. (e.g., 99 percent M–F, 8 a.m. to 6 p.m., and 90 percent S & S, 8 a.m. to 5 p.m.)
System functionality (meets customers'/users' needs)	Measure how well customer needs are being met	Positive trend in customer satisfaction survey(s)
Absence of defects (that impact customer)	Number of defects removed during project life cycle	90 percent of defects expected were removed
Ease of learning and use	Measure time to becoming productive	Positive trend in training survey(s)
Time it takes to answer calls for help	Manage/reduce response times	95 percent of severity one calls answered within three hours
Rating of training course	Assess effectiveness and quality of training	90 percent of responses of "good" or better
Business Goals/Mission		
Functionality tracks reportable inventory	Validate system supports program mission	All reportable inventory is tracked in system
Turnaround time in responding to Congressional queries	Improve customer satisfaction and national interests	Improve turnaround time from two days to four hours

Focus	Purpose	Measure of Success
Maintenance costs	Track reduction of costs to maintain system	Reduce maintenance costs by two thirds over three-year period.
Standard desktop platform	Reduce costs associated with upgrading user's systems	Reduce upgrade costs by 40 percent
Productivity		
Time taken to complete tasks	To evaluate estimates	Completions are within 90 percent of estimates
Number of deliverables produced	Assess capability to deliver products	Improve product delivery 10 percent in each of the next three years.

Index